David Edgar
Plays: 2

Ecclesiastes, The Life and Adventures of Nicholas Nickleby, Entertaining Strangers

This second selection from David Edgar's dramatic work examines the historical roots of our contemporary world to explore its moral basis.

Ecclesiastes, a late 70s radio play, explores the conflict over what human beings are capable of, morally as well as socially, through the rise and fall of a radical clergyman.

Nicholas Nickleby: '"Adaptation" is a feeble word for the structural invention, tonal emphasis, and stylistic definition of David Edgar's text, and for its skill in re-creating the realities of 1838 from the vantage point of 1980.' *The Times*

Entertaining Strangers: 'Edgar's tale triumphs because it captures the cliché simplicities of the old morality, the emotional power of melodrama, while weaving them into a more ambitious tapestry.' *Times Literary Supplement*
'Generous, sprawling and highly enjoyable.' *Observer*

David Edgar was born in 1948 in Birmingham. His stage work includes *Excuses Excuses* (1972); *Dick Deterred* (1974); *Saigon Rose* (1976); *Wreckers* (1977); *Mary Barnes* (1978); *Teendreams* (with Susan Todd, 1979); *That Summer* (1987) and *Entertaining Strangers*, a community play first commissioned by Ann Jellicoe and the Colway Theatre Trust and adapted for performance at the National Theatre, London in 1987–8. He has written five plays for the Royal Shakespeare Company: *Destiny* (1976); *The Jail Diary of Albie Sachs* (1978); *Nicholas Nickleby* (1980); *Maydays* (1983); and *Pentecost* (1994). Plays for the National Theatre include *Entertaining Strangers* (revised version 1987) and *The Shape of the Table*. He received the John Whiting award for *Destiny*, the Society of West End Theatres Best Play award for *Nicholas Nickleby* (which also won him a Tony award in New York), the *Plays and Players* Best Play award for *Maydays* and the *Evening Standard* Play of the Year award for *Pentecost*. His television work includes adaptations of *Destiny, Jail Diary* and *Nicholas Nickleby, Buying a Landslide* (1992) and a three-part play *Vote for Them* (BBC, 1989). His radio work includes *Ecclesiastes* (1977), *A Movie Starring Me* (1991) and *Talking to Mars* (1996). His first film, *Lady Jane*, was released in 1986. He is Professor of Playwriting Studies at the University of Birmingham.

D0234365

by the same author

DAVID EDGAR PLAYS: 1*
The Jail Diary of Albie Sachs, Mary Barnes,
Saigon Rose, O Fair Jerusalem, Destiny

DAVID EDGAR PLAYS: 3*
Teendreams, Our Own People,
That Summer, Maydays

THE SHAPE OF THE TABLE
THE STRANGE CASE OF DR JEKYLL AND MR HYDE
PENTECOST

EDGAR: SHORTS
Ball Boys, The National Theatre, Bloodsports,
The Midas Connection, Baby Love

THE SECOND TIME AS FARCE
A book of essays

also available
by Susan Painter

EDGAR THE PLAYWRIGHT*

* published by Methuen Drama

DAVID EDGAR

Plays: 2

Ecclesiastes
a radio play

The Life and Adventures of Nicholas Nickleby
(Parts One and Two)
from the novel
by Charles Dickens

Entertaining Strangers
a new version of
'Entertaining Strangers: A Play for Dorchester'

with an introduction by the author

Methuen Drama

METHUEN CONTEMPORARY DRAMATISTS

This collection first published in Great Britain 1990 by Methuen Drama
Reissued with a new cover design 1994; reissued in this series in 1997
by Methuen Drama
an imprint of Reed International Books Ltd
Michelin House, 81 Fulham Road, London SW3 6RB
and Auckland, Melbourne, Singapore and Toronto
and distributed in the United States of America
by Heinemann, a division of Reed Elsevier Inc
361 Hanover Street, Portsmouth, New Hampshire NH 03801 3959

Ecclesiastes copyright © David Edgar, 1990

The Life and Adventures of Nicholas Nickleby (Parts One and Two) first
published in 1982 in the USA by Dramatists Play Service Inc. and fully revised
in the 1990 edition. Copyright © 1982, 1990

Entertaining Strangers first published as a Methuen New Theatrescript in 1986,
re-set as a Methuen Modern Play in 1988 by Methuen London and reprinted
with minor corrections and revised for the reissue in 1994. Copyright © 1986,
1988, 1990, 1994

This collection © 1990, 1994 by David Edgar
Introduction © 1990 by David Edgar.

The author has asserted his moral rights

A CIP catalogue record for this book is available from the British Library

ISBN 0–413–63050–1

Printed and bound in Great Britain by Cox & Wyman Ltd, Reading, Berkshire

SPECIAL NOTE ON MUSIC
The incidental music and lyrics composed by Stephen Oliver for the original
production of *The Life and Adventures of Nicholas Nickleby* are copyrighted by
Novello and Company Ltd, Borough Green, Sevenoaks, Kent TN15 8DT,
England. Sole distributor for the United States is Theodore Presser Company,
Presser Place, Bryn Mawr, PA 19010. Terms quoted on request. Copyright ©
1981, by Novello and Company Limited (PAu 352-229). Lyrics reprinted by
permission

To Sean and Veronica

Contents

David Edgar

A Chronology of Plays and Screenplays

Two Kinds of Angel (Bradford University, July 1970; Basement Theatre, London, February 1971) Published by Burnham House, London, 1975

The National Interest (General Will Theatre Group, July 1971)

Tedderella (Pool Theatre, Edinburgh, December 1971; Bush Theatre, London, January 1973)

Excuses Excuses (Belgrade Theatre Studio, Coventry, May 1972; Open Space, London, July 1973)

Death Story (Birmingham Repertory Theatre Studio, November 1972; New End Theatre, London, November 1975)

Baby Love (Soho Poly Theatre, London, May 1973; BBC-TV Play for Today, November 1974)

The Eagle Has Landed (Granada Television, April 1973)

Operation Iskra (Paradise Foundry Theatre Group, September 1973)

Dick Deterred (Bush Theatre, February 1974) Published by Monthly Review Press, New York, 1974

I Know What I Meant (Granada Television, July 1974)

O Fair Jerusalem (Birmingham Repertory Theatre Studio, May 1975) Published by Methuen, London, 1987

Blood Sports/Ball Boys (Birmingham Arts Lab, July 1975; Bush Theatre, June 1976) *Ball Boys* published by Pluto Press, London, 1978

The National Theatre (Open Space, London, October 1975)

Saigon Rose (Traverse Theatre, Edinburgh, July 1976; BBC Radio Three, April 1979) Published by Methuen, London, 1987

Destiny (Royal Shakespeare Company at the Other Place and subsequently the Aldwych Theatre, September 1976, May 1977; BBC-TV Play for Today, January 1978; BBC Radio Four, January 1979) Published by Methuen, London, 1976/78

Wreckers (7:84 Theatre Company, February 1977) Published by Methuen, London, 1977

Ecclesiastes (BBC Radio Four, April 1977)

Our Own People (Pirate Jenny Theatre Company, November 1977) Published by Methuen, London, 1988

The Jail Diary of Albie Sachs (Adaptation) (Royal Shakespeare Company at the Warehouse, June 1978; Manhattan Theatre Club, New York, October 1979; productions in Los Angeles, San Francisco and Seattle; BBC Television, 1981) Published by Rex Collings, London, 1978 and Methuen, London, 1988

Mary Barnes (Based on the book by Mary Barnes and Joe Berke) (Birmingham Repertory Studio 1978; Royal Court, January 1979;

Introduction

One of the characteristics of my generation of political playwrights is that for a long time we tended to set almost all our plays in our own country in the present day. If this seems unremarkable, it's worth pointing out how much political theatre – from Brecht and Shaw to Arden and Bond – has been set in other countries and other times, and has sought to explore the characteristics and needs of the present by way of analogy with an often distant past.

There was – as you might detect – an element of polemic in our insistence that the best way to address the decline of Britain in the 70s was not necessarily by way of the Hundred Years War, Renaissance Italy or feudal China. It's therefore of interest to note how – in the immediate wake of Mrs Thatcher's election victory – there was something of a flight from the here-and-now (Hare to India, Brenton to Roman Britain), as we tried to assess the implications of that unexpected happening. In my case, an invitation to adapt a long nineteenth-century novel was something of a relief: after a year enjoying a British Council fellowship in America, I welcomed the RSC's invitation to dramatise Charles Dickens' *Nicholas Nickleby*, not least because it would allow me a breathing-space, in which to reassess the architecture of the social and political model on which I had previously relied, and which had been found so spectacularly wanting.

In fact, *Nickleby* proved to be more important than that, in a number of ways. First of all, it was cheering to note that the 70s movement towards democratic collectivism in the theatre had not entirely run out of steam (it was to do so later in the decade); second, its length (both of preparation and performance) and its success (on both sides of the Atlantic) led it to dominate my life in a way I couldn't have predicted. But I believe also that its success owed much to the beginnings of something else; a feeling that if the urge towards egalitarianism and social justice had indeed lost its sap and vigour, then their cultural roots should be preserved and nurtured, against the day when they would put forward new buds and blossoms in the future.

In that sense, *Nickleby* was an early – if not the first – shot in the war that was to dominate the cultural landscape in the later 80s, about the uses of history and heritage (in general) and the nature of Victorian values (in particular). The message of Dickens' novel and our adaptation – that material self-interest is neither the first nor the most effective motor of human behaviour – was clearly an attractive one, even to people who felt that taxation needed cutting and union bosses taming.

For that reason, I was keen to return to the human nature theme, obliquely in *Maydays* and more directly in another Victorian piece. Like *Nickleby, Entertaining Strangers* began life as an attractive invitation, and discovered its content as it went along. I had, of course, known of the director and writer Ann Jellicoe's pioneering work in community theatre in the South West, but it wasn't until I saw the production of her own play for Lyme Regis – *The Western Women* – that I understood how much her brilliant combination of large-scale theatrical spectacular with genuine community involvement answered my then current needs (not least, to get away from metropolitan theatreland). So when she asked me to write a play for the county town of Dorchester, I was happy to accept.

The story we hit upon – of a titanic if historically unlikely 20-year contest of wills between a fundamentalist pastor and a businesswoman – gave ample opportunity to explore the tension at the heart of the mid-nineteenth century period, a tension I'd already touched on in *Nickleby*, between feudal atavisms and commercial energies, between the ancient mysteries of the countryside and contemporary certainties of town. (Its scale also provided scope for the required provision of upwards of 150 parts). It was not however until I began to rewrite the play for professional performance at the National Theatre that I realised the simple geometry already at its heart. One of the sharpest accusations Conservatives fire at the Left concerns the supposed contradiction between love for all humanity and caring for people you actually know (as Burke puts it, the apparent mutual exclusiveness of love of 'kind' and 'kindred'). In the course of *Entertaining Strangers*, the cleric Henry Moule discovers an almost superhuman care for strangers, but he cannot apply this lesson to relations with his own son. While the brewer Sarah Eldridge, desperately loving of her own, cannot extend that love beyond her doors.

It seems to me clear that both forms of love are limited and insufficient. The first has blighted the socialist experiment, the second challenges the moral pretensions of the enterprise culture. It was already a theme of the first version of *Entertaining Strangers*; it was central to my reworking of it for the National, cunningly enticed from me by Peter Hall (I *think* I am still the only living writer to have worked with the directors of both our national theatres; certainly to have been both Nunned and Halled is a most agreeable distinction). And I'm surprised by how clearly that theme is present also in my late 70s radio play *Ecclesiastes*, another play about a clergyman, but this time a radical one (indeed, much of John Hammond's theology is based on a book I read by a then relatively unknown Anglican academic called David Jenkins).

But in fact the conflict over what human beings are capable of, morally as well as socially, is at the very centre of the narratives that presently contend for mastery; it is the real battleground on which the New Conservatism has fought, and on which it will ultimately lose.

The bulk of this book consists of plays which go back to the historical roots of our contemporary world to explore its moral basis. I am more certain than I was when I wrote them that the industrial world created during the period of *Nicholas Nickleby* and *Entertaining Strangers* is now in decline, and that a new kind of world, with new dangers (but also new opportunities) is emerging from it. In the 70s most of what I wrote was set in the present, and in the 80s I seem to have spent much time in the past. How to write of new times – how, in a sense, to write futuristically – is the next challenge.

David Edgar, 1989

Ecclesiastes

a radio play

Ecclesiastes is my only original radio play (a fact of which I am not proud, and which I plan to correct). I owe a lot to Michael Rolfe, its director, who taught me much that I needed to know about the form, and who subsequently directed adaptations of my stage plays *Destiny* and *Saigon Rose*.

Ecclesiastes was first broadcast on BBC Radio Four on 1 April 1977, with the following cast:

JOHN HAMMOND	Eric Allan
JUDITH HAMMOND	Elizabeth Proud
LUKE/AMERICAN PREACHER	Peter Marinker
BISHOP OF STANTON/MR ATTWOOD	Haydn Jones
PROVOST	Clifford Rose
BISHOP PUGH	Geoffrey Matthews
BILL CROSBY/CUSTOMS OFFICER	Sean Barrett
CANON SIDNEY WILLCOX	Brian Hewlett
MRS GILLOT/MIDDLE-CLASS WOMAN/APPOINTMENTS SECRETARY	Patricia Gallimore

The play was produced and directed by Michael Rolfe.

Scene One

A hymn, sung rather badly in a poorly attended church, intercut with:

Open air, a crowd. An American PREACHER, using a microphone.

HYMN.
> The king of love my shepherd is
> His goodness faileth never
> I nothing lack if I am his
> And he is mine for ever.

PREACHER. Brothers and sisters, we have come together in the sight of the Lord, 'cos we know, that you turn on to Jesus and he'll never let you down.

Brothers and sisters, we have come together, in the sight of the Lord, 'cos we know, that when you rush with Jesus, then you'll never crash.

Brothers and sisters, we have come together, in the sight of the Lord, 'cos we know, you drop Jesus, that's a high that's everlasting.

HYMN.
> In Death's dark vale, I fear no ill
> With thee, dear Lord, beside me
> Thy rod and staff my comfort still . . .

PREACHER. And, brothers and sisters, we have come together, here, in God's sight, to baptise and make anew the good Lord's newest servant, Brother Zepheniah, let me hear you praise the Lord.

CONGREGATION. Praise the Lord.

PREACHER. Let me hear a J.

CONGREGATION. J.

PREACHER. Let me hear an E.

CONGREGATION. E.

PREACHER. Let me hear an S.

CONGREGATION. S.

PREACHER. Let me hear a U.

CONGREGATION. U.

PREACHER. Let me hear an S.

CONGREGATION. S.

PREACHER. What does it spell?

CONGREGATION. Jesus!

PREACHER. I can't hear you.

CONGREGATION. JESUS!

PREACHER. Praise be to God. And —

HYMN.

> . . . so through all the length of days
> Thy goodness faileth never;
> Good Shepherd, may I sing thy praise
> Within thy house for ever.

Fade out.

Scene Two

Fade in, interior.

Voice of the BISHOP *of Stanton.*

BISHOP. May the words of my mouth, and the meditation of all our hearts, be ever gracious in thy sight, O Lord, our strength and our redeemer.

CONGREGATION (*mumbles*). Amen.

Chairs scrape, coughing as they sit.

BISHOP. The Book of Ecclesiastes, Chapter Four, Verse One: 'So I returned, and considered all the oppressions that are done under the sun: and behold the tears of such that were oppressed, and they had no comforter; and on the side of the oppressors there was power; but they had no comforter.'

My friends. I have chosen today this strange text, from this strange old book, for one reason alone. And that is contained within the text's last phrase: stating, as it does, that the oppressors, just as much as the oppressed, need comfort.

My friends, how often have we heard, from pulpits, from this pulpit, that the message of Christ Jesus, Jesus coming not with peace but a sword, is that of violent revolution. Furthermore, that the oppressors, tares beneath the flail, have put themselves beyond salvation. Further, that the reapers of those tares, the risen poor, are holy in precisely that, because they're poor and rising.

Well. Fine. But what I want to ask these, worthy clerics, these, idealist ecclesiastics, who believe in Christ as Freedom Fighter, all I'd ask them is to read, to re-read, just this verse, this passage from Ecclesiastes.

Now, yes, of course, it says, the poor, the suffering, they have no comforter; but also it asserts that those on the oppressors' side, they too lack comfort. And when we look at our society, our system, with all its inequalities and ghastliness, should we not remember that the message of Jesus Christ, the Good Shepherd, is not just delivered to the poor, but everyone. And should we not, as well —

Pause.

And should we not . . .

Long pause. Shuffling. Suddenly, with energy, banging the pulpit.

And should we not, as well as that . . .

Slight pause. Suddenly, in great pain.

On God. . . .

A body falling against wood. Papers falling. Hubbub from the congregation. Another voice, thin, reedy: the PROVOST *of Stanton.*

PROVOST. Mm . . . I think we, now, while we . . . the next hymn, mm, Hymn 217. . . . (*Pause.*) The next hymn, mm, please, 217 . . .

Over the hubbub, the organ plays. Sound of much scuffling and movement, as the congregation sings.

HYMN.
        Jesus calls us, o'er the tumult
        Of our life's wild restless sea
        Day by day his sweet voice soundeth . . .

Fade out.

Scene Three

Fade in.

Ten Downing Street. A phone is dialled. We don't hear the rings, but it's answered quickly. We hear the APPOINTMENTS SECRETARY *to the Prime Minister.*

SECRETARY. Hello, is that the Bishop's Palace? (*Slight pause.*) I wonder if I could speak to Bishop Pugh. It's the Prime Minister's Appointments Secretary. Thank you. (*Pause.*) Ah, good morning, my lord. It's the . . . Yes, my lord, that's right. The vacancy at Stanton. (*Pause.*) Yes, of course, he had several coronary attacks before, but nonetheless, quite tragic, yes . . . (*Slight pause.*) Well, we have received a fairly detailed submission from the Vacancy-in-See Committee, type of man they want . . . Obviously, we want to cast the net as wide . . . (*Slight pause.*) Yes, that's right, my lord, the Usual Discrete Consultations. And I wondered if . . . (*Pause.*) Right, my lord. Wed. p.m. it is. Thank you so much.

Ting of phone down. Buzzer.

Margaret? Trains to Westford, Berkshire, Wednesday, early afternoon. To see Bishop Pugh. All right?

Fade out.

Scene Four

Fade in the Bishop's Palace, Westford.

A slow, deep chime as the clock strikes four. Silence.

SECRETARY. Well, my lord?

PUGH. Mm? What?

SECRETARY. That's the list, my lord. Those are the people who have been suggested. For the Bishopric of Stanton.

PUGH. Yes. (*Grunts as he rises.*) Milk and sugar?

SECRETARY. Lemon, please. My lord.

Tinkling for a moment or two.

PUGH. Here you are. Help yourself to bikkies.

SECRETARY. Thank you.

PUGH *grunts as he sits down.*

PUGH. Right. Very impressive list. Grafton I've lots of time for, beta plus, might be rather old, p'raps not. Bishop Sanders *is* too old, unless they want a stopgap. Laundimer I don't know, but they say at Oxford he's not only bright but also approachable. Beta query plus, I s'pose. Provost Ridgway is sound on everything, of course, 'cept race. Apparently he got a toe shot off in Delhi, 1946, and had a blind spot ever since. So, for

Stanton, gamma plus-ish. Stork's fine on race, of course, but pretty Muggeridge on matters sexual. So not so sure.

SECRETARY. There have been reservations, too, on Mrs Stork.

PUGH. Oh, why?

SECRETARY. Apparently, some ugly fracas, some reception.

PUGH. And with whom?

SECRETARY. The wife of the Precentor.

PUGH. Splendid. She's a gruesome woman. Thought to put him beta query minus, but that edges him to beta. So, I s'pose, it's him or Laundimer or Grafton.

SECRETARY. Well, I think that's probably –

PUGH. And now, perhaps, you'll tell me why you came to see me.

SECRETARY. Beg your pardon?

PUGH. Well, there's no one likes a gossip more than I, but really I know nothing of these men that any curate couldn't tell you. So. Who is it that you want to know about?

SECRETARY. Hammond.

PUGH. Hammond. Ah. I should have known.

SECRETARY. His name has been suggested. Twice. We think, a rather strange idea . . .

PUGH. Yes, yes, of course, the man's a Trot. A God-Trot, but a Trot. Not likely to be the blue-eyed boy at number ten.

SECRETARY. I don't know, really, very much about him. Hence —

PUGH. You're here. Of course. Right. John Hammond. Born in Yorkshire, circa 40 years ago. Studied at Durham. Married the girl next door at 32, she's Judith and a toughie . . . Well, what then. A few hard parishes, a book . . . And then, of course, my Dean, here in Westford. Seemed set fair, his first foot on the escalator. Lots of bits and pieces, up at Church House, including, importantly for my little tale, a seat on the Investments Committee of the Church Commissioners. Now, as you know, our men who labour in the city, raising the cash to keep us going, rendering to Caesar so that we can render unto God, do tend to view their ecclesiastical partners with little more than rank contempt. Not so with John. He was – they told me, charmingly – a bloody ace. If IBM were needing to design a new computer, so the saying went, they needn't look beyond the inside of John Hammond's head. So, everything is fine. Then, perhaps foolishly, I let him go for two months to Bolivia.

SECRETARY. I see.

PUGH. It must seem rather unfair of God to curse a man with a genius for capital accumulation *and* a social conscience. The cynics, by the by, regard the conscience as belonging to his wife. But there it is, the Almighty has a sense of irony. Hammond, quite soon, resigns from his various finance committees. But that's not enough. He's zipping up the escalator, and he wants a bash at running down. He resigns the Deanery, spots a vacant benefice in the most deprived and blighted area of Stanton, writes to the Bish as bold as brass, and ends up with the worst parish south of the Trent.

SECRETARY. Yes.

PUGH. So? You want my opinion? Should he have the diocese?

SECRETARY. Indeed I do.

PUGH. Don't know. You see, the problem is, with Hammond, as I see it . . .

SECRETARY. Yes?

PUGH. To be a Bishop, anywhere, perhaps particularly in the Church of England, needs a certain, social sense, a sense, perhaps, of compromise. You know?

SECRETARY. Indeed I do, my lord.

PUGH. Yes, I imagine . . . Anyway, the problem with John Hammond is . . . The man's a monk. No sense of compromise. That's the problem. He's a very bright, attractive, personable, and compassionate, Mad Monk.

Fade out.

Scene Five

Fade in. JOHN HAMMOND's *house. Sounds of lunch.*

JUDITH. Bill, soup?

CROSBY. Oh, thank you, Judith.

Clink of plate.

JUDITH. There you are.

JOHN. Well, Bill, so how's the world of big city finance?

CROSBY. Big and shitty. Well, John, and how's the world of urban deprivation and blight?

JOHN. Deprived and blighted.

CROSBY. Mm. Your congregation?

JOHN. Small. But that's not really what the job's about.

CROSBY. Oh, no, of course. There's the pastoral work. Soup to the needy. Or, for the radical vicar like yourself, ammunition, factual or actual, for the socially disprivileged. Since your Pauline conversion on the road to South America.

JUDITH. I don't think it was quite like that, Bill. For starters, John didn't go blind.

CROSBY. Oh, you disappoint me. We'd had this splendid vision, that it happened one fine morning, the Very Rev John Hammond at his toilette, suddenly realising, in a flash of shaving foam, that capitalism is a terrible thing, lather lather, that the Stock Exchange is a den of vipers, scrape scrape, that the system is doomed and all history's the history of the class struggle, rinse rinse, glad that's sorted out and what's for breakfast.

JOHN. Well, not quite, Bill. Just the understanding that if you're contributing to the problem, you can't be part of the solution.

CROSBY. And Bolivia.

JOHN. Oh, yes, indeed, Bolivia.

CROSBY. We hadn't really realised, you see, Judith, the point about Bolivia. We thought, oh well, he's gone, but at least he'll turn up in some Oxford college, pottering around the New Testament, redating here a gospel, querying there the authorship of an epistle, as happy as the day is long . . . But no . . . and here he is, in the land God forgot, taking vengeance on his class, his friends and his life so far, fomenting revolt among the lower orders.

JUDITH (*warning note*). Bill –

CROSBY. Not that he isn't, still, pocketing his stipend, raised through the satanic doings of sharks like myself, who slosh about knee-deep in the gore of the equity market so that saints like John can overthrow the state.

(*Slight pause.*)

JUDITH. His grossly inadequate stipend.

CROSBY. Yes, indeed, and one of the reasons for that, of course, is because the Church Commissioners are the most insanely responsible investors in Christendom . . . Nothing in South Africa, of course, nor armaments, nor nicotine or alcohol . . .

JUDITH. Another glass of wine, Bill?

CROSBY. Thank you so much.

Slight pause. Clink.

JOHN. Yes, of course, Bill. And you're absolutely right. We certainly require some of your dividends of sin.

CROSBY. Go on.

JOHN. Oh, just, I never really saw the need to send bailiffs smashing into people's homes, to raise the rent that's going to pay for 51-room Bishop's Palaces. Or chauffeur-driven cars.

CROSBY. John, you know full well that's just a tiny drop –

JOHN. I also know the church's treatment of its tenants has been –

CROSBY. And it strikes me, sometimes, if you're so agin the pomp and palaces and cars and circumstance, you might just be, just be in the wrong institution? Don't you think?

JOHN. Well –

Doorbell.

Callers, and at a time like this. Excuse me.

Scrape of chair and door.

JUDITH. Well. Bash Hammond day, I see, Bill.

CROSBY. Oh, I'm sorry. Perhaps it's all getting a bit heavy, for Sunday lunch.

JUDITH. Oh, don't worry. I'm enjoying it. Probably only slightly less than John.

Door.

JOHN (*approaching*). It's Sid Willcox, darling.

JUDITH. Oh, hello, Sid. To what do we owe –

WILLCOX (*approaching*). Oh, I just wanted to talk to John about this conference I'm organising, I didn't realise you were . . .

CROSBY *coughs.*

JOHN. Oh, I'm sorry. Canon Sidney Willcox, Residentiary of Stanton; Bill Crosby, stockbroker.

WILLCOX. Oh.

JUDITH. With the Commissioners. An old mate from John's sordid past.

CROSBY. Hello.

WILLCOX. Hello.

JUDITH. Sid, have you eaten?

WILLCOX. Yes, thanks.

JUDITH. A glass of wine, at least.

WILLCOX. Oh, yes, ta.

Chairs as WILLCOX *and* JOHN *sit.*

Do, please, go on with whatever you were . . .

CROSBY. Right. I will. John, answer the question.

JOHN. Oh, yes. The reason why I'm in the Church of England.

CROSBY. That's the one.

JOHN. Well. Father Crosby. I'll confess. I have erred. I was for many years an ecclesiastical bureaucrat. I have strayed. In that I adored it. I have done things I should not have done, like coming here for motives that are graced by the description 'righteous pride'. And I have not done things I should perhaps have done, like leaving the Anglican Communion to stew in its own contradictions. And there is no health in me. But, somehow, in a way . . . You know the old joke, the Church of England is the Tory Party on its knees. It needn't be. Because it is the C *of* E, of people, in this city. The fact it has been the church of privilege, doesn't mean it must be so. So I beg absolution. All right?

Slight pause.

CROSBY. Well, that's a splendid credo, John, and suitably flagellatory, you'll have to say 20 Hail Mary's at least, but it doesn't quite tell us how you change the Church of England. And what to.

WILLCOX. Why don't you come and hear him, Mr Crosby?

CROSBY. I'm sorry?

WILLCOX. At this conference. John is, I hope, going to be speaking about precisely that.

CROSBY. Well I . . . Well, why not. If I'm available. I will. I'd be delighted.

Fade out.

Scene Six

Fade in. Ten Downing Street. The APPOINTMENTS SECRETARY *is on the telephone.*

SECRETARY. Yes, of course, Archdeacon. (*Slight pause.*) Yes, I shall certainly be talking to the Provost of Stanton . . . Yes, I know, you're basically the industrial side. (*Pause.*) No, that's what I wanted . . . what you thought of him, on the industrial side . . . (*Pause.*) No, please, Archdeacon, do go on . . .

Fade out.

Scene Seven

Fade in. A factory. Noise of machines. People need to shout.

JOHN (*approaching*). Hey. Mr Attwood.

ATTWOOD. 'Lo, Padre. What can I do for you?

JOHN. Think it may be the other way round, Mr Attwood.

ATTWOOD. Oh, well, that means it can't be money. Shoot.

JOHN. I've just been a week in Düsseldorf, at a convention.

ATTWOOD. Well, that's nice. I've just been a week in Blackpool, at a Congress.

JOHN. Yes, I know you have. Discussing, Wednesday a.m., 10 to 10.45, relative EEC/UK wage rates in the motor industry.

Slight pause.

ATTWOOD. Well, go on.

JOHN. Now, my conference was worker-priests, Lutheran, Catholic, the lot, from all over Europe. But particularly Germany. And, naturally, a lot of information was swapped about, you know? And I thought, as Works Convenor, you might like a glance at this.

Rustle of papers.

ATTWOOD. Ta very much. What is it?

JOHN. It's comparative wage breakdowns of a number of major car firms in the Federal Republic. Comparative in that the calculations are on a cost of living basis, ie you can compare yourself with them in realistic terms. You don't, in fact, compare that favourably.

ATTWOOD. That has got to be right, Mr Hammond.

JOHN. Well, there it is.

ATTWOOD. Ta muchly. Can I ask a question?

JOHN. Sure.

ATTWOOD. Very grateful for this nugget, more than nugget, but what I'm keen to know is, why d'you bother?

JOHN. What d'you mean?

ATTWOOD. Our last industrial chaplain seemed to see his function as essentially blessing peacemakers. The poor and meek inheriting the earth, on that he wa'n't as keen.

JOHN. I'm not your last industrial chaplain.

ATTWOOD. There, you're not wrong.

JOHN. I'm an Anglican Socialist. It's not a total contradiction.

ATTWOOD. Ah. Well. I'm a Red Methodist. And that is.

Machines grind to a halt. Lovely silence.

Ah. Thank God for that. The line's broke down. D'you want a cup of tea?

Fade out.

Scene Eight

The Cathedral offices, Stanton. The APPOINTMENTS SECRETARY *and the* PROVOST. *Another, different, clock chime. Five.*

SECRETARY. So, Provost, what d'you think?

PROVOST. Well, I think it must be, mm, from Ridgway, Laundimer and Sanders.

SECRETARY. The Bishop not too old?

PROVOST. The stock response to that is, mm, Pope John.

SECRETARY. Indeed. John Hammond?

PROVOST. Hammond. Yes. (*Slight pause.*) Mm, let me make it clear, I've always thought, the virtue of this, mm, this system that we have, mm, for selecting Bishops in the Church of England, though of course it's logically indefensible, the old boy network, backstairs chat, all highly, mm, undemocratic, yet it does mean that, in fact, our choices are much wider, more, mm, if you like, eccentric, freer, than they would be with elections, canvassing, and so on, all the stuff they have, mm, in America. You see?

SECRETARY. Of course.

PROVOST. But I will say, quite frankly, that I'd vote in Synod, for elections, universal suffrage, mm, mob rule, if by that I could guarantee that Hammond would not be a Bishop, here or anywhere. Mm? To be frank.

SECRETARY. Why's that? Because of his politics?

PROVOST. Oh, no, unless all, mm, radicals are by their nature quite as arrogant. Or, mm, to use the word the Bible gives us, proud.

SECRETARY. Hammond's proud?

PROVOST. John Hammond's possibly the proudest –

Knock on door.

Yes, yes, come in.

Door opens as:

Do people really want John Hammond?

SECRETARY. Some people, very much.

PROVOST. Mm. Mm. Ah, this is our Canon Willcox.

SECRETARY. How d'you do, Canon –

WILLCOX. Fine, sir, thank you, how –

PROVOST. Who's at the moment busy organising us a conference, you know, some radical assembly, session on St Paul As Urban Guerrilla, and A Christian View Of Gelignite, you know the kind of thing . . . The Canon, mm, himself is working on a paper on the new Theology of Rape.

WILLCOX. Look, Provost, I think, if you don't mind, I'll come back in a few –

PROVOST. That's all right, Sidney. I'll be through in half an hour.

Door closes.

Hammond star speaker, mm, of course.

Slight pause.

In answer to your question. Mm. There is a form of pride, mm, that we know. The pride of hypocrites, and puritans and holiers-than-thou. But there's a greater pride, in my view, and that states not that everyone is sinful, but that there's no sin. Or anyway, that, mm, society's so rotten that there's no sin that is blamable on anyone. And that is pride, and harmful, hurtful pride because it takes from people that one prop that makes their, mm, their wickedness a weight that's bearable. And that is consciousness of sin. You have no sin, you leave men isolated in their evil, with no one or thing to aid them. And that's why, mm, I regard John Hammond as a man of, mm, an unforgivable pride.

SECRETARY. Yes. No other reason?

Pause.

PROVOST. All right. I'll tell you, mm. About John Hammond's son.

SECRETARY. His son? I didn't know –

PROVOST. You wouldn't, would you? Well, you see, John Hammond, the apostle of free living, mm, does have his skeleton, mm, rattling round. Which for a man who preaches that our lusts are all from God and, thus, indulging them is somehow doing the creator's will . . . You should hear some of the things he's reputed to tell his parishioners . . .

Fade out.

Scene Nine

Fade in. A private house. Sound of noisy children in another room. MRS GILLOT, JOHN HAMMOND *and* JANET GILLOT.

MRS GILLOT. I said she should have it adopted.

JOHN. Yes, Mrs Gillot?

MRS GILLOT. But she said she couldn't bear the thought.

JOHN. Yes, I see. So, it's a matter of having the baby and keeping it?

MRS GILLOT. Well, of course it isn't, Vicar.

JOHN. Oh, why not?

MRS GILLOT. 'Cos then she'd be a single mother with a bastard, wouldn't she?

JOHN. Yes, well, that's not a word I often –

MRS GILLOT. And that's obviously impossible.

JOHN. I see. And so –

MRS GILLOT. She wanted an abortion. Well.

JOHN. Yes, well – ?

MRS GILLOT. What d'you think of that?

JOHN. What d'you think?

MRS GILLOT. I'm asking you, Vicar.

JOHN. Well, I'm not that keen –

MRS GILLOT. Well, you should say so.

JOHN. I just have.

Pause.

MRS GILLOT. Then she could get married.

JOHN. Well, that does seem a possible course of action.

MRS GILLOT (*in some triumph*). Even though she's three months pregnant?

JOHN. That, Mrs Gillot, is what is called a given fact.

MRS GILLOT. Even though that'd mean her standing up in church and –

JOHN. Mrs Gillot, there is always –

MRS GILLOT. Even though he does just happen to be a Muslim –

JOHN. Oh, does that really matter very much?

Pause.

MRS GILLOT. Mr Hammond, I do think you're talking rather oddly, for a Christian.

JOHN. Well, Mrs Gillot, I think you're talking rather oddly, for a human being.

Pause.

MRS GILLOT (*icily matter of fact*). Do you believe in sin, Vicar?

JOHN. Yes, Mrs Gillot, I believe in sin. However, I do not believe that life's a hurdle-race across the ten commandments and you've won salvation, if you fall you're doomed to hellfire. That I don't think. And I think that how the vast majority are forced to live, and you and Janet too, that's a sin as great as any, if not greater . . . (*Slight pause.*) Sorry. I'm bullying you. I shouldn't do that. But I really think, you should, we should just listen to what Janet has to say.

MRS GILLOT. She wants to —

JOHN. Janet. Please. Just tell us what you want to do. Go on.

Pause.

JANET. I want it getting rid of.

Slight pause.

JOHN (*a note of weariness in his voice*). Yes? Go on?

Fade out.

Scene Ten

Fade in. A conference centre. Foyer area. Slight hubbub, quite far away.

WILLCOX. John!

JOHN. Sid. How are you?

WILLCOX. Fine. Glad you could make it.

JOHN. Glad to be asked. Where are they all?

WILLCOX. Oh, they're — John, a word, before we go in.

JOHN. Shoot.

WILLCOX. You feeling strong?

JOHN. Why?

WILLCOX. Some news, I shouldn't tell you.

JOHN. Well, then, don't.

WILLCOX. I think I must.

JOHN. Then do.

Slight pause.

WILLCOX. You're up for Stanton.

JOHN. Come again?

WILLCOX. You're being discussed. I heard, or overheard. For the Bishopric of Stanton.

JOHN. Sid, I don't believe it, one, and second, were it true, I shouldn't know.

WILLCOX. One. It is true. Two, you're quite right, you shouldn't know, it's a holy mystery, the workings of the C of E, just wake up one fine morning, find the letter from 10 Downing Street among your bills and circulars. I know. But in this case, if there's a chance, and so it seems there is, if there's a chance, I had to talk to you, if only just to stop you writing back that morning, by return, and saying no.

JOHN. It's academic, but, of course I would. Say no.

WILLCOX. Why, John?

JOHN. Well, obviously, because –

WILLCOX. Look, John, you're in it. As you've said, you're in it, 'cos it is, it should be, what it says, the Church of all of England, bits of England like this diocese, you said that.

JOHN. So I did.

WILLCOX. So? Then? You'd turn it down? The chance to –

JOHN (almost desperate). It isn't going to happen, Sid.

WILLCOX (echoing his tone). It might and if it does what do you do?

Pause.

JOHN. I wish you hadn't told me.

WILLCOX. Well I did. That's what you'd call a given fact.

Pause.

JOHN. Sid. The reason why I'm certain, absolutely certain, that it's academic . . .

WILLCOX. Yes?

JOHN. Did you ever meet Luke?

WILLCOX. Luke?

JOHN. My son.

WILLCOX. No, I didn't realise you –

JOHN. No. He hasn't been around, of course. I don't, in fact, know where he is, we haven't been in touch, two years, ever since he jumped the clinic in Los Angeles.

WILLCOX. Go on.

JOHN. However liberal and cranky they may be, they don't make Bishops, in the Church of England, when their sons are dying of heroin addiction. They're just not that, eccentric.

Pause.

WILLCOX. I'm sorry. Really didn't know.

JOHN. Well, now you do. (Pause.) Holiday, in 1971. Had, you

know, his joints at University. Supply in California, same pusher, why not try a little something, stronger buzz, you know? One of a million casualties, street corners all across the world.

WILLCOX. John, you're wrong, they wouldn't —

JOHN. Sid, I've got a lecture to deliver.

WILLCOX. Yuh. Of course.

JOHN. Let's go and meet the people.

Fade out.

Scene Eleven

Fade in. Conference hall. Slight echo.

JOHN. Fellow Christians. Friends. About six months ago, I was in a factory, in Stanton, talking to a Communist worker. He was, as it happened, an ex-Catholic. And we were talking about contemporary theology — a preoccupation, I have discovered, of Communist ex-Catholics, they talk of little else — (*Some laughter.*) — and he said, look, with reference to the highly vaunted Christian—Marxist dialogue, the problem is that Christians only ever read Marx to pick holes in him, and to find ways to convert Marxists. It isn't a true dialogue at all.

And I think he's right. And I think when we read Marx — which we should, voraciously — we should look, like all good academics, not for what we want to find, divergence, conflict, but for what, perhaps, we don't want to find.

Slight pause.

Agreement, and convergence. Where we, as Christians, find a common ground with Marx, the Jewish atheist. Now I think we do find some convergence, in the principle of Hope. I think we do have common ground on the idea of history as progress. But what I want to speak of now, is that I think there is agreement on the fact that there are systems, of which capitalism is one, that prevent men and women from fulfilling their potential, to its fullest. The Marxists have a word for this phenomenon: they call it alienation. We Christians have a word as well. We call it sin.

Now, of course, if we view sin as just an individual phenomenon, then this comparison is worse than odious, it's irrelevant. But if we don't believe that salvation is just a matter of an individual's relation to his God, that there are barriers to the kingdom of heaven, then we must extend the concept into collectivity. A state of sin can mean a sinful state.

I think a system that denies the elementary physical needs of people is sinful. I think the Army and the police-force and indeed the established church of a country like Bolivia or Uruguay, or Chile, or South Africa, or even the United States, are sinful. I think there is room, indeed there must be room, in our theology, for the concept of structural sin. And I believe that concept has relevance to the misery and poverty and emptiness of people living here in England, and in this city. And insofar as our church is exclusive, tribal, denying full humanness to those outside it, then it too is sinful.

Now, there will be those who say that what I've just said is a view so social, so wrapped up with men and their affairs, that it is hardly a theological view at all. But, in fact, I don't believe this is so. The concept of Christ's divinity, I think, the doctrine of the Incarnation is *more* central to this vision, *more* vital to its logic, than to most theologies . . . Why is this so? Because, in Jesus Christ as God, the impossible becomes possible. The Incarnation is the impossible made flesh. And, furthermore, and here, my friends, we're leaving Marx, we can just see him through the mirror, a receding pinprick back along the road, it is precisely the impossible made flesh, that can prevent our Christian revolution from the kind of ugly, vicious inhumanity, that, rightly, we accuse the Marxists of. Our view is not inhuman. It's precisely opposite. We say one man cannot be human until all are human. All. Not just the poor, indeed. Not just the freedom fighters. *Christ* Jesus proves to us that it's possible to make everybody, and everything, new.

I'd like to end by quoting to you something that expresses my feelings with far more eloquence than I can muster. It is part of the Manifesto of the Young Churches of Chile, nailed to the door of Santiago Cathedral on the 11th of August 1968. And that date itself, five years before the newest darkness fell on Chile, contains its own bitter irony.

'We want', these young Christians wrote, 'once again to become the church of the people, as in the gospel, living in the same poverty, simplicity and struggle. That is why we say, *no* to a church that is enslaved to the structures of social compromise, *yes* to a church which is free to serve all men. *No* to a church which compromises with power and wealth, *yes* to a church which is prepared to be poor in the name of its faith in men and in Jesus Christ. *No* to the established disorder, *yes* to the struggle for a new society which will give human beings back their dignity and make love a possibility.' Note that word. A possibility. It's no more, but, as well, no less, than that.

Fade out.

Scene Twelve

Fade in. Heathrow Airport. Busy hubbub. Ting of announcement bell. Then:

ANNOUNCER. To passengers recently arrived on TWA Flight 301 from New York, your baggage is now ready for collection prior to customs. Will those passengers who have nothing to declare proceed through the green channel. Passengers with items to declare please proceed through the red channel. TWA Flight 301 from New York, baggage now available for collection.

Ting of bell. Hubbub fades slightly.

CUSTOMS. Yes, sir? Can I help you.

LUKE. Praise the lord. God loves you.

CUSTOMS. I beg your pardon?

LUKE. Praise the lord. God loves you.

CUSTOMS. What have you to declare, sir?

LUKE. I have nothing to declare.

CUSTOMS. Then you've come through the wrong channel, sir. This is the Red Channel. Those with nothing to declare go through the green channel.

LUKE. I have nothing to declare except, as God says through John, that God so loved the world, that he gave his only begotten Son, that whosoever believed in him should not perish, but have everlasting life.

CUSTOMS. Come again, sir?

LUKE. Everlasting life.

CUSTOMS. Oh, I *see*. Would you open your bag, please, sir?

LUKE (*clunk of case*). As God says through Matthew, ask and it shall be given to you.

CUSTOMS. Now what have we here?

LUKE. Seek and ye shall find.

CUSTOMS. Is this all you've brought with you, sir?

LUKE. Knock, and it shall be opened unto you.

CUSTOMS. Well, I have, sir, knocked and opened, and it strikes me that your suitcase contains nothing except a number of pieces of wood, attached together, at right angles to each other, in pairs. Are these your personal possessions, sir, or are you importing them for retail purposes?

LUKE. Lay not up for yourselves treasures upon earth, where moth or rust doth corrupt, and where thieves break in and steal.

CUSTOMS. I wouldn't dream of it, sir. Could you tell me where you purchased these articles?

LUKE. But lay up for yourselves treasures in heaven, where neither moth nor rust doth corrupt.

CUSTOMS. Yes, absolutely, sir, and were these articles indeed in heaven, they would not be liable to duty. But as they are in the temporal territory of Her Majesty's Customs and Excise, I am empowered to enquire if you have a receipt.

LUKE. It is more blessed –

CUSTOMS. To give than to receive.

Case is shut.

Thank you so much, sir, I think under the circumstances, we may release you to your friends, relatives and the promise of life eternal.

LUKE. God thanks you.

CUSTOMS. I thank God.

LUKE. Smile.

CUSTOMS. Smile? Whatever for?

LUKE. God loves you. Praise the Lord.

CUSTOMS. Jesus Christ.

Fade out.

Scene Thirteen

Fade in. A social session, at the Conference. Hubbub of conversation.

WILLCOX. Well, Mr Crosby? What did you think?

CROSBY. John's speech? Striking.

JOHN. But did you agree with it?

CROSBY. Ah, well, there I'd have to –

PUGH (*approaching*). John.

JOHN. Oh, hello, my lord. How are you?

PUGH. I'm splendid.

JOHN. Do you know Canon Willcox? This is the Bishop of Westford. And this is Bill Crosby, of the Church Commissioners.

PUGH. Aha. Strange company you keep.

CROSBY. Strange company he kept, my lord.

PUGH. And what did you think of John's peroration, then?

CROSBY. I think I can say, I was struck.

PUGH. As was I. Struck is the *mot juste*. But I must confess to one or two teeny reservations.

JOHN. Go on, my lord.

PUGH. Well, you know, I've done my reading, not as much as you, I'm sure, but what I find fascinating about these new theologies of revolution, liberation and so on, taken as a whole, is the direction that they've taken, not theoretically, so much as geographically . . . Yes?

JOHN. Not with you, my lord.

PUGH. Well, where are these ideas applied?

JOHN. In many places, but, of course, most extensively in Latin America.

PUGH. Indeed. Where you can see the meek, and poor in spirit, naked wretches wheresoe'er they are, on every corner. Mm?

JOHN. Go on, my lord.

PUGH. Whereas, in our first world, the meek are . . . well, hardly leading revolutions. In the West, it tends to be the rich, in spirit and elsewhere . . . And I wonder where that leaves the revolutionary theologies, in our complicated world?

JOHN. With respect, my lord, although you don't see beggars, or not that many, on English streets, that doesn't mean –

PUGH. I just wonder, John . . . I mean, I'm sure if I was, say, a Bishop in Bolivia or Argentina, then, no doubt, the power of my gospel would proceed from the barrel of a gun. But I am ministering to a quiet and cosy, doubtless Tory, country diocese in England. Am I to say that the Incarnation is less, what's the new word, 'valid' there?

JOHN. It's valid in the slums of Stanton.

PUGH. Perhaps. Just – remember, what your congregation needs, John. Mm? To each according to his spiritual needs. Don't be so proud and holy that you stop your ears to what the Christians in your care require.

WILLCOX. Bishop, are you saying John said –

PUGH. Nothing, Canon, nothing. Just a pompous old Bishop, prattling on. Now I must go and persecute your Provost. Looking far too smug, and on to his third sherry. 'Scuse me.

Footsteps away.

CROSBY. Well. What a bright Bishop.

WILLCOX. You think so?

CROSBY. Oh, yes. I think he put John right on the spot. Not, of course, that John won't wriggle off it.

JOHN. Well, now –

Door slams. Hubbub hubs and bubs.

LUKE (*from afar*). Praise be to God!

WILLCOX. What's that?

JOHN. I dunno, someone –

LUKE (*approaching*). Praise be to God! I have come with good news, for everyone!

CROSBY. Good lord. I think we've been invaded by some class of Jesus Freak.

LUKE. For Jesus Christ is risen, and if you repent your sins and follow him, you will be saved!

JOHN. Oh, God, it isn't –

LUKE. And thus I have come home.

PUGH (*approaching*). What is this? Who are you?

LUKE. Brother Zepheniah is my name in Christ.

PUGH. Why have you come bursting in – ?

LUKE. For I must make a witness to these people, that I Zepheniah was in sin. I have worshipped the false Gods of pleasure and revolt and oriental lushness. I looked at strange pictures that weren't really there. I've sworn and used bad language. I have not remembered it was Sunday. I was ungrateful to my father and my mother. I have had violent thoughts, and I have had sex outside marriage. I have stolen, and told lies. And I've been envious of those who have more than me, when it is God's will that they should. But then I opened my heart to Jesus Christ and –

JOHN. Luke.

LUKE. Yes, Father?

JOHN. Stop it, Luke.

PUGH. John, do you know this –

JOHN. I do. My lord the Right Reverend the Bishop of Westford. This is Luke, my son.

LUKE. Praise be to God. For it is written by God through Matthew that he rejoices more in the sheep that was lost, more than the 99 which went not astray. Who will pray with me?

JOHN. Luke.

LUKE. Who will go down on their knees, right here and now, and pray with me?

Fade out.

Scene Fourteen

Fade in. A phone is dialled. No rings. It's answered.

PUGH. Ten Downing Street? Good morning. I'd like to speak to the Appointments Secretary. (*Slight pause.*) No, not his office. Him. (*Slight pause.*) Name of Pugh. (*Slight pause.*) B.I.S.H.O.P. Pugh. (*Slight pause.*) Thank you so much. (*Pause.*) Ah, hello, old chap. Pugh here. Think there's something you should know about. An incident. To do with Hammond. Yes, that's right . . .

Fade out.

Scene Fifteen

Fade in. JOHN HAMMOND's *house. Silence for a few moments, apart from the clink of cutlery and glassware.*

LUKE. I want to tell you what's happened in my life. I want to give you my testimony.

JUDITH. Go on, Luke. Tell us.

LUKE. I was abusing my body and my mind. I didn't understand that Jesus died for me. I didn't realise I was in sin. All I thought about was drugs and revolt, abusing my body and my mind. And then I met these people, Brother Zadok, and repented of my sin.

JUDITH. Brother Zadok?

JOHN. As, I assume, in The Priest.

LUKE. And I was born again, and spoke in tongues. I got loaded on Jesus, and I didn't need the rest. I took the gospel, and dropped Matthew, Mark, Luke and John.

JUDITH. You 'dropped'?

JOHN. I think, um, Luke could tell us, it's a drugs expression.

LUKE. I realised, you see, they told me, if someone hates you, then you've just got to praise God. If someone hits you, praise God. 'Cos that's what it says in the Bible, and all those guys who throw bricks at the police, they're trying to change things when it's against God's will.

JOHN. You don't believe Christians should try and alter things that they think are wrong?

LUKE. It says in Matthew, render unto Caesar the things that are Caesar's.

JOHN. Yes, but, Luke, it's how you —

LUKE. But it says it, Father. There it is.

JOHN. Yes, but I've always thought, it's a matter of how you interpret —

LUKE. Of course it's true. The Word Made Flesh. John One.

Pause.

JUDITH. Luke, can I ask you a question?

LUKE. Yes, of course, Mother.

JUDITH. Do you believe in Genesis? Do you believe that heaven and earth and men were made in six days?

LUKE. And on the seventh day he rested. Genesis One.

JUDITH. Mm. And do you think, there's hell and Satan?

LUKE. Why, yes, of course. And everyone who isn't saved will burn for all eternity.

JUDITH. I see. (*Slight pause. Brightly.*) Well, do you want some more?

LUKE. No, thank you. I've had a sufficiency, praise the Lord. Excuse me, I have to pray now.

Scrape of chair.

I pray for five minutes six times a day. Prayer is a hot-line to heaven.

Door shuts.

JOHN. And he's never off the phone.

JUDITH. I'd be more convinced of his conversion if he'd spent his five minutes on the washing up.

JOHN. Yes.

Pause.

JUDITH. John, it isn't rosy memories, is it? I mean, he was a bright, intelligent young bloke; he questioned, he had a sense of humour, he was –

JOHN. Yes, he was.

JUDITH. He's been brainwashed. Automaton. An amplifier for the Lord.

JOHN. Godwashed.

JUDITH. What a thought.

JOHN. Judy.

JUDITH. Yes.

JOHN. You wouldn't, in a way, prefer . . . I mean, if he was like he was, in the States, before . . .

JUDITH. John, that's an awful thing to say.

JOHN. Yes, I'm sorry.

JUDITH. Of course, I'm glad he's back. I just wish, I mean it's very ironical, I just wish he hadn't come back quite like he has . . .

JOHN. As you say. Ironical.

Slight pause.

JUDITH. D'you want some more?

JOHN. What? No thanks. (*Pause.*) He wants to come, you know. Tonight.

JUDITH. To the Stanton League of Decency?

JOHN. The very same. I don't s'pose I can stop him.

JUDITH. I don't know why *you're* going. You always say they're the most ghoulish gang of –

JOHN (*firm*). Because they're my parishioners. As Luke's my son. I can't exclude them. Either of them.

JUDITH (*a warning note, something bothering her*). John . . .

JOHN (*almost snapped*). Yes?

JUDITH. Doesn't matter. (*Slight pause.*) What's the meeting about?

JOHN. Oh, they've drawn up some petition. I assume they want me to sign it, and preach it from the pulpit, and so on. Generally commit myself to its doubtless luridly Calvinist contents.

JUDITH. Can I come too?

JOHN. Oh, Judy, no, you know how these harpies get your –

JUDITH. In good times and bad, in sickness and in health. Even in the clutches of the Stanton League of Decency. Love, honour and obey.

JOHN. You didn't say obey, as I recall.

JUDITH. No more I did.

Pause. Clink of cutlery.

Well, better get our hats on.

Scrape of chairs.

JOHN. Judy, you know what really frightens me.

JUDITH. What?

JOHN. To be so certain, and so happy.

JUDITH. Luke? Or the harpies?

JOHN. Both.

Door opens.

LUKE. Praise the Lord. I'm ready.

Fade out.

Scene Sixteen

Fade in. A small meeting hall. A middle-class woman is reading a petition.

WOMAN. 'We, the undersigned Citizens of Stanton, are appalled by the state of our nation. Specifically we oppose the following manifestations of a sick society: 'First, the fact that filth and pornography are peddled on every street corner.'

JOHN. Well, yes, I –

LUKE. Right on. For as God says through Matthew, out of the heart proceed evil thoughts, murders, adulteries, fornications, thefts, false witness, blasphemies. These are the things which defile a man.

WOMAN. 'Second, the permissive attitude that sexual relations outside marriage are acceptable and healthy.'

JOHN. Well, indeed, but –

LUKE. Right on. As God said through Paul to the Corinthians, to avoid fornication, let every man have his own wife, it is better to marry than to burn.

WOMAN. 'Third, the acceptance of homosexuality and other perversions as natural and permissible.'

JOHN. Now, look, I –

LUKE. Right on. Romans. And likewise also the men, leaving the natural use of the women, burned in their lust one toward another, men with men working that which is unseemly.

WOMAN. 'Fourth, the idea of so-called Women's Liberation that threatens the sanctity of the Family.'

JOHN. Um –

LUKE. Right on. One Peter. Likewise, ye wives, be in subjugation to your own husbands.

WOMAN. 'Furthermore, we deplore the modern trend to deride authority, both in the family and in the country as a whole.'

LUKE. Children, obey your parents in the Lord; for this is right. Servants, be obedient to them that are your masters.

WOMAN. 'We are disturbed by a society that puts material possessions and the envy of the rich above spiritual values.'

LUKE. The poor always ye have with you; but me ye have not always.

WOMAN. 'And we see all these manifestations as part of a wider attack on the unity and morale of the nation.'

LUKE. Right on. As God says through Luke, every kingdom divided against itself is brought to desolation.

WOMAN. 'And finally – '

JOHN (*interrupts in some passion*). All right. All right. Luke 12.51. Suppose ye that I am come to give peace on earth? I tell you, nay, but rather division. Proverbs 21.13. He who closes his ear to the cry of the poor will himself cry out and not be heard. John 15.15. Henceforth I call ye not servants; but I have called ye friends. Luke 23.13. Woe unto you, scribes and hypocrites; for ye shut up the kingdom of heaven against men. All right?

LUKE. It's Matthew.

JOHN. What?

LUKE. Woe unto you, scribes and hypocrites. It's Matthew 23.13.

JOHN (*after a pause, suddenly fading*). I'm sorry, you must excuse me, I'm very sorry . . .

JUDITH (*also fading*). John. *John* . . .

Fade out.

Scene Seventeen

Fade in. Faint traffic noises. Rain. Running feet.

JUDITH (*approaching*). John! John, stop —

Running feet stop. JUDITH *breathless.*

John. What are you doing?

JOHN. I'm running away.

JUDITH. Grown men don't run away. Even grown vicars.

JOHN. Don't they? Most of them?

JUDITH. Is that a statistical or a philosophical point?

JOHN. Why are you so angry?

JUDITH. Why did you go in the first place? (*Pause.*) Why did you go to a meeting of the Stanton League of Decency, and have to put up with all that grimy neo-fascism . . . John, why did you go? That's why I'm so angry.

JOHN. Had to go. (*Pause.*) You're dripping wet.

JUDITH. It's raining.

JOHN. So it is. Let's –

JUDITH. *No.*

Slight pause.

JOHN. Judy, I didn't tell you something.

JUDITH. Christ, confession time, again?

JOHN. Confession time again. Apparently, I'm being put forward, as a possible, for Stanton.

JUDITH. John, you speak in tongues.

JOHN. The diocese.

JUDITH. The Bishop?

JOHN. Yuh.

JUDITH. John, why didn't you –

JOHN. I shouldn't know.

JUDITH. So then *I* shouldn't know?

JOHN. I didn't want to think about it. But, I did, of course, mention it, because, I mean it's academic now, of course, after, events, it's in the past, but I did think and pray about it, and I came to the conclusion –

JUDITH (*still impatient*). Yes?

JOHN. That if we work within this institution, then –

JUDITH. Oh, don't go on.

JOHN. Why not?

JUDITH. I know what you're going to –

JOHN. No you don't.

Pause.

JUDITH. Go on then.

JOHN. Don't you want to go inside? It's pouring.

JUDITH. *No.*

JOHN. OK. The Stanton League of Decency. And Luke.

JUDITH. Go *on.*

JOHN. Both need the same thing. As I said.

JUDITH. What's that?

JOHN. Need certainty. (*Slight pause.*) They live, or Luke lived, if you can call it living, in a prison cell without windows. Gnawed by demons.

JUDITH. Demons?

JOHN. Demons. All right, chemicals, demons of the mind, that we can say, with our ruddy sophistication, we can say drugs or paranoia, but for them they're demons, and they're all around, and their demand, their *right*, from me, is that I exorcise those demons. Give them comfort, just a little. That's my job, to give them, in this darkness of that prison cell, a little spitting candle in the gloom. I can't deny them that.

JUDITH. Lead kindly light, amid the encircling.

JOHN. Sure.

JUDITH. Oh, John. All this. All that you've turned your back on and rejected, coming here to Stanton. And now you're here, you compromise.

Pause. The rain.

You try and have it both ways. Radical, conservative, revolution and reaction. All in one. You just can't do it, John.

JOHN. I can't? I can.

JUDITH. Well? *Well?*

JOHN (*simply*). That's what it is. Belief. One foot in the slime, and one eye on the heavens. Being a Christian means just that: you have it both ways. See?

Fade out.

Scene Eighteen

Fade in. A hymn cuts in. Big, a great choir.

HYMN. Thou whose almighty word
       Chaos and darkness heard
       And took their flight
       Hear us, we humbly pray
       And where the Gospel-day
       Sheds not its glorious ray
       Let there be light.

Fade out.

The Bishop's Palace, Westford. Phone rings. It's answered.

PUGH. Hello? Who? Ten Downing Street? . . . Oh, yes, put him on. (*Pause.*) Hello. Pugh here. (*Pause.*) Well, isn't that interesting . . . Yes. (*Pause.*) No, I'm surprised as, um, anyone . . . A very courageous choice under the circumstances . . . You've told him, have you? (*Slight pause.*) Yes, well, thanks so much for calling.

Phone put down.

Well, glory be.

Fade out.

Scene Nineteen

Fade in. The hymn cuts in again.

HYMN. Spirit of truth and love,
        Life-giving, holy dove
        Speed forth thy flight!

Fade as PUGH speaks, with echo.

PUGH. And on the day of the consecration, the new Bishop moves through the ranks of the assembled clergy, to kneel at the feet of the Archbishop. Behind him the other Bishops, Senior, Diocesan and Suffragan . . . The Deans and Provosts, and Archdeacons and Precentors . . . The Canons and the Rural Deans and Parish Priests, the Deacons, all according to their place . . . the great and multi-storeyed wedding cake that is the hierarchy of the Church of England . . .

Fades as the hymn fades up again.

HYMN. Move on the waters' face,
        Bearing the lamp of grace,
        And in earth's darkest place
        Let there be light!

Fades again.

Scene Twenty

Fade in. The Cathedral.

JOHN. In the name of God, Amen. I, John, chosen Bishop of the Church and See of Stanton, do profess and promise all due reverence and obedience to the Archbishop and to the Metropolitical Church of Canterbury, and to their successors:

So help me God, through Jesus Christ . . .
Fade down and fade up PUGH *again*.

Scene Twenty-one

No echo.

PUGH. John Hammond. The Mad Monk. Man who couldn't be a
  Bishop, for he would not compromise. But every man has his
  Achilles heel. And I saw Hammond's, when he first confronted
  his transfigured son. A look, just crossed his face. A look that
  said: embarrassment. I'm socially embarrassed. And a man who
  is embarrassed is a' social animal. And social animals are
  animals that compromise. Mad Monks don't compromise. He
  did, and would and will. Luke, his son, his dad's Achilles heel.
  And so I said, I told them: Hammond is the right man to be
  Bishop in the Church of England.

Fade down and fade up hymn again.

HYMN.   Blessed and Holy Three
        Glorious Trinity
        Wisdom, love, might . . .

Fade down and continue PUGH.

PUGH. The Church of England. Like the rest of England. Like its
  institutions. Liquid, open, with an all-encompassing embrace.
  An English institution: velvet glove, on velvet skin, on velvet
  flesh; shot through with bones of iron. Iron compromise.

Fade as fade up end of the hymn.

HYMN.   Boundless as ocean tide
        Rolling in fullest pride,
        Through the world far and wide
        Let there be light!

Fade out.

Scene Twenty-two

Fade in. Conference hall. Slight echo.

JOHN. Fellow Christians, friends. It's now a year since this
  conference was last convened, and since I last spoke to you.
  Since then, I have been — somewhat translated.

Some laughter.

When I spoke to you then, I said that, in fact, far from the Incarnation being a kind of added bonus for those Christians who saw themselves and their religion as an integral part of the struggle for a better world, that in fact the concept was absolutely central. My thinking, since that time, has deepened and enriched that belief.

Reading back over my notes, I find, indeed, a certain blandness, almost arrogance; I think I grossly over-simplified. Because I said to you, of course, that those sinful structures which bar men from God, are as much present in our world, the first world, as they are in Latin America or Southern Africa. I wonder, now, how true that is.

Oh, of course, there's misery. But there is also massive wealth, and, yes, that wealth extends now to the very class that Marxists claim to be the fount of all eternal goodness. And I wonder if, transplanting the theology that works in South America to the council estates of industrial England, I wonder if we're not guilty of an over-simplification, if we're not avoiding facing up to the complexities of a confused and confusing world.

And then I read a passage from the Old Testament. It's the book of Ecclesiastes. Let me read it to you.

'So I returned, and considered all the oppressions that are done under the sun: and behold the tears of such that were oppressed, and they had no comforter; and on the side of the oppressors there was power; but they had no comforter.'

Now, what does Ecclesiastes mean here. Note: he doesn't gloss over the realities of oppression. But he does say that both the poor and the rich have need of comfort. They have solidarity in that. We must recognise their humanity even if they don't recognise the humanity of the people they oppress. And I think I said that last time. But I said it in parenthesis and rather quietly, and now I want to say it very loudly.

And it may be that what I am saying conflicts directly with the theory that changing the world is so important that those who oppose it are fit only for the dustbin of history. To use the well-known culinary image, I could be accused of trying to make the proverbial omelette without breaking the proverbial eggs.

A little laughter.

True. I think I am. Impossible. But so, also, is it impossible that a dead man with a broken body can rise again in three days. Jesus makes what is impossible – politically – a possibility in the spirit by his death and resurrection. Jesus is in fact that miraculous chef who can make an omelette and the eggs stay in their shells.

And, perhaps, you know, in our delving into the great explosion of revolutionary consciousness in the world, over the last ten years, we have ignored another, rather quieter explosion, or implosion, of a kind of spirituality, or at least an urge toward it, expressed in Eastern religion, and, yes, even, in the junkies and the potheads who are searching, however fruitlessly, for spiritual grace.

And perhaps that is the difference. Between us and the Marxists. That we believe we can transcend the world and its diseases, through the spirit, in dark places, contemplation, mystically, we can transcend the greed and pride that traps us all, oppressed, and, yes, oppressors.

We can synthesise the movement to a better world collectively, and find, as well, salvation for the individual soul.

Oppressors, too, have souls. Or don't they?

Pause. Slightly different tone.

Don't they?

Fade out.

Scene Twenty-three

Fade in. Number One, Millbank, HQ of the Church Commissioners. Telex clatter. People chatter. Phones ring. One rings and is answered.

CROSBY. Hello. It's Bill Crosby. (*Slight pause.*) Oh, hello, Nick. What can I do for you? (*Pause.*) Well, with things as they are, on gilts, we're tending to move a bit shorter. Particularly in view of what's likely to happen to MLR. (*Pause.*) No, no, all depending on flat yield, old son. (*Pause, laughs.*) Yes, delighted about John. Did you see him, in all the gear? A sight for sore. (*Slight pause.*) Oh, yes, indeed. More joy in heaven over one lost sheep, and all.

Pause.

Look, actually, Nick, glad you rang, 'cos want to pick your brains. Apparently, it's whispered that ICI's interim's looking bullish, and I wondered what you thought of hedging bets and thinking of a grand or two . . .

Fade out.

Scene Twenty-four

Fade in. Open air. Wind. LUKE's voice, hoarse, unmiked.

LUKE. Brothers and sisters, we have come together, in the sight of the Lord, 'cos we know, that you turn on to Jesus, and he'll never let you down.

Brothers and sisters, we have come together, in the sight of the Lord, 'cos we know, that when you rush with Jesus, then you'll never crash.

Brothers and sisters, we have come together, in the sight of the Lord, 'cos we know, you drop Jesus, that's a high that's everlasting. So let me hear you praise the Lord.

Silence.

Let me hear a J. (*Nothing.*)
Let me hear an E. (*Nothing.*)
Let me hear an S. (*Nothing.*)
Let me hear a U. (*Nothing.*)
Let me hear an S. (*Nothing.*)
What does it spell?

Pause.

What does it spell?

Long silence.

Can't hear you.

Nothing but the wind.

Fade out.

The Life and Adventures of Nicholas Nickleby

from the novel by Charles Dickens

PART ONE

My adaption of Charles Dickens' *Nicholas Nickleby* emerged out of five weeks of discussions, workshops and experiments undertaken by 45 members of the Royal Shakespeare Company in the autumn of 1979. The script that I produced out of that work then went through massive changes as directors Trevor Nunn and John Caird rehearsed what was initially assumed would be a single play of sensible length, but which turned out to be two plays of extraordinary size.

The plays were originally presented in June 1980, at the Aldwych Theatre in London, and were revived twice. The production then transferred to Broadway, and was also televised. The cast list is that of the final Aldwych (and television) cast (in which, for the statistically-minded, 39 performers played 123 speaking parts in 95 scenes); but where necessary I have inserted the names of those performers who created the characters against their principal parts.

It should be noted that everyone participated in the crowd scenes and in the narration (without regard to size of part, age, or – on occasions – sex). Indeed, it is absolutely essential that everybody does so: for the essence of this version of Dickens' considerable and under-rated novel is that it is a tale of the early nineteenth century, written perhaps 20 years after it is set, told by late-twentieth century actors to a contemporary audience.

The *Life and Adventures of Nicholas Nickleby* was first performed by the Royal Shakespeare Company at the Aldwych Theatre from 6 June to 26 July 1980. The production was subsequently revived at the Aldwych in November 1980 and January 1981, and opened at the Plymouth Theatre, New York, on 4 October 1981. The following is the third Aldwych cast, with the original cast members listed, with an asterisk, against their principal roles.

THE NICKLEBY FAMILY

NICHOLAS NICKLEBY	Roger Rees
KATE NICKLEBY	*Susan Littler/Emily Richard
RALPH NICKLEBY	John Woodvine
MRS NICKLEBY	Jane Downs

LONDON

NEWMAN NOGGS	Edward Petherbridge
HANNAH	Hilary Townley
MISS LA CREEVY	Rose Hill
SIR MATTHEW PUPKER	David Lloyd Meredith
MR BONNEY	*Terence Harvey/ Andrew Hawkins
IRATE GENTLEMAN	Patrick Godfrey
FLUNKEY	Timothy Kightley
MR SNAWLEY	William Maxwell
SNAWLEY MAJOR	Janet Dale
SNAWLEY MINOR	Hilary Townley
BELLING	Stephen Rashbrook
WILLIAM	John McEnery
WAITRESSES	Sharon Bower, Sally Nesbitt
COACHMAN	Clyde Pollitt
MR MANTALINI	John McEnery
MADAME MANTALINI	Thelma Whiteley
FLUNKEY	Griffith Jones
MISS NAG	Janet Dale
RICH LADIES	Sharon Bower, Shirley King
MILLINERS	Suzanne Bertish, Sharon Bower, Ian East, Lucy Gutteridge, Cathryn Harrison, William Maxwell, Sally Nesbitt, Stephen Rashbrook, Hilary Townley

YORKSHIRE

MR SQUEERS	*Ben Kingsley/ Alun Armstrong
MRS SQUEERS	Lila Kaye
SMIKE	David Threlfall
PHIB	Sally Nesbitt
FANNY SQUEERS	Suzanne Bertish
YOUNG WACKFORD SQUEERS	*Timothy Spall/Ian McNeice
JOHN BROWDIE	Bob Peck
TILDA PRICE	*Julie Peasgood/ Cathryn Harrison

Boys

TOMKINS	William Maxwell
COATES	Andrew Hawkins
GREYMARSH	Alan Gill
JENNINGS	Patrick Godfrey
MOBBS	Christopher Ravenscroft
BOLDER	Mark Tandy
PILTCHER	Sharon Bower
JACKSON	Nicholas Gecks
COBBEY	John McEnery
PETERS	Teddy Kempner
SPROUTER	Lucy Gutteridge
ROBERTS	Ian East

LONDON AGAIN

MR KENWIGS	Patrick Godfrey
MRS KENWIGS	Shirley King
MORLEENA KENWIGS	*Clare Travers-Deacon/ Hilary Townley
MR LILLYVICK	Timothy Kightley
MISS PETOWKER	Cathryn Harrison
MR CROWL	Ian East
GEORGE	Alan Gill
MR CUTLER	Jeffrey Dench
MRS CUTLER	Janet Dale
MRS KENWIGS' SISTER	Sharon Bower
LADY FROM DOWNSTAIRS	Rose Hill
MISS GREEN	Jane Downs
BENJAMIN	Teddy Kempner
PUGSTYLES	Roderick Horn
OLD LORD	Griffith Jones

YOUNG FIANCÉE	Lucy Gutteridge
LANDLORD	Jeffery Dench

PORTSMOUTH

MR VINCENT CRUMMLES	*Graham Crowden/ Christopher Benjamin
MRS CRUMMLES	Lila Kaye
THE INFANT PHENOMENON	Hilary Townley
MASTER PERCY CRUMMLES	Teddy Kempner
MASTER CRUMMLES	Mark Tandy
MRS GRUDDEN	Rose Hill
MISS SNEVELLICCI	Suzanne Bertish
MR FOLAIR	Clyde Pollitt
MR LENVILLE	*Neil Phillips/ Christopher Ravenscroft
MISS LEDROOK	Lucy Gutteridge
MISS BRAVASSA	Sharon Bower
MR WAGSTAFF	Alun Armstrong
MR BLIGHTEY	Jeffery Dench
MISS BELVAWNEY	Janet Dale
MISS GAZINGI	Sally Nesbitt
MR PAILEY	William Maxwell
MR HETHERINGTON	Andrew Hawkins
MR BANE	Stephen Rashbrook
MR FLUGGERS	Griffith Jones
MRS LENVILLE	Shirley King
MR CURDLE	Hubert Rees
MRS CURDLE	Emily Richard
MR SNEVELLICCI	John McEnery
MRS SNEVELLICCI	Thelma Whiteley

LONDON AGAIN

SCALEY	Ian McNeice
TIX	Teddy Kempner
SIR MULBERRY HAWK	Bob Peck
LORD FREDERICK VERISOPHT	Nicholas Gecks
MR PLUCK	Teddy Kempner
MR PYKE	*John Matshikiza/ Mark Tandy
MR SNOBB	Chistopher Ravenscroft
COLONEL CHOWSER	Timothy Kightley
BROOKER	Clyde Pollitt

MR WITITTERLEY	Roderick Horn
MRS WITITTERLEY	Janet Dale
ALPHONSE	Stephen Rashbrook
OPERA SINGERS	Sharon Bower, Andrew Hawkins, John Woodvine
CHARLES CHEERYBLE	David Lloyd Meredith
NED CHEERYBLE	Hubert Rees
TIM LINKINWATER	Griffith Jones
THE MAN NEXT DOOR	Patrick Godfrey
KEEPER	Alan Gill
FRANK CHEERYBLE	Chrisopher Ravenscroft
NURSE	Thelma Whiteley
MADELINE BRAY	*Juliet Hammond-Hill/ Lucy Gutteridge
ARTHUR GRIDE	Jeffery Dench
WALTER BRAY	*Norman Tyrrell/ Christopher Benjamin
PEG SLIDERSKEW	Suzanne Bertish
HAWK'S RIVAL	Edward Petherbridge
CAPTAIN ADAMS	Andrew Hawkins
WESTWOOD	Alan Gill
CROUPIER	Ian McNeice
CASINO PROPRIETOR	Patrick Godfrey
SURGEON	Timothy Kightley
UMPIRE	Roderick Horn
POLICEMEN	Andrew Hawkins, Mark Tandy
MRS SNAWLEY	Janet Dale
YOUNG WOMAN	Hilary Townley

Directed by Trevor Nunn and John Caird
Assisted by Leon Rubin
Designed by John Napier and Dermot Hayes
Costumes by John Napier
Lighting by David Hersey
Music and Lyrics by Stephen Oliver
Script Assistant Sarah Spare

ACT ONE

Scene One

The whole company assembles on stage. Each member of the company takes at least one of the lines of opening narration:

NARRATION.

There once lived in a sequestered part of the county of Devonshire, one Mr Godfrey Nickleby, who, rather late in life, took it into his head to get married.

And in due course, when Mrs Nickleby had presented her husband with two sons, he found himself in a situation of distinctly shortened means,

Which were only relieved when, one fine morning, there arrived a black-bordered letter, informing him that his uncle was dead and had left him the bulk of his property, amounting in all to five thousand pounds.

And with a portion of this property, Mr Godfrey Nickleby purchased a small farm near Dawlish,

And on his death some fifteen years later, he was able to leave to his eldest son three thousand pounds in cash, and to his youngest, one thousand and the farm.

The younger boy was of a timid and retiring disposition, keen only to attach himself to the quiet routine of country life.

The elder son, however, resolved to make much use of his father's inheritance.

For young Ralph Nickleby had commenced usury on a limited scale even at school, putting out at interest a small capital of slate pencil and marbles,

And had now in adulthood resolved to live his life by the simple motto that there was nothing in the world so good as money.

And while Ralph prospered in the mercantile way in London, the young brother lived still on the farm,

And took himself a wife,

Who gave birth to a boy and a girl,

And by the time they were both nearing the age of twenty, he found his expenses much increased and his capital still more depleted.

Speculate. His wife advised him.

Think of your brother, Mr Nickleby, and speculate.

And Mr Nickleby did speculate,

But a mania prevailed,

A bubble burst,

Four stockbrokers took villa residences at Florence,

Four hundred nobodies were ruined,

And one of them was

Mr Nickleby.

And Mr Nickleby took to his bed,

Apparently resolved to keep that, at all events.

Cheer up, sir!

Said the apothecary.

You mustn't let yourself be cast down, sir,

Said the nurse.

Such things happen every day,

Remarked the lawyer,

And it is very sinful to rebel against them,

Whispered the clergyman,

And what no man with a family ought to do,

Added the neighbours.

But Mr Nickleby shook his head,

And he motioned them all out of the room

And shortly afterwards his reason went astray,

And he babbled of the goodness of his brother and the merry times they'd had at school,

And one day he turned upon his face,

Observing that he thought that he could fall asleep.

And so, with no one in the world to help them but Ralph Nickleby,

MRS NICKLEBY, KATE *and* NICHOLAS *are emerging from the crowd.*

MRS NICKLEBY. The widow,

KATE/NICHOLAS. And her children,

NARRATOR. Journeyed forth to – LONDON!

And immediately, the company becomes the population of London, jostling and bustling round, past and through the Nicklebys, until we can see them no more, and the next scene has emerged.

Scene Two

The London Tavern. A public meeting. On stage, some seated, some standing, are the organisers of the meeting: SIR MATTHEW PUPKER, MR BONNEY, *a* FLUNKEY, *several gentlemen, and, sitting a little apart,* RALPH NICKLEBY. *In and around the audience are representatives of the lower classes: in particular, a large number of* MUFFIN BOYS, *who distribute muffins to the audience from the trays they carry round their necks. There are also a few* POLICEMEN *to keep public order, and, as we shall discover, an* IRATE GENTLEMAN *and a* FURIOUS GENTLEMAN *as well. The* FLUNKEY *bangs his staff for silence.*

FLUNKEY. My lords, ladies and gentlemen. Pray give silence for Sir Matthew Pupker, Honourable Member of the Commons of England in Parliament assembled.

Applause. The odd cat-call. The Police finger their truncheons.

SIR MATTHEW. Good morning. It falls to me today to announce the opening of a public meeting to discuss the propriety or otherwise of petitioning Parliament in urgent condemnation of the appalling, deplorable, and generally heinous state of the Hot Muffin Baking and Delivery Industry.

The IRATE GENTLEMAN *shouts from the audience.*

IRATE GENTLEMAN. Crumpets.

Polite applause.

SIR MATTHEW. Ladies and gentlemen, in troubled times like these, when naked riot stalks the frightened streets at home and overseas the Russian bear is pawing at the very vitals of the Empire, there could not be a greater nor a nobler task than this we face today.

Applause. To stop it, SIR MATTHEW *raises his hand.*

So, Mr Bonney will now read the resolution.

BONNEY *stands, coughs, and reads.*

BONNEY. The Resolution. That this meeting views with alarm and apprehension, the present state of the Muffin trade.

IRATE GENTLEMAN (*shouts*). And crumpet trade.

BONNEY. . . . that it considers the present constitution of the Muffin Boys –

IRATE GENTLEMAN (*shouts*). And crumpet boys!

SOME. Order – shh –

BONNEY (*after a slight pause*). . . . wholly undeserving of the confidence of the public, and that it deems the whole Muffin System –

IRATE GENTLEMAN. Crumpet!

BONNEY *turns to* SIR MATTHEW *in frustration.*

SIR MATTHEW. Now, what –

The IRATE GENTLEMAN *has marched up on to the stage.*

IRATE GENTLEMAN. Sir, I must protest.

SIR MATTHEW. I beg your pardon?

IRATE GENTLEMAN. Sir, I must protest and I must insist. I must insist and I must demand.

SIR MATTHEW. Yes? What?

IRATE GENTLEMAN. And crumpets, sir. And *crumpets*. Not just muffins. Crumpets.

Pause.

SIR MATTHEW. Is that an amendment?

IRATE GENTLEMAN. It's a demand. And an amendment, too.

SIR MATTHEW. I see. Well, then. All those in favour?

ALMOST EVERYONE. Aye!

One FURIOUS MAN, *however, shouts.*

FURIOUS MAN. No! no! a thousand times, no!

And he strides out.

SIR MATTHEW. The ayes appear to have it. Mr Bonney.

BONNEY. And it deems the whole Muffin and Crumpet system prejudicial to the best interests of a great mercantile community.

Applause.

My lords, ladies, and gentlemen: I must state that I have visited the houses of the poor, and have found them destitute of the slightest vestige of a muffin, or a crumpet, which there appears to be much reason to believe some of these persons to not taste from year's end to year's end.

Boos and expressions of shock and horror: 'It's a scandal', 'This must stop', 'Fancy that'.

It is this melancholy state of affairs that the company proposes to correct.

During the following a certain amount of protest develops among those sectors of the audience who are in fact muffin and crumpet sellers themselves, and have thus far been sympathetic to the emotional description of their sad and miserable lot.

. . . firstly, by prohibiting under dire penalties all private muffin and crumpet trading of every description;

Applause – dies down, and we hear MUFFINEERS.

1st MUFFINEER. Eh?

2nd MUFFINEER. What's he saying?

BONNEY. . . . and secondly, by ourselves providing the public generally, with muffins and crumpets of first quality at reduced prices –

Applause – dies down, we hear MUFFINEERS.

1st MUFFINEER. He must be joking.

2nd MUFFINEER. It's our livelihood!

BONNEY. . . . and it is with this object that a bill has been introduced into Parliament.

The MUFFINEERS are striding up towards the stage.

. . . it is this bill that we have met to support;

1st MUFFINEER. What about the Muffin Boys!

Some MUFFINEERS have reached the stage. Others are throwing their muffins on to the stage. Some disreputable members of the audience probably join in too.

MUFFINEERS: So what about the Muffin Boys.
So what about the Muffin Boys.
So what about the –

The MUFFINEERS are roundly truncheoned by the Police for this anarchic display, and are ejected, as BONNEY:

BONNEY. . . . and, finally, it is the supporters of this bill who will confer undying brightness and splendour upon England, under the name of the United Metropolitan Improved Hot Muffin and Crumpet Baking and Punctual Delivery Company! Capital five millions, in five hundred thousand shares of Ten – Pounds – Each!

Wild applause. BONNEY *accepts hand-shakes from supporters and wipes his brow. Eventually, the applause dies.*

SIR MATTHEW. Well, thank you, Mr Bonney.

Pause. Something should have happened. SIR MATTHEW *looks to* RALPH NICKLEBY, *who has sat, impassively, throughout the proceedings.*

Mr Nickleby?

RALPH. Seconded.

SIR MATTHEW. All those in favour?

EVERYONE! Aye!

SIR MATTHEW. Carried by an acclamation! Meeting closed.

And suddenly, SIR MATTHEW, MR BONNEY, *the gentlemen, and everyone else disperse, and* RALPH *walks forward.*

Scene Three

Street. RALPH NICKLEBY *is greeted by his clerk* NEWMAN NOGGS, *a sallow-faced man in rusty-brown clothes.* NOGGS *carries a letter.*

RALPH. Noggs.

NOGGS. That's me.

RALPH. What is it?

NOGGS. It's a letter.

RALPH. Oh. The Ruddles mortgage, I suppose?

NOGGS. No. Wrong.

RALPH. What *has* come, then?

NOGGS. I have.

RALPH (*irritated*). What else?

NOGGS (*handing over the letter*). This. Postmark Strand, black wax, black border, woman's hand, C.N. in the corner.

RALPH. Black wax. I know the hand, too. Newman, I shouldn't be surprised if my brother was dead.

He opens the letter and reads.

NOGGS. I don't think you would.

RALPH (*reading*). Why not, sir?

NOGGS. You are never surprised at anything, that's all.

RALPH (*folding the letter*). It's as I thought. He's dead.

NOGGS. Children alive?

RALPH. Yes, well, that's the point. They're both alive.

NOGGS. Both?

RALPH. And a widow too, and all three of 'em in London, damn 'em.

Slight pause. RALPH looks at NOGGS, who is looking neutral. Enter MR BONNEY.

NOGGS (*unconvincingly*). Terrible.

Slight pause.

RALPH. Go home.

BONNEY *coughs. RALPH turns to BONNEY. NOGGS does not go.*

Ah, Bonney. Put me down for 500, would you?

BONNEY. They'll nearly double in a three-month, Mr Nickleby.

RALPH. I'm sure of it.

BONNEY. And when they have . . . You'll know just what to do with 'em.

Slight pause. Embarrassingly confidential.

Back quietly out, at just the right time, eh?

RALPH. Indeed.

He notices NOGGS is still there.

I told you to go home.

NOGGS. I'm going.

NOGGS *snaps his knuckles and goes out.*

BONNEY. What a very remarkable man that clerk of yours is.

RALPH. Kept his own hounds and horses, once. But squandered everything, borrowed at interest, took to drinking . . . I'd done a little business with him, as it happens, and he came to me to borrow more, I needed to employ a clerk . . .

BONNEY. Yes, yes, just so.

RALPH. So, then – five hundred, Bonney.

BONNEY *goes. RALPH waves the letter. To himself.*

What are they to me? I've never even seen 'em. Damn 'em.

And he turns to go.

Scene Four

Outside and inside a house in the Strand, RALPH *walks round the stage, as* NARRATORS *describe the journey:*

NARRATORS. And so Ralph Nickleby proceeded to the Strand . . .

And found the number of the house . . .

And gave a double-knock,

Someone bangs a stick twice on the floor.

And waited for an answer.

A dirty-faced servant, HANNAH, *appears.*

HANNAH. Yes?

RALPH. Mrs Nickleby at home?

HANNAH. La Creevy.

RALPH. Beg your pardon?

HANNAH. Name, in't what you said. It's Miss La Creevy.

RALPH (*waving the letter*). But –

A female voice from off.

MISS LA CREEVY. Who is it, Hannah?

HANNAH. There's a man here, wanting something.

Enter MISS LA CREEVY, *a small lady of 50 in a yellow bonnet, carrying a paintbrush.*

MISS LA CREEVY. Who? And wanting what?

HANNAH *shrugs, nods at* RALPH.

Oh, sir –

RALPH. Madam, to whom –

MISS LA CREEVY. Oh, sir, I'm Miss La Creevy, sir, I am a painter of portraiture in miniature, sir, and if I may presume to speak such, you have a very strongly marked countenance for such a purpose, sir, should that be your –

RALPH. Is there a widow lodging here? A Mrs Nickleby?

MISS LA CREEVY. Oh, you're for Mrs Nickleby?

RALPH. That's right. I am Mr Ralph Nickleby.

MISS LA CREEVY. Oh, Hannah, what a stupid thing you are. Why, sir, yes, they have their apartments just across the hall from mine, just there, sir, and I must say what an extremely affable lady she is, though of course very low in her spirits, and the children too, most pleasant –

RALPH. Over here, you say?

MISS LA CREEVY. That's right, sir, but may I remark, that if you should ever wish to have a miniature . . .

RALPH turns back, looks darkly at MISS LA CREEVY, who retains sufficient composure to produce a small card.

Perhaps you will have the kindness to take a card of terms.

RALPH takes the card. With a humourless smile.

RALPH. Of course.

MISS LA CREEVY. Now, Hannah, go on, and announce Mr Nickleby to Mrs Nickleby.

RALPH. I thank you.

MISS LA CREEVY goes out, as NICHOLAS, KATE and MRS NICKLEBY come forward. NICHOLAS carries a chair, on which MRS NICKLEBY sits. HANNAH leads RALPH to them. HANNAH tries to make a proper announcement.

HANNAH. Uh, Mrs Nickleby, here's . . . Mr Nickleby.

HANNAH withdraws.

RALPH. Ah, young Nicholas, I suppose. Good morning sir. And, Kate.

MRS NICKLEBY. That is correct, sir. These are my –

Unable to get out the word 'children', MRS NICKLEBY bursts into tears.

RALPH. Well, ma'am, how are you? You must bear up against sorrow, ma'am, I always do. You didn't mention how he died.

MRS NICKLEBY. The doctors could attribute it to no particular disease. We have reason to fear that he died of a broken heart.

RALPH. Hm. What?

MRS NICKLEBY. I beg your pardon?

RALPH. I don't understand. A broken leg or head, I know of them, but not a broken heart.

NICHOLAS. Some people, I believe, have none to break.

RALPH. What's that? How old is this boy, ma'am?

MRS NICKLEBY. Nineteen.

RALPH. And what's he mean to do for bread?

NICHOLAS. To earn it, sir. And not look for anyone to keep my family, except myself.

RALPH. I see. Well, ma'am, the creditors have administered, you say, and you spent what little was left, coming all the way to London, to see me.

MRS NICKLEBY. I hoped . . . It was my husband's wish, I should appeal to you —

RALPH. I don't know why it is. But whenever a man dies with no property, he always thinks he has the right to dispose of other people's. If my brother had been acquainted with the world, and then applied himself to make his way in it, then you would not now be in this — in your situation. I must say it, Miss Nickleby: my brother was a thoughtless, inconsiderate man, and no one, I am sure, can feel that fact more keenly than you do.

MRS NICKLEBY. Well, well. That may be true. I've often thought, if he had listened to me . . . Yes. It may well be true.

NICHOLAS *and* KATE *give an uncertain glance at each other.* RALPH *notes this.*

RALPH. So, what's your daughter fit for, ma'am?

MRS NICKLEBY. Oh, Kate has been well educated, sir.

KATE. I'm willing to try anything that will give me home and bread.

RALPH (*slightly affected by* KATE). Well, well.

To NICHOLAS, *briskly.*

And you, sir? You're prepared to work?

NICHOLAS. Yes, certainly.

RALPH *takes a newspaper cutting from his pocket.*

RALPH. Then read that. Caught my eye this morning.

NICHOLAS *takes the cutting and reads.*

NICHOLAS. Education. The Master of the Academy, Dotheboys Hall, near Greta Bridge in Yorkshire, is in town, and attends at the Saracen's Head, Snow Hill. Able assistant wanted. Annual salary five pounds. A Master of Arts would be preferred.

RALPH. Well. There.

MRS NICKLEBY. But he's not a Master of Arts.

RALPH. That I think can be got over.

KATE. And the salary is so small, and it is so far away —

MRS NICKLEBY. Hush, Kate, your uncle must know best.

RALPH. And I'm convinced that he will have you, if I recommend
it.

Pause.

Ma'am, if he can find another job, in London, now, which
keeps him in shoe leather . . . He can have a thousand pounds.

Pause.

KATE. We must be separated, then, so soon?

NICHOLAS. Sir, if I am appointed to this post, what will become
of those I leave behind?

RALPH. If you're accepted, and you take it, they will be provided
for. That will be my care.

Pause.

NICHOLAS. Then, uncle, I am ready to do anything you wish.

RALPH. That's good. And, come, who knows, you work well,
and you'll rise to be a partner. And then, if he dies, your
fortune's made.

NICHOLAS. Oh, yes?

To his family, to cheer them up, but becoming convinced himself.

Oh, yes, to be sure. Oh, Kate, and who knows, perhaps there
will be some young nobleman or other, at the school, who takes
a fancy to me, and then I'll become his travelling tutor when he
leaves . . . And when we get back from the continent, his father
might procure me some handsome appointment, in his
household, or his business. Yes? And, who knows, he might fall
in love with Kate, and marry her . . .

To RALPH.

Don't you think so, uncle?

RALPH (*unconvincingly*). Yes, yes, of course.

KATE goes to RALPH.

KATE. Uncle. We're a simple family. We were born and bred in
the country, we have never been apart, and we are
unacquainted with the world.

RALPH. Well, then, my dear –

KATE. It will take time for us to understand it, to apply ourselves
to make our way in it, and to bear that separation which
necessity now forces on us. I am sure you understand.

Pause.

RALPH. Oh, yes, indeed I do.

NICHOLAS *embraces his mother and sister.*

Now, sir . . . shall we go?

NICHOLAS *follows* RALPH *out one way, as* MRS NICKLEBY *and* KATE *leave the other.*

Scene Five

The coffee house of the Saracen's Head. A table, on which WACKFORD SQUEERS *is sitting, reading a newspaper. Near him is a little trunk, on which a small boy,* BELLING, *is sitting. This scene is set up during:*

NARRATOR. And so the uncle, and his nephew, took themselves with all convenient speed towards Snow Hill, and Mr Wackford Squeers.

The narration is carried on by WILLIAM, *a waiter at the Saracen's Head.* TWO MAIDS *enter; and stare at* MR SQUEERS.

WILLIAM. And in Snow Hill, near to the jail and Smithfield, is the Saracen's Head, and outside the Saracen's Head are two stone heads of Saracens, both fearsome and quite hideously ugly, and inside, on this January afternoon, stood Mr Squeers, whose appearance was not much more prepossessing.

SQUEERS *lowers the newspaper. We see him as the* TWO MAIDS *describe him to each other.*

1st MAID. He's only got one eye.

WILLIAM. While the popular prejudice runs in favour of two.

2nd MAID. And, look, the side of his face is all wrinkled and puckered.

WILLIAM. Which gave him a highly sinister appearance, especially when he smiled.

1st MAID. And the eye he's got's a very funny colour.

WILLIAM. Which indeed it was, a kind of greenish grey, in shape resembling the fanlight of a street-door, through which Mr Squeers was glaring at a tiny boy, who was sitting on a tiny trunk, in front of him.

And indeed SQUEERS *and* BELLING *are looking at each other.* BELLING *sneezes as* WILLIAM *and* THE MAIDS *withdraw.*

SQUEERS. Hello, sir! What's that, sir?

THE MAIDS *withdraw.*

BELLING. Nothing, please, sir.

SQUEERS. Nothing, sir?

BELLING. Please, sir, I sneezed, sir.

SQUEERS (*taking the boy by the ear*). Sneezed? You Sneezed? Well, that's not nothing, is it?

BELLING. No, sir.

SQUEERS. Wait till Yorkshire, my young gentleman. And then I'll give you something to remember.

BELLING *is crying. Re-enter* WILLIAM.

WILLIAM. Mr Squeers, there's a gentleman who's asking for you.

SQUEERS. Show him in, William, show him in.

WILLIAM *goes out.* SQUEERS *looks at* BELLING, *who is still sniffing.* BELLING *cringes at this look, and is somewhat surprised when* SQUEERS *sits on the bench, and puts his arm round the tiny boy.*

Now, dear child, why are you weeping? All people have their trials, but what is yours? You are losing your friends, that is true, but you will have a father in me, my dear, and a mother in Mrs Squeers.

WILLIAM *admitting* SNAWLEY, *a sleek, flat-nosed man in sombre garments, and two little Snawley boys.*

At the delightful village of Dotheboys, near Greta Bridge in Yorkshire, where youth are boarded, clothed, booked, furnished with pocket-money, provided with all necessaries,

SNAWLEY *checks* SQUEERS' *speech against a newspaper advertisement he carries. It is the same.*

. . . instructed in all languages, living and dead, mathematics, orthography, geometry, astronomy, trigonometry, the use of the globes, algebra, single stick (if required), writing, arithmetic, fortification, and every other branch of classical literature. Terms, 20 guineas per annum, no extras, no vacations, and diet unparalleled, why good day, sir, I had no idea . . .

And SQUEERS *turned to* SNAWLEY *and extended his hand.*

SNAWLEY. Mr Squeers?

SQUEERS. The same, sir.

SNAWLEY. My name is Snawley. I'm in the oil and colour way.

SQUEERS. Well, how do you do, sir?

And to the little Snawleys.

And how do *you* do, young sirs?

SNAWLEY. Mr Squeers, I have been thinking of placing my two boys at your school.

SQUEERS. Sir, I do not think you could do a better thing.

SNAWLEY. At – £20 per annum?

SQUEERS. Guineas.

SNAWLEY. Pounds for two, perhaps? They're not great eaters.

SQUEERS. Then we will not be great feeders, sir. I am sure that we can reach accommodation.

SNAWLEY. And this is another boy, sir?

SQUEERS. Yes, sir, this is Belling, and his luggage that he's sitting on. Each boy requires two suits of clothes, six shirts, six pairs of stockings, two nightcaps, two pocket handkerchiefs, two pairs of shoes, two hats and a razor.

SNAWLEY. Razor? Sir, whatever for?

SQUEERS. To Shave With.

Pause. SNAWLEY *takes* SQUEERS *aside. The little boys look at each other.*

SNAWLEY. Sir, up to what age . . .?

SQUEERS. As long as payment's regularly made.

SNAWLEY. I see.

Slight pause.

SQUEERS. Sir, let us understand each other. Are these boys legitimate?

SNAWLEY. They are.

SQUEERS. They are?

SNAWLEY. But I am not their father.

Slight pause.

SQUEERS. Go on.

SNAWLEY. I'm the husband of their mother.

Slight pause.

And as it's so expensive, keeping boys . . . And as she has so little money of her own . . .

Slight pause.

And hearing of a school, a great distance off, where there are none of those ill-judged comings-home three times a year, that do unsettle the children so . . .

Pause.

SQUEERS. And payments regular, and then, no questions asked.

Slight pause.

SNAWLEY. I should . . . I should want their morals particularly attended to.

WILLIAM *brings in* RALPH *and* NICHOLAS.

SQUEERS. Well, you've come to the right shop for morals, sir. I think we do, now, understand each other.

RALPH. Mr Squeers.

SQUEERS. Yes? What is it?

RALPH. A matter of business, sir. My name is Ralph Nickleby. Perhaps you recollect me.

SQUEERS. Why, yes, sir . . . Did you not pay me a small account for some years . . . on behalf of parents of a boy named Dorker who . . .

RALPH. That's right. Who died, unfortunately, in Yorkshire.

SQUEERS. Yes, sir, I remember well.

SNAWLEY *looking at* SQUEERS.

And I remember too, how Mrs Squeers nursed the boy . . . Dry toast and warm tea when he wouldn't swallow, and a candle in his bedroom on the night he died, a dictionary to lay his head upon . . .

RALPH. Yes, yes. So, shall we come to business? You have advertised for an able assistant, and here he is.

SQUEERS *looks at* NICHOLAS.

My nephew Nicholas, hot from school, with everything he learnt there fermenting in his head, and nothing fermenting in his pocket.

Pause.

His father lies dead, he is wholly ignorant of the world, he has no resources whatever, and he wants to make his fortune.

SQUEERS. Well . . .

NICHOLAS. I fear, sir, that you object to my youth, and my not being a Master of Arts?

SQUEERS. Well, the absence of a college degree is an objection . . .

RALPH. And if any caprice of temper should induce him to cast aside this golden opportunity, I shall consider myself absolved from extending any assistance to his mother and sister. Now the question is, whether, for some time to come, he won't exactly serve your purposes.

Pause. SQUEERS a little gesture. He and RALPH withdraw a little.

SNAWLEY (*to convince himself*). A fine gentleman, sir. That Mr Squeers, a gentleman of virtue and morality.

NICHOLAS (*to convince himself*). I'm sure of it.

RALPH and SQUEERS back.

RALPH. Nicholas, you are employed.

NICHOLAS (*delighted*). Oh, sir —

SQUEERS. The coach leaves eight o'clock tomorrow morning, Mr Nickleby — and you must be here a quarter before.

NICHOLAS. I shall be. Surely.

RALPH. And your fare is paid.

SQUEERS takes SNAWLEY aside, taking money from him and inserting something in a ledger. NOGGS enters.

NICHOLAS. Well, thank you, uncle. I will not forget this kindness.

RALPH. See you don't.

SQUEERS. Mr Snawley . . .

SQUEERS, SNAWLEY, the little SNAWLEYS and BELLING withdraw as RALPH and NICHOLAS meet NOGGS.

RALPH. Noggs.

NOGGS (*hands RALPH a letter*). Mortgage letter's come. And Mr Bonney says —

RALPH (*taking the letter and opening it*). Oh, yes. I know what Mr Bonney says. A matter of investment.

He opens the letter and reads. NOGGS is looking fixedly at

NICHOLAS. NICHOLAS *doesn't quite know what to do. After a few moments, to break the silence.*

NICHOLAS. Um, I'm

NOGGS. Yes, I know.

RALPH *pocketing the letter.*

RALPH And we're late. You'd best go home and pack, sir. Early in the morning, you heard Mr Squeers.

Exit RALPH and NOGGS.

Scene Six

The Nicklebys' rooms. MRS NICKLEBY and KATE, carrying a suitcase, books and clothes, enter to NICHOLAS as he speaks:

NICHOLAS. And there was so much to be done,

KATE. And so little time to do it in. (*The Nicklebys quickly packing NICHOLAS' suitcase.*)

MRS NICKLEBY. So many kind words to be spoken,

KATE. And so much bitter pain to be suppressed,

NICHOLAS. That the preparations for the journey were mournful indeed.

KATE (*putting a book in the suitcase*). A hundred things deemed indispensable for his comfort, Nicholas left behind,

NICHOLAS (*taking the book out again*). As they might prove convertible into money if required.

MRS NICKLEBY. A hundred affectionate contests on such points as these took place;

NICHOLAS. And as they grew nearer and nearer to the close of their preparations,

KATE. Kate grew busier and busier, and wept more silently.

During the following, KATE and MRS NICKLEBY leave NICHOLAS, alone with his suitcase.

NICHOLAS. And bed at last, and at six the next morning, Nicholas rose up, and wrote a few lines in pencil to say goodbye, and resolved that, come what may, he would bear whatever might be in store for him, for the sake of his mother and his sister, and giving his uncle no excuse to desert them in their need.

And by now, the Saracen's Head has reappeared behind him.

Scene Seven

The Saracen's Head. SQUEERS *sitting at the table with a plate of eggs and ham. The two* SNAWLEYS *and* BELLING *sitting with nothing. A maid stands next to* WILLIAM, *carrying a tray, on which is a jug of water, and a plate of one piece of bread-and-butter.* SQUEERS *is holding up a mug of milk.* NICHOLAS *stands apart, watching.*

SQUEERS. This is two penn'orth of milk, is it, William?

WILLIAM. S'right, sir.

SQUEERS. What a rare article milk is in London, to be sure. Now fill it up with water, will you?

WILLIAM. To the top, sir?

SQUEERS (*starting to eat*). That's correct.

WILLIAM. But, sir, you'll drown the milk.

SQUEERS. Well, serve it right for being so expensive. Now. Where's bread-and-butter?

WILLIAM. Here, sir.

He puts the bread-and-butter on the table. The little boys quickly reach for it.

SQUEERS. Wait!

The boys freeze. Their hands go back. WILLIAM *goes away.* SQUEERS *divides the slice of bread into three, as* NICHOLAS *approaches.*

Good morning, Nickleby. Sit down. We're breakfasting.

NICHOLAS. Good morning, sir.

SQUEERS. Now, boys, when I say 'One', young Snawley takes a drink of milk and eats his bread. When I say 'two', the older Snawley, and then three is Belling. Clear?

BOYS. Oh, yes, sir.

SQUEERS (*eating*). Right. Now, wait. Subdue your appetites, my dears, you've conquered human nature. One!

SNAWLEY JNR. *eats and drinks.*

Say 'thank you',

SNAWLEY JNR. (*eating*). 'Ank 'ou.

Pause. SQUEERS *eats.*

SQUEERS. Two!

SNAWLEY SNR. *eats and drinks.*

Well!

SNAWLEY SNR. Thank you, sir.

SQUEERS *finishes his food.*

SQUEERS. And –

He is interrupted by the blowing of a horn.

Oh, dear Belling, there's the horn. You've missed your turn. Come, my dears, let's bustle.

And at once there is tremendous bustle, and the sudden, noisy entrance of coachmen, passengers, porters, flower- and newspaper-sellers and passers-by gives the impression that the coach has arrived. SQUEERS marshalls the little boys, and NICHOLAS is collared by NOGGS, who appears out of the crowd.

NOGGS. Psst.

NICHOLAS. I'm sorry? Mr Noggs!

NOGGS (*handing him a letter*). Hush. Take it. Read it. No one knows. That's all.

He is going. MRS NICKLEBY and KATE appear.

NICHOLAS. Stop!

NOGGS. No.

Exit NOGGS.

NICHOLAS. But –

MRS NICKLEBY. Nicholas!

NICHOLAS. Oh mother, Kate – you shouldn't.

KATE. How could we just let you go . . .

SQUEERS, *dragging BELLING, comes to NICHOLAS.*

SQUEERS. Now, Nickleby, I think you'd better ride behind. I'm feared of Belling falling off, and there goes 20 pounds a year.

NICHOLAS. Right, I, uh –

SQUEERS (*dragging BELLING away*). And, dear Belling, if you don't stop chattering your teeth and shaking, I'll warm you with a severe thrashing in about half a minute's time. Come Nickleby!

KATE. Oh, Nicholas, who is that man? What kind of place can it be that you're going to?

NICHOLAS. Well, I suppose – that Yorkshire folk are rather rough and uncultivated –

SQUEERS (*calling*). Nickleby, God damn you!

And now it is clear from waving passers-by and exiting passengers that the coach's departure is imminent.

NICHOLAS. Goodbye, mother. To our meeting, one day soon. And goodbye, Kate.

KATE. You'll write?

NICHOLAS. Of course I will.

COACHMAN. Stage leaving! Stage leaving! Everyone for the stage, up and sit fast!

And NICHOLAS *runs out past the waving passers-by.* NARRATORS *speak to the audience.*

NARRATORS.

And a minute's bustle,

And a banging of the coach doors,

A swaying of the vehicle,

A cry of all right,

A few notes from the horn –

The horn sounds. The coach departs, everyone waving.

NARRATOR. And the coach was gone, and rattling over the stones of Smithfield.

And everyone except KATE *is gone.*

Scene Eight

Miss La Creevy's House: MISS LA CREEVY *with her painting equipment in front of her on a little table: opposite a chair on a little platform. This is set up as* KATE *speaks to the audience:*

KATE. And on the second morning after Nicholas' departure, Kate found herself sitting in a very faded chair, rasied upon a very dusty throne, in Miss La Creevy's room, giving that lady a sitting for a portrait.

KATE *sits on the other chair and poses.* MISS LA CREEVY *painting.*

MISS LA CREEVY. Well, I think I have caught it now. And it will be the sweetest portrait I have ever done, certainly.

KATE. It will be your genius that makes it so, I'm sure.

MISS LA CREEVY. Well, my dear, you are right, in the main though I don't allow that it's of such importance in the present case. Ah! The difficulties of art, my dear, are very great.

KATE. I have no doubt.

MISS LA CREEVY. They are beyond anything you can form the faintest perception of. What with bringing out eyes and keeping down noses, and adding to heads, and taking away teeth altogether, you have no idea of the trouble one little miniature can be.

KATE. The remuneration can scarcely repay you.

MISS LA CREEVY. Well, it does not, and that's the truth. And then sitters are so dissatisfied and unreasonable, that nine times out of ten there's no pleasure in painting them. Sometimes they say, "Oh how very serious you have made me look, Miss La Creevy", and at others, "La, Miss La Creevy, how very smirking!", when the very essence of a good portrait is that it must be either serious or smirking, or it's no portrait at all.

KATE. Indeed! And which, dear Miss La Creevy, which am I?

MISS LA CREEVY *beckons* KATE, *who goes to look at the portrait.*

Oh!

MISS LA CREEVY. Dear, now what's the matter?

KATE. Oh, it's just the shade. Is my face, really, that —

MISS LA CREEVY. Oh, that's my salmon pink, my dear. Originally, I hit upon it for an officer. But it went down so well, among my patrons, that I use it now for almost everything. It is considered, in the art world, quite a novelty.

KATE (*returning and sitting*). I am convinced of it.

MISS LA CREEVY (*continuing to paint*). And now, my dear, when do you expect to see your uncle again?

KATE. I scarcely know. I'd thought to, before now.

MISS LA CREEVY. Hm. I suppose he has money, hasn't he?

KATE. I'm told he's very rich.

MISS LA CREEVY. Hm. You may depend upon it, or he wouldn't be so surly.

KATE. Yes, he is a little rough.

MISS LA CREEVY. A little rough! A porcupine's a featherbed to him.

KATE. It's only his manner, I believe. I should be sorry to think ill of him unless I knew he deserved it.

MISS LA CREEVY. Well, that is very right and proper. But mightn't he, without feeling it himself, make you and your mama some nice little allowance . . . What would a hundred a year, for instance, be to him?

KATE. I don't know what it would be to him. But it would be unacceptable to me.

MISS LA CREEVY. He is your uncle, dear . . .

KATE (*stands*). From anyone. Not him, particularly. Anyone.

Pause.

I'm sorry. I have moved.

MISS LA CREEVY. It doesn't matter, dear.

HANNAH is there. Someone knocks.

Now, who can that be? Yes, come in.

HANNAH steps into the room.

HANNAH. Um . . . It's Mr – um . . .

MISS LA CREEVY. It's who?

Enter RALPH NICKLEBY.

RALPH. Your servant, ladies.

KATE (*standing*). Uncle.

RALPH. Hm. Where's Mrs Nickleby?

MISS LA CREEVY. Hannah.

Exit HANNAH.

RALPH. Is it my niece's portrait, ma'am?

MISS LA CREEVY. Well, yes it is, sir, and between you and me and the post, sir, it will be a very nice portrait too, though I say it myself as shouldn't.

RALPH. Well, don't trouble yourself to show it to me, ma'am, I have no eye for likenesses. Is it nearly finished?

MISS LA CREEVY. Why, yes. Two more sittings will –

RALPH. Have them done at once, ma'am, for she'll have no time to idle over fooleries. Have you let your lodgings, ma'am?

MISS LA CREEVY. I have not put a bill up yet, sir.

RALPH. Then do so, at once. For neither of them's going to need your rooms, or if they do, can't pay for 'em.

KATE. Uh – uncle, we are moving? Where?

RALPH. I'm not yet sure where either of you will be placed.

KATE. Oh, uncle, do you mean we're to be separated?

HANNAH *admits* MRS NICKLEBY.

MRS NICKLEBY. Brother-in-law.

RALPH. Ma'am. I've found a situation for your daughter.

MRS NICKLEBY (*sitting in* KATE's *chair.*) Well. This is good news. But I will say it is only what I would have thought of you.

RALPH *about to say something.*

"Depend on it", I said to Kate only yesterday at breakfast, "that after your uncle has provided in that most ready manner for Nicholas, he will not leave us until he has done at least the same for you!"

RALPH *about to say something.*

Those were my very words, as near as I can remember. Kate, my dear, why don't you thank your –

RALPH. Let me proceed, ma'am, pray.

MRS NICKLEBY. Kate, my love, let your uncle proceed.

KATE. I am most anxious that he should, mama.

MRS NICKLEBY. Well, if you are, you had better allow your uncle to say what he has to say, without interruption.

RALPH. I am very much obliged to you, ma'am. An absence of business habits in this family apparently leads to a great waste of words before business is arrived at at all.

MRS NICKLEBY (*with a sigh*). I fear it is so, indeed. Your poor brother –

RALPH. My poor brother, ma'am, had no idea what business was.

Pause. MRS NICKLEBY *says nothing.*

The situation that I have made interest to procure for your daughter, is with a milliner and dressmaker.

MRS NICKLEBY. A milliner.

RALPH. Yes, and milliners in London, as I need not remind you, ma'am, are persons of great wealth and station.

MRS NICKLEBY. Well, now, that's very true. That's very true, Kate, for I recollect when your poor papa and I came to town after we were married, that a young lady brought me home a chip cottage bonnet, with white and green trimming, and a green persian lining, in her own carriage, which drove up to the door at a full gallop – at least, I am not quite certain whether it was her own carriage or a hackney chariot, but I remember very well that the horse dropped down dead as he was turning round, and that –

RALPH. The lady's name is Madame Mantalini. She lives near Cavendish Square. If your daughter is disposed to try the situation, I'll take her there on Monday. Now, I must –

MRS NICKLEBY. Kate, have you nothing that you wish to say? To tell your uncle?

KATE. Yes, I have. But I'd prefer to speak to him alone.

MRS NICKLEBY. Now Kate, I'm sure –

KATE. I'll see you out then, uncle.

She firmly gestures RALPH out of the room.

RALPH. Then – I'm your servant, ma'am.

RALPH and KATE leave the room, and come downstage together.

So? What d'you want to say?

KATE. I must ask one question of you, uncle. Am I to live at home?

RALPH. At home? Where's that?

KATE. I must – we must, me and my mother, have some place we can call home. It may be very humble –

RALPH. "May be!" Must be. "May be" humble!

KATE. Well, then, must be. But, my question, uncle. You must answer it.

Pause.

RALPH. I'd some idea . . . providing for your mother, in a pleasant district of the country . . .

KATE. Out of London?

RALPH. Yes, I'd thought so, but if you're quite determined that you want to stay with her . . .

KATE. I am.

RALPH. Yes. I had thought you would be.

Slight pause.

Well, I have an empty house. It's in the East End. Till it's rented, you can live in it. I'll send my clerk on Saturday to take you there. So — is that satisfactory?

KATE is cracking.

KATE. I'm very much, obliged to you, dear uncle.

Pause.

Very much —

RALPH. Please don't begin to cry.

KATE. It's very foolish, I know, uncle.

RALPH. Yes, it is. And most affected, too.

To KATE.

Let's have no more of it.

RALPH goes out. KATE goes out another way.

Scene Nine

Outside and inside Dotheboys Hall. A bare stage. Snow falls. Wind blows. SQUEERS, NICHOLAS, BELLING and the two SNAWLEYS walk downstage with the luggage. They stop.

NICHOLAS. Dotheboys Hall.

SQUEERS. Oh, sir, you needn't call it a hall up here.

NICHOLAS. Why not?

SQUEERS. 'Cos the fact is, it ain't a hall.

As SQUEERS leads the party round to the side of the stage, NICHOLAS speaks to the audience.

NICHOLAS. A host of unpleasant misgivings, which had been crowding upon Nicholas during the whole journey, thronged into his mind. And as he considered the dreary house and dark windows, and the wild country round covered with snow, he felt a depression of heart and spirit which he had never experienced before.

SQUEERS. No, we call it a hall up in London, because it sounds better, but they don't know it by that name here.

He bangs an imaginary door.

A man may call his house an island if he likes; there's no Act of Parliament against that, I believe?

NICHOLAS. No, I think not, sir.

SQUEERS (*banging*). Well, then. Hey! Door!

From the darkness, SMIKE *appears. He is about 19, but bent over with lameness, and dressed in ragged garments which he has long since outgrown. He pulls open the huge door, and the wind howls as* SQUEERS *strides into the house.*

Smike. Where the devil have you been?

SMIKE. Please, sir, I fell asleep.

SQUEERS. You fell awhat?

SMIKE. Please, sir, I fell asleep over the fire.

SQUEERS. Fire? What fire? Where's there a fire?

During the following, SQUEERS, SMIKE, NICHOLAS *and the boys with their luggage move round the stage — as if passing along corridors — as the Squeers' servant* PHIB *brings on a big chair and then a table to centre stage. This is the Squeers' parlour, and* PHIB *goes out again to being on a tray of brandy, glasses and water, placing it on the table.*

SMIKE. Please, sir, Missus said as I was sitting up, I might be by the fire for a warm . . .

SQUEERS. Your missus is a fool. You'd have been a deuced deal more wakeful in the cold.

From off, we hear the voice of MRS SQUEERS.

MRS SQUEERS (*off*). Squeers!

SQUEERS (*calls*). My love!

MRS SQUEERS. Squeers!

By now SQUEERS *is in the parlour area, the boys are standing in the corridor with their luggage, and* NICHOLAS *is between them, not knowing quite what to do.*

SQUEERS (*to* SMIKE). There's boys. The boys, to bed.

SMIKE *takes the boys out, leaving their luggage, as* MRS SQUEERS *enters.*

MRS SQUEERS. Oh, Squeers. How is my Squeery, dearie.

The SQUEERSES *embrace.*

SQUEERS. Well, well, my love. How are the cows?

MRS SQUEERS. All right, every one of 'em.

SQUEERS. And the pigs?

MRS SQUEERS. As well as they were when you went.

SQUEERS. Well, that's a great blessing.

These sweet nothings over, SQUEERS leaves MRS SQUEERS and takes letters and documents from his pocket. As an afterthought:

The boys all as they were, I suppose?

MRS SQUEERS, taking the letters from SQUEERS and placing them on the table, glancing at one or two.

MRS SQUEERS. Oh yes, they're well enough. But young Sprouter's had a fever.

SQUEERS (*taking off his greatcoat*). No! Damn the boy, he's always at something of that sort.

PHIB takes Squeers's huge coat, and stands there, holding it. SQUEERS goes to the table, sits, MRS SQUEERS pours him a brandy and tops it up with water. As:

MRS SQUEERS. Never was such a boy, I do believe. Whatever he has is always catching, too. I say it's obstinacy, and nothing shall ever convince me that it isn't. I'd beat it out of him, and I told you that six months ago.

SQUEERS. So you did, my love. We'll try what can be done.

Slight pause. MRS SQUEERS nods in the direction of NICHOLAS, who is still standing near the door, not knowing what to do.

Ah, Nickleby. Come, sir, come in.

NICHOLAS comes a little further into the room.

This is our new young man, my dear.

MRS SQUEERS (*suspiciously*). Oh. Is it?

SQUEERS. He can shake down here tonight, can't he?

MRS SQUEERS (*looking round*). Well, if he's not particular . . .

NICHOLAS (*politely*). Oh, no, indeed.

MRS SQUEERS That's lucky.

She looks at SQUEERS and laughs. SQUEERS laughs back. They laugh at each other. Meanwhile, SMIKE reappears. MRS SQUEERS looks at PHIB, and snaps her head towards the door.

PHIB *goes out with the big coat. Slight pause. Then, with a drink to* SQUEERS, *as if to ask if* NICHOLAS *should be given a drink.*

Another brandy, Squeers?

SQUEERS (*nodding back*). Certainly. A glassful.

MRS SQUEERS *pours a large brandy-and-water for* SQUEERS, *and a small one for* NICHOLAS. *She takes the drink to* NICHOLAS. SQUEERS *is looking through the letters.* NICHOLAS *takes the drink.* SMIKE *stands, staring fixedly at the letters on the table.* MRS SQUEERS *goes and picks up one of the boys' bags and takes it back to the table.*

Bolder's father's short.

MRS SQUEERS. Tt tt.

SQUEERS. But Cobbey's sister's sent something.

MRS SQUEERS *starts going through the boys' luggage, picking out the bits and pieces she fancies.*

MRS SQUEERS. That's good.

SQUEERS. And Greymarsh's maternal aunt has written, with no money, but two pairs of stockings and a tract.

MRS SQUEERS. Maternal aunt.

SQUEERS. My love?

MRS SQUEERS. More likely, in my view, that she's Greymarsh's maternal mother.

THE SQUEERSES *look at each other. Then* SQUEERS *notices that* SMIKE *is very close, craning to see the letters.*

SQUEERS. Yes? What's to do, boy?

SMIKE. Is there –

SQUEERS. What?

SMIKE. Is there . . . there's nothing heard . . .?

SQUEERS. No, not a word. And never will be.

MRS SQUEERS. (*The very idea.*) Tt.

Pause. SQUEERS *decides to rub it in.*

SQUEERS. And it is a pretty sort of thing, that you should have been left here all these years and no money paid after the first six – nor no notice taken, nor no clue to who you belong to? It's a pretty sort of thing, is it not, that I should have to feed a great fellow like you, and never hope to get one penny for it, isn't it?

SQUEERS *looking at* SMIKE.

NICHOLAS (*out front*). The boy put his hand to his head, as if he was making an effort to remember something, and then, looking vacantly at his questioner, gradually broke into a smile.

SQUEERS. That's right. Now off with you, and send the girl.

SMIKE *limps out.* MRS SQUEERS *has finished sifting the boy's bag. She looks for something on the table.*

MRS SQUEERS. I tell you what, Squeers, I think that young chap's turning silly.

SQUEERS (*wiping his mouth*). I hope not. For he's a handy fellow out of doors, and worth his meat and drink anyway.

He stands.

But come, I'm tired, and want to go to bed.

MRS SQUEERS. Oh, drat the thing.

SQUEERS. What's wrong, my dear?

MRS SQUEERS. The school spoon. I can't find it.

SQUEERS. Never mind, my love.

MRS SQUEERS. What, never mind? It's brimstone, in the morning.

SQUEERS. Ah, I forgot.

He helps the search.

Yes, certainly, it is.

NICHOLAS. Uh . . .?

SQUEERS. We purify the boys' bloods now and then, Nickleby.

MRS SQUEERS (*crossly*). Purify fiddle-sticks. Don't think, young man, that we go to the expense of flour of brimstone and molasses just to purify them; because if you think we carry on the business in that way, you'll find yourself mistaken, and so I tell you plainly.

SQUEERS *is not sure this intelligence is quite discreet. Enter* PHIB, *who tidies round the table, putting things back on the tray.*

SQUEERS. My dear . . . should you . . .

MRS SQUEERS. Nonsense. If the young man comes to be a

teacher, let him understand at once that we don't want any foolery about the boys. They have the brimstone and treacle, partly because if they hadn't something or other in the way of medicine they'd always be ailing and giving a world of trouble, and partly because it spoils their appetites and comes cheaper than breakfast and dinner. So it does them good and us good at the same time, and that's fair enough, I'm sure.

SQUEERS *looking embarrassed.* MRS SQUEERS *shoots a glance at him.*

Now, where's the spoon?

PHIB *has picked up the tray.*

PHIB. Uh. Ma'am.

MRS SQUEERS. What is it?

PHIB. S'round your neck.

And indeed the spoon is round MRS SQUEERS' *neck. She cuffs* PHIBS *lightly for telling her.*

MRS SQUEERS. Why did you not say *before.*

PHIBS. M'sorry, ma'am.

PHIBS *picks up the tray, leaving the brandy bottle, and goes out.*

MRS SQUEERS (*pleasantly*). And so, dear Mr Nickleby, good night.

MRS SQUEERS *goes out. Pause.*

SQUEERS. A most invaluable woman, Nickleby.

NICHOLAS. Indeed, sir.

SQUEERS. I do not know her equal. That woman, Nickleby, is always the same: always the same bustling, lively, active, saving creature that you see her now.

NICHOLAS. I'm sure of it.

SQUEERS. (*Warming further to his theme.*) It is my custom, when I am in London, to say that she is like a mother to those boys. But she is more, she's ten times more. She does things for those boys, Nickleby, that I don't believe half the mothers going would do for their sons.

NICHOLAS. I'm certain of it.

SQUEERS. And so, goodnight, then, Nickleby.

He tries to make a solemn exit, undermined by spotting the brandy, which he returns to pick up.

NICHOLAS. Goodnight, sir.

SQUEERS nods gravely and goes out. NICHOLAS stands a moment, then takes off his coat. He sits, on the floor. He notices Noggs' letter in his coat pocket. He opens it and begins to read. NOGGS himself appears, with a glass of brandy. He speaks his letter as we see NICHOLAS read it.

NOGGS My dear young man. I know the world. Your father did not, or he would not have done me a kindness when there was no hope of return. You do not, or you would not be bound on such a journey. If ever you want a shelter in London, they know where I live at the sign of the Crown, in Silver St., Golden Square. You can come at night. Once, nobody was ashamed – never mind that. It's all over. Excuse errors. I have forgotten all my old ways. My spelling may have gone with them.

NICHOLAS (*reads*). Yours obediently, Newman Noggs.

NOGGS. P.S.: If you should go near Barnard Castle, there is good ale at the King's Head. Say you know me, and I am sure they will not charge you for it. You may say Mr Noggs there, for I was a gentleman then. I was indeed.

NOGGS shambles out. NICHOLAS crumples to the floor. He is crying.

Blackout.

Scene Ten

Dotheboys Hall. The school bell rings, the lights come up. The parlour chair and table have gone. SQUEERS shouts to NICHOLAS, who wakes.

SQUEERS. Past seven, Nickleby! It's morning come, and well-iced already. Now Nickleby, come, tumble up, will you?

SQUEERS, with his cane, strides on. NICHOLAS jumps up and, pulling on his coat, goes to him. MRS SQUEERS enters, followed by SMIKE, who carries a bowl of brimstone and treacle. SQUEERS and NICHOLAS arrive at one side of the stage. MRS SQUEERS and SMIKE at the other. Then, through the darkness at the back of the stage, we see, approaching us, THE BOYS of Dotheboys Hall. They are dressed in the ragged remains of what were once school uniforms. They move slowly, through lameness and sullenness and fear. Then they form themselves into a kind of line, and each boy goes to MRS SQUEERS to receive a spoonful of brimstone and treacle.

There. This our shop, Nickleby.

Each boy gives his number, name, age and reason for being at the school before receiving his dose. Clearly, this is an accepted ritual.

TOMKINS. First boy. Tomkins. Nine. A cripple.

COATES. Second boy. Coates. Thirteen. A bastard.

GREYMARSH. Third boy. Greymarsh. Twelve. Another bastard.

JENNINGS. Fourth boy. Jennings. Thirteen. Disfigured.

MOBBS. Fifth boy.

Pause.

Mobbs. Uh – 'leven.

Pause. He doesn't know what's wrong with him. MRS SQUEERS *hits him on the side of the head.*

MRS SQUEERS. Simpleton!

MOBBS. Fifth. Mobbs. Eleven. Sim-pull-ton.

BOLDER. Sixth. Bolder. Fourteen. Orphan.

PITCHER. Seventh. Pitcher. Ten.

MRS SQUEERS. Yes!

Pause.

PITCHER. I'm very. Very. Slow.

MRS SQUEERS. Move on. Move *on.*

JACKSON. Eighth. Johnny.

MRS SQUEERS. Johnny?

JACKSON. Jackson. Thirteen. Illegitimate.

COBBEY. Ninth. Cobbey. Fifteen. Cripple.

PETERS. Tenth. Uh – Peters. Seven. Blind.

SPROUTER. Eleventh. Sprouter. Seven. My father killed my mother.

MRS SQUEERS. Yes?

SPROUTER. Sent away.

ROBERTS. Twelfth. Roberts. Ten. There's something wrong — my brain.

Squeers' young son, WACKFORD, well-dressed and stout, pushes forward the two SNAWLEY boys and BELLING.

SNAWLEY SNR. Robert Arthur Snawley.

MRS SQUEERS. Number!

SNAWLEY SNR. I'm eleven.

MRS SQUEERS (*twisting SNAWLEY SNR's ear*). Number, is thirteen.

SNAWLEY SNR. Thirteen.

SNAWLEY JNR. Uh — fourteen-th. Snawley, H. Uh — seven.

BELLING. Fifteen. Anthony Belling. Seven years of age. A classical and modern — moral, education.

MRS SQUEERS wipes her hands on SMIKE. SQUEERS to WACKFORD.

SQUEERS. Thank you, young Wackford. Thank you, son. And what do you say? And what d'you say, to this?

Pause.

BOYS. For what we have received, may the Lord make us truly thankful.

SQUEERS. Amen.

BOYS. Amen.

SQUEERS. That's better. Now, boys, I've been to London, and have returned to my family and you, as strong and well as ever.

Pause. MRS SQUEERS gestures to a boy.

COATES (*feebly*). Hip hip.

BOYS (*Equally feebly*). Hooray.

COATES. Hip hip.

BOYS. Hooray.

COATES. Hip hip.

BOYS. Hooray.

SQUEERS takes various letters from his pockets and wanders around among the boys as he speaks.

SQUEERS. I have seen the parents of some boys, and they're so glad to hear how their sons are doing, that there's no prospect at all of their going home, which of course is a very pleasant thing to reflect upon for all parties.

He continues to perambulate.

But I have had disappointments to contend with. Bolder's father, for instance, was two pound ten short. Where is Bolder?

The boys around BOLDER kick him and he puts up his hand. SQUEERS goes to BOLDER.

Ah, Bolder. Bolder, if you father thinks that because –

SQUEERS suddenly notices warts on BOLDER's hand. He grabs the boy's arm.

What do you call this, sir?

BOLDER. Warts, sir.

SQUEERS. What, sir?

BOLDER. Warts, sir.

SQUEERS. Warts?

BOLDER. I can't help it, sir. They will come . . . It's working in the garden does it sir, at least I don't know what it is, sir, but it's not my fault . . .

SQUEERS. Bolder. You are an incorrigible young scoundrel, and as the last thrashing did you no good, we must see what another will do towards beating it out of you.

BOLDER looks terrified.

La – ter.

He lets BOLDER go and walks on, reading.

Now, let's see . . . A letter for Cobbey. Cobbey?

COBBEY puts his hand up. SQUEERS hardly acknowledges, but walks on.

Oh. Cobbey's grandmother is dead, and his uncle John has took to drinking, which is all the news his sister sends, except eighteenpence, which will just pay for that broken square of glass. Mobbs!

MOBBS, not sure whether this will be good or bad news, nervously puts up his hand. It is clear it is not good news when SQUEERS walks to him and stands near.

Now, Mobbs' step-mother took to her bed on hearing that he would not eat fat, and has been very ill ever since. She wishes to know by an early post where he expects to go to, if he quarrels with his vittles; and with what feelings he could turn up his nose at the cow's liver broth, after his good master had asked a blessing on it. She is disconsolate to find he is discontented, which is sinful and horrid, and hopes Mr Squeers will flog him into a happier state of mind.

Into MOBBS' ear.

Which – he – will.

Long pause to let this sink in to everyone. Then:

Right, boys. I'd like you all to meet my new assistant, Mr Nickleby. Good morning, Mr Nickleby.

BOYS. Good morning, Mr Nickleby.

NICHOLAS. Good, morning.

SQUEERS. Now, this is the first class in English spelling and philosophy, Nickleby. We'll soon get up a Latin one and hand that over to you.

NICHOLAS *joins* SQUEERS.

Now, then, where's Smallpiece?

BOYS. Please, sir . . .

SQUEERS. Let any boy speak out of turn and I'll have the skin off his back!

He points to JENNINGS.

JENNINGS. Please, sir, he's cleaning the back parlour window.

SQUEERS. So he is, to be sure. We go on the practical mode of teaching, Nickleby; C-l-e-a-n, clean –

BOYS. Clean.

SQUEERS. Verb active, to make bright, to scour. W-i-n, win, –

BOYS. Win –

SQUEERS. D-e-r, der –

BOYS. Der, winder –

SQUEERS. Winder, a casement. When a boy knows this out of a book, he goes and does it. It's just the same principle as the use of the globes. Where's Grinder?

COATES *puts his hand up.* SQUEERS *points to* COATES.

COATES. Please, sir, he's weeding the garden.

SQUEERS. To be sure. So he is. B-o-t-, Bot –

BOYS. Bot –

SQUEERS. T-i-n, tin –

BOYS. Tin –

SQUEERS. Bottin –

BOYS. Bottin –

SQUEERS. N-e-y-, Ney –

BOYS. Ney –

SQUEERS. Bottiney –

BOYS. Bottiney –

SQUEERS. Noun substantive, a knowledge of plants. When he has learned that bottiney means a knowledge of plants, he goes and knows 'em. That's our system, Nickleby. What do you think of it?

NICHOLAS. It's a very useful one, at any rate.

SQUEERS. I believe you. Greymarsh, what's a horse?

GREYMARSH. A beast, sir.

SQUEERS. So it is. A horse is a quadroped, and quadroped's Latin for beast, as anybody that's gone through the grammar knows, or else where's the use in having grammars at all?

NICHOLAS. Where indeed.

SQUEERS (*to* GREYMARSH). And as you're so perfect in that, go to *my* horse, and rub him down well, or I'll rub *you* down. The rest go and draw water up till somebody tells you to leave, for it's washing day tomorrow, and they'll want the coppers filled.

THE BOYS *hurry out,* MOBBS *and* BOLDER *hurrying more than the others.*

Except – for Mobbs and Bolder.

Everyone stops. Some of THE BOYS *push* MOBBS *and* BOLDER *forward, towards* SQUEERS. *Then the others go out, as* MRS SQUEERS *and* WACKFORD *go too.* SMIKE *tries to go as well.*

Stay there, Smike. They'll need taking to their beds.

He turns to NICHOLAS.

This is the way we do it, Nickleby.

SQUEERS *lifts his cane. Blackout.* NARRATORS *appear in a little light. As they speak this narration, we see* NICHOLAS *sit morosely down at the side.* SQUEERS, SMIKE, MOBBS *and* BOLDER *have gone.*

NARRATORS. And Nicholas sat down, so depressed and self-degraded that if death could have come upon him then he would have been happy to meet it.

The cruelty of which he had been an unwilling witness,

The coarse and ruffianly behaviour of Squeers,

The filthy place,

The sights and sounds about him,

All contributed to this feeling.

And when he recollected that, being there as an assistant, he was the aider and abetter of a system which filled him with disgust and indignation,

He loathed himself.

Blackout.

Scene Eleven

Outside Dotheboys Hall. Bare stage. Enter MRS SQUEERS, and, from the other side, her 20-year old daughter, FANNY.

FANNY. Mama! Mama, I'm home!

MRS SQUEERS. Fanny.

Enter Fanny's friend TILDA PRICE, followed by her swain JOHN BROWDIE, carrying luggage.

FANNY. Tilda Price brought me home, mama.

MRS SQUEERS. Miss Price.

TILDA (*a little bob*). Good morning, ma'am.

JOHN. Ah, 'allo, missus. How's thissen?

FANNY. And John as well.

MRS SQUEERS. I see.

FANNY (*aside to MRS SQUEERS*). Mama, do ask them in.

MRS SQUEERS. Hm. Would you care for a glass of something, Miss Price?

Slight pause.

Mr Browdie?

JOHN. Ay. We would that, certainly.

MRS SQUEERS. Well, then –

JOHN. As soon as tied me 'orse.

JOHN goes out to tie his 'orse. FANNY confidentially to MRS SQUEERS.

FANNY. Engaged.

MRS SQUEERS. Who is?

FANNY. She is.

MRS SQUEERS. To who?

FANNY. To him.

MRS SQUEERS. At her age?

Pause.

Well, I suppose, she is quite easy on the eye.

FANNY. And, after all, he's hardly what you'd call a gentleman.

Re-enter JOHN.

JOHN. Right then. Let's have that glass of summat, missus, and let's have it sharpish, eh?

He and TILDA go out, as:

FANNY (*to MRS SQUEERS*). No. Certainly. Not what you'd call a gentleman, at all.

FANNY and MRS SQUEERS follow out JOHN and TILDA.

Scene Twelve

The Squeers' parlour. THE BOYS drag on a sofa. SQUEERS is drinking, MRS SQUEERS is trying Belling's clothes on young WACKFORD. PHIB is in attendance.

SQUEERS. Well, my dear, so what do you think of him?

MRS SQUEERS. Think of who?

FANNY comes in, having just said her goodbyes to TILDA and JOHN. She sits, knits, and listens, as:

SQUEERS. The new man.

MRS SQUEERS. Oh. Young Knuckleboy.

SQUEERS. Young Nickleby.

MRS SQUEERS. Well, if you want to know, Squeers, I'll tell you that I think him quite the proudest, haughtiest, turned-up nosediest –

SQUEERS. He is quite cheap, my dear. In fact, he's very cheap.

MRS SQUEERS. I don't see why we need another man at all.

SQUEERS. Because it says in the advertisement quite clearly —

MRS SQUEERS. Fiddlesticks it *says*. You *say*, in the advertisement, it's "Education by Mr Wackford Squeers and his able assistants", but that don't mean you have to have 'em, does it? Sometimes, Squeers, you try my patience.

SQUEERS. Sometimes, you try mine.

MRS SQUEERS. What's that?

SQUEERS. Well, my love, any slave-driver in the West Indies is allowed a man under him, to see his blacks don't run away, or get up a rebellion; and I want a man under me, to do the same with our blacks, till such time as little Wackford is able to take charge.

WACKFORD. Oh, am I?

MRS SQUEERS (*impatiently*). Am you what?

WACKFORD. Oh, am I to take charge of the school when I grow up father?

SQUEERS. Yes, of course you are.

WACKFORD. Oh. Oh. Oh, won't I give it to 'em. Won't I make 'em shriek and squeal and scream.

The SQUEERSES *look at each other. This exemplary attitude on the part of their son has brought them back together.*

SQUEERS. Of course you will, my boy, of course you will.

FANNY (*unable to keep silence*). Papa . . .

SQUEERS *and* MRS SQUEERS *look at* FANNY.

Who is this — person? This young man?

MRS SQUEERS (*impatient again*). Oh, he's the new assistant, and your father has got some nonsense in his head he's the son of a gentleman that died the other day.

FANNY. A gentleman.

MRS SQUEERS. Yes, but I don't believe a word of it. If he's a gentleman's son at all, he's a fondling, that's my opinion.

SQUEERS. Foundling, and he's nothing of the kind. His father was married, *to* his mother years before he was born, and she's alive now.

MRS SQUEERS. Well, all I can say —

SQUEERS (*stands*). And if you do dislike him, dear, I don't know anyone who shows dislike better than you do, and if there's a touch of pride about him, then I do not believe there is a woman living that can bring a person's spirit down as quick as you.

MRS SQUEERS. Oh, is that so.

SQUEERS. My love.

Pause. MRS SQUEERS looks at SQUEERS. Then she laughs. SQUEERS laughs too.

MRS SQUEERS. Come, Wackford.

MRS SQUEERS, still laughing, gestures WACKFORD to follow her, and goes out, SQUEERS, laughing too, goes out. FANNY and PHIB left.

FANNY. Well? So what's he like?

PHIB. He's lovely.

Scene Thirteen

The common dormitory. THE BOYS asleep. SMIKE is sitting. NICHOLAS, still sitting at the side of the stage, now stands, and goes to SMIKE. NICHOLAS carries a book.

NICHOLAS. Hello.

SMIKE looks up, scared, and flinches a little.

Please, don't be frightened.

NICHOLAS crouches down near SMIKE. He puts down his book.

You're shivering.

Pause. NICHOLAS stands to go. He stops when SMIKE speaks.

SMIKE. Oh, dear.

NICHOLAS turns back.

Oh, dear. Oh, dear. My heart. Will break. It will.

Louder, more forceful.

It *will*. I know it *will*.

NICHOLAS (*embarrassed, looking round*). Shh, shh.

SMIKE. Remember Dorker, do you?

NICHOLAS. Dorker?

SMIKE. I was with him at the end, he asked for me. Who will I ask for? Who?

Pause. NICHOLAS *doesn't know what* SMIKE *is talking about.*

NICHOLAS. Who will you ask for when?

SMIKE *back into himself again.*

SMIKE. No One. No Hope. Hope Less.

Slight pause.

NICHOLAS *(feebly).* There's always hope.

SMIKE *(to himself).* Is there?

SMIKE *turns again to* NICHOLAS. *Forcefully.*

O-U-T-C-A-S-T. A noun. Substantive. Person cast out or rejected. Abject. And foresaken. Homeless. Me.

NICHOLAS *looks at* SMIKE. *He doesn't know what to say. Pause. Then* FANNY *enters, behind* NICHOLAS. *She takes in the scene.*

FANNY. Oh – I'm sorry.

NICHOLAS *turns.*

I was looking for my father.

NICHOLAS. He's not here.

FANNY. I see.

Pause.

I beg your pardon, sir. How very awkward.

NICHOLAS. Please, please don't apologise.

FANNY. I thank you, sir. Oh . . . Sir.

FANNY *curtseys, turns, turns back, turns again and goes.* NICHOLAS *turns to go out too, when he realises he's left his book. He looks back to* SMIKE, *who has picked up the book and is holding it to himself.* NICHOLAS *decides to leave* SMIKE *with the book.* SMIKE *is left alone, with the sleeping boys.*

Blackout.

Scene Fourteen

Miss La Creevy's house in the Strand. Enter KATE *and* HANNAH, *with luggage, from upstage.*

HANNAH. Is it the East End that you're going to, Miss?

KATE. That's right. Is that unusual, as a place to live?

HANNAH (*trying to avoid answering 'yes'*). Well, uh . . .

Enter MRS NICKLEBY *and* MISS LA CREEVY.

MISS LA CREEVY. Well, I'm afraid that millinery is not a healthy occupation, for your dear Kate or anyone else. For I remember getting three young milliners to sit for me, and they were all very pale and sickly.

MRS NICKLEBY. Oh, Miss La Creevy, that's not a general rule by any means. For I recall employing one to make a scarlet cloak, at the time when scarlet cloaks were fashionable, and she had a very red face – a very red face indeed.

MISS LA CREEVY. Perhaps she drank.

MRS NICKLEBY. Well, I don't know how that may have been, but I do know she had an extremely red face, so your argument goes for nothing.

Pause.

Think. Nickleby and Mantalini. How well it would sound. And, who knows, Dr Nickleby, the headmaster of Westminster School, living in the same street . . .

Pause.

It's not impossible, at all.

Enter HANNAH, *followed by* NEWMAN NOGGS.

HANNAH. Uh – it's a gentleman. I think.

MISS LA CREEVY *looks peevishly at* HANNAH.

NOGGS. Name's Noggs. From Mr Nickleby. To Thames Street.

KATE. Yes. We'll need a coach, I fear.

NOGGS. I'll get one.

MRS NICKLEBY. Uh, Mr Noggs . . . did not we see you on the morning when my son departed on the coach for Yorkshire?

NOGGS. Me? Oh, no.

MRS NICKLEBY. I'm sure of it –

NOGGS. No. First time I've been out, three weeks. I've had the gout. You ready?

KATE. Yes. (*She turns to* MISS LA CREEVY). We are sorry, very sorry, to leave you, Miss La Creevy.

MISS LA CREEVY. Oh, that's stuff. You cannot shake me off that easily. I'll see you very often, come and call, and hear how you get on.

KATE *smiles*.

And if, in all the world, there's no one else to take an interest in your welfare, there will still be one poor, lonely heart that prays for it night and day.

NOGGS. Uh – can we go?

And The NICKLEBYS *leave with MR NOGGS, MISS LA CREEVY and HANNAH waving, the former with a handkerchief pressed to her nose.*

Scene Fifteen
The parlour at Dotheboys Hall. Early evening. Enter TILDA *and* FANNY, *both dressed up to the nines.* PHIB *enters, too, setting the table with tea and a plate of bread-and-butter.*

TILDA. Engaged!

FANNY. No, not exactly. Not exactly, as it were, engaged. But going to be, there is no question.

They sit on the sofa.

TILDA. Fanny, that is *wonderful*.

FANNY. Because, you see, his very presence, coming here to live with us, beneath this roof, and under the most mysterious circumstances . . .

TILDA. Fanny, what's he said?

Slight pause.

FANNY. What do you mean?

TILDA. I mean – what has he *said*?

Pause.

FANNY. Don't ask me what he said, my dear. If you had only seen his look . . .

TILDA. Was it like this?

TILDA gives a love-lorn look.

FANNY. Like that?

TILDA. John looked at me like that.

FANNY. Well, so did he. Like that, entirely, only rather more genteel.

TILDA. Well, then, that's it.

FANNY. That's what?

TILDA. He must mean something, if he looks like that. He must feel . . . something very strong.

FANNY. Oh, I'm so jealous of you, Tilda!

TILDA. Why?

FANNY. Because you are so fortunate. That your mama and papa are so readily agreeable to your engagement, indeed appear not to have thought twice about it, whereas my mother and my father are so bitterly opposed to my dear Nicholas; and will throw all kinds of obstacles in our way; and will force us to meet in secret, and deny our passion . . . Oh that my course of love were half as simple, quiet and smooth as yours!

Pause.

TILDA. I cannot wait to see him.

FANNY. Oh, I'm shaking!

TILDA. Yes, I know just how you feel.

Knock, knock.

FANNY. Oh, there he is! Oh, Tilda!

TILDA. Shh. Just say, come in.

FANNY (*almost silently*). Come in!

TILDA *a glance at* PHIB, *who looks away. Nothing.*

TILDA. Come in!

NICHOLAS *comes in.*

NICHOLAS. Good evening. I understood from Mr Squeers that –

FANNY. Oh, yes. It's all right. Father's been called away, but you won't mind that, I dare venture.

NICHOLAS (*out front*). And Nicholas opened his eyes at this, but he turned the matter off very coolly – not minding particularly about anything just then – and went through the ceremony of introduction to the miller's daughter with as much grace as he could muster. (*Bowing to* TILDA.) Your servant, ma'am.

FANNY. We are only waiting for one more gentleman.

NICHOLAS (*out front*). It was a matter of equal moment to Nicholas whether they were waiting for one gentleman or twenty; and being out of spirits, and not seeing any especial reason why he should make himself agreeable, looked out of the window and sighed.

Looks 'out of the window' and sighs.

TILDA. Oh, Mr Nickleby.

NICHOLAS (*with a start*). I'm sorry.

TILDA. Please, don't apologise. Perhaps your languor is occasioned by my presence. But, please, don't heed me. You may behave just as you would if you two were alone.

FANNY (*blushing*). Tilda! I'm ashamed of you!

The young women giggle.

NICHOLAS (*out front*). And here the two friends burst into a verity of giggles, glancing from time to time at Nicholas, who, in a state of unmixed astonishment, gradually fell into one of irrepressible amusement.

TILDA. Come, now, Mr Nickleby. Will you have tea?

NICHOLAS (*cheerfully, going over to sit*). Oh, certainly. I'm honoured. And delighted.

The women look at each other. TILDA a little nod, FANNY a deep breath.

FANNY. Some — bread-and-butter?

NICHOLAS. Please.

NICHOLAS *being poured tea and helping himself to bread-and-butter when there's another knock.* TILDA *stands,* FANNY *gestures to* PHIB, *who admits* JOHN BROWDIE, *looking scrubbed and uncomfortable in a huge collar and white waistcoat.*

TILDA. Well, John.

JOHN. Well, lass.

FANNY. I beg your pardon, Mr Nickleby — Mr John Browdie.

JOHN. You servant, sir.

NICHOLAS. Yours to command, sir.

FANNY. Please, Mr Browdie, sit down.

JOHN. (*as he sits*). Old woman gone awa, be she?

FANNY. She has.

JOHN (*helping himself to bread-and-butter*). And schoolmaster as well?

FANNY. Yes, yes.

JOHN. An' just the four o' us?

FANNY. That's right. Do have some bread-and-butter.

JOHN, *in mid-bite, grins hugely. Then, to* NICHOLAS.

JOHN. Tha won't get brea-and-butter ev'ry night, eh, man?

NICHOLAS *a weak smile.*

In fact, I tell thee, if tha stay here long enough, tha'll end up nowt but skin and bone.

JOHN *laughs hugely.* NICHOLAS *annoyed by this criticism of his employer.* JOHN *elbows* FANNY.

Just skin and bone, eh, Fanny?

JOHN *looks back to* NICHOLAS. *To explain.*

I tell tha, man, last teacher, 'ad 'ere, when turned sideway, couldn't tell were there!

NICHOLAS *suddenly to his feet.*

NICHOLAS. Sir, I don't know whether your perceptions are quite keen enough, to enable you to understand that your remarks are highly offensive, to me and my employer, but if they are, please have the goodness to —

TILDA *stops* JOHN's *response.*

TILDA. If you say one more word, John, only half a word, I'll never speak to you again.

JOHN. Oh. Weel. I'll shut me mouth, then. Eh?

JOHN *eats bread-and-butter and slurps his tea.* FANNY, *overcome, stands and runs to the side.* TILDA *follows.* NICHOLAS *looks alarmed.*

TILDA. Fanny, what's the matter?

FANNY. Nothing.

TILDA. There was never any danger of an altercation, was there, Mr Nickleby?

NICHOLAS (*a step towards the women*). No, none at all.

TILDA *to* NICHOLAS, FANNY *still sniffing.*

TILDA. Say something kind to her.

NICHOLAS. Why, what —

TILDA. Or better, why don't John and I go off next door, and leave you two together? For a little while.

NICHOLAS. Whatever for?

TILDA. Whatever for? And her dressed up so beautifully, and looking really almost handsome. I'm ashamed of you.

NICHOLAS. My dear girl, what is it to me how she is dressed, or how she looks? It's hardly my concern.

TILDA *quickly to the table.*

TILDA. Don't call me a dear girl, or Fanny will be saying it's my fault. We will play cards. Phib, dear, please clear the table.

PHIB *clears the table,* TILDA *whispers to* FANNY, *and* JOHN *finishes the bread-and-butter, as* NICHOLAS *speaks out front.*

NICHOLAS. And all of this was completely unintelligible to Nicholas, who had no other distinct impression, than that Miss Squeers was an ordinary-looking girl, and her friend Miss Price a pretty one, and that he had been called to join in a game of Speculation.

FANNY *and* TILDA *both standing near the chair opposite* JOHN.

TILDA. So, who's to partner whom?

NICHOLAS (*obviously, moving to a chair opposite an empty chair*). I'll partner you, Miss Price.

TILDA. Oh, *sir.*

NICHOLAS (*Taking this response as meaning assent.*) It will be my great pleasure.

TILDA *glances at* FANNY, *and sits opposite the chair beside which* NICHOLAS *is standing.* FANNY *sits opposite* JOHN. NICHOLAS *tearing up cards for chips.*

FANNY (*hysterically*). Well, Mr Browdie, it appears we're to be partners.

JOHN (*dumbfounded*). Aye.

NICHOLAS. I'll deal?

FANNY. Oh, please, do deal.

NICHOLAS *deals five cards to each player. They look at their cards.*

Well, Mr Browdie?

JOHN (*pushing two chips into the centre*). Two on spades.

NICHOLAS. Miss Price?

TILDA (*Three chips.*) Bid three. On hearts.

FANNY (*putting one chip in*). I'll – pass.

NICHOLAS (*putting one chip in*). Then hearts it is.

FANNY *a sharp intake of breath. The hand is played out in total silence. The principle is the same as whist, with each player laying a card for each trick, hearts being trumps.* TILDA *and* NICHOLAS *win.*

Well, then. We've won.

FANNY. And Tilda something that she'd not expected to win, I think.

TILDA (*ingenuously*). Oh, only seven, dear.

JOHN *dealing another hand.*

FANNY (*to* TILDA). How dull you are.

TILDA. Oh, no, indeed. I am in excellent spirits. I was thinking you seemed out of sorts.

FANNY. Oh, me? Why, no.

TILDA. Your hair's coming out of curl, dear.

FANNY. Pray, dear, don't mind me. You'd better attend to your partner.

NICHOLAS. Thank you for reminding her. She had.

JOHN *looking black.*

TILDA. One diamond.

FANNY. Two clubs.

NICHOLAS. Two diamonds.

JOHN. Three clubs.

TILDA. Pass.

FANNY. Pass.

NICHOLAS. Pass.

JOHN *looks round.* NICHOLAS *and* TILDA *indicate they have no further bid. The hand is played, and, surprisingly,* NICHOLAS *and* TILDA *win again, on the last trick, with Nicholas's king of clubs.* NICHOLAS *pulls in the chips.* TILDA *deals again during:*

TILDA. Well, I never had such luck. It's all you, Mr Nickleby, I'm sure. I should like to have you for a partner always.

NICHOLAS. Well, I wish you had.

TILDA. Though if you win at cards, of course, you'll have a bad wife, sure as sure.

NICHOLAS. Not if your wish is gratified, Miss Price.

He picks up his cards. Aware of the silence of the others.

We have all the talking to ourselves, it seems.

FANNY. Oh, but you do it so well, Mr Nickleby. It would be quite an outrage to interrupt you, wouldn't it? Two hearts.

NICHOLAS. Pass.

Pause.

TILDA. John, dear, your bid.

JOHN. My what?

TILDA. Your bid.

JOHN (*throwing down his cards.*) Well, damn me if I'm going to take this longer.

Pause. The young women very shocked.

NICHOLAS. Erm . . .

JOHN (*stands*). And you are coming home with me, now, Tilda, and him o'ert there can look sharp for a broken head next time he comes near me.

TILDA. Mercy on us, what is all this?

JOHN. Home! Home, now, home!

FANNY crying.

TILDA. And here's Fanny in tears, now. What can be the matter?

FANNY. Oh, don't you bother, ma'am. Oh, don't you trouble to enquire.

TILDA. Well, you are monstrous polite, ma'am.

FANNY. Well, I shall not come to you to take lessons in the art, ma'am.

TILDA. And you need not take the trouble to make yourself plainer than you are, ma'am, because it's quite unnecessary.

FANNY. Oh! Oh, I can thank God that I haven't the boldness of some people!

TILDA (*standing*). And I can thank God I haven't the envy of others. While wishing you a good night, ma'am, and pleasant dreams attend your sleep.

FANNY. Tilda, I hate you!

TILDA sweeps out, followed by JOHN, with a dark look at NICHOLAS. FANNY, weeping, thumps PHIB. NICHOLAS, out front:

NICHOLAS. This is one consequence, thought Nicholas, of my cursed readiness to adapt myself to any society into which chance carries me. If I had sat mute and motionless, as I might have done, this would not have happened.

Pause. End of reportage. NICHOLAS flails.

What did I do? What did I do?

NICHOLAS *withdraws.*

FANNY. Oh, I swear that there is no one in the world more miserable than I. And never has been. And never will be.

Pause.

PHIB (*Carefully*). Well, I can't help saying, miss, if you were to kill me for it, that I never saw anyone look so vulgar as Miss Price this night.

FANNY. Oh, Phib, how you do talk.

Pause.

PHIB. And I know it's very wrong of me to say so, Miss, Miss Price being a friend of yours and all, but she do dress herself out so, and go on in such a manner to get noticed: well, if people only saw themselves.

FANNY. Now, Phib, you know you musn't talk like that.

PHIB. So vain. And so, so plain.

FANNY. And I will hear no more of this. It's true, Miss Price has faults, has many, but I wish her well. And above all, I wish her married. And I think it desirable – most desirable, from the nature of her failings – that she is married as soon as possible.

PHIB. Yes, miss.

A knock.

FANNY. Who's that? Come in.

Enter TILDA. PHIB exit.

TILDA. Well, Fanny.

Slight pause.

Well, Fanny, you see I have come back to see you. Although we had bad words.

FANNY. I bear no malice, Tilda. I am above it.

TILDA. Don't be cross, please, Fanny. I have come to tell you something.

FANNY. What may that be, Tilda?

TILDA. Well . . . Well, this. After we left here, John and I had the most dreadful quarrel. But after a great deal of wrangling, and saying we would never speak again, we made it up, and John has promised that first thing tomorrow morning he'll put our names down in the church, and I give you notice to get your bridesmaid's frock made now. There!

FANNY. Oh, *Tilda*. Oh, dear Tilda.

And the two women burst into tears and embrace each other.

Oh, I'm so *happy*.

TILDA *decides to strike while the iron is cool.*

TILDA. But, now, Fanny, there's the matter of young Mr Nickleby.

FANNY. Oh, him. He's nothing to me.

TILDA. Oh, come now, Fanny, that's not true.

FANNY. It is. I hate him. And I wish that he was dead. And me as well.

TILDA. Now, dear. You know you'll think differently in five minutes, and wouldn't it be much nicer to take him back in favour?

FANNY. Oh, Tilda. How could you have acted so mean and dishonourable. I wouldn't have believed it of you.

TILDA. Now, Fanny, you're talking as if I murdered someone.

FANNY. Very near as bad.

TILDA. Oh, don't be silly. It's not my fault I've got enough good looks to make some people civil. Persons don't make their own faces, and it's no more my fault if mine is a good one than it is other people's fault if their's is not.

FANNY (*in horror*). Oh, *Tilda*.

TILDA. Fanny, I don't mean –

FANNY. Now, go. Go back home at once.

TILDA. Oh, Fanny –

FANNY. Now, at once, d'you hear me?

TILDA. Very well, but –

FANNY. NOW.

> FANNY *turns firmly away.* TILDA *to the exit. She turns back.*
> FANNY *turns slowly to* TILDA. TILDA *gives a little, shruggy,*
> *affectionate gesture, as if to apologise. Pause. Then* FANNY
> *runs to her friend, crying.*

Oh, I'm so *happy* for you, Tilda.

Scene Sixteen

The Nicklebys' new house in Thames St. Two meagre, broken
chairs and a threadbare carpet. MRS NICKLEBY, KATE *and*
NOGGS – *who carries their luggage* – *enter during the narration.*

NARRATION.

And at that moment, Kate and Mrs Nickleby arrived at their
new home.

Around, the squalid slums of the East End of London –

And behind, a wharf that opened to the river –

And nearby, an empty kennel, and some bones of animals –

Past which they quickly walked,

And went inside.

NOGGS (*putting down the luggage*). Well, here it is.

KATE. I see.

NOGGS. It's not, of course . . . There are some bits of furniture.
And there's a fire made up. I'm sure, although it looks a little
gloomy, it can be made, quite . . .

KATE. Yes.

> *Pause.*

MRS NICKLEBY. Well, well, my dear. Is it not thoughtful and
considerate of your kind uncle? To provide us with . . .

NOGGS. Your uncle, yes.

> NOGGS *picks up the luggage and takes it to another room.*

KATE. Oh, mama, this house is so depressing. I – one could
imagine that some dreadful – that some awful thing had –

MRS NICKLEBY. Lord, dear Kate, don't talk like that, you'll
frighten me to death.

KATE. It's just a foolish fancy.

MRS NICKLEBY. Well, Kate, I'll thank you to keep your foolish fancies to yourself, and not wake up my foolish fancies to keep them company.

KATE. Yes, I'm sorry.

The two women look at each other. Then, quite suddenly, they embrace. NOGGS enters.

Mr Noggs, we need detain you no longer.

NOGGS. Is there nothing more?

KATE. No, nothing, really. Thank you.

MRS NICKLEBY (*fumbling in her purse*). Perhaps, dear, Mr Noggs would like to drink our healths.

KATE. I think, mama, you'd hurt his feelings if you offered it.

NOGGS bows and withdraws. The women sit.

NARRATION.

Gloomy and black in truth the old house was –

No life was stirring there –

And everything said coldness, silence and decay.

Scene Seventeen

Outside Dotheboys Hall. Day. Enter NICHOLAS.

NICHOLAS. And so it happened that, the next day, during the short daily interval that was suffered to elapse between what was pleasantly called the dinner of Mr Squeers' pupils and their return to the pursuit of useful knowledge, Nicholas was engaged in a melancholy walk, and brood, and listless saunter.

NICHOLAS perambulates as TILDA and FANNY enter, arm-in-arm.

TILDA. And Miss Price, who had stayed the night with Miss Squeers, was at that same time being taken by her best friend at least as far home as the second turning of the road.

FANNY (*seeing NICHOLAS*). Ah! Him!

TILDA. Oh, Fanny, shall we turn back? He hasn't seen us yet.

FANNY. No, Tilda . . . It is my duty to go through with it, and so I shall.

NICHOLAS walks straight past TILDA and FANNY.

NICHOLAS (*as he passes*). Good morning.

FANNY (*nudging TILDA violently*). He's going. I shall faint.

TILDA. Oh, Mr Nickleby, come back!

FANNY (*staggering slightly, and needing to be supported by* TILDA). I know I shall –

TILDA. Oh, Mr Nickleby –

NICHOLAS *turns back, and comes to* TILDA *and* FANNY.

NICHOLAS. Um, what's the –

TILDA. Just, please, help –

NICHOLAS *to hold* FANNY, *when that young lady expertly twists and falls backwards into his arms. For a moment, they stand there, and then* NICHOLAS, *unable to prevent himself, falls over backwards,* FANNY *on top of him.*

NICHOLAS. Miss Squeers . . .

FANNY (*coming around*). Oh, dear, this foolish faintness –

TILDA. It's not foolish, dear. You have no reason to feel shamed. It's others, who provoke it, who should –

NICHOLAS. Ah. I understand.

NICHOLAS *manhandles* FANNY *to a sitting position.*

You are still resolved to fix it upon me. I see. Although I told you last night it was not my fault.

TILDA. There, he says it was not his fault. Perhaps you were too jealous, or too hasty with him? He says it was not his fault. I think that is apology enough.

NICHOLAS. Um –

FANNY. All right, Tilda. you've convinced me. I forgive him.

FANNY *lies back on* NICHOLAS *again.*

NICHOLAS. Oh, dear. This is more serious than I supposed. Allow me –

He dislodges FANNY, *and stands.* FANNY *stands with* TILDA. May I speak?

The two women look at him with eager anticipation.

I must say – that I am very sorry – truly and sincerely so – for having been the cause of any difference among you last night. I reproach myself most bitterly for having been so unfortunate as to cause the dissension that occurred, although I did so, I assure you, most unwittingly and heedlessly.

Pause.

TILDA. Well, that's not all you have to say, surely.

NICHOLAS. No, it is not, I fear there is something more.

Slight pause.

It is a most awkward thing to say, as the very mention of such a supposition makes one look like a puppy – but, still . . . May I ask if that lady supposes that I entertain . . . a sort of . . .

Quickly.

Does she think that I'm in love with her?

FANNY. Oh!

Change of tack.

Oh, answer for me, dear.

TILDA. Of course she does.

NICHOLAS. She does?

TILDA. Of course.

FANNY. And you may say, dear Tilda, that if Mr Nickleby had doubted that, he may set his mind at rest. His sentiments are completely recipro –

NICHOLAS. Stop!

FANNY. Whatever for?

NICHOLAS. Pray hear me. This is the grossest and wildest delusion, the completest and most signal mistake, that ever human being laboured under or committed. I have scarcely seen the young lady half a dozen times, but if I had seen her sixty times, or sixty thousand, it would be and will be precisely the same. I have not one thought, wish, or hope, connected with her unless it be – and I say this, not to hurt her feelings, but to impress her with the real state of my own – unless it be the one object dear to my heart as life itself, of being one day able to turn my back on this accursed place, never to set foot in it again or to think of it – even think of it – except with loathing and disgust.

Pause. Then NICHOLAS, *out front.*

And with this particlarly plain and straightforward declaration, Nicholas bowed slightly, and waiting to hear no more, retreated.

NICHOLAS *retreats.*

TILDA. But oh, poor Fanny! Her anger, rage and vexation are not to be described.

FANNY. Refused!

FANNY *starts to push at* TILDA, *to make her go away, as punishment for encouraging her.*

TILDA (*being pushed, and beginning to enjoy* FANNY's *fury, and find it amusing*). Refused by a teacher picked up by advertisement at an annual salary of five pounds payable at indefinite periods . . .(*Really taunting now.*) . . and this too in the presence of a little chit of a miller's daughter of eighteen,

FANNY (*pushing and shoving*). . . . who was going to be married, to a man who had gone down on his very knees to ask her!

And, with a little, dismissive gesture, FANNY *turns, runs to the side and weeps, while* TILDA *still laughing, dances out the other way, and* NICHOLAS *speaks out front.*

NICHOLAS. And it may be remarked, that Miss Squeers was of the firm opinion that she was prepossessing and beautiful, and that her father was, after all, master, and Nicholas man, and that the father had saved money and Nicholas had none, all of which seemed to her conclusive arguments why the young man should feel only too honoured by her preference, and all too grateful for her deep affection . . .

And NICHOLAS *turns and sees* FANNY. *She has composed herself now, but this has the effect of making her look even more crumpled. She marches to* NICHOLAS, *with an effort at dignity, but then breaks down.*

FANNY. Sir . . . I pity you.

She turns and runs back, as MRS SQUEERS *and* SMIKE *appear, as if from the house.*

You're right, mama.

MRS SQUEERS. Right? What about?

FANNY (*crying*). About that Knuckleboy.

She runs out, as if into the house.

MRS SQUEERS (*To* NICHOLAS). You, sir!

NICHOLAS. Yes, ma'am?

MRS SQUEERS. You've been wanted in the classroom for ten minutes.

NICHOLAS. Certainly.

He goes towards MRS SQUEERS, *as if into the house.*

MRS SQUEERS. Not through the house, sir. Round that way.

Pause. Then NICHOLAS *turns his collar up against the cold, and goes out another way.* SMIKE *makes to follow him.*

Smike!

SMIKE *turns back to* MRS SQUEERS.

In here. You haven't finished.

She cuffs SMIKE *on the head as he passes her into the house.*

Scene Eighteen

The dormitory at Dotheboys Hall. Night. The boys enter and lie down on the bare stage. SMIKE *enters and sits, with Nicholas' book.* NICHOLAS *enters with a candle, to see* SMIKE *trying to read the book.* SMIKE *can't work out what to do.*

SMIKE. Can't do it. With the book. Can't do it, with the book, at all.

NICHOLAS. Oh, please. Don't cry.

SMIKE *crying.*

Don't. For God's sake. I cannot bear it.

SMIKE *whimpering*

They are more hard on you, I know. But, please . . .

SMIKE. Except for you, I die.

NICHOLAS. No, no. You'll be better off, I tell you, when I'm gone.

SMIKE *picks it up after a second.*

SMIKE. You gone.

NICHOLAS. Shh. Yes.

SMIKE. You going?

NICHOLAS. I was speaking to my thoughts.

SMIKE. *Tell* me. Will you? Will you go?

Pause.

NICHOLAS. I shall be driven to it. Yes. To go away.

Pause.

SMIKE. Please tell me. Is away as bad as here?

Pause.

NICHOLAS. Oh, no. Oh, no, there's nothing —

SMIKE. Can I meet you there? Away?

NICHOLAS. Well, yes . . . you can, of course . . .

SMIKE. Can I meet you there? Away? And I will find you, in away?

NICHOLAS. You would. And, if you did, I'd try to help you.

Pause. NICHOLAS moves away with the candle and sits. He takes out a paper and a pen. He is writing a letter to KATE.

I miss you terribly, but at least I feel that if my work here prospers — I miss you terribly.

Pause.

I took a Latin class today. The boys are — they are not advanced and there is much to do.

Pause.

The countryside is —

Pause. He puts away the letter. He blows out the candle. Darkness.

Scene Nineteen

The same. A bell rings offstage, and then cold, morning light. The boys and NICHOLAS are in the same positions, but, in the blackout, SMIKE has slipped away.

SQUEERS (*off*). Hey! Hey, you up there? Are you going to sleep all day?

NICHOLAS. We shall be down directly, sir.

He gestures to the boys, who speed up.

SQUEERS (*off*). Well, you'd better be, or I'll be down on some of you in less — Where's Smike?

NICHOLAS *goes to* SMIKE's *place, but sees he isn't there. The boys nearly fully up.*)

Off: I said — where's Smike?

NICHOLAS *turns and calls.*

NICHOLAS. He isn't here, sir.

SQUEERS (*off*). What? Not there?

Pause. SQUEERS *enters, rushes to* SMIKE's *place. He sees* SMIKE *is absent.*

What does this mean? Where have you hid him?

NICHOLAS. I have not seen him since last night.

SQUEERS. Oh, no?

Turning to the boys.

And you? You boys? Have any of you —

JENNINGS, *who is obscured from* SQUEERS *by other boys.*

JENNINGS. Please, sir . . .

SQUEERS. Yes? What's that?

JENNINGS. Please, sir, I think he's run away.

SQUEERS. Who said that?

BOYS. Jennings, sir.

SQUEERS. And, where is Jennings?

BOYS. Here, sir.

JENNINGS *is pushed forward by his fellows.* SQUEERS *to* JENNINGS.

SQUEERS. So you think he's run away, do you?

JENNINGS. Yes, sir. Please, sir.

SQUEERS. And what, sir, what reason have you to suppose that any boy would *want* to run away from this establishment?

SQUEERS *hits* JENNINGS *on the face.*

Eh, sir?

JENNINGS *says nothing.* SQUEERS *looks to* NICHOLAS, *who is looking away.* SQUEERS *to* NICHOLAS.

And you, Nickleby. I s'pose you think he's run away?

NICHOLAS. I think it's highly likely, yes.

SQUEERS. You do? Perhaps you *know* he's run away?

NICHOLAS. I do not know, sir. And I'm glad I did not, for it would then have been my duty to have warned you.

SQUEERS. Which, no doubt, you would have been devilish sorry to do.

NICHOLAS. I should indeed, sir.

MRS SQUEERS *enters.*

MRS SQUEERS. What's going on? Where's Smike?

SQUEERS. He's gone.

MRS SQUEERS (*an order, to* SQUEERS). Gone? Well, then, we'll find him, stupid. We must search the roads. He hasn't any money, any food. He'll have to beg. He must be on the public road.

SQUEERS (*going towards the exit*). That's true.

MRS SQUEERS (*following*). And when we catch him, oh . . .

SQUEERS *turns his back to the boys. Slowly.*

SQUEERS. And when we catch him, I will only stop just short of flaying him alive. So, follow your leader, boys, and take your pattern by Smike. If you dare.

The SQUEERSES *go out.* NICHOLAS *and the boys follow.*

Scene Twenty

The streets of the West End of London. Early morning. During this opening narration, we set up the breakfast room of the MANTALINIS: *a table and two chairs on the one side, and a single chair on the other. The Narration is delivered by* KATE NICKLEBY *and four or five* MILLINERS.

KATE. It was with a heavy heart, and many sad forebodings, that Kate Nickleby left the city when its clocks yet wanted a quarter of an hour of eight, and threaded her way, alone, amid the noise and bustle of the streets, towards the West End of London.

MILLINERS.

At this early hours many sickly girls,

Whose business, like that of the poor worm, is to produce with patient toil the finery that bedecks the thoughtless and luxurious,

Traverse our streets, making towards the scene of their daily labour,

And catching, as if by stealth, in their hurried walk,

The only gasp of wholesome air and glimpse of sunlight which cheers their monotonous existence during the long train of hours that make up the working day.

The MILLINERS *dispersing, as a tall, old* FOOTMAN *enters, a little unsteadily.*

KATE. Kate saw, in their unhealthy looks and feeble gait, but too clear an evidence that her misgivings were not wholly groundless.

KATE *goes to the* FOOTMAN, *as:*

NARRATOR. She arrived at Madame Mantalini's at the appointed hour, and was admitted to a small, curtained room, by a tall, elderly footman.

During the following, MR *and* MADAME MANTALINI *enter to the breakfast table and sit.* MADAME MANTALINI *is a handsome, well-dressed middle-aged woman. Her husband wears a morning gown, with a green waistcoat and Turkish trousers, a pink kerchief, bright slippers, black curled whiskers and a moustache. He is younger than his wife.*

KATE. Excuse me – Mantalini? Are they Italian?

FOOTMAN. Muntle.

KATE. I beg your pardon?

FOOTMAN. Changed his name. From Mr Muntle. To Mr Mantalini.

KATE. Oh, I see.

The FOOTMAN *nods gravely and goes out.* KATE *sits on the single chair. We gather from the fact that the* MANTALINIS *do not notice her that the room is divided by an imaginary curtain. There is a bad-tempered silence between the Mantalinis, which is broken when* MR MANTALINI *speaks.*

MANTALINI. I tell you again, my soul, that if you will be odiously, demnibly, outrageously jealous, you will make yourself most horrid miserable.

MADAME MANTALINI (*pouting*). I *am* miserable.

MANTALINI. And I tell you, my fastness, that it is a pretty bewitching little countenance you have, but if it is out of humour, it quite spoils itself, and looks very much like a hobgoblin's.

MADAME MANTALINI. It's very easy to talk.

MANTALINI. Not so easy when one is eating an egg and one is provoked into a passion by demned false accusations, my jewel, for the yolk runs down the waistcoast, and yolk of egg don't match it. 'Cept, of course, a yellow waistcoat. Which this ain't.

Pause. MADAME MANTALINI *breaks.*

MADAME MANTALINI. You flirted with her all night long.

MANTALINI. No, no, my love.

MADAME MANTALINI. I watched you all the time.

MANTALINI. Oh, bless the little winking eye – was on me all the time?

MADAME MANTALINI. And I say, Mantalini, that you waltz with anyone but me again, I will take poison. I will swear it, now.

MANTALINI. Take poison?

MADAME MANTALINI. Yes.

MANTALINI. You'll take demned poison on account of Mantalini, preciousness?

MADAME MANTALINI. I will.

MANTALINI. He who could have had the hands of a dowager and two countesses –

MADAME MANTALINI. *One* countess.

MANTALINI (*stands and goes round to his wife's side of the table*). But who at a morning concert saw the demndest little fascinator, and married it, and fiddlesticks to every countess in the world?

MADAME MANTALINI. Oh, Mantalini.

MANTALINI. Oh, my little cherub. I'm forgiven?

MADAME MANTALINI. Well . . . Oh, well.

MANTALINI (*moving briskly back to his seat*). Now, tell me, sapphire, how are we for cash? For there's a horse for sale at Scrubbs, for next to nothing, and if I can raise some discount from Ralph Nickleby, a hundred guineas buys him, mane and crest and legs and tail, all of the demdest beauty.

KATE *looks up in alarm.* MADAME MANTALINI *turns her head away.*

Then I can ride him in the park, before the very chariots of the rejected countesses.

Moving back to his wife.

My little – princess.

MADAME MANTALINI. Oh, my – Mantalini.

KATE *coughs loudly.* MANTALINI *stands and mimes pulling back the curtain – we hear the swish and rattle from offstage.*

MANTALINI *sees* KATE.

MANTALINI. Well. What's this?

MADAME MANTALINI. Child, who are you?

KATE (*standing*). I – I am sent here, by my uncle. I am sent here for a situation.

MANTALINI (*coming closer to* KATE). And, my dear, you'll have one.

MADAME MANTALINI. Mantalini.

KATE *thrusts* RALPH's *letter at* MADAME MANTALINI.

KATE. There's a letter. From my uncle, Mr Nickleby.

MADAME MANTALINI (*taking the letter, opening it, a little tartly*). Oh, yes.

MANTALINI (*trying to look at the letter*). Ralph Nickleby?

KATE. I'm sorry, I was – I was left here, by your footman.

MANTALINI. What a rascal is that footman, dear. To keep this sweet young creature waiting –

MADAME MANTALINI (*folding* RALPH's *letter*). Well, dear, I must say that that's your fault.

MANTALINI. My fault, my joy?

MADAME MANTALINI. Of course. What can you expect, dearest, if you will not correct the man?

Slight pause.

MANTALINI. Well, then. Indeed. He shall be horsewhipped.

MADAME MANTALINI. Well, my dear. Your uncle recommends you, and we are connected with him, in commercial matters. Now, do you speak French?

KATE. Yes, ma'am, I do.

MANTALINI. But do you speak it like a native?

MADAME MANTALINI (*ignoring* MR MANTALINI). Miss Nickleby, we have twenty young women constantly employed in this establishment.

MANTALINI. Some of them demned handsome, too.

MANTALINI *a knowing smirk at* KATE. MADAME MANTALINI *clocks it.*

MADAME MANTALINI. Of whom, I am pleased to say, Mr Mantalini knows nothing, as he is never in their room, as I will not allow it.

MANTALINI *shrugs, poutishly, and lies down on the sofa.*

Now, our hours are from nine to nine, with extra if we're busy, for which there's a little payment, and I'd think your wages would be in the region of five to seven shillings. Is that satisfactory?

KATE. Oh, yes. It's . . . Certainly.

MANTALINI. Demned satisfactory.

MADAME MANTALINI. Miss Nickleby, you will pay no attention, please, to anything that Mr Mantalini says.

KATE. I will not, ma'am.

MADAME MANTALINI. So, then, let me take you to the workroom, now, Miss Nickleby.

MADAME MANTALINI *leads* KATE *out.* MANTALINI *goes too.*

Scene Twenty-one

The MANTALINIS' *workroom and showroom. In the workroom are clothesrails, tailors' dummies, hatboxes, and uncompleted dresses and hats. In the showroom are display tailors' dummies, more hatboxes, a chaise longue and a tall mirror. For the moment, the showroom is empty, and the workroom is full of working* MILLINERS, *presided over by a short, bustling, over-dressed lady called* MISS KNAG. MADAME MANTALINI *and* KATE *enter. The* MILLINERS *look* KATE *up and down, whisper and giggle.*

MADAME MANTALINI. Miss Knag?

MISS KNAG. Madame Mantalini.

MADAME MANTALINI. Ah, Miss Knag, this is the young person I spoke to you about.

MISS KNAG. Oh, good morning, miss.

To the gawping MILLINERS.

Come on, come on, no gawping, is there no work to be done?

The MILLINERS *set about their tasks with bad humour.*

MADAME MANTALINI. I think, for the present, it will be better for Miss Nickleby to come into the showroom with you –

MISS KNAG. Showroom, yes.

MADAME MANTALINI. And try things on for people.

MISS KNAG. People, yes.

MADAME MANTALINI. She'll not be much use yet in any other way,

MISS KNAG. Way, no.

MADAME MANTALINI. And her appearance will –

MISS KNAG. Suit very well with mine.

MISS KNAG *to* KATE.

For, yes, I see, Miss Nickleby and I are very much a pair – although I am just a little darker, and I have, I think, a slightly smaller foot. Miss Nickleby will not, I am sure, be too much offended at my saying that, as our family has always been quite celebrated for its feet – the smallness of them – ever since the family had feet at all.

MADAME MANTALINI. You'll take care, Miss Knag, that she understands her hours,

MISS KNAG. Hours,

MADAME MANTALINI. And so forth.

MISS KNAG. So forth, yes.

MADAME MANTALINI. And I'll leave her with you.

MISS KNAG. Yes, of course, dear Madame Mantalini.

MADAME MANTALINI. Good morning, ladies.

EVERYONE. Good morning, madame.

MADAME MANTALINI *goes out. As she leaves, she finds* MANTALINI *skulking near the doorway. She looks at him, and shakes her head, near tears, and runs off.* MANTALINI, *dramatically, follows.*

MISS KNAG. Well, what a charming woman.

KATE. Yes. I'm sure she is.

MISS KNAG. And what a charming husband.

KATE. Is he?

MISS KNAG. You don't think so?

KATE. Well –

MISS KNAG. Oh, goodness gracious mercy – where's your taste? And such a dashing man, with such a head of hair and teeth.

KATE. Well, p'raps I'm very foolish –

MISS KNAG (*with a conspiratorial look at the* MILLINERS). Well, I should say you –

KATE. But as my opinion is of very little importance to him or anyone else, I think I shall keep it, just the same.

Pause. MISS KNAG, *slightly thrown. The odd* MILLINER, *aware of this, giggles.* MISS KNAG *turns to them.*

MISS KNAG. Well, come on, girls, where are your manners? Make Miss Nickleby welcome. Take her shawl.

The MILLINERS *bustle round* KATE.

1st MILLINER. Your shawl, miss?

2nd MILLINER. Can I take your bonnet?

KATE (*giving the* MILLINER *her shawl*). Oh, thank you.

1st MILLINER. Oh, *miss.* And all in black.

KATE. Well, yes, I –

3rd MILLINER. Don't you find it quite intol'r'ble hot? And dusty?

KATE (*almost in tears*). Yes. I do. Oh, yes, I do.

Embarrassed pause.

1st MILLINER. Was it a near relation, miss?

KATE. My father.

MISS KNAG (*calls*). For what relation?

2nd MILLINER. Father.

MISS KNAG. A long illness, was it?

2nd MILLINER. I don't know.

KATE. Our misfortune was very sudden. Or I might, perhaps, be able to support it better now.

And the MILLINERS *turn out front.*

MILLINERS.

And then there came a knock at Madame Mantalini's door,

And there entered a great lady,

Well, a rich one,

Who had come with her daughter for approval of some court dresses,

Long in preparation,

Upon whom Miss Nickleby was told to wait,

MADAME MANTALINI, MISS KNAG, KATE, *a* RICH LADY *and her* RICH DAUGHTER *are in the showroom. The* RICH

LADY *sits on the chaise, the* RICH DAUGHTER *stands trying on a coat and hat, near the mirror.*

MADAME MANTALINI. Bonjour, madame.

1st MILLINER. With Miss Knag,

MISS KNAG. Mademoiselle –

3rd MILLINER. And officered of course by –

MILLINERS. Madame Mantalini.

KATE (*bustling about with clothes and hats*). Kate's part in the pageant was humble enough –

MISS KNAG (*taking something from* KATE). Là, ma chère –

KATE. Her duties being limited to holding the articles of costume until Miss Knag was ready to try them on . . .

MISS KNAG (*taking something else*). Ici . . .

KATE. And now and then tying a string,

MISS KNAG. Or fastening a hook and eye . . . Merci . . .

KATE. And thinking that she was beneath the reach of all arrogance and ill-humour.

MISS KNAG (*surveying the effect*). Ah. Mais oui.

RICH LADY (*off-hand*). Alors . . .

MILLINERS.

But as it happened, both the rich lady and her rich daughter were in a terrible temper,

And Miss Nickleby came in for a considerable share of their displeasure.

KATE *steps backwards from the* RICH DAUGHTER, *nearly stepping on the foot of the* RICH LADY.

RICH LADY. She's so awkward.

1st MILLINER. They remarked.

KATE *fumbling, trying to tie a hat on the* RICH DAUGHTER.

RICH DAUGHTER. Her hands are cold.

2nd MILLINER. They said.

KATE *accidentally pushes the hat forward, so it falls over the* RICH DAUGHTER's *face.*

RICH LADY. Can she do nothing right?

The RICH DAUGHTER *takes off the hat,* MISS KNAG *takes*

her coat, the DAUGHTER *and the* RICH LADY *preparing to go, as:*

3rd MILLINER. And they wondered how Madame Mantalini could have such girls about her —

MADAME MANTALINI. Madame, je regrette infiniment . . .

1st MILLINER. And requested they might see some other young person the next time they came . . .

RICH LADY. Chère Madame, au revoir!

The RICH LADY *and her* RICH DAUGHTER *sweep out.*

2nd MILLINER. And so on,

3rd MILLINER. And so forth.

The MILLINERS *disperse.* KATE *moves into the workroom area, leaving* MADAME MANTALINI *and* MISS KNAG *in the showroom.*

KATE. And so common an occurrence would hardly be worthy of mention, but for its effect on Kate, who shed many bitter tears when these people were gone, and felt, for the first time, humbled by her occupation. She had, it is true, quailed at the prospect of hard work and drudgery; but she'd felt no degradation in the thought of labour, till she found herself exposed to insolence and pride.

KATE stays.

MISS KNAG. Well, now, Madame Mantalini. That Miss Nickleby is certainly a very creditable young person, indeed.

MADAME MANTALINI. Well, Miss Knag, beyond putting an excellent client out of humour, Miss Nickleby has not done anything very remarkable thus far that I'm aware of.

MISS KNAG. Aware of, no. But, dear Madame, you must make allowances for inexperience. And such.

MADAME MANTALINI. Well, yes, Miss Knag, of course, but in my view she still remains among the awkwardest young girls I ever saw. And not, despite the opinion of her uncle, not that pretty either.

MISS KNAG. Pretty, no. But, Madame Mantalini. That is not her fault, now is it? She should not be blamed for that, and be denied our friendship, should she?

Slight pause. MADAME MANTALINI *goes out. A great beam is spreading around* MISS KNAG's *face, as* KATE *takes out a letter.*

KATE: Oh, Nicholas. How happy it makes me to hear from you, in such good spirits. It consoles me so, to think that you at least are comfortable and happy.

Exit KATE. MISS KNAG, *quickly*.

MISS KNAG. I love her. I quite love her. I declare I do.

Scene Twenty-two

The Dotheboys Hall schoolroom. Bare stage. The boys enter, two of them dragging a pair of steps, the thrashing-horse. They put it centre stage. The boys form two lines either side of it.
NICHOLAS enters, and looks in horror at the thrashing-horse.
SQUEERS enters, with a long cane.

SQUEERS. Is every boy here? Every boy keep his place.

Pause.

Nickleby, to your place, sir. Coates. Jackson.

COATES *and* JACKSON *go out.* NICHOLAS *moves near the thrashing-horse.* MRS SQUEERS, FANNY, YOUNG WACKFORD *and* PHIB *enter, and stand to one side.* COATES *and* JACKSON *re-enter, dragging* SMIKE, *who is bound, and filthy, clearly having been caught after spending the night rough. He is brought down to the thrashing-horse.*

SQUEERS. Untie him, sirs.

The two boys untie SMIKE.

Now, sir, what do you have to say for yourself?

Pause.

Nothing, I suppose?

Pause. SMIKE *glances at* NICHOLAS, *who is looking away.*

Well, then. Let's begin.

SMIKE. Oh, spare me, sir.

SQUEERS. What's that?

SMIKE. Oh, spare me, sir.

SQUEERS. Oh, that's all, is it? Well, I'll flog you within an inch of your life, but I will spare you that.

Pause.

Coates, Jackson.

COATES *and* JACKSON *help* SMIKE *on to a step of the*

thrashing-horse. COATES *and* JACKSON *tie* SMIKE *to the horse.*

SMIKE. I was driven to it, sir.

SQUEERS. Driven to it? Not your fault, but mine?

MRS SQUEERS. Hm. That's a good one.

SQUEERS *goes a little upstage, turns, runs, and delivers the first blow.* SMIKE *cries out,* SQUEERS *grunts. He goes upstage again, runs, and delivers the second blow. He is back upstage again, when* NICHOLAS *takes a slight step forward.*

NICHOLAS. Uh . . . This must stop.

SQUEERS *looks round.*

SQUEERS. Who said that? Who said stop?

NICHOLAS. I did. I said that it must stop, and stop it will.

Pause.

I have tried to intercede. I have begged forgiveness for the boy. You have not listened. You have brought this on yourself.

SQUEERS (*dismissively, preparing for his next stroke*). Get out. Get out.

NICHOLAS *walks to stand between* SQUEERS *and* SMIKE.

NICHOLAS. No sir. I can't.

SQUEERS. Can't? You can't? We'll see.

SQUEERS *walks to* NICHOLAS *and strikes his face.*
NICHOLAS *doesn't respond.*

Now leave, sir, and let me to my work.

NICHOLAS *turns, as if to go, then suddenly turns back, grabs* SQUEERS, *pulls him round, and hits him.*

What?

NICHOLAS. You have –

SQUEERS *tries to hit* NICHOLAS, *but* NICHOLAS *seizes the cane and beats* SQUEERS *with it. During the ensuing, the following things happen:* MRS SQUEERS, WACKFORD *and eventually* FANNY *come to* SQUEERS' *aid – somewhat ineffectually; The boys crush round to see, and eventually to obscure, the fight. And* SMIKE, *let go, slips away. There is much shouting.*

MRS SQUEERS. What do you think you're doing, you madman?

FANNY. Get off him! Get off him, you monster!

WACKFORD. Beastly! Beastly, man! You beast!

And NICHOLAS, finished, breaks through the boys and runs out.

MRS SQUEERS. After him! After him, you vermin! Move, run after him!

The boys, who have no intention of doing anything of the sort, nonetheless disperse, revealing SQUEERS, sitting on the ground, holding himself.

Oh, Squeery, Squeery.

She helps SQUEERS to his feet.

Oh, my Squeery.

MRS SQUEERS takes SQUEERS out. WACKFORD and FANNY follow.

Scene Twenty-three

In the countryside. Bare stage. Darkness. NICHOLAS running. JOHN BROWDIE enters with a lamp. He carries a stout staff.

JOHN. Hey! Hey! Who's that, who's there? Hey!

John's light reveals NICHOLAS.

Eh. It's tha. From school.

NICHOLAS. Yes, I'm afraid so.

JOHN. What's tha mean, afraid?

NICHOLAS. Well, only –

JOHN. Eh, man, what's the matter with thy face?

NICHOLAS. Oh, it's a cut. A blow. But I returned it to the giver, and with interest, too.

JOHN. Nay. Did tha?

NICHOLAS. Yes. For I have been the victim of considerable mistreatment.

JOHN. Eh?

NICHOLAS. At, from the hands of Mr Squeers. But I have beaten him quite soundly, and am leaving here as a result.

JOHN. Tha what?

NICHOLAS. I said – I've beaten him.

And JOHN BROWDIE *goes into strange, silent convulsions. It is not immediately clear that he is vastly amused.*

Uh – what . . .?

JOHN. Tha beat the schoolmaster!

NICHOLAS. Yes, I'm afraid –

JOHN. Who ever heard the like!

NICHOLAS. I'm very sorry, but I was –

JOHN. Give me tha hand.

NICHOLAS. Give you my hand?

JOHN (*taking* NICHOLAS's *hand and pumping it firmly*). That's right. Give me tha hand. Tha beat the schoolmaster!

NICHOLAS. Yes, I did, and as a consequence –

JOHN. Eh, man, where is tha going?

NICHOLAS. Well, to London . . .

JOHN. Has tha owt, in way of cash?

NICHOLAS. Well, no, but as I plan to walk –

JOHN. To walk to Lunnon? Look, man, tha needs cash. At least, for food, and suchlike.

Finds his purse.

So, here's money.

NICHOLAS. Oh, I couldn't possibly –

JOHN. Tha couldn't possibly? Tha couldn't possibly without. So, come on, man. At least, accept a sovereign.

NICHOLAS. Well, I don't know . . .

JOHN. And, p'raps, tha'll not use all of it, and send the surplus back, eh? Oh, and take this timber. If tha's walking that far, need this too.

NICHOLAS *takes the staff. Pause.*

Now, go be off with thee.

Pause.

NICHOLAS. I cannot thank you, sir, enough. I – after what, the words we had – I cannot –

JOHN. Beat the schoolmaster. I've not heard good as that, for twenty year.

And JOHN *gives* NICHOLAS *a big, bear-like hug, and goes out.* NICHOLAS *follows.*

Scene Twenty-four.

The parlour at Dotheboys Hall. Bare stage. Enter FANNY, furious, clutching a letter she has written. To the audience:

FANNY. To Mr Ralph Nickleby. Golden Square. In London. Sir. My pa requests me to write to you, the doctors considering it doubtful whether he will ever recover the use of his legs, which prevents him holding a pen. We are in a state of mind beyond everything, and my pa is one mask of bruises both blue and green . . . When your nephew, which you recommended for a teacher, had done this to my pa, and jumped upon his body, with his feet, and language I will not pollute my pen with describing, he assaulted my ma with dreadful violence, dashed her to the earth, and drove her back comb several inches into her head. A little more and it must have entered her skull. We have a medical certificate that if it had, the tortoiseshell would have affected the brain. Me and my brother were then the victims of his fury; I am screaming out loud all the time I write and so is my brother which takes off my attention rather, and I hope will excuse mistakes. The monster, having satiated his thirst for blood, ran away, taking with him a boy of desperate character that he had excited to rebellion. I remain yours, and — cetrer, Fanny Squeers.

FANNY *folds the letter. A knock at the door.*

Phib!

PHIB *enters.*

Someone at the door. P.S.: I pity his ignorance, and despise him.

PHIB *goes to the "door". BROOKER enters. He is an old man, dressed in rags, and covered in mud and snow.*

PHIB (*frightened, turning to FANNY*). Uh . . .

FANNY *looks at BROOKER. She looks scared, too.*

BROOKER (*takes a step into the room*). Boy. I've come about a boy. Lived here.

FANNY *looks at PHIB in panic. PHIB runs out. BROOKER takes another step into the room.*

My name is Brooker. Come about a boy.

FANNY *runs out, BROOKER following.*

Scene Twenty-five.

NICHOLAS *on his own in the countryside. Bare stage.*

NICHOLAS. It's morning.

NICHOLAS *turns to walk out. Something he hears makes him stop. He turns back.* SMIKE *stands there.*

Oh, Smike. Oh – Smike.

NICHOLAS *quickly to* SMIKE, *who falls to his knees.*

Why do you, kneel to me?

SMIKE. To go. Go anywhere. Go everywhere. To the world's end. To the churchyard grave.

Pause.

I can. You'll let me. Come away with you.

Pause.

You are my home.

NICHOLAS *stands there. He doesn't know what to do.* SMIKE *turns his face away. He's crying.* NICHOLAS *puts his hand out to* SMIKE. SMIKE *looks back. He sees the hand.* NICHOLAS *helps* SMIKE *to his feet, and the two of them go slowly out together.*

END OF ACT ONE.

ACT TWO

Scene One

A group of NARRATORS *on the bare stage. During the following,* NOGGS *enters and sits in his old armchair. A hard-featured, thin-faced man, wearing a dirty nightcap and carrying an unlit candle, is behind him. This man is* MR CROWL.

NARRATION.
In that quarter of London where Golden Square is situated,
There is a bygone, tumbledown old street,
Two rows of blackened, battered houses,
At the top of one of which there is a meagre garret room;
Where, on a wet and dismal winter's evening,
Newman Noggs,
The clerk to that great man of business Ralph Nickleby,
Sat studying a letter,
Written to his master,
Which had arrived that very afternoon.

NOGGS (*reading*). My pa requests – one mask of bruises – language – thirst for blood. Oh, dear. And cetrer, Fanny Squeers. Oh, dear, oh, dear.

MR CROWL *knocks.*

What's that?

CROWL (*unnecessarily loud*). It's Mr Crowl. Your Neighbour. Have you got a light?

NOGGS. Oh, yes, do come in, Mr Crowl.

NARRATORS *withdraw as* CROWL *to* NOGGS.

CROWL. A nasty night, Mr Noggs.

NOGGS. Oh, does it rain outside?

CROWL. Oh, does it rain? I'm wet through.

NOGGS (*looking at his threadbare sleeve*). Well, it doesn't take much to wet you and me through, does it, Mr Crowl.

CROWL. Well, but that only makes it more vexatious, doesn't it?
Pause.

NOGGS. You'll forgive me, Mr Crowl. I must go downstairs to supper.

CROWL. To the Kenwigses?

NOGGS. That's right. It is their wedding anniversary, and Mrs Kenwigs' uncle is expected, the collector of the water-rate, and I am invited to make up the punch and the numbers. So, you'll let me —

CROWL. Well, now, think of that.

NOGGS. Yes, what?

CROWL. I was invited too.

NOGGS. You were?

CROWL. Indeed I was, but I resolved not to go, thinking you were not invited, and planning to spend the evening in your company.

NOGGS. Well, um . . . I was obliged . . .

CROWL. And now, what's there for me to do?

Pause. NOGGS gestures vaguely.

I know. I've got it. I'll spend the evening here. And keep your fire up for you. Hm?

NOGGS. Oh . . . very well.

NOGGS *turns to go.*

CROWL. Um, Mr Noggs, it being such a night . . . Where do you keep your coals?

NOGGS. They're in the coal scuttle. Where coals ought to be.

NOGGS *goes out,* CROWL *pushes out the armchair.*

CROWL (*out front*). The following, having the misfortune to treat of none but common people, is necessarily of a mean and vulgar character.

Scene Two

The Kenwigs' living room. A small, cluttered room, full of furniture and people. They are the pregnant MRS KENWIGS, her eldest daughter MORLEENA, two other LITTLE KENWIGSES — both girls, MR and MRS CUTLER, MISS GREEN, MRS KENWIGS' SISTER, a young man called GEORGE, a fierce-looking STOUT LADY, in a book-muslin dress, and MISS PETOWKER, an actress. NOGGS sits by a small table on which are glasses, trays and a bowl of punch. MRS KENWIGS is just greeting him.

MRS KENWIGS. Dear Mr Noggs. Now, Miss Petowker, have you met my husband's old friend, George?

GEORGE. I'm most delighted. ·

MRS KENWIGS. Miss Petowker's from the Theatre Royal, Drury Lane, and later on she may recite for us.

MISS PETOWKER. Oh, Mrs Kenwigs . . .

MRS KENWIGS *going to her* SISTER.

GEORGE. Miss Petowker, tell me, how do you fill your days?

SISTER (*referring to the* STOUT LADY). My dear, who is that woman?

MRS KENWIGS. Oh, she's the lady from downstairs.

SISTER. What *does* she think she's wearing?

MRS KENWIGS. Well, she wouldn't wear it here, but for the fact our supper's cooking on her grate.

SISTER. I see. ·

KENWIGS *enters, briskly.*

KENWIGS. Now, Mrs Kenwigs, if everything's prepared, wouldn't it be best to begin with a round-game?

MRS KENWIGS. Kenwigs, my dear, I am surprised at you. Would you begin without my uncle?

KENWIGS. Ah. I forgot the collector.

MRS KENWIGS (*to* MRS CUTLER). He's so particular, that if we begin without him, I shall be out of his will forever.

MRS CUTLER. Oh, my dear!

MRS KENWIGS. You have no *notion* how he is.

To KENWIGS.

And yet, of course, as good a creature as ever breathed.

KENWIGS. Indeed. The kindest-hearted man that ever was.

GEORGE. It brings the very tears to his eyes, I believe, to be forced to cut the water off when people don't pay.

MRS KENWIGS. Now, George, if you please.

GEORGE. Oh, I'm sorry. Just my —

MRS KENWIGS. We'll have none of that.

GEORGE. Was just my little joke.

KENWIGS. Now, George. A joke is a good thing, an excellent

thing, but when a joke is made at the expense of Mrs Kenwigs' feelings I set my face against it. And, even putting Mrs Kenwigs out of the question — if I *could* put Mrs Kenwigs out of the question on such an occasion as this — I myself have the honour to be connected with the collector by marriage, and I cannot allow these remarks in my . . . in my apartments.

Pause.

GEORGE. Just my little joke.

KENWIGS. The subject is now closed.

A ring.

The bell!

MISS PETOWKER. That's him?

MRS CUTLER. The collector?

STOUT LADY. Who?

MRS KENWIGS. Yes, yes, it must be, dear Morleena, run straight down and let your uncle in and kiss him most directly when the door is open. Hurry, girl!

MORLEENA. Yes, yes, mama.

Exit MORLEENA.

MRS KENWIGS. And, everyone, we must appear to be engaged in light and easy conversation of a general character.

MISS GREEN. Light and easy?

MRS KENWIGS. Yes, so as to look —

MR CUTLER. And of a general character?

MRS KENWIGS. Yes, yes, now Miss Petowker, tell us, if you'd be so kind —

MRS CUTLER. So as to look —

MRS KENWIGS *has turned and sees* MR LILLYVICK, *who has been admitted by* MORLEENA.

MRS KENWIGS. Oh, uncle, I'm so pleased to see you.

LILLYVICK. Susan.

MRS KENWIGS. Oh, so glad.

LILLYVICK. As I, my dear, as I. And may I wish you every happiness.

MR LILLYVICK *kisses* MRS KENWIGS.

MRS CUTLER. Well, look at that.

MR CUTLER. A tax-collector.

MISS GREEN. Kissing.

GEORGE. Actually.

MRS KENWIGS. And so, uncle, where will you sit?

LILLYVICK (*standing*). Oh, anywheres, my dear. I'm not particular, at all.

MRS CUTLER. You hear that?

MR CUTLER. Anywheres.

MISS GREEN. He's not particular.

GEORGE. At all.

KENWIGS. Um, Mr Lillyvick, some friends of mine, sir, very anxious for the honour . . .

LILLYVICK. As I am, Kenwigs, just as I am . . .

KENWIGS. Mr and Mrs Cutler, Mr Lillyvick.

MR CUTLER. I'm proud to know you, sir. As having heard of you so often. In your professional capacity.

KENWIGS. My old friend George you know, I think; of course, Mrs Kenwigs' sister; Miss Green, who makes up Mrs Kenwigs' dresses, Mr Lillyvick; and Mrs, um, downstairs . . . And, Mr Lillyvick, this here is Miss Petowker of the Theatre Royal Drury Lane, and very glad I am indeed, to make two public characters acquainted.

MISS PETOWKER. I am so pleased to meet you, sir.

LILLYVICK. Yes, yes, most privileged, I'm sure.

KENWIGS. Now, Morleena, where's your sisters, so they can kiss your uncle?

MORLEENA *pushes forward the two* LITTLE KENWIGSES, *and* MR LILLYVICK's *attention is reluctantly removed from* MISS PETOWKER *so he can kiss them; meanwhile* MRS KENWIGS *is whispered to about* MR NOGGS *by her* SISTER.

SISTER. Why doesn't he . . . the threadbare gentleman?

MRS KENWIGS. Oh, Mr Noggs, he'd be embarrassed, to be taken notice of. He was a gentleman, you see, before.

LILLYVICK. And where is little Lillyvick?

MRS KENWIGS. Oh, uncle, in safe hands, in Miss Green's bed, and sleeping like a baby . . .

LILLYVICK. Well, he is a baby.

MRS KENWIGS. Yes, and minded by a girl, of course.

MISS GREEN. Who's being paid nine pence,

MRS KENWIGS. And thus will see to it no harm befalls your namesake, uncle.

LILLYVICK. Yes, it should be so.

Pause.

Well. Susan. Kenwigs. Anniversary.

KENWIGS. Eight years.

LILLYVICK. Eight years. I still recall my niece . . .

STOUT LADY. Recalls his niece?

LILLYVICK. That very afternoon, she first acknowledged to her mother a partiality for Kenwigs. "Mother," she says, "I love him."

MRS KENWIGS. Actually, 'adore him,' I said, uncle.

LILLYVICK. 'Love him,' you said, Susan, I remember it, and instantly her mother cries out 'what?' and falls at once into convulsions.

MRS CUTLER. What?

MISS GREEN. Convulsions?

LILLYVICK. Into strong convulsions. For, I'm sure that Kenwigs will forgive me for saying so, there was a great objection to him, on the grounds that he was so beneath the family, and would disgrace it. You remember, Kenwigs?

KENWIGS. Certainly.

LILLYVICK. And I, I must confess, I shared that feeling . . . and perhaps it's natural, and perhaps it's not . . .

MRS CUTLER. Well, I'd say –

STOUT LADY. *Quite* natural.

LILLYVICK. And after they were married, I was the first to say that Kenwigs must be taken notice of. And he *was* taken notice of, because I said so; and I'm bound to say, and proud to say, that I have always found him a most honest, well-behaved and upright sort of man. Kenwigs, shake hands.

KENWIGS (*doing so*). I am proud to do it, sir.

LILLYVICK. And so am I.

KENWIGS. And a very happy life I have led with your niece, sir.

LILLYVICK. And it would have been your own fault if you hadn't, sir.

MRS KENWIGS (*overcome*). Oh, dear Morleena, kiss your uncle once again.

LILLYVICK. Oh. Well . . .

MRS KENWIGS. And all of you, dear children, come and kiss your uncle . . .

LILLYVICK. Well, indeed, and now to see these three young lively girls . . .

MRS KENWIGS. Oh, yes, oh, yes, they are too beautiful.

LILLYVICK. Too beautiful for what, my dear?

MRS KENWIGS. Too beautiful to live.

MISS GREEN. Oh, Mrs Kenwigs . . .

MRS KENWIGS *in tears*.

MRS KENWIGS. Oh far, far too . . .

MRS CUTLER. Oh, dear Mrs Kenwigs, please . . .

SISTER. Oh, come now, Susan, don't distress yourself.

MISS GREEN. Don't give way, dear . . .

MRS KENWIGS. I'm sorry, but I cannot help it, it don't signify. They're just . . . they are too beautiful.

KENWIGS. Um, Mrs Kenwigs, should, perhaps . . . While Mr Noggs makes up the punch, Morleena do her figure dance for Mr Lillyvick?

MISS GREEN. Oh, yes. It's a spectacle.

MRS KENWIGS. Oh, no, my dear, it will only worry my uncle.

MISS PETOWKER. Come, I'm sure it won't, now will it, Mr Lillyvick?

LILLYVICK. I'm sure, dear lady, it is most –

MRS KENWIGS (*recovered*). Well, then, I'll tell you what. Morleena does the steps, if uncle can persuade Miss Petowker to recite for us afterwards the Blood Drinker's Burial.

Much applause and encouragement.

GEORGE. Oh, yes, indeed.

MISS GREEN. Oh, that would be a treat.

STOUT LADY. Blood Drinker's what?

MISS PETOWKER. Oh, now, you know that I dislike doing anything professional at private parties.

MRS KENWIGS. Oh, but not here? We're all so very friendly and pleasant, that you might as well be going through it in your own room; besides, the occasion . . .

MISS PETOWKER. Well . . . I can't resist that. Anything in my humble power, I shall be delighted.

More applause.

KENWIGS. Come, then, everyone, form a space here . . .

MRS KENWIGS. Morleena, dear, have you chalked your shoes?

STOUT LADY. She's going to do a poem?

MRS CUTLER. No, a dance.

MISS PETOWKER. All ready?

MORLEENA *nods. Some musical accompaniment – from* MISS PETOWKER, *humming or otherwise; or perhaps another member of the party.* MORLEENA *does her dance – "a very beautiful figure, comprising a great deal of work for the arms," and it is received with unbounded applause. During this,* NOGGS *hands round punch.*

GEORGE. Bravo!

MRS CUTLER. Quite wonderful.

MISS GREEN. Oh, Mr Kenwigs, you must be so proud . . .

MR CUTLER. Can say with confidence, have never seen the like.

MRS CUTLER. I wouldn't like to meet her teacher, that's all I can say.

MR CUTLER. I say, I'd like to shake her teacher by the hand.

KENWIGS. Ah, Noggs, please, the collector first . . .

MRS KENWIGS (*to* LILLYVICK). You see, how beautifully she . . . Oh, dear me . . .

MISS PETOWKER. You know –

MISS PETOWKER *gains attention.*

If I was ever, blessed . . . And if my child were, such a genius as that . . . I'd have her in the opera at once.

KENWIGS. The opera?

MISS PETOWKER. What's wrong?

MRS KENWIGS. I think that Kenwigs thinks . . . the younger dukes and marquises . . .

LILLYVICK. Yes, very right.

MISS PETOWKER. Oh, sir, one only needs to keep one's pride. I've kept my pride, and never had a thing of that sort. Not a thing.

KENWIGS. Well, then. Perhaps we should give it serious consideration.

MISS PETOWKER *graciously prepares herself. She whispers to* GEORGE, *and they put out some of the lights to give a better effect.*

STOUT LADY. What's she doing now? Another dance?

MRS CUTLER. She's going to recite.

STOUT LADY. What, in the dark?

KENWIGS. Ladies and gentlemen. Pray silence, please, for Miss Petowker.

Applause. MISS PETOWKER *strikes an attitude. During this,* CROWL *enters and goes towards the party.*

MISS PETOWKER.
'Twas in a back-street tavern that one night it did perchance,
While the wind was howling fiercely, all the bottles were
   a-dance,
The candle gutted fitful as they, fearful, drank their ale,
When a dark-eyed stranger entered, bought a drink, and
   told a tale.
Oh, he was a –

CROWL *knocks loudly.*

What?

MRS KENWIGS. What's that?

KENWIGS. It sounded like a –

CROWL. It's Mr Crowl, and Mr Noggs is wanted.

KENWIGS (*admitting* CROWL). Mr Noggs?

NOGGS. Who, me?

CROWL. Two people in his room. Both very queer-looking. And covered up with rain and mud.

NOGGS. What, me? By name?

CROWL. By name. (*To* KENWIGS.). The one's a kind of scrawny chap, and not quite right, it seems to me; the other's straighter, darkish, twenty years or so . . .

MISS PETOWKER *shrugs at* GEORGE, *who relights candles.* NOGGS, *who has been going towards the exit, turns back.*

NOGGS. Dark? Twenty years?

CROWL. Or so.

Suddenly, NOGGS *rushes back into the room, grabs a candle, and takes the cup of punch from* MR LILLYVICK.

Excuse me. Please.

NOGGS *rushes out.*

Well, look at that —

MRS KENWIGS. Well, suppose it should be an express sent up to say his property has all come back again, and the express accounting for the mud and —

KENWIGS. Well, it's not impossible, perhaps, in that case, we should send a little extra punch up —

LILLYVICK. Kenwigs. I'm surprised at you.

KENWIGS. Why, what's the matter, sir?

LILLYVICK (*standing*). Why, making such a remark as that, sir. He has had punch already, has he not? My punch, in fact. Now, it may well be customary to allow such things here, but it's not the sort of thing I have been used to, when a gentleman is raising up a glass of punch and then another comes and collars it without a "with your leave" or "by your leave" . . . This may be called good manners, but it's not by me, and now it's past my hour to go to bed, and I can find my own way home.

MRS KENWIGS. Oh, uncle!

KENWIGS. Sir, I'm very sorry, sir.

LILLYVICK. Then it should have been prevented, sir, that's all.

KENWIGS. Well, sir, I didn't . . . Just a glass of punch, to put you out of temper . . .

LILLYVICK. Out of temper? Me? Morleena, get my hat.

MISS PETOWKER (*bewitchingly*). Oh, you're not going, sir . . .

LILLYVICK. I am not wanted here. My hat!
    (MORLEENA, *terrified, goes to find Lillyvick's hat.*

MRS KENWIGS. Oh, do not speak so, uncle, please . . .

LILLYVICK. My hat!

KENWIGS (*grabbing the hat from* MORLEENA). Sir, I must grovel at your feet, and beg you, for your niece's sake, that you'll forgive me.

LILLYVICK. Hm?

KENWIGS. For, for your niece's sake. And little Lillyvick.

LILLYVICK. Well, then.

Pause.

Well, then. You are forgiven.

Applause.

But let me tell you, Kenwigs, that even if I'd gone away without another word, it would have made no difference respecting that pound or two which I shall leave among your children when I die.

MRS KENWIGS. Morleena Kenwigs. Now, go down upon your knees, next to your father, and beg Mr Lillyvick to love you all his life, for he is more an angel than a man, and I have always said so.

LILLYVICK *smiles benignly as* MORLEENA, *rather uncomfortably, kneels beside her Father.*

MORLEENA. Uh. Uncle Lillyvick. Uh . . .

Suddenly, three high-pitched screams from another room.

KENWIGS. What's that?

GEORGE. Where is it?

MRS KENWIGS (*to* MISS GREEN). Oh, it's your – oh, my baby!

MRS KENWIGS *trying to run out, stopped by her* SISTER.

Oh, my blessed, blessed –

SISTER. Susan, please –

KENWIGS. Now, I will go at once and –

MRS KENWIGS. Let me go!

KENWIGS. Come, George –

GEORGE. Of course. Where is the –

MISS GREEN. Up the stairs, just –

MRS KENWIGS. Oh, my own dear darling, innocent – Oh, let me go–

LILLYVICK. What: Little Lillyvick!

KENWIGS *is nearly out of the room, followed by* GEORGE, *when* NICHOLAS *bursts into the room, holding little* LILLYVICK *in his arms.*

KENWIGS. Oh, sir.

LILLYVICK. What's this? Who's this?

NICHOLAS (*breathlessly*). Don't be alarmed. Here is the baby. Safe and sound.

MRS KENWIGS (*rushing to take the baby from* NICHOLAS). Oh, oh, my baby . . .

NICHOLAS. It was – a nothing. All that happened was the little girl who watched the baby fell asleep, and the candle set her hair on fire.

MISS GREEN. The wretch.

MISS GREEN strides out.

NICHOLAS. I heard her cries. And ran down. And the baby was not touched. I promise you.

MISS PETOWKER. Oh, sir, without you, he would certainly have burned to death.

NICHOLAS. Well, no, I'm sure you would have heard it too, and rushed to her assistance.

Enter MISS GREEN, *pushing a little girl with singed hair.*

MISS GREEN. Here is the wretch! Look, here she is. Her head all singed.

MRS CUTLER. And costing ninepence.

MISS GREEN. Which she *won't* receive. Be off with you!

MRS CUTLER. Yes, off, off, now!

The poor little girl is pushed out, the LITTLE KENWIGSES *running to catch a glimpse of her singed head before she's gone.*

LILLYVICK. Now, sir. You have done service, and we must all drink your health.

NICHOLAS. Well, in my absence, I'm afraid, sir. I have had a very tiring journey, and would be most indifferent company. So please forgive me if I go back up to Mr Noggs. Good night.

NICHOLAS goes out.

MRS KENWIGS. That is – the man.

SISTER. And quite delightful.

KENWIGS. Quite uncommonly. Now, don't you think so, Mr Lillyvick?

LILLYVICK. Well, yes, he is – he seems to be a gentleman.

MISS PETOWKER. Oh, yes . . . There's something in him, looks, now what's the word?

MISS GREEN. What word?

MISS PETOWKER. You know, when lords and dukes and things go breaking knockers, and playing at coaches, and all that sort of thing?

LILLYVICK. Aristocratic.

MISS PETOWKER. Yes, that's right. That's what he is.

MISS GREEN. Indeed.

KENWIGS. Well, now, perhaps . . . There is still supper to be had . . .

STOUT LADY. Downstairs.

KENWIGS. Downstairs.

EVERYONE, *going out, as:*

LILLYVICK. I shall . . . I should esteem it a great honour, Miss Petowker, soon to hear the ending of your recitation.

LILLYVICK. Oh, dear Mr Lillyvick, you shall. I swear you shall.

And MR LILLYVICK *takes the arm of* MISS PETOWKER, *and leads her into supper.*

Scene Three
Noggs' garret room. NICHOLAS *and* SMIKE, *and* NOGGS, *who has a bottle and two glasses.* NICHOLAS *sits in Noggs' chair, reading Fanny Squeers' letter.*

NICHOLAS. Monster . . . boy of desperate character . . . So, has my uncle yet received this outrageous letter?

NOGGS. Yes, he has –

NICHOLAS. Then, I must go to him at once –

NOGGS. No, no, you mustn't –

NICHOLAS. Mustn't? Why?

NOGGS. Because he hasn't read it yet. And he's, gone away from town. Three days.

NICHOLAS. My mother and sister do not know of this?

NOGGS. They don't.

NICHOLAS. Well, then. At once, I must go to them. Tell me,
quick, where are they living? I must go there now.

NOGGS. No, no, you mustn't.

NICHOLAS. Mustn't? Why?

NOGGS (*handing glasses to* NICHOLAS *and* SMIKE). Because . . .
please, be advised by me. Your uncle — Do not be seen to be
tampering with anyone. You do not know this man. And also —
He pours a drink for each of them. They don't yet drink it.

NICHOLAS. Yes? And also?

NOGGS. You come home, after just three weeks. No money, no
position. What — what will your mother —

NICHOLAS. Mr Noggs, I tell you, that three weeks or three
hours, if I had stood by —

NOGGS. I know, I know, but still, my dear young man . . . you
can't, you mustn't give way to — this sort of thing will never do,
you know, and if you want to get on in the world, if you take
the part of everybody that's ill-treated . . .
Suddenly, clapping NICHOLAS *on the arm.*
Damn it, I'm proud of you. I would have done the same myself!

NICHOLAS. Oh, Newman, Newman, thank you. But you're
right, at least . . . I must find something. Something to keep
myself in shoe-leather. Before I see them.
Cheerfully.
Well, tomorrow, I will set about it.
Depressed again.
We haven't even got a place to stay.

NOGGS. Well, tonight you stay with me. Tomorrow, there's a
room downstairs to let. It's hardly less a mean one than my
own, but . . .

NICHOLAS. Mr Noggs. Your kindness. Unsurpassable.
Pause.
I have three friends. Three friends, in all the world. That bluff
young fellow up in Yorkshire; Smike, yourself; and Mr Noggs,
our benefactor.
Slight pause.

And it is enough. It is enough, indeed.

NICHOLAS *drinks his drink.* SMIKE, *in imitation drinks his.
After a second, the effect hits* SMIKE. *His eyes pop. He bangs
his chest.* NICHOLAS *and* NOGGS *look alarmed. Firmly,*
SMIKE *puts his glass out to* MR NOGGS *for more.*

Scene Four

*Westminster. At once, sounds of many busy people. On one side
of the stage, the office of Sir Matthew Pupker, consisting of a
desk, an impressive map of the world, and* SIR MATTHEW
*himself, sitting on a chair, his feet up on the desk, his head
covered by* The Times, *asleep. On the other, a sturdy*
DEPUTATION, *consisting of many firm-faced Gentlemen.*

NICHOLAS. And the next morning, Nicholas proceeded to the
General Employment Office, in search of a position; where,
much to his surprise, he was informed that the great member of
Parliament, the renowned Sir Matthew Pupker, was seeking a
young man of conscientiousness and character, to fill the
position of his secretary, at the Palace of Westminster.

He turns to the passing DEPUTATION.

Excuse me . . . I have business with Sir Matthew Pupker —

A DELEGATE. What, you as well? Come, follow me.

The DEPUTATION *is at Sir Matthew's door. It knocks.*

SIR MATTHEW. Wait!

SIR MATTHEW *removes* The Times *from his face, adjusts
the map, as* NICHOLAS *catches up with the rest of the*
DEPUTATION.

Come!

The DEPUTATION, *and* NICHOLAS, *enter the room.*

Gentlemen, I am rejoiced to see you. Please, come in.

SIR MATTHEW *returns to his desk as the leader of the*
DEPUTATION, *a* MR PUGSTYLES, *pushes himself to the front.*

Now, gentlemen. I see by the newspapers that you are
dissatisfied with my conduct as your member.

PUGSTYLES. Yes, we are.

SIR MATTHEW. Well, now, do my eyes deceive me? Or is that
my old friend, Pugstyles?

PUGSTYLES. I am that man.

SIR MATTHEW. Give me your hand, my worthy friend. Pugstyles, I am so sorry you are here.

PUGSTYLES. I am sorry too, but your conduct has rendered this deputation quite imperative.

SIR MATTHEW. My conduct, Pugstyles? You speak of my conduct?

PUGSTYLES. Yes.

SIR MATTHEW. Well, then . . . (*Rhetorically*.)My conduct, gentlemen, has been, and ever will be, regulated by a sincere regard for the true interests of this great and happy country. Whenever I behold the peaceful, industrious communities of our island home, I clasp my hands, and turning my eyes to the broad expanse above my head, exclaim, 'Thank heaven, that I am a Briton!'

Long pause.

A DELEGATE. Gammon.

SIR MATTHEW. The meaning of that term, I must confess, is quite unknown to me. But if it means you think I'm too benign, too sanguine, too complacent, sir, you would be right.

He goes to the map and gestures.

For e'en as we sit here, and lightly chatter, Russia's surly armies, fixed on vile conquest, surge across her borders, threatening the very jugular. Sir, do you know Kabul?

THIRD DELEGATE. No, sir.

SIR MATTHEW. Or have you met the Amir of the Afghans, he whose ~~name~~ is perfidy?

THIRD DELEGATE. I have not, sir.

SIR MATTHEW. Or heard the hideous war-cry of the Slavic hordes, intent on rape and pillage?

THIRD DELEGATE. No, I have not heard the Slavic hordes, sir, or their hideous war-cry.

SIR MATTHEW. Well . . . well, then. What is the little matter you would speak of? Fishing rights, or water-rates, or timber duty?

PUGSTYLES *puts on his spectacles and takes out a list of questions. The rest of the* DEPUTATION *also take out lists of questions, to check* PUGSTYLES' *reading.*

PUGSTYLES. Question number one. Whether, sir, you did not give a voluntary pledge, that in the event of your being returned you would immediately put down the practice of coughing and groaning in the House of Commons. And whether you did not submit to being coughed and groaned down in the very first debate of the session?

Pause.

SIR MATTHEW. Go on to the next one, my dear Pugstyles.

PUGSTYLES. Have you any explanation to offer with reference to that question, sir?

SIR MATTHEW. Certainly not.

The DEPUTATION *looks at each other.* PUGSTYLES *breathes deeply, and continues.*

PUGSTYLES. Question number two. Whether, sir, you did not likewise give a voluntary pledge that you would support your colleagues on every occasion; and whether you did not, the night before last, desert them and vote upon the other side, because the wife of a leader on that other side had invited Lady Pupker to an evening party?

Pause.

SIR MATTHEW. Go on.

PUGSTYLES. Nothing to say on that either, sir?

SIR MATTHEW. Nothing whatever.

Pause.

PUGSTYLES. So, Question number three. If, sir, you did not state upon the hustings, that it was your firm and determined intention, if elected, to vote at once for universal suffrage and triennial parliaments?

SIR MATTHEW. Oh, no!

DEPUTATION. Oh! Oh!

SIR MATTHEW. No, not at all. What happened was, that an illiterate voter in the crowd inquired if I would vote for universal suffering and triangular parliaments. To which I replied, in jest of course, "why, certainly."

A groan from the DEPUTATION.

So, is that all?

PUGSTYLES. No. Question four? Will you resign?

SIR MATTHEW. No.

PUGSTYLES. Sorry?

SIR MATTHEW. I said, no.

PUGSTYLES. You won't resign, under any circumstances?

SIR MATTHEW. Absolutely not.

PUGSTYLES. Then . . . Then, good morning, sir.

The DEPUTATION *turns to go.*

SIR MATTHEW. Good morning to you all.

As the DEPUTATION *leaves.*

God bless you! Every one!

Left alone, as he thinks, SIR MATTHEW *notices* NICHOLAS.
What? Who's this?

NICHOLAS. It's me, sir.

SIR MATTHEW. Ha! A secret voter! Out, sir, out, you've heard my answer. Follow out your deputation.

NICHOLAS. I should have done so if I had belonged to it.

SIR MATTHEW (*tossing down the map*). You don't? Then what the devil are you in here for?

NICHOLAS. I wish to offer myself as your secretary.

SIR MATTHEW. That's all you came for, is it?

NICHOLAS. Yes.

SIR MATTHEW. You've no connection with the papers?

NICHOLAS. No.

SIR MATTHEW. And what's your name?

NICHOLAS. My name is Nickleby.

Slight pause. SIR MATTHEW *eyes* NICHOLAS *beadily.*

SIR MATTHEW. Related to Ralph Nickleby?

NICHOLAS. I am.

SIR MATTHEW. Well, then, sit down.

SIR MATTHEW. So, you want to be my secretary, do you?

NICHOLAS. Yes.

SIR MATTHEW. Well, what can you do?

NICHOLAS. Well, I suppose that I can do what usually falls to the lot of other secretaries.

SIR MATTHEW. What's that?

NICHOLAS. Well, I presume, correspondence . . .

SIR MATTHEW. Good.

NICHOLAS. The arrangement of papers and documents —

SIR MATTHEW. Very good, what else?

NICHOLAS. Well, um — the general one, of making myself as agreeable and useful as I can.

SIR MATTHEW. Well, now, that's all very well, young Mr Nickleby, as far as it goes, but it don't go far enough. I should require, for example, to be crammed, sir.

NICHOLAS. Crammed?

SIR MATTHEW. Yes, crammed. My secretary would need to make himself acquainted with all domestic and all international affairs, to scan the newspapers for paragraphs of lasting or of passing interest, for revolutions, wars, disturbances in Birmingham, "the mysterious disappearance of a potboy", on which I might found a speech or question; he would be required, as well, to study all the printed tables, and to work up arguments about the dire consequences of a raise in tax, or else the terrible result of lowering it, on why we need to increase government expenditure on the national defence, or else decrease it, to encourage thrift among the lower classes; of gold bullion, and the supply of money, all those things it's only necessary to talk fluently about, as no one understands 'em; and that's just a hasty, basic outline of your duties, except of course waiting in the lobby every night, and sitting in the gallery, and pointing me out to the populace, and noting that that sleeping gentleman's none other than the celebrated and renowned Sir Matthew Pupker, and, for salary, I'll say at once, although it's much more than I'm used to give, it's fifteen shillings every week and find yourself. So. Any questions?

Pause.

NICHOLAS. One. While I'm performing all your duties, sir, may I inquire what you'll be doing?

SIR MATTHEW. Eh?

NICHOLAS. I said, while I'm performing all your duties, sir, may I inquire what you'll be doing?

Pause.

SIR MATTHEW. Out! Get out! Out, now!

NICHOLAS (*turns to go*). I'm sorry to have troubled you.

SIR MATTHEW. Well, so am I! Out, upstart! Troublemaker!

NICHOLAS *has been going, but he turns back.*

NICHOLAS. Humbug.

SIR MATTHEW. Chartist!

NICHOLAS. Charlatan!

SIR MATTHEW. Potboy!

NICHOLAS. Politician!

This is too much. SIR MATTHEW *goes, and* NICHOLAS *does too.*

Scene Five

The MANTALINIS' *workroom and showroom. In the workroom, the* MILLINERS, MISS KNAG *entering, and* KATE. *In the showroom, an* OLD LORD, *his* YOUNG FIANCEE *and* MADAME MANTALINI.

MISS KNAG. Well, bless you, dear, how very clumsy you were yesterday, again.

KATE. I know, Miss Knag.

MISS KNAG. But don't you worry, I can do all that needs doing, and all you have to do is stay quiet before company and your awkwardness will not be noticed.

KATE. No, indeed.

MISS KNAG. Oh, I do take the liveliest of interests in you, dear, upon my word. It's a sister's interest, actually. It's the most singular circumstance I ever knew.

MADAME MANTALINI *pulls a bell pull.*

Ah, that's the showroom. Now, perhaps it's best dear, after yesterday, if you do not come up.

Unlikely:

Unless, of course, you're called for.

MISS KNAG *to the showroom.*

1st MILLINER. Well.

2nd MILLINER. *Well.*

3rd MILLINER. Has herself took a shine to you.

The focus shifts to the showroom, as the MILLINERS *narrate.*

MILLINERS. And it so happened that an old lord of great family,

Who was going to marry a young lady of no family in particular,

Came with the young lady to witness the ceremony of trying on two nuptial bonnets,

Which were presented to her by Miss Knag,

In a charming if not breathless state of palpitation.

MISS KNAG *now in the showroom. The* OLD LORD *is very upper class, very lecherous, and a bit gaga. The* YOUNG FIANCEE *is not very upper class at all.*

YOUNG FIANCEE. Well, now. How d' I look?

MADAME MANTALINI. Oh, mademoiselle, trés élégante.

MISS KNAG. Mais oui. C'est entierement exquise, n'est ce pas?

YOUNG FIANCEE. Exsqueeze?

MISS KNAG. Exquisite.

YOUNG FIANCEE. Oh, yes? Is that so?

A slight hiatus.

MADAME MANTALINI. So, what do you think, my lord?

YOUNG FIANCEE. Yur, do you think that I'll look fitting, darling?

OLD LORD. Fitting?

YOUNG FIANCEE. For our wedding day.

OLD LORD. Oh, yes. Oh, very fitting. For our wedding day.

The YOUNG FIANCEE *blushes, grins, and pokes the* OLD LORD.

YOUNG FIANCEE. Oh, you are, really.

OLD LORD. Am I? Am I, really?

YOUNG FIANCEE. Yur, you are.

MISS KNAG *a clucking, disapproving look at* MADAME MANTALINI. *The* YOUNG FIANCEE *notices it.*

Mm? Can I help you?

MISS KNAG. Peut-être –

YOUNG FIANCEE. Pardon?

MISS KNAG. Would madam care to try –

YOUNG FIANCEE. Yur, why not?

The YOUNG FIANCEE, *trying on another bonnet.*

Oh, by the way, dear Madame Mantalini?

MADAME MANTALINI. Mademoiselle?

YOUNG FIANCEE. Tell me, where is that pretty creature we saw yesterday? The young one.

MADAME MANTALINI. Pretty . . . young . . .

MISS KNAG (*helpfully*). Miss Nickleby.

YOUNG FIANCEE. That's right. 'Cos if there's one thing that I can't abide, it's being waited on by frights.

MISS KNAG. Frights, no.

MADAME MANTALINI. By – what?

MISS KNAG has got there.

YOUNG FIANCEE. By frights. By old frights, in particular. Well, elderly.

Pause.

MADAME MANTALINI. Mais oui. Certainement. Miss Knag, send up Miss Nickleby.

MISS KNAG. Bring up?

MADAME MANTALINI. Send up. You need not return.

Pause. MISS KNAG *goes out as the* YOUNG FIANCEE *looks at her new bonnet in the mirror.*

YOUNG FIANCEE. Oh, yur. Mais oui. C'est entirement exquise.

Focus shifts back to the workroom as MISS KNAG *enters.*

MISS KNAG (*to* KATE). You're wanted in the showroom.

KATE. Me?

MISS KNAG. Yes, you. You have been Asked For.

KATE. Oh, I . . . very well.

She goes to the door. MISS KNAG *rather obviously not following.*

Are you not coming?

MISS KNAG. I? Why should I come? A fright like me?

Pause.

1st MILLINER. What's that?

2nd MILLINER. A fright?

MISS KNAG. Why should I come? You chit, you child, you upstart!

KATE. Please, Miss Knag, what have I done?

MISS KNAG. What have you done? She asks me, what she's done?

3rd MILLINER (*whispers to* 2nd MILLINER.) What has she done?

MISS KNAG. I'll tell you what I've done, my dear Miss Nickleby, what I've done is to be, for fifteen years, the ornament of this room and the one upstairs. And what have you done? Nothing.

KATE. Well, I would not –

MISS KNAG. And never, fifteen years, have I been victim of the vile arts, a creature who disgraces us with her proceedings, and makes proper people blush to see her machinations.

KATE. Miss Knag, what have I –

MISS KNAG. Yes, here she is, look carefully . . . the one who everyone is talking of, the belle, the beauty . . . Oh, you boldfaced thing!

KATE. Miss Knag, please tell me –

MISS KNAG. I will tell you. Go! You're asked for in the showroom. Go!

KATE *stands a moment, shrugs desperately and goes out. Pause.* MISS KNAG *throws herself into a chair. She is surrounded by* MILLINERS.

Oh, have I worked here, fifteen years. And to be called a fright.
Pause.

1st MILLINER. Oh, no.

2nd MILLINER. Oh, absolutely not.

MISS KNAG. And have I laboured, all these years, to be called elderly.

2nd MILLINER. What, elderly?

1st MILLINER. Well, what a thing to say.

MISS KNAG (*stands*). I hate her. I detest and hate her. Never let her speak to me again. And never let anyone who is a friend of mine have words with her. The slut. The hussy. Impudent and artful, hussy!

Scene Six

Downstage, Noggs' garret, with NOGGS *and* SMIKE. *Upstage, the Kenwigs' room, with* MRS KENWIGS, MORLEENA. *the two* LITTLE KENWIGSES, MR LILLYVICK *and* MISS PETOWKER. MR LILLYVICK *has a glass of brandy and a jug of water. Enter* NICHOLAS.

NICHOLAS. And so, with a sad and pensive air, Nicholas retraced his steps homewards.

NOGGS. Come back?

NICHOLAS. Yes, and tired to death, and might have stayed at home for all the good I've done.

NOGGS. Couldn't expect too much, one morning.

NICHOLAS. Well, I did. And so am disappointed. I see little to choose between assisting a brutal pedagogue and being a toad-eater to a mean and ignorant upstart, member or no member. Oh, Newman, show me in all this wide waste of London, any honest means by which I could at least defray the hire of our poor room; I would not shrink from it, I will do anything, except that which offends my common pride.

NOGGS. Well, then . . . I hardly know . . .

NICHOLAS. Yes? What?

NOGGS. There is a prospect I could offer . . .

NICHOLAS. Please, dear Newman, tell me.

NOGGS. It concerns the Kenwigses, downstairs. I told them you were Mr Johnson, thinking perhaps, your circumstances being, as it were . . .

NICHOLAS. Yes, yes.

NOGGS. And said you were a teacher, and she said, well, having talked to Mr Kenwigs, as is only right, she said that she had long been searching for a tutor for her little ones, to teach them French as spoken by the natives, at the weekly stipend of four shillings current coin, being at the rate of a one a week per each Miss Kenwigs, with a shilling over for the baby. That's all, and I know it's beneath you, but –

NICHOLAS. Dear Newman. I accept at once. Please tell the worthy mother, now, without, delay.

NOGGS (*delighted*). Right, then.

Narration into the Kenwigs' room, in which will be MR

LILLYVICK, MISS PETOWKER, MRS KENWIGS, MORLEENA, *the* LITTLE KENWIGSES *and* NICHOLAS. SMIKE *goes*.

NOGGS. And Newman hastened with joyful steps to inform Mrs Kenwigs of his friend's acquiescence,

NICHOLAS. And soon returning, brought back word that they would be happy to see Mr Johnson in the first floor as soon as convenient,

NOGGS. And that Mrs Kenwigs had upon the instant sent out to secure a second-hand French grammar and dialogues,

MISS PETOWKER. Which had long been fluttering in the sixpenny box at the bookstall round the corner,

MRS KENWIGS. And that the family,

LILLYVICK. Highly excited at the prospect of this addition to their gentility,

MRS KENWIGS. Wished the initiatory lesson to come off

MORLEENA. Immediately!

Exit NOGGS.

MRS KENWIGS. Now, uncle, this is Mr Johnson.

LILLYVICK. How d'ye do, sir?

NICHOLAS. Splendid, thank you sir.

MRS KENWIGS. Mr Johnson, this is Mr Lillyvick, my uncle, The Collector Of The Water Rate.

NICHOLAS (*uncertain of how he is supposed to react to this intelligence*). The Water Rate? Indeed.

MRS KENWIGS. And this is Miss Petowker, of the Theatre Royal Drury Lane.

NICHOLAS. Oh, I am highly honoured.

Wrong.

To make, both of your acquaintances.

MRS KENWIGS. Now, Mr Johnson is engaged as a private master to the children, uncle.

LILLYVICK. Yes, Susan, so you said.

MRS KENWIGS. But I hope, Mr Johnson, that they don't boast about it to the other children, and that if they must say anything about it, they don't say no more than: "We've got a private master comes to teach us at home, but we ain't proud, because ma says it's sinful." Do you hear, Morleena?

MORLEENA. Yes, ma.

MRS KENWIGS. Then mind you recollect, and do as I tell you. Shall Mr Johnson begin, then, uncle?

LILLYVICK. In a moment, Susan, in a moment. First, I'd like to ask a question. Sir, how do you think of French?

NICHOLAS. What do you mean, sir?

LILLYVICK. Do you view it as a good language, sir? A pretty language? Sensible?

NICHOLAS. A pretty language, certainly. And as it has a name for everything, and admits of elegant conversation on all topics, I assume it's sensible as well.

LILLYVICK. I see. (*Gesturing with his glass.*)
So, what's the French for this, then, sir?

NICHOLAS. For brandy?

LILLYVICK. No, for water. As in, "water rate."

NICHOLAS. Oh, water, sir, is "l'eau."

LILLYVICK. I thought as much. You hear that, Miss Petowker? Water. Low. I don't think anything of that. I don't think anything of French at all.

MRS KENWIGS. But, still, the children, may –

LILLYVICK. Oh, yes. Oh, let them learn it. I have no wish to prevent them.
Pause. MISS PETOWKER *a slight smile.* MRS KENWIGS *nervously.*

MRS KENWIGS. Well, then . . . Mr Johnson?

NICHOLAS. Well, then . . . Lesson One.
Enter NOGGS, *breathless.*

NOGGS. Oh – oh, Mr Johnson, this is terrible –

LILLYVICK. What's this?

MRS KENWIGS. Why, Mr Noggs!

NOGGS. He's back again – he's gone off to your mother's –

NICHOLAS. What?

NOGGS. – your uncle, and I got the wrong day and I'm terribly –

LILLYVICK (*To* MISS PETOWKER). It's him again.

NICHOLAS. Oh, I must go there now.

NOGGS. Yes. yes, I s'pose you must.

MRS KENWIGS. But Mr Johnson –

NICHOLAS. Oh – uh – mes enfants . . . on doit continuer la leçon demain. Pardon.

To LILLYVICK, *taking his drink and giving it to* NOGGS. Pardon.

NICHOLAS *rushes out.*

Scene Seven

The Nicklebys' house in Thames St. One chair for MRS NICKLEBY. MISS LA CREEVY, KATE *and* RALPH *are there.* RALPH *is folding up Fanny Squeers' letter.*

KATE. No, I won't believe it. Never. It's a lie, that they've invented.

RALPH. No, my dear, you wrong the worthy man. These aren't inventions. Mr Squeers has been assaulted, Nicholas is gone, the boy goes with him. It's all true.

KATE. It can't be true. Mama, how can you stand there, listening to this?

RALPH. She's no choice, my dear. Her son's committed conduct for which he might well hold up his head at the Old Bailey.

Pause.

And it would be my duty, if he came my way, to give him up to justice. As a man of honour and of business, I would have no other course. Though I wish to spare the feelings of his mother, and his sister.

MISS LA CREEVY. Perhaps I'd better . . .

KATE. No, please, Miss La Creevy, stay.

RALPH (*suddenly, forcefully, waving the letter*). Madam, everything combines to prove the truth of this. He steals away at night, he skulks off with an outlaw boy. Assault, and riot? Is this innocent?

Unnoticed by anyone, NICHOLAS *stands there.*

MRS NICKLEBY. Well, I don't know, I'm sure.

KATE. Oh, mother!

MRS NICKLEBY. And I never would have thought it of him, certainly.

KATE. You never *would have* thought?

MRS NICKLEBY. Your uncle — is your uncle, dear.

NICHOLAS. But what he says is still untrue.

RALPH. Oh. You.

MRS NICKLEBY. Oh, Nicholas!

NICHOLAS *marching towards* RALPH, KATE *getting in the way*.

KATE. Oh, Nicholas, be calm, consider.

NICHOLAS. What?

KATE. Please, please, consider . . . and refute these accusations.

NICHOLAS. What are they? Tell me what he's said to you.

RALPH. I've said, sir, what is true. That you attacked your master, and you nearly killed him, and you ran away.

Pause. NICHOLAS *is calmer now.*

NICHOLAS. I see.

NICHOLAS *speaks to* KATE *and* MRS NICKLEBY, *not to* RALPH.

I interfered to save a miserable creature from the vilest cruelty. In doing so, I did inflict punishment upon the wretch who was abusing him. And if the same scene was repeated now, I'd take exactly the same part. Except, that I would strike him heavier and harder.

RALPH. Hm. The penitent.

KATE. Please, Nicholas, where is this boy?

NICHOLAS. He's with me now.

RALPH. Will you restore him?

NICHOLAS. No. Not to that man. Not ever.

MRS NICKLEBY. Oh, I don't know what to think . . .

RALPH. Now, sir, you'll listen to a word or two?

NICHOLAS. Say what you like. I shan't take heed of it.

RALPH. Then I won't speak to you, but to your mother. She may find it worth her while to listen, because what I have to say is, that he, Nicholas, shall not have access to one penny of my

money, or one crust of my bread, or one grasp of my hand that
might save him from the gallows. I will not meet him, and I will
not hear his name. I will not help him, nor help anyone who
helps him. So now he knows what he has brought on you, by
coming back, and as I will not ask you to renounce him, I must
renounce you.

Pause.

MRS NICKLEBY. Oh, I can't help it –

RALPH. What?

MRS NICKLEBY. I know you have been good to us. But still, I –
even if he has done everything you say –

KATE. You heard what he said, mother –

MRS NICKLEBY. Still. I can't renounce my son. I really can't.

Pause. MRS NICKLEBY weeping.

And all that, thinking that he'd be headmaster . . .

RALPH. Then I'll go.

NICHOLAS. You needn't.

RALPH. Needn't I?

NICHOLAS. Because I will.

KATE *runs to* NICHOLAS *and embraces him.*

KATE. Nicholas, oh, Nicholas, don't say so, or you'll break my
heart . . . Mama, please speak to him. Mama, don't let him go.
Don't leave us here, with no one to protect us. Please.

NICHOLAS. I can't protect you. How can I protect you?

RALPH. My dear, there is your answer.

MRS NICKLEBY. Oh, Kate. We'll go to rack and ruin. To the
workhouse, or the Refuge for the Destitute. Or Magdalen
Hospital. One or the other. Or the third.

NICHOLAS *takes* KATE's *arms from him.*

NICHOLAS. No, mother. I'm the one that's going.

KATE (*horrified*). Where? Where, Nicholas?

NICHOLAS. Don't know.

Pause.

It is hard. To have done nothing, but be proscribed, just like a
criminal. And to be forced to leave the ones I love. It is quite
hard to bear. But still, I must, or else . . . you're destitute.

KATE. It might be – years.

NICHOLAS. Don't know.

NICHOLAS *turns to go.* KATE *runs after him, embraces him.*

KATE. Please, you won't –

NICHOLAS. I must –

KATE. You won't forget us. Everything we had. The days, the years we spent together.

NICHOLAS (*taking her arms from him*). And I don't need to entreat your sympathy. I know you won't forget them.

MISS LA CREEVY. No.

NICHOLAS (*to* RALPH). This isn't over. You will hear from me.

To KATE.

Oh, my darling girl.

NICHOLAS *goes out, leaving* MRS NICKLEBY, MISS LA CREEVY, *and* KATE.

Scene Eight

The street. Early morning. Bare stage. NICHOLAS, SMIKE *and* NOGGS *appear during the narration.* NICHOLAS *and* SMIKE *have bundles.* NOGGS *has a can.*

NARRATORS.

It was a cold, foggy morning in early Spring . . .

And a few meagre shadows flitted to and fro in the misty streets.

At intervals were heard the tread of slipshod feet,

And the chilly cry of the sweep as he crept shivering to his early toil;

The sluggish darkness thickened as the day came on,

And those who had the courage to rise and peep at the gloomy street from their curtained windows,

Crept back to bed again,

And coiled themselves up to sleep.

NICHOLAS. But Nicholas and Smike were up,

NOGGS. And Newman too, who had expended a day's income on a can of rum and milk to prepare them for their journey.

SMIKE *shoulders the bundles.*

Which way are you going?

NICHOLAS. Kingston first.

NOGGS. And afterwards?

Slight pause.

Why won't you tell me?

NICHOLAS. Because I scarcely know myself.

NOGGS. I am afraid you have some deep scheme in your head.

NICHOLAS. So deep that even I can't fathom it. Don't worry, I'll write soon.

NOGGS. You won't forget?

NICHOLAS. Oh, I'm not likely to. I've not so many friends that I can grow confused about the number, and forget the very best.

NOGGS. And, despite Newman's insistence, that he be allowed to walk an hour or two with them,

NICHOLAS. Nicholas and Smike eventually made their farewells and turned, and left, and turned again,

NOGGS. To see their friend still waving to them,

NICHOLAS. Till they turned the corner, and could see old Newman Noggs no more.

NOGGS *has gone.* SMIKE *and* NICHOLAS *trudging on.*

NICHOLAS. Now, listen to me, Smike. We're bound for Portsmouth.

SMIKE. Ports – mouth.

NICHOLAS. Yes, because it is a seaport town, and I am thinking we might board some ship. I'm young and active, so are you.

SMIKE. And I am very willing.

NICHOLAS. Yes, you are. Too willing, for example, with that bundle. Let me carry it a while.

SMIKE (*stops*). No. No.

NICHOLAS (*stops*). Why not?

SMIKE. Because I thought of carrying it. For you.

They walk on. Narration:

NARRATORS.
It was by this time within an hour of noon, and although dense

vapour still enclosed the city they had left,

As if to clothe its schemes of gain and profit,

In the open country it was clear and fair.

SMIKE. Hey. I –

NICHOLAS. Yes, Smike?

SMIKE. The ship. On ship. I, when I was at – that – place –

He doesn't want to name Dotheboys Hall.

NICHOLAS. Yes?

SMIKE. I used to milk the cows and groom the horses.

NICHOLAS. Um – it is a ship, Smike. Not that many cows and horses on board ship. Well, I don't believe . . .

SMIKE *looks at* NICHOLAS. *He gets the joke. It's infectious.* NICHOLAS *laughs too. Music play and the* NARRATORS *sing. As they sing,* SMIKE *jumps on* NICHOLAS' *back, and the two of them career round the stage, blissfully happy.*

NARRATORS (*sing*).

A broad fine honest sun
Lighted up the green pasture
And dimpled water with the semblance of summer,
Leaving the travellers with the freshness of spring.

The ground seemed to quicken their feet,
The sheep bells were music to their ears,
And hoping made them strong
And strength awakened hope
And they pushed onward with the courage of lions.

And so the day wore on
And so the day wore on
And so the day wore on.

NICHOLAS *and* SMIKE *stop, put down the bundles, and sit.*

NICHOLAS. Smike. Do you have a good memory?

SMIKE. I don't know. I had once, I think. But now all gone.

NICHOLAS. Why do you think you had one once?

SMIKE. Because I could remember when I was a child.

NICHOLAS. Do you remember, when you went to Yorkshire? What the day was like. The weather, hot or cold?

SMIKE. Wet. Very wet. And afterwards. When it was raining. I could see myself. The day I came.

NICHOLAS. Did you come there alone?

SMIKE. No. No. A man — a dark and withered man, they used to say. And I think I remember, too. Remember — being frightened of him. Glad he went away. But frightened at the place he left me, too.

NICHOLAS. Now look at me. Don't turn away. Do you remember, anything or anyone or anywhere, before that house in Yorkshire? Think, Smike, think.

Pause.

SMIKE. A room.

Slight pause.

I slept once in a room, a large and lonesome room, beneath the attic, there was a hook in the ceiling above me. I was frightened of it, covered up my head.

Pause.

Used to dream. Dream terribly about the room. And people in it. Things, that changed. But that room — never changes.

Pause.

Till now, I have not known two days together when I haven't been afraid.

A LANDLORD enters, as a table and a bench are brought in behind him.

LANDLORD. And the sun went down, and in the morning it rose up again, and they rose with it, and walked onwards, until Smike could go no further. And they found a little inn, yet twelve miles short of Portsmouth.

Scene Nine

The courtyard of a roadside inn. The LANDLORD sits on the bench beside the table. NICHOLAS and SMIKE standing there, looking bedraggled and tired.

NICHOLAS. Ah. How far to Portsmouth, sir?

LANDLORD. Twelve miles. Long miles.

NICHOLAS. A good road?

LANDLORD. No. A bad one.

NICHOLAS. We must get to Portsmouth by tonight.

LANDLORD. Well, don't let me influence you, in any way . . .
But if I were you, I wouldn't go.

NICHOLAS. You wouldn't?

LANDLORD. No.

NICHOLAS. Look, I . . . Look here, it's obvious enough. We are
both, very humble, and we can't afford to stay the night. But if
you had a little food . . .?

LANDLORD. What would you like?

NICHOLAS. Cold meat?

LANDLORD. No, sorry.

NICHOLAS. Mutton chops?

LANDLORD. Clean out.

NICHOLAS. An egg?

LANDLORD. No, yesterday, had more than we could cope with.
And tomorrow, mountains of 'em coming in.

NICHOLAS. And today?

LANDLORD. No eggs today.

Enter MR VINCENT CRUMMLES *and his sons,* MASTER
CRUMMLES *and* MASTER P. CRUMMLES. MR CRUMMLES
*is a theatrical manager. His sons are dressed in sailor suits, and
are presently practising a stage fight with wooden swords. The
fight finishes spectacularly, with the defeat of the taller*
MASTER CRUMMLES *by the shorter* MASTER P.
CRUMMLES. CRUMMLES *himself applauds.*

CRUMMLES. That's capital! You'll get a double encore if you
take care, boys. You'd better go and get your travelling clothes
on now.

The boys go out, one of them leaving his sword where it fell.
NICHOLAS *to the* LANDLORD.

NICHOLAS. Well, then, we'll have to walk on hungry.
Portsmouth, twelve bad miles.

NICHOLAS *and* SMIKE *turn to go.*

CRUMMLES. Portsmouth?

NICHOLAS. Sir?

CRUMMLES. You're set for Portsmouth?

NICHOLAS. Yes, we –

CRUMMLES. So am I.

NICHOLAS. I'm pleased to hear it, sir.

CRUMMLES *comes over.*

CRUMMLES. And may I venture, short of money for the stage?

NICHOLAS. You've guessed it, sir.

CRUMMLES. Why, then, you'll ride with me, upon my phaeton.

NICHOLAS. Um –

CRUMMLES. That's settled. Landlord, see my pony's fetched.

The LANDLORD *goes out.* CRUMMLES *sees the dropped sword, picks it up, and waves it.*

So, what d'you think of that, sir?

NICHOLAS. What? Oh, very good indeed. Quite – capital.

CRUMMLES. You won't see such as that too often.

NICHOLAS. No. And if they'd been, perhaps, a little better matched –

CRUMMLES. Matched? Why sir, it's the very essence of the combat that there should be a foot or two between 'em. Otherwise, how are you to get up the sympathies of the audience in a legitimate manner?

NICHOLAS. Oh, I see. They are – you are – theatricals?

CRUMMLES. Why yes, of course. And playing Portsmouth from tonight. Yes, I am Vincent Crummles, and I am in the theatrical profession, my wife is in the theatrical profession, and my children are in the theatrical profession. I had a dog that lived and died in it from a puppy, and my chaise-pony goes on in Timour the Tartar.

The MASTER CRUMMLESES *re-enter with baggage. Re-enter, too, the* LANDLORD, *and a* STABLE-BOY. *During the following, they convert the table, bench and baggage into the small carriage that Crummles calls his "phaeton". The final additions are two washing tubs and a water-pump, piled on top, and two reins, running out from the front.*

Ah, now it's just my baggage, and we're set to go.

NICHOLAS. This is – this is most generous.

CRUMMLES. Oh, not at all. It's my self-interest. I have an eye for talent, Mr . . .

NICHOLAS. Oh, uh, Johnson.

CRUMMLES. Johnson? And yours struck me immediately.

NICHOLAS. Talent for what?

CRUMMLES. Why, for the stage! There's genteel comedy, your walk and manner, juvenile tragedy, your eye, and touch-and-go farce in your laugh.

NICHOLAS. But, sir –

CRUMMLES (*dropping his voice*). And as for your, associate, I've never seen a better for the starving business. Only let him be quite tolerably well-dressed for the Apothecary – Romeo and Juliet – the slightest red dab on his nose, and he'll be guaranteed three rounds the moment he pops his head round the practicable door.

NICHOLAS. The practicable –

CRUMMLES. In the front grooves, O.P. Sir, can you write?

NICHOLAS. Well, I am not illiterate.

CRUMMLES. Well, that could not be better. You will write our new piece, for a week on Monday, if you'd be so kind. Now, boys –

NICHOLAS. But, sir – I can't – I've never written anything.

CRUMMLES. What stuff! Do you speak French?

NICHOLAS. Yes, like a native.

CRUMMLES *takes a script from a bag and tosses it to* NICHOLAS.

CRUMMLES. Then turn that into English, put your name on it and there's the play. Oh, but for one thing . . . I've just bought a real pump and two fine washing tubs – I got 'em cheap – and you must work them in. You know, the bills, we'll advertise 'em: "Splendid Tubs", "A Real Pump", that kind of thing, you'll probably be writing out the bills yourself, now are we set and can we go?

NICHOLAS. Sir, I must ask one more question.

CRUMMLES *turns back*.

CRUMMLES. Ask away.

NICHOLAS. Will I be paid for this?

CRUMMLES. Will you be paid? Will you be paid? Dear sir, with your own salary, your friend's, and royalties, you'll make a pound a week!

NICHOLAS. A pound a week.

CRUMMLES. At least. Now come, sirs, come.

NICHOLAS turns to SMIKE who is looking rapt.

NICHOLAS. Well, Smike, what times we've fallen on, who could have . . . Smike?

SMIKE. The stage!

Everyone now on the phaeton. CRUMMLES has picked up the reins. The LANDLORD and STABLE-BOY have gone.

CRUMMLES (*with a nod at the pony*). He's a good pony at bottom.

NICHOLAS. I am sure of it.

CRUMMLES. And quite one of us. His mother was on the stage, of course.

NICHOLAS. She was?

CRUMMLES. Yes, yes, ate apple-pie at a circus for upwards of fourteen years, fired pistols, went to bed in a nightcap, and in short, took the low comedy entirely.

CRUMMLES, *confidentially, to* NICHOLAS.

His father was a dancer.

NICHOLAS. Oh? Distinguished?

CRUMMLES. No, not very. The fact is, that he'd been jobbed out in the days originally, and never lost his bad habits. He was cleverish in melodrama, but too broad, too broad. And when the mother died, he took the port-wine business.

NICHOLAS. Port-wine business.

CRUMMLES. Yes, you know, the drinking of the port-wine with the clown. But he was greedy, and one night he bit the bowl right off, and choked himself to death. Vulgarity – the end of him at last.

And they have arrived. Everyone gets off the phaeton.

Well, here we are boys, Portsmouth, for three weeks. All men have their trials, and this is ours. Come on, boys, bustle, bustle.

NICHOLAS. And Nicholas jumped out, and, giving Smike his arm, accompanied the manager up the High Street towards the theatre, feeling nervous and uncomfortable at the prospect of an introduction to a scene so new to him.

Scene Ten

The stage at the Portsmouth Theatre. It is bare, and looks very dusty and dour. Enter most of the Crummles Theatre Company. They are MR BANE, MR WAGSTAFF, MR PAILEY, MR FLUGGERS, MR HETHERINGTON, MR BLIGHTEY, MISS BRAVASSA, MISS BELVAWNEY, MISS GAZINGI, MRS LENVILLE, and, at the centre of it all, MRS CRUMMLES. A moment as they survey the scene. Then MRS GRUDDEN, the Stage Manager, pulls a clothes rail across the stage. A certain amount of animation follows: MR BANE and MR HETHERINGTON fetch a chair and table for MRS CRUMMLES, others open luggage, practise attitudes, look round. The bustle continues throughout the scene. Enter CRUMMLES, NICHOLAS, SMIKE and the MASTER CRUMMLESES.

CRUMMLES. Well, here we are. Good afternoon to one and all. And welcome to Portsmouth.

The PERFORMERS look back, not very enthusiastically. MRS CRUMMLES calls to her husband.

MRS CRUMMLES. Vincent.

CRUMMLES (*going to her*). Ah – Mrs Crummles.

MRS CRUMMLES. Vincent.

They embrace. MRS CRUMMLES notices NICHOLAS and SMIKE.

Who are those men, so withered and so wild in their attire?

CRUMMLES *whispers to* MRS CRUMMLES.

SMIKE. Is this a theatre? I thought it would be a blaze of light and finery.

NICHOLAS. Why, so it is. But not by day, Smike, not by day.

CRUMMLES. Uh, Mr Johnson. Please, meet Mrs Crummles.

NICHOLAS *and* SMIKE *come over.*

MRS CRUMMLES. I am so glad to see you see, so glad. And overcome to welcome you,

To CRUMMLES.
provisionally,

To NICHOLAS.

as a promising new member of our corps.
She looks at SMIKE.

And this — yet more? An undernourished friend. You too are welcome, sir.

SMIKE *is brought forward to shake the hand of* MRS CRUMMLES *as the* INFANT PHENOMENON *dances on. She is of doubtful age, though dressed in a little girl's ballet costume. She pirouettes and falls in an attitude of terror. She is followed on by* MR FOLAIR, *a pantomimist, not in the first flush of youth, who wears buff slippers and is brandishing a walking stick.* MRS GRUDDEN *appears with a list and tries to attract* MR CRUMMLES' *attention as it becomes clear that* FOLAIR *and the* PHENOMENON *are practising a dance.*

FOLAIR. And one and two and three —

CRUMMLES. What's this?

MRS CRUMMLES. It's the Indian Savage and the Maiden.

FOLAIR. Pose and one and two and growl and threaten —

CRUMMLES (*explaining to* NICHOLAS). Oh, yes, the little ballet interlude. Capital, capital.

FOLAIR. And attitude . . . and he loves her, and she loves him, and spin . . .

The PHENOMENON *executes a little spin, aided by* FOLAIR. *A trailing hand hits* FOLAIR *in the mouth.*

. . . Thank you, and climax . . .

A complicated and uncertain climax, culminating with FOLAIR *kneeling, and the* PHENOMENON *standing with one foot on his knee, her hand over his face.* CRUMMLES *applauds.*

CRUMMLES. Bravo, bravo!

CRUMMLES *takes the* PHENOMENON *to introduce her to* NICHOLAS. *During the following, two late-comers,* MISS SNEVELLICCI *and* MISS LEDROOK, *appear. The former is the leading young actress of the company, and knows it. She whispers to* MISS BRAVASSA, *asking her about* NICHOLAS.

And this, sir, is Miss Ninetta Crummles, better known to half the nobility of England, as the Infant Phenomenon.

NICHOLAS. Your daughter?

CRUMMLES. Our daughter, sir, and the idol of every place we go into. The talent of this child is not be imagined. She must be seen, sir, seen — to be even faintly appreciated. Now, kiss your mother, dear.

The INFANT PHENOMENON *kisses* MRS CRUMMLES.
Something unpleasant transfers itself from daughter to mother.

MRS CRUMMLES. What has the child been eating, Mrs
Grudden? Where are you?

MRS CRUMMLES *drags the* PHENOMENON *off.*

NICHOLAS. May I ask how old she is?

CRUMMLES. You may, sir. She is ten years of age, sir.

NICHOLAS. Not more!

CRUMMLES. Not a day.

NICHOLAS. Dear me, it's quite — extraordinary!

FOLAIR *joins the conversation.* SMIKE *has wandered off, and
soon he will be collared by* MRS GRUDDEN, *who tries
costumes on him.*

FOLAIR. Oh, great talent, there, sir. Great talent.

NICHOLAS. Well, yes, ind —

FOLAIR. Oh, yes, she shouldn't be in the provinces, she really
shouldn't.

CRUMMLES (*suspiciously*). What do you mean?

FOLAIR. I mean that she is too good for country boards, and that
she ought to be in one of the large houses in London, or
nowhere; and I tell you more, that if it wasn't for envy and
jealousy in some quarters, she would be. Perhaps you'll
introduce me here, Mr Crummles.

CRUMMLES. Mr Folair. This is Mr Johnson, who's to write our
new piece for Monday, and when he's done that he's to study
Romeo — oh, don't forget the tubs and pumps, sir, by-the-by . . .

CRUMMLES *is presenting* NICHOLAS *with bits of script from
his pockets.*

and Rover, too, of course, you might as well while you're about
it, and Cassio and Jeremy Diddler. You can easily knock them
off; one part helps all the others so much. Here they are, cues
and all.

NICHOLAS. But —

CRUMMLES. Ah, here's Miss Belvawney.

CRUMMLES *goes off after* MISS BELVAWNEY.

FOLAIR. Happy to know you, sir.

He shakes NICHOLAS's hand.

Well, did you ever see such a set-out as *that*.

He tosses his head in the general direction of the
PHENOMENON *and pulls a face.*

NICHOLAS. Do you mean the Infant Phenomenon?

FOLAIR. Infant humbug, sir. With half a pint of gin a morning,
every day since infancy, you could look ten for life, I'd venture.

NICHOLAS. I see. You seem to take it to heart.

FOLAIR. Yes, by Jove, and well I may. Isn't it enough to make a
man crusty to see that sprawler put up in the best business
every night, and actually keeping money out of the house? Why,
I know of fifteen and sixpence that came to Southampton to see
me dance the Highland Fling, and what's the consequence? I've
never been put up in it since – never once – while the Infant
Phenomenon has been grinning through artificial flowers at five
people and a baby in the pit, and two boys in the gallery, every
night. Oh, halloa, fellow, how are you?

For some moments, NICHOLAS *has been aware of* MR
LENVILLE, *the Tragedian, fencing towards him.*

LENVILLE. Well, Tommy, do the honours, do the honours.

FOLAIR. Ah, yes. This is Mr Johnson, joined us suddenly, this
afternoon. Mr Lenville, who does our first tragedy.

NICHOLAS. First tragedy.

FOLAIR. Oh, yes, the major tragic roles, and –

LENVILLE. What's he joined to play, then, Tommy?

NICHOLAS. Well, I've been asked to –

FOLAIR (*interrupts*). Bits and pieces, bits and pieces. Cassio, and
other things, and such.

LENVILLE. What other things?

FOLAIR. And writing a new piece as well.

LENVILLE. A new piece, eh? What's in it?

NICHOLAS. Well, the play is based on a fascinating French fable –

LENVILLE. I meant for me. Something, you know, in the tragic
and declamatory line –

Luckily, MR LENVILLE *has said this while looking round at
other activity, so* FOLAIR *can whisper to* NICHOLAS.

FOLAIR. But Not Too Young.

NICHOLAS. Oh, yes. Well, sir, there is a character who turns his wife and child out of doors, and in a fit of jealousy stabs his eldest son in the library.

LENVILLE. Ah yes, that's very good.

NICHOLAS. After which, he is troubled by remorse till the last act, and then makes up his mind to destroy himself. But just as he — or, you — are raising the pistol to your head, a clock strikes ten.

LENVILLE. I see. Yes, excellent.

NICHOLAS. You pause. You recollect to have heard a clock strike ten in your infancy. The pistol falls from your hand, you burst into tears, and become a virtuous and exemplary character for ever afterwards.

LENVILLE. Capital. Yes, sir, that will definitely serve. Ha.

FOLAIR (*anxiously*). Anything for me?

NICHOLAS (*enjoying himself*). Well, let me see . . . I imagine you would play the faithful and attached servant who is turned out of doors with the wife and child —

FOLAIR. Always coupled with that infernal phenomenon!

He strides off. SMIKE, who has been dressed in a vaguely renaissance costume — a long grey gown and velvet hat — rushes forward to NICHOLAS, waving in delight, and rushes back again to MRS GRUDDEN. MISS SNEVELLICCI glides over to NICHOLAS.

MISS SNEVELLICCI. I beg your pardon, sir. But did you ever play at Canterbury?

NICHOLAS. Uh . . . No, never.

MISS SNEVELLICCI. It's just — I recollect meeting a gentleman at Canterbury, only for a few moments, for I was leaving the company as he joined it, so like you that I felt almost certain it was the same.

NICHOLAS. Well, I do assure you that you are mistaken, for I'm certain, if we had met, I'd remember it.

MISS SNEVELLICCI. Oh, I'm sure that's very flattering of you to say so. But now, as I look at you again, I see that gentleman had not your eyes. You'll think me foolish, doubtless, that I take notice of such things.

NICHOLAS. Why, not at all. How can I feel otherwise than flattered by your notice in any way?

MISS SNEVELLICCI. Oh, Mr Johnson. All you men are such vain creatures, aren't you? Mm?

MISS SNEVELLICCI *has been gesturing with a hand to* MISS LEDROOK, *who refuses to come over, so* SNEVELLICCI *turns and calls.*

SNEVELLICCI. Led, my dear.

MISS LEDROOK. Yes, what is it?

MISS SNEVELLICCI. It's not the same.

MISS LEDROOK. The same what?

MISS SNEVELLICCI. He never was at Canterbury, come here, I want to speak to you.

CRUMMLES *appears.* MISS LEDROOK *doesn't move, so* MISS SNEVELLICCI *has to go to her, and they have a little argument, as:*

CRUMMLES. A genius, sir, a genius. I'm thinking, that we will bring out your new piece for her bespeak.

NICHOLAS. Bewhat?

CRUMMLES. Her benefit, when her friends and patrons bespeak the play. In fact, sir, you might do us some other little assistance. There is a little – what shall I call it – a little canvassing on these occasions –

NICHOLAS. Among the friends and patrons?

MISS SNEVELLICCI *aware of this conversation.*

CRUMMLES. Yes, just half an hour tomorrow morning, calling on the houses, drumming up support . . . You know, new author, all the way from London, book now to avoid a disappointment, all that kind of thing . . .

NICHOLAS. Now, sir, I am afraid that I should not like to do that.

CRUMMLES. Not even with the infant?

NICHOLAS. No.

MISS SNEVELLICCI *rushes to* CRUMMLES *and* NICHOLAS.

MISS SNEVELLICCI. Oh, Mr Johnson. Sir, you surely aren't so cruel, so heartless . . . and after I have been so looking forward to it, too.

NICHOLAS. Well, I'm very sorry, but –

MRS CRUMMLES *sails in.*

MRS CRUMMLES. What's this? A problem, with the canvass?

CRUMMLES. Yes, dear. Mr Johnson seems to have objections.

MRS CRUMMLES. What? Object? Can this be possible?

NICHOLAS. Well, it's –

MRS CRUMMLES. This Mr Johnson, is it, with objections? This one, plucked, as 'twere, from dank obscurity, took off the streets – the highway – and presented with a chance that half of London would donate a vital limb for? Vincent, this is inconceivable. I am convinced his sense of what is proper, nay is chivalrous, nay once again is gallant, all will sweep him to enlistment in this noble cause.

Looking at NICHOLAS. *Slightly coquettishly.*

Is this not so?

NICHOLAS. Well . . . It is not in my nature to resist any entreaty, unless it is to do something positively wrong. I know nobody here, and nobody knows me. So be it, then. I yield.

MRS CRUMMLES (*with a look at* CRUMMLES, *as if to say, "must I cope with everything?"*). Well. There.

MRS CRUMMLES, CRUMMLES *and* MISS SNEVELLICCI *leave* NICHOLAS, *and join the Company.* NICHOLAS *now sees the full Company ranged before him.*

MRS GRUDDEN. Quiet. Quiet, everybody!

CRUMMLES. Ladies and gentlemen! May I introduce to you Mr Johnson and Mr –

NICHOLAS (*giving a new name to* SMIKE). Digby.

CRUMMLES. Thank you. Mr Johnson, you have met Mr Folair and Mr Lenville, Miss Snevellicci and my wife and family. This is Mr Bane, who does the tenor lovers;

MR BANE *waves weakly.*

Mr Wagstaff, who's our virtuous old gentleman;

MR WAGSTAFF *is holding a suitcase, and as he stands to nod at* NICHOLAS, *we hear the clink of many bottles inside it. This confirms the impression that his red nose and uncertain gait has already given us.*

And Mr Fluggers, who does the cloth, and can do everything from country parsons to the Pope.

MR FLUGGERS *looks up from his newspaper.*

Now, that is Mr Blightey, who's irascible –

BLIGHTEY (*benignly*). Hallo.

CRUMMLES. Mr Hetherington, who swaggers, and Mr Pailey who is country comical;

MR PAILEY *grins.*

There's Miss Ledrook, who's our secondary romance, Miss Belvawney, who does the pages in white hose; Mrs Lenville, who's the wife to Mr Lenville; Miss Bravassa, Miss Gazingi, and Mrs Grudden. Now, tomorrow morning, ten o'clock, we'll call The Mortal Struggle and then it's all the Chorus for the Raising of the Siege of Ghent. Good evening, everyone!

As all the company except for the CRUMMLES FAMILY *itself disperse:*

MRS GRUDDEN. Ten o'clock, call, ten o'clock, The Mortal Struggle. Half past Siege of Ghent. All those with lodgings, go to 'em. All those without, see me. Good evening, everyone.

MRS CRUMMLES *leads her* FAMILY *to* NICHOLAS *and* SMIKE. NICHOLAS *a little shrug, which* MRS CRUMMLES *interprets as a request that he should be put out of his agony.*

MRS CRUMMLES. Yes, sir, I think you'll do.

CRUMMLES *relieved. The* FAMILY *sweep out.* NICHOLAS *and* SMIKE *follow.*

Scene Eleven

The Mantalinis' showroom. The mirror, a clothes rail, clothes stands, and tailors' dummies. MISS KNAG *crossly fiddling about. Enter* KATE.

KATE. Um, Miss –

MISS KNAG. Oh, well. If it isn't that young and pretty creature, Miss Kate Nickle –

KATE. Please, Miss Knag. You're wanted in the workroom.

MISS KNAG. Workroom. Thank you.

As she goes.

Well, one might have thought, some people would have had the sensitivity, to seek alternative employment. Yes, one might have thought, but it's a queer world.

MISS KNAG *goes out. Enter* MADAME MANTALINI.

MADAME MANTALINI (*adjusting a dress on a stand*). Well, Miss Nickleby, and how are you?

KATE. I'm quite well, thank you, Madame Mantalini.

KATE *starting to help*.

MADAME MANTALINI. Hm. I wish that I could say the same.

KATE. Why, Madame Mantalini, what's the matter?

MADAME MANTALINI. Nothing, nothing. Now, get these things in order, do.

MANTALINI'*s head pops into the room*.

MANTALINI. Now, is my life-and-soul present?

MADAME MANTALINI. No.

MANTALINI. But how can that be so, when I see it blooming in the room before me like a little rose in a demd flowerpot? So, may its poppet enter?

MADAME MANTALINI. No, he may not. For he knows he's not allowed in here. So, go along.

MANTALINI *enters the room and embraces* MADAME MANTALINI.

MANTALINI. Oh, will it vex itself?

MADAME MANTALINI. I said that –

MANTALINI. Will it twist and crunch its little face?

MADAME MANTALINI. Oh, I can't bear you –

MANTALINI. What, can't bear me? I, whose only joy is gaining such a lovely creature, such a Venus, such a demd enchanting, and bewitching, and engrossing, captivating little Venus?

MADAME MANTALINI (*breaking away*). Mantalini, you, your debts, extravagances, they will ruin me.

MANTALINI (*airily*). Oh, that. Oh, it's a nothing, money will be made, and if it don't get made, enough, old Nickleby can stump up once again, or else I'll cut his jugular from ear to –

MADAME MANTALINI. Hush. Hush, don't you see?

MANTALINI. Oh, Dear Miss Nickleby. Well, I'll be demd.

Pause.

Well, then, as I am commanded, and quite demnibly admonished, by my little rapture . . . I'll withdraw.

He goes to the door. Then turns back.

Unless . . . My little joy and bliss . . . Would care to join her slave for breakfast?

Pause. Then, after a look to KATE, MADAME MANTALINI *follows* MANTALINI *to the door. They go.* KATE *carries on, working alone, for a moment. Then a new head pops round the door. It belongs to* MR SCALEY, *a rather rough-and-ready, though completely professional, gentleman.*

SCALEY. Psst.

KATE. Oh! What?

SCALEY (*coming into the room*). Please don't alarm yourself, Miss. Is this the millinery concern, proprietor one Mister Muntlehiney?

KATE. Yes, what do you want?

SCALEY (*calling out of the door*). Yes, Mr Tix, we have the right establishment.

Enter MR TIX, *another professional gentleman.* KATE, *fearing that these men are thieves, backing away.*

Oh, please don't go yet, Miss. I haven't yet presented you my card.

He hands a square, white card to KATE.

My name is Scaley. This is Mr Tix. Perhaps you'd be so kind as to aquaint your guv'nor with our presence.

KATE *backs to the wall and pulls the bell pull. Bell rings.*

Thank you ever so.

Pause. KATE *stands there, by the bell pull.* MR TIX *is looking up at the ceiling.*

TIX. I like the ceiling. Nice high ceiling.

SCALEY. Isn't it.

TIX. A boy could grow up here, grow up to be a man, a tall 'un too, and never bump his head on that.

SCALEY. Now, that is very true.

Tapping a mirror.

Good plate here, Tix.

TIX. Oh, yur.

Fingering a dress.

And this here article weren't put together without outlay of considerable expense, nor, neither.

Pause as they continue looking round the room. Then TIX, *to lighten the atmosphere, to* KATE.

And a very pretty colour.

Enter MADAME MANTALINI.

MADAME MANTALINI. Kate, what's the – oh? Oh!

SCALEY. Ah. Mrs Muntlehinney?

KATE. Madame.

SCALEY. Scaley.

He waves at TIX.

Mr Tix.

He waves a document.

This is a writ of execution, and if it's not immediately convenient to settle, we'll set to work at once, please, taking the inventory.

MADAME MANTALINI *stumbles in horror, grabs the bell, pulls it, and falls into a chair.* KATE *to her.*

Oh, dear. I do suspect, Tix, that we'd better make a brisk commencement.

TIX *has already taken out his inventory book. He stands behind a dress on a stand, to note its features, so that, to us, he appears to be wearing it.*

TIX. Dress. One. Fetching shade of blue.

Enter MANTALINI.

SCALEY. Ah. Um, monsieur?

MANTALINI *stands there a moment. He is not unused to this situation, or to men like* SCALEY *and* TIX.

MANTALINI. So, what's the total, demn you?

TIX. Fifteen hundred, twenty-seven pound, and four and ninepence ha'penny.

MANTALINI. The ha'penny be demd.

SCALEY. By all means. And the ninepence, too. But with regard to the outstanding . . .?

MANTALINI *shrugs, and waves his hand.* MADAME
MANTALINI *is in tears.*

SCALEY. Oh, well. I fear that Mrs Tix and all the little Tixes'll be
minus their papa for a day or two.

TIX (*looks around*). Or even three.

SCALEY (*to comfort* MADAME MANTALINI). Now, come on,
madam, take a little consolation, for I'll warrant half of this
stuff in't been paid for, eh?

SCALEY *and* TIX *set about their business as* MANTALINI *goes
to his wife.*

TIX. Two cheval-glasses. One with damaged frame.

MANTALINI. Now, dear, my cup of happiness's sweetener, will
you listen to me for two minutes?

MADAME MANTALINI (*suddenly, in great passion*). Oh, don't
you speak to me. You've ruined me, and that's enough.

TIX. Three bonnets. Styling, various.

MANTALINI (*recoiling, as if from a blow*). What? Do not speak
to you? All this, and I, your drudge and potboy, I am not to
speak to you?

KATE *looking at* MANTALINI *with some cynicism, as are
Messrs* SCALEY *and* TIX.

TIX. One bust. A Roman gentleman.

MANTALINI. Oh, it's too much! Too much!

MANTALINI *rushes from the room.* MADAME MANTALINI
stands, quickly.

MADAME MANTALINI. Quick! Quick, Miss Nickleby! Make
haste, for heaven's sake, he will destroy himself.

She runs to the exit.

I spoke unkindly to him, and he cannot bear it. Alfred, Alfred!

She runs out. Chase music. MANTALINI, *who has found a pair
of scissors, runs on, pursued by* MILLINERS *and* MADAME
MANTALINI.

MANTALINI. No, I'm going to do it. Right now. No question.
Going to do it. Yes, I'm going to do it. I will do it now!

Everyone is back in the showroom. MISS KNAG *appears on the
sidelines.* MR SCALEY *and* MR TIX *carry on their work
calmly.*

1st MILLINER. Eh, what's he doing?

2nd MILLINER. Got my scissors.

1st MILLINER. Lor.

MADAME MANTALINI (*flinging her arms round her husband*). Oh, Alfred, stop, I didn't mean to say it, promise you, I didn't mean to say . . .

2nd MILLINER. That's highly dangerous.

MANTALINI. I have brought ruin on the best and purest creature ever threw herself away on some demned vagabond. I'll do it! Demmit, let me go!

He pulls himself away from her.

MADAME MANTALINI. Compose yourself, my angel, please, someone, disarm him!

MANTALINI *raises the scissors, to plunge them in his breast. The two* MILLINERS, *without much difficulty, grab him and disarm him.*

2nd MILLINER. Now, come on, Mr Mantalini –

1st MILLINER. Drop the scissors, like a nice man.

2nd MILLINER. There!

MANTALINI. No! No! You, fetch me poison!

2nd MILLINER. Poison?

MADAME MANTALINI. It was no one's fault.

MANTALINI (*banging his head against an absent wall*). Fetch me a pistol. You, ma'am, blow my brains out.

1st MILLINER. Me?

MADAME MANTALINI. It was my fault as much as yours –

MANTALINI *grabs the scissors back from the* 2nd MILLINER.

2nd MILLINER. Hey –

MANTALINI. Rope! A rope to hang myself –

He tries to hang himself by the bell pull. The bell rings. He looks at MADAME MANTALINI.

What did you say?

MADAME MANTALINI. I said – that it was no one's fault. Or, if it was, then mine as much as yours. My love.

Pause. MANTALINI *raises the hand, in which he holds the scissors.*

MANTALINI. Oh, my little pepperpot. Demnation, gravy-boat.

He drops the scissors.

SCALEY. One pair, scissors . . .

MANTALINI. My – little – apfel strudel.

MADAME MANTALINI aware for the first time of the open-mouthed MILLINERS and the faintly smiling MISS KNAG.

MADAME MANTALINI. Please, now, Alfred. Come.

MADAME MANTALINI puts out her hand to MANTALINI. He walks to her, and they go out together. MISS KNAG picks up the scissors.

1st MILLINER. Well, hark at that.

2nd MILLINER. Well, hark at *her.*

MISS KNAG. Well, now, young ladies. After all this, wild excitement, shall we return, and recommence our labours? Hm?

The MILLINERS turn out front to narrate.

MILLINERS.
And return they did, but after half-an-hour they were informed their services would be immediately dispensed with;

And on the next day Mr Mantalini's name appeared among the list of bankrupts;

And on the third day, the young ladies were all re-engaged,

Except for Miss Kate Nickleby.

MISS KNAG (*maliciously, to* KATE). Miss Nickleby. I think *you* needn't recommence your labours. I think that *you* Need Not Return.

She goes out, the MILLINERS go out too, and finally KATE.

Scene Twelve

Portsmouth, various locations. Bare stage. Enter NICHOLAS.

NICHOLAS. And at the hour next morning stipulated for the canvassing of Miss Snevellicci's friends and patrons, Nicholas repaired to the lodgings of that lady, which were at the house of a tailor in Smollet St. And having been admitted to her apartments by the tailor's daughter, he was told to wait.

Enter MISS SNEVELLICCI, carrying a pile of sheets and towels,

and, on top of them, a scrapbook. She is followed by the
INFANT PHENOMENON.

MISS SNEVELLICCI. Oh, Mr Johnson. Please forgive me. We're all at sixes and sevens this morning.

NICHOLAS. Oh, I'm sorry to —

MISS SNEVELLICCI. My darling Led — Miss Ledrook, from the company . . .

NICHOLAS. Oh, yes.

MISS SNEVELLICCI. — was taken so ill in the night, we had to all move rooms. I thought she would expire, there, in my arms!

NICHOLAS. Well, such a fate is almost to be envied. But —

MISS SNEVELLICCI. Oh, Mr Johnson, what a flatterer you are.

MISS SNEVELLICCI, *moving towards the exit, artfully drops the scrapbook.*

Oh, dear, look —

NICHOLAS (*picking up the scrapbook*). Allow me, please.

MISS SNEVELLICCI. Oh, thank you, sir. Forgive me for a moment.

MISS SNEVELLICCI *goes out.* NICHOLAS *reads the scrapbook.*

NICHOLAS.
"Sing, God of Love, and tell me in what dearth,
Thrice-gifted Snevellicci came on earth,
To thrill us with her smile, her tear, her eye,
Sing, God of Love, and tell me quickly why."

MISS SNEVELLICCI *has reappeared, without the sheets and towels.*

MISS SNEVELLICCI. Mr Johnson!

NICHOLAS. Oh, I'm —

MISS SNEVELLICCI. Mr Johnson, I'm surprised at you.

NICHOLAS. I'm sorry, I —

MISS SNEVELLICCI. You are a cruel creature, I'm ashamed to look you in the face.

NICHOLAS. I thought, perhaps . . . You'd dropped it here on purpose?

MISS SNEVELLICCI. Mr Johnson. I would not have had you see it For The World. Now, shall we go?

NICHOLAS *out front, as* MISS SNEVELLICCI *and the* PHENOMENON *move to the area which will represent the home of the Curdles.*

NICHOLAS. And go at once they did, and the first house to which they bent their steps was situated in a terrace of respectable appearance, where lodged the Curdles, to whose apartments they were instantly directed.

NICHOLAS *joins the* PHENOMENON *and* MISS SNEVELLICCI.

MISS SNEVELLICCI. Now, Mrs Curdle is well-known to have quite the London taste in matters relating to the drama; and as to Mr Curdle, he has written a pamphlet of sixty-four pages,

NICHOLAS (*out front*). Proving that by altering the received mode of punctuation, any one of Shakespeare's plays could be made quite different, and the sense completely changed.

Enter MR *and* MRS CURDLE. MR CURDLE *has a chair for his wife.*

CURDLE. To be or not? To be that, is the question! Hm?

NICHOLAS. Oh, yes, indeed.

MRS CURDLE. Dear Miss Snevellicci, and how do you do?

MISS SNEVELLICCI. Oh, I'm alarming well, dear Mrs Curdle, and ventured to call for the purpose of asking whether you would put your name to my bespeak.

MRS CURDLE. Oh, I really don't know what to say . . . It's not as if, now is it, that the theatre was in high and palmy days – the drama's gone, perfectly gone.

MISS SNEVELLICCI. Well, p'raps, but surely –

CURDLE. As an exquisite embodiment of the poet's visions, and laying upon a new and magic world before the mental eye, the drama is gone, perfectly gone.

MRS CURDLE. What man is there now living who can present before us all those changing and prismatic colours with which the character of Hamlet is invested?

CURDLE. What man indeed – upon the stage; why, Hamlet! Pooh! He's gone, perfectly gone!

Pause.

MISS SNEVELLICCI. The play is new.

MRS CURDLE. Oh, yes, what is the play?

MISS SNEVELLICCI. A new one, written by this gentleman, and in which he will make his first appearance on the stage.

CURDLE. I trust he has preserved the unities.

NICHOLAS. The piece is in French — originally — there is an abundance of incident, sprightly dialogue, well-fleshed, three-dimensional characters, two tubs, a pump —

CURDLE. All unavailing — pump and all — without the unities.

NICHOLAS. May I inquire, sir, as to what are the unities?

CURDLE. The unities, sir, are a completeness — a kind of universal dove-tailedness, and oneness, and general warmth, and harmony, and tone . . .

MISS SNEVELLICCI. And I am sure that Mr Johnson will preserve the unities — all three of them — most closely. May I put your names . . .?

CURDLE (*taking a sheet of paper from* MISS SNEVELLICCI). Well, I suppose . . . We must accept it as our duty to the drama, even if — Four Shillings?

MISS SNEVELLICCI. Yes, that's right?

MRS CURDLE. Four shillings for *one box*?

MISS SNEVELLICCI. Yes, that's correct.

CURDLE. Four shillings for *one play*?

  MISS SNEVELLICCI *looks desperately at* NICHOLAS.

NICHOLAS. Well. With a lot of people in it.

  Slight pause.

  And it is very long.

CURDLE. Well, it had better be.

NICHOLAS (*out front*). And Miss Snevellicci took the money with many smiles and bends, and Mr Curdle rang the bell as a signal for breaking up the conference.

  The CURDLES *going.*

CURDLE. Oh, what? A rogue and peasant slave, am I?

  Exit the CURDLES.

NICHOLAS. What odd people.

MISS SNEVELLICCI. Oh, I assure you, Mr Johnson, they get even odder.

  MISS SNEVELLICCI *and the* PHENOMENON *leaving during:*

NICHOLAS. As indeed they did, and three hours later, with two pounds and nine shillings taken –

MISS SNEVELLICCI (*calls*). And a further ten and sixpence definitely promised –

NICHOLAS. Nicholas repaired, as he had been instructed, to the lodgings of the Vincent Crummleses.

Enter CRUMMLES *in a dressing gown.*

CRUMMLES. Ah, Johnson, there you are. Come in, come in. How goes it, Johnson?

NICHOLAS. Uh – the canvass?

CRUMMLES. No, the play.

NICHOLAS. It's not quite finished yet.

CRUMMLES. Thank heavens.

NICHOLAS. Oh?

CRUMMLES. I have another novelty, that must at all costs be included, in a prominent position.

NICHOLAS. Uh . . . I'm sorry, I can't guess.

CRUMMLES. What would you say to a young lady up from London? Say, Miss Someone, of the Theatre Royal, Drury Lane?

NICHOLAS. Well, that would look excellently, on the bills.

CRUMMLES. Exactly.

CRUMMLES *produces a poster, unrolls it, on which is prominently displayed the name of Miss Petowker, of the Theatre Royal, Drury Lane.*

So, what d'you think of that?

NICHOLAS. Dear me, Miss Petowker, I know that lady.

CRUMMLES. Then you are acquainted, sir, with as much talent as was ever compressed into one young person's body. The Blood Drinker, sir, the Blood Drinker will die with that girl; and she's the only sylph *I* ever saw who could stand upon one leg, and play the tambourine on her other knee, *like* a sylph.

NICHOLAS. When is she expected?

CRUMMLES. Why, today. She is an old friend of Mrs Crummles's, who taught her, as it happens, everything she knows. And here she comes.

MRS CRUMMLES *entering*.

You're probably aware that Mrs Crummles was the original Blood Drinker.

NICHOLAS. I didn't know that, no.

MRS CRUMMLES. Why, yes, indeed, sir. I was obliged to give it up, however.

NICHOLAS. Oh, I'm sorry, why?

MRS CRUMMLES. Oh, the audiences, sir. They couldn't stand it. It was too tremendous. Vincent, there's a letter here – from Miss Petowker.

CRUMMLES. Ah.

CRUMMLES *reads the letter*. NICHOLAS *feels it necessary to converse with* MRS CRUMMLES.

NICHOLAS. You teach, I gather, ma'am.

MRS CRUMMLES. Oh, yes, I do. I did receive some pupils here in Portsmouth, on a previous occasion. I imparted some tuition in the art of acting to the daughter of a dealer in marine provisions. Sadly, it emerged that all the time she was coming to me she'd been totally insane.

NICHOLAS. Insane! How – most extraordinary.

MRS CRUMMLES. Well, I thought so too, until I learnt she was of the strong opinion she was living on the moon, which sad delusion went a long way to explain the style of her performances, which were distinctly lunar. So, then, Vincent, it *is* true!

For MR CRUMMLES *has finished the letter*.

CRUMMLES. Well, so it must appear. Who would have thought it?

MRS CRUMMLES. I would, Vincent. Any woman would. It is – demonstrably – her mission.

MISS PETOWKER (*off*). Mrs Crummles! Mr Crummles!

MRS CRUMMLES. Ah, and here she is. Boys, boys!

The MASTER CRUMMLESES *run on, and help* MISS PETOWKER *and her luggage into the room*.

MISS PETOWKER. Oh, Mrs Crummles, Mr Crummles . . . Oh, why, Mr Johnson!

MRS CRUMMLES. You two are acquainted?

NICHOLAS. Yes, we . . .

MISS PETOWKER. Mr *Johnson*. We met — oh, I don't recall, on two or three occasions, Lady — Thing, and Mrs Whatsit's salon, at the opera . . . Well, Mr Johnson, what a pleasure.

NICHOLAS *is embraced by* MISS PETOWKER. MISS PETOWKER *to* MRS CRUMMLES.

Why, Mrs Crummles, I had no *idea* . . .

MRS CRUMMLES. We are all quite delighted, Henrietta, with The News.

MISS PETOWKER (*confidentially*). Oh, but now, Mrs Crummles, there must be no *word*, no *hint*, of anything . . .

MRS CRUMMLES. My lips, my dear, are glued. Now, at this instant, dinner.

MRS CRUMMLES *has been escorting* MISS PETOWKER *into another room. She changes her mind, however, and turns back to* NICHOLAS, *who is moving towards the door.*

Mr Johnson?

NICHOLAS. Mrs Crummles?

MRS CRUMMLES. We have but a shoulder of mutton with onion sauce, but such as our dinner is, we beg of you to partake of it.

NICHOLAS. Oh, Mrs Crummles, I should be delighted.

MRS CRUMMLES (*as she escorts* MISS PETOWKER *out*). Then let the mutton and onion sauce appear!

Exit the two women as the MASTER CRUMMLESES *and the* PHENOMENON *run on and drag* NICHOLAS *into dinner.*

Scene Thirteen

Ralph Nickleby's office and Noggs' room. To one side, Ralph's desk, at which RALPH *sits, working. To the other side, a high stool and ledger table, on which are account books and a bell.* NOGGS *is in Ralph's part of the office at present.* MR MANTALINI *is banging the bell on Noggs' desk.* NOGGS *goes out of the "door" and round into his own area.*

MANTALINI. What a demnation long time you have kept me ringing at this confounded old cracked tea-kettle of a bell, every tinkle of which is enough to throw a strong man into blue convulsions.

NOGGS. Didn't hear it more than once, myself.

MANTALINI. Then you are most demnibly and outrageously deaf. Now, where's Ralph Nickleby?

NOGGS. Might not be home. What purpose?

MANTALINI (*striding past* NOGGS *into Ralph's office*). Purpose? It's to melt some scraps of paper into bright and shining, clinking, trinkling demd mint sauce.

RALPH NICKLEBY *looks at* MR MANTALINI.

Ah. Nickleby. You are at home.

RALPH *a look at* NOGGS, *who has followed*.

NOGGS (*shrugs*). He wouldn't wait.

RALPH *tosses his head at* NOGGS. NOGGS *returns to his desk*.

MANTALINI. Well, Nickleby, you're looking well today. You look quite juvenile and jolly, demmit?

RALPH. What do you want with me?

MANTALINI. Demnation discount.

RALPH. Money's scarce.

MANTALINI. Demnd scarce, or else I wouldn't want it.

RALPH. But – as you're a friend . . . Bills of exchange?

MANTALINI. Yes, two. One for £40, and one for thirty-five.

RALPH. So, seventy-five in all. When are they due for payment?

MANTALINI. Two months one, the other four.

RALPH. Names of the guarantors?

MANTALINI *hands over the Bills. The front doorbell rings again.* NOGGS *goes to answer it.*

Well, they are not cast-iron . . . But they're safe enough. I'll give you fifty for 'em.

MANTALINI. Only fifty.

RALPH. Yes.

MANTALINI. Not even, just a little more, as we are friends . . .

RALPH. But this is business, Mr Mantalini. You'll not get a better rate.

NOGGS *admits* MADAME MANTALINI *and* MISS KNAG.

And so? Do you accept?

MANTALINI. I must.

RALPH (*opening a cash box*). Well, then . . .

MADAME MANTALINI *followed by* MISS KNAG, *has stridden in past* NOGGS *and into Ralph's office.*

MADAME MANTALINI. Oh, here you are.

MANTALINI. Oh. You.

MADAME MANTALINI. Yes. Me. Forgive us, Mr Nickleby, for this intrusion. Which is attributable to the gross and most improper misbehaviour of, of Mr Mantalini.

MANTALINI *stands and tries to embrace* MADAME MANTALINI.

MANTALINI. What's this you're saying, juice of pine-apple?

MADAME MANTALINI. No, none of that. I won't allow it. I will not be ruined by your profligacy any more.

MANTALINI *sits.*

Mr Nickleby, I call on you to witness what I'm going to say.

RALPH. Pray, do not ask me, madam. Settle it amongst yourselves.

MADAME MANTALINI. Well, settle it is what I plan to do.

To MANTALINI.

This morning, you appropriated, from my desk, some bills belonging to the company, without permission. Is that not the case?

MANTALINI. It is, my precious, it is true, my tulip. I'm the demdest villain ever lived.

MADAME MANTALINI. And, knowing of my debts and obligations, caused by your extravagance, you have come here to change those bills of mine to cash. Do you deny it?

MANTALINI. No, I cannot. Oh, I'll fill my pockets up with ha'pennies, and drown myself.

MADAME MANTALINI. Well then, I tell you, Mr Nickleby, Miss Knag, once and for all, that I never will supply this man's extravagance again.

Pause. MANTALINI *looks up at his wife. He says nothing.*

I have been his dupe and his fool for long enough, and in future, he shall support himself if he can, and he may spend all that he pleases, and on whom he likes, but it shall not be mine.

MANTALINI. What are you saying, seraphim?

MADAME MANTALINI. I am insisting on a separation.

RALPH. Madam, you are not in earnest.

MADAME MANTALINI. Oh, I am.

RALPH. Madam, consider. A married woman has no property. The company belongs to Mr Mantalini.

MADAME MANTALINI. Oh, no, sir. It does not. That company is bankrupt. But, to save what little has been left, of the furnishings and stock, I was obliged to call upon another party, who had, I'm pleased to say, sufficient capital to meet outstanding bills, to re-employ the staff, and to engage me as the manager of her new company.

MISS KNAG. New company.

Slight pause. MANTALINI *looks at* MISS KNAG *in horror.*

Yes, it's quite true, Mr Nickleby. It's very true indeed. And I never was more glad in all my life, that I had the strength of mind to resist all offers of marriage, however advantageous, than I am when I think of my present position as compared with your most unfortunate and most undeserved one, Madame Mantalini.

To RALPH.

Otherwise, where would I be today?

MANTALINI. Oh, demmit, demmit, will it not slap and pinch the envious dowager, that dares so to reflect upon its own delicious?

MADAME MANTALINI. No, of course not. For Miss Knag is now, perforce, my very greatest friend.

MANTALINI. This a dream, a demned, demned horrid dream.

MADAME MANTALINI. You have brought it on yourself.

MANTALINI. Oh, has it come to this? Oh, have I cut my heart into a demned extraordinary number of little pieces, and given them away one after another to the same little engrossing captivator, and it's come to this.

MADAME MANTALINI. It has. You know it has.

Slight pause. MADAME MANTALINI *goes to* RALPH *and puts out her hand.* RALPH *hands over the Bills of Exchange.* MISS KNAG *trots over, and puts out her hand.* MADAME MANTALINI *gives the Bills to* MISS KNAG. *To* RALPH.

I did . . . A long time. I did love that creature, Mr Nickleby.

MADAME NICKLEBY *and* MISS KNAG *go out.* MANTALINI
runs, and cries after them.

MANTALINI. Oh, I will drown myself!

But they have gone. Back to RALPH.

Oh, Nickleby, how can you sit there, watching such a cruel,
brazen chick-a-biddy savaging the very heart of one who –

RALPH. Come, sir, you must put away these fooleries, now.

MANTALINI. You – what?

RALPH. And live by your own wits again.

Pause.

MANTALINI. But, demmit, you'll help me, won't you, Nickleby?

RALPH. No, I will not. Good day.

MANTALINI. You can't be serious.

RALPH. I seldom joke. Good day.

MANTALINI. Now, look here, Nickleby, you know, without me,
you'd've not got one brass farthing out of –

RALPH. Without you, sir, my credit would not have been needed.
As well you know. And now, good day to you.

Pause.

MANTALINI. Well. Well, demnation – cruelty.

He makes to go, turns back. He can't believe it.

It's over.

MANTALINI *goes out.*

RALPH. Hm. Love him. Love that. All love, is cant and vanity.

NOGGS *has appeared. He coughs.*

Yes, what?

NOGGS (*presenting a card to* RALPH). Two gentlemen. Are out
the back. Their card.

Enter MR SCALEY *and* MR TIX.

SCALEY. Well, good day, Mr Nickleby. Here is the tally. Thirteen
hundred pounds. That's plus or minus the odd bonnet, or an
underskirt or two.

RALPH. I thank you.

SCALEY. And dare I venture, you'll be kindly helping out the
business once again? Another loan? And in a threemonth, when
the interest falls due . . .

RALPH. No, I think not, Mr Scaley. There has been a change of ownership. The business is now in more able hands.

TIX. Oh, dear.

SCALEY. Oh, very sorry, sir.

RALPH. So, then, your task's complete. How much?

SCALEY *hands* RALPH *a bill, which* RALPH *signs and hands back to* SCALEY.

SCALEY. It's always such a pleasure doing business with you, Mr Nickleby.

TIX. It's such a joy.

Scene Fourteen

Portsmouth. In the wings of the theatre. The CRUMMLES COMPANY *runs on from their curtain call. We hear applause. They have been performing Nicholas' play for Miss Snevellicci's benefit. The women are mostly clustering round* NICHOLAS, *the men round* MISS PETOWKER. SMIKE *looks on.*

MISS GAZINGI. Oh, Mr Johnson, what a triumph.

NICHOLAS. Well, I — Was it?

MISS BRAVASSA. Oh, my dear, you quite divided the applause, despite it being for Miss Snevellicci —

NICHOLAS. Well, I'm sure I —

CRUMMLES *comes to* NICHOLAS, *as* MRS CRUMMLES *sweeps back on to the stage.*

CRUMMLES. Johnson. Sir. This has been magnificent. Why, quite magnificent. I have not, sir, seen such a debut since the Phenomenon herself first danced the Fairy Porcupine.

The INFANT PHENOMENON *curtseys and does a twirl.*

And everyone, well done.

The PHENOMENON *bumps into* MISS BRAVASSA *and there is a little altercation.* LENVILLE *and* FOLAIR *step forward.*

LENVILLE. Hm. In my view, grossly over-rated.

FOLAIR (*leading him aside*). Oh, come on, now, old man . . .

CRUMMLES (*taking* NICHOLAS' *arm.*) So what did you think of Miss Petowker, sir?

NICHOLAS. Oh, quite extraordinary.

CRUMMLES *looks at* NICHOLAS *quizzically. During this a knock at the outer door and the Page-clad* MISS BELVAWNEY, *out of force of habit, goes out to answer it.*

Good, is not the word. But what I did observe, additional to all her talents, was that every time she spoke, or even entered, there was quite a fearful opening and closing, in the upper boxes, of a green umbrella.

CRUMMLES. Was there? I can't say I noticed.

NICHOLAS. Yes, it was most striking. Every time she –

MISS SNEVELLICCI *approaches bearing vast numbers of flowers, followed by* MISS LEDROOK, *carrying the rest.*

MISS SNEVELLICCI. Mr Johnson.

NICHOLAS. Oh, Miss Snevellicci.

MISS SNEVELLICCI. Mr Johnson, I –

But even MISS SNEVELLICCI *is interrupted by the entrance of* MRS CRUMMLES.

MRS CRUMMLES. So, are you *all* deaf?

CRUMMLES. Why, Mrs Crummles, what's the matter?

MRS CRUMMLES. What's the matter? The audience is what's the matter, the great Portsmouth public is the matter, they are calling for an encore from the shepherdesses, they're insisting Miss Petowker does another dance, they're shrieking out for anything from Mr Johnson, there is a concerted move to rip the cupids and muses from the lower boxes if Miss Snevellicci doesn't –

CRUMMLES. Then, come, let's return! Come, come, at once!

MRS CRUMMLES. If you'd all be so kind.

The COMPANY *running back on, as* MISS BELVAWNEY *appears.*

MISS BELVAWNEY. Psst, Mr Johnson.

NICHOLAS. Yes?

MISS BELVAWNEY. There's someone here to see you.

NICHOLAS. But –

MISS BELVAWNEY. He says it's very urgent.

NICHOLAS. But I –

NICHOLAS *sees that* MR LILLYVICK *has come in.*

Why, in the name of wonder, Mr Lillyvick!

MISS BELVAWNEY *scuttles across and out.*

LILLYVICK (*a little bow*). Sir, I am your servant.

He puts down a large, green umbrella.

NICHOLAS. And I yours. Why, there's the green umbrella!

LILLYVICK. Ah, yes, that it is. What did you think of that performance?

NICHOLAS. Your performance with the – ?

LILLYVICK. What? No, I refer to Miss Petowker's.

NICHOLAS. Well, as far as I could judge, I found it most agreeable.

LILLYVICK. Agreeable? I would say, sir, it was much more than agreeable. I'd say, in fact, it was delicious.

NICHOLAS. Well, she is a clever girl.

LILLYVICK. She's a divinity. I have known divine actresses before now, sir; I used to collect the water rate at the house of a divine actress, but never in all my experience did I see a diviner creature than Miss Henrietta Petowker.

NICHOLAS. Well, yes –

LILLYVICK (*grasping* NICHOLAS's *arm*). A bachelor's a miserable wretch, sir.

NICHOLAS. Is he?

LILLYVICK. I have been one nigh on sixty years. I ought to know.

NICHOLAS. That's certain.

LILLYVICK. But you know that the reason, the great reason, against marriage, is expense. That's what has kept me off it, or else, lord! I might have married fifty women.

NICHOLAS. Fifty.

LILLYVICK. But, you see: the wondrous Miss Petowker earns a salary herself.

Pause. LILLYVICK *leaves* NICHOLAS's *arm. He moves a step or two away and eyes* NICHOLAS *inquiringly.*

NICHOLAS. Uh, Mr Lillyvick, d'you mean you're going to marry Miss Petowker?

LILLYVICK. Day after tomorrow, sir.

NICHOLAS. Well . . . Mr Lillyvick. Congratulations.

LILLYVICK. The only problem is, the family.

NICHOLAS. What family?

LILLYVICK. The Kenwigses, of course. If my niece and her husband had known a word of it before I came away, they'd have gone into fits at my feet, and never have come off 'em till I took an oath not to marry anybody, or they'd have got out a commission of lunacy, or some such dreadful thing.

NICHOLAS. Yes, they would certainly have been quite jealous.

LILLYVICK. To prevent which, we resolved to marry here, in fact, to be married from the Crummleses, old friends of Miss Petowker, and should be most pleased if you were there for breakfast, nothing fancy, muffins, coffee, p'raps a shrimp or something for a relish . . .

NICHOLAS. Mr Lillyvick, I'd be delighted. And I am most happy for you both.

LILLYVICK. Most happy? Yes. Yes – I should think it is a pleasant life, the married one – eh?

NICHOLAS. There is no doubt about it.

LILLYVICK. Um. No doubt. Oh, yes. Yes, certainly.

Enter MRS CRUMMLES.

MRS CRUMMLES. Ah, Mr Johnson. *Here* you are.

NICHOLAS. Oh, Mrs Crummles

LILLYVICK *slips out, as:*

MRS CRUMMLES. Mr Johnson, you are called for, in the lower circle. You're demanded in the gallery, which is, in fact, quite near collapse from all the stamping. Your appearance was entreated by dear Mrs Curdle, till she had a palpitation and was rushed off horizontal in a fly . . . Without, of course, the wish in any way to interrupt your evening – would you be so kind, sir, as to come?

NICHOLAS. Of course I will

MRS CRUMMLES *sweeps out.* NICHOLAS *turns out front to introduce the next scene.*

Scene Fifteen

Portsmouth. Miss Snevellicci's apartment, and the Crummles' lodgings. As NICHOLAS *speaks,* MISS SNEVELLICCI, MISS

PETOWKER *and* MISS LEDROOK *enter with a chair on one side; and* FOLAIR, LENVILLE, LILLYVICK *and the rest of the* CRUMMLES' COMPANY MEN *enter the other.*

NICHOLAS. And on the morning designated for the nuptial coupling of Mr Lillyvick and Miss Petowker, the parties were assembling; with the bridegroom and his best man Tom Folair already at the Crummleses; and Miss Petowker being finally prepared at the apartments of Miss Snevellicci.

MISS PETOWKER *is sitting, having a sustaining glass of something.*

MISS PETOWKER. Oh, Lillyvick! If you only knew what I am undertaking . . . Leaving all my friends, the friends of youthful days, for you!

MIS LEDROOK. Of course he knows it, love, and never will forget it.

MISS PETOWKER. Are you sure? You're sure that he'll remember?

MISS SNEVELLICCI. Oh, yes, I'm absolutely sure that he'll remember.

Focus shifts to LILLYVICK.

FOLAIR. Come, sir, cheer up, it is soon done.

LILLYVICK. What is?

FOLAIR. The tying up, the fixing of one with a wife. It is quickly o'er. Just like a hanging, what?

LILLYVICK. Like hanging?

LENVILLE. Come on, now, Tommy, none of that.

FOLAIR. Yes, yes, you know, to hang oneself takes but a moment –

LILLYVICK. Do you compare, sir, do you draw a parallel –

FOLAIR *miming a hanging.*

Between my matrimony and a hanging?

FOLAIR (*still miming*). Yes, yes, the —

LILLYVICK. You say this in the house of Mr not to mention Mrs Crummles, who have brought up such a family, chock full of blessings and phenomena, you call their state a noose?

FOLAIR. Well, just a little joke –

The BRIDAL PARTY *has arrived.*

MISS PETOWKER. Oh, Lillyvick.

LILLYVICK (*turning to* MISS PETOWKER). My dear, d'you know what this, your actor friend —

MISS PETOWKER. Oh, Lillyvick . . .

LILLYVICK *stops, realising his Bride has arrived in her full finery on her wedding morning. He embraces* MISS PETOWKER.

MISS PETOWKER. Oh, Lillyvick . . . You will remember, won't you? Always, always, always?

LILLYVICK. Uh, remember what, my dear?

Enter CRUMMLES *in 18th Century costume, clearly dressed as the Heavy Father, followed by the* INFANT PHENOMENON, *covered in artificial flowers, and* MRS CRUMMLES, *as the Distraught Mother. Some "oohs" and "ahs" from the rest.* MRS CRUMMLES *kisses* MISS PETOWKER, *and is overcome.*

CRUMMLES. Come, stir, stir, stir! The second cock hath crow'd, the curfew bell has rung, 'tis —

He looks at an enormous fob watch.

Nine o'clock.

MISS PETOWKER (*dramatically*). 'Tis nine o'clock, dear Lillyvick. Come, stir.

A wedding anthem plays. MR CRUMMLES *takes the arm of the bride, and walks upstage with a feeble gait. The* COMPANY *form into a procession, two by two: the* BRIDESMAIDS, MRS CRUMMLES *with the* PHENOMENON, *the other* ACTRESSES; *then* LILLYVICK *and* FOLAIR, *the other* ACTORS, NICHOLAS *and* SMIKE, *and, at the rear, the drunken* MR WAGSTAFF.

THE ANTHEM.
How blest are they that fear the Lord
And walk in His way
For thou shalt eat the labour of thine hands
Well, well is thee and happy shalt thou be.
Thy wife shall be
The fruitful vine on the walls of thy house
Thy children like the olive branches
Growing, growing round about thy table.
Lo, thus shall the man be blest
That fearest the Lord.

Lo, thus shall the man be blest
That feareth the Lord.

Narration as the BRIDE *and* GROOM *run out, the former throwing her bouquet, which is caught by* MISS SNEVELLICCI.

NARRATORS.
And Mr Lillyvick and his bride departed to take the steamboat to Ryde where they were to spend the next two days in profound retirement.

The COMPANY *beginning to disperse, leaving only* NICHOLAS *and* SMIKE.

And Mr Crummles declared his intention of keeping the celebrations going till everything to drink was disposed of;

But Nicholas, having to play Romeo for the first time on the ensuing evening, and anxious on account of Smike – who would have to sustain the character of the apothecary – contrived to slip away.

And only NICHOLAS *and* SMIKE *are left.*

Scene Sixteen

Portsmouth and London. Bare stage. This is a double scene, counterpointing NICHOLAS' *rehearsal of* SMIKE *as the Apothecary with* RALPH's *dealings in London. First,* NICHOLAS *and* SMIKE; *during which* RALPH *and* NOGGS *enter.* NICHOLAS *has a copy of* Romeo *and* Juliet *with him.*

NICHOLAS (*prompting*). Who calls so loud?

SMIKE. Who calls so loud.

NICHOLAS.
Come hither, man. I see that thou art poor.
Hold, there is forty ducats. Let me have
A dram of poison, such soon-speeding gear
As will disperse itself through all the veins
That the life-weary taker may fall dead
And that the trunk may be discharged of breath
As violently as hasty powder fired
Doth hurry from the fatal cannon's womb.

Pause. Prompting.

Such mortal drugs I have –

SMIKE.
Such mortal drugs I have . . .

NICHOLAS.
But Mantua's law –

SMIKE.
But Mantua's law . . .
Is death to anyone who utters them.

NOGGS. Are you at home?

RALPH. I'm not.

NOGGS. You're sure?

RALPH. Of course I'm sure.

NOGGS. Well, they're downstairs.

RALPH. Who are?

NOGGS. Two gentlemen.

RALPH. You didn't tell me.

NOGGS. Didn't ask. Ah, here they are.

Enter SIR MATTHEW PUPKER and MR BONNEY. NOGGS
remains in the background.

RALPH. Sir Matthew, Bonney. What can I –

BONNEY. Look, Nickleby. This matter, your investment in our
company –

RALPH. Yes, yes. I have resolved to realise my capital.

BONNEY. But, Nickleby – withdrawal of a sum of that
proportion, now – nine thousand?

RALPH. Ten.

BONNEY. At this stage, when the stock's still going up –

RALPH. Will make the price fall. Yes, I know.

BONNEY. The bubble – bursts!

RALPH. Yes, certainly. But I have need of it.

SIR MATTHEW. Now, Nickleby . . .

RALPH. Sir Matthew?

SIR MATTHEW. Have you not considered this, this matter, who's
involved? The highest level? Have you no thought for your
country?

RALPH. I have thought of it, my country, to the same extent as
you have, sir. Good day.

SIR MATTHEW *looks at* BONNEY, *who shrugs apologetically.*
SIR MATTHEW, *with a huge gesture of rage and frustration,
storms out followed by* BONNEY. RALPH *to* NOGGS.

My hat and stick.

NOGGS. Your hat and stick.

RALPH. Well, then? Don't stand, repeating what I've said. You're
not a parrot.

NOGGS. Wish I was.

RALPH. Well, so do I. Then I could wring your neck. And I'd be
done with you.

RALPH *strides out.* NOGGS *stands there for a few moments, as*
SMIKE *and* NICHOLAS *re-enter.*

NICHOLAS.
Art thou so bare and full of wretchedness,
And fearest to die? Famine is in thy cheeks,
Need and oppression starveth in thy eyes,
Contempt and beggary hangs upon thy back:
The world is not thy friend, nor the world's law;
The world affords no law to make thee rich;
Then be not poor, but break it, and take this.

Pause. Prompting.

My poverty —

SMIKE.
My poverty . . .

MRS NICKLEBY (*off.*) Kate. Kate, my dear.

NICHOLAS. But not my will —

KATE (*off*). Mama?

SMIKE. But not my will — consents.

SMIKE *and* NICHOLAS *go as* MRS NICKLEBY, *with* RALPH,
enters to KATE.

MRS NICKLEBY. You are to dine, dine with your uncle, half-past
six tomorrow.

KATE. Uncle, what is this?

RALPH. I have a party of — of gentlemen, to whom I am
connected in business, at my house tomorrow, and your
mother's promised that you shall keep house for me. I'm not
much used to parties, but such fooleries are often part of
business — and I hope that you won't mind obliging me.

MRS NICKLEBY. Mind? Mind? My dear Kate, tell —

KATE. I shall be very glad, of course — but I'm afraid you'll find me very awkward and embarrassed.

RALPH. No, oh no . . . Come when you like, and take a hackney coach. I'll pay for it. Good night and, um, God bless you.

Exit RALPH.

MRS NICKLEBY. Well, Kate. Your uncle's taken quite a fancy to you, that is clear, and if good fortune doesn't come to you from this, I shall be most surprised.

KATE *and* MRS NICKLEBY *go out during:*

SMIKE.
My poverty and not —

NICHOLAS.
My will —

SMIKE.
Consents.
My poverty and not my will consents.

NICHOLAS.
I pay thy poverty and not thy will.

SMIKE.
My poverty and not my will consents.

NICHOLAS. Uh — no —

NICHOLAS *takes* SMIKE *out, as a* MAN *enters one side, and on the other,* RALPH *and* NOGGS. NOGGS *has a plate of muffins, which he gives to* RALPH.

NOGGS. He's here. I got him tea. But he's not eating it.

RALPH *gestures to* NOGGS, *who goes.* RALPH *to the* MAN.

RALPH. Sir Mulberry.

SIR MULBERRY HAWK *is an elegant, though dissipated, rake. He holds a bottle and a glass.*

HAWK (*pouring a drink*). Hm. Nickleby, Is everything arranged?

RALPH. It is. Um — have you taken tea?

SIR MULBERRY HAWK *raises his glass, in answer.*

The gull will come?

HAWK. Lord Frederick? Of course. I told him that the evening would be both — an entertainment, and of profit. Will it be?

RALPH. Oh, yes. For us, at least. And, for the first, I think . . .
there will be an attraction, for his lordship, present. For the
second, I am able to advance . . . as much as he, and you, will
need.

HAWK. You're sure of that?

RALPH. Oh, yes. I am prepared.

Offering the plate.

Look, please, Sir Mulberry, at least . . . Do have a muffin. Hm?

*Enter SMIKE and NICHOLAS. They are in costume for the
performance: NICHOLAS as Romeo and SMIKE in a grey
gown as the Apothecary.*

NICHOLAS.
There is thy gold — worse poison to men's souls,
Doing more murder in this loathsome world,
Than these poor compounds that thou mayst not sell.
I sell thee poison; thou hast sold me none.
Farewell.

*RALPH goes. MRS GRUDDEN, dressed as Juliet's Nurse,
marches across the stage.*

MRS GRUDDEN. Act Three! Act Three! Beginners, orchestra!

NICHOLAS and SMIKE smile at each other.

SMIKE. Who calls so loud?

NICHOLAS. Who calls so loud.

They go out.

Scene Seventeen

*Ralph's drawing room, in London. A chaise longue, surrounded
by men in evening dress, including SIR MULBERRY HAWK, his
young friend LORD FREDERICK VERISOPHT, and his acolytes
MR PLUCK and MR PYKE. On another chair sit the elderly
COLONEL CHOWSER, near to him stand the HONOURABLE
MR SNOBB and a MAKEWEIGHT. A FLUNKEY is in
attendance. RALPH enters with KATE.*

RALPH. Gentlemen. My niece, Miss Nickleby.

KATE notices they're all men.

VERISOPHT. Eh. What the devil.

PYKE (*to* PLUCK). Hm . . . Hm.

RALPH. My niece, my lord. Kate, Lord Frederick Verisopht.

VERISOPHT (*coming forward*). Well, then me ears did not deceive me, and it's not a waxwork. How d'ye do, Miss Nickleby.

KATE *curtseys.*

PYKE (*coming forward*). Now, don't you leave me out, now, Nickleby.

RALPH. And this is Mr Pyke.

PLUCK. Nor me.

RALPH. And Mr Pluck, my dear.

KATE *curtseys again.* SNOBB *stands.*

And the Honourable Mr Snobb, and

CHOWSER *getting to his feet, not without difficulty.*

this is Colonel Chowser.

The MAKEWEIGHT *obviously isn't going to be introduced, but takes advantage of the situation to go and get another drink from the* FLUNKEY.

CHOWSER. Pleased. So very. Pleased.

A slight hiatus, broken as SIR MULBERRY HAWK, *in one assured movement, takes the* MAKEWEIGHT's *glass of wine,* KATE's *arm, and everyone's attention.*

HAWK. Miss Nickleby, forgive us. Let me sit you down.

KATE. Why, sir I —

HAWK (*gliding* KATE *to the chaise*). And, as I'm left out, damn you, Nickleby, I'll do the offices myself.

KATE *sits.*

Hawk, Miss Nickleby, and at your service.

HAWK *gives* KATE *the glass of wine.*

KATE. Why, thank you, sir.

RALPH (*to explain to* KATE). Sir Mulberry.

VERISOPHT *to* RALPH.

VERISOPHT. An unexpected pleasure, Nickleby. Indeed, one might say, it'd almost warrant the addition of an extra two and a half per cent.

HAWK (*turns to* PLUCK). Eh, Nickleby should take the hint, and tack it on to the other five-and-twenty, and give me half for the advice.

PLUCK *and* PYKE *laugh uproariously as* VERISOPHT *comes to stand on the other side of* KATE's *chair.*

VERISOPHT. Well, certainly, if he'll see to it you're not monopolising dear Miss Nickleby all night, Sir Mulberry.

RALPH (*lightly, as he goes to the* FLUNKEY). Well, my lord, he does have a tolerable share of everything you lay claim to.

VERISOPHT. Gad, so he has. Devil take me, sometimes, if I know who's master in me own house. But I swear . . . I'll cut him off with but a shilling, if he —

HAWK. Sir, when you're at your last shilling, I'll be cutting you. While here is poor Miss Nickleby who's doubtless bored to tears with all this talk of discount, and hoping that some gallant fellow'll make love to her. Now, ain't that so, Miss Nickleby?

KATE. No, sir, indeed . . .

HAWK. In fact, I'll hold you, any of you, fifty pounds, that Miss Nickleby can't look me in the face, and then deny that she was not hoping so.

To LORD FREDERICK VERISOPHT.

My Lord?

KATE. Oh, sir . . .

VERISOPHT. Well, why not? Done! Within a minute.

HAWK. Done. Now, Mr Snobb, you'll take the stakes, and keep the time?

SNOBB (*coming to them*). Of course.

The GENTLEMEN *produce money.* KATE *standing and going to* RALPH.

PYKE. That's fifty pounds . . .

CHOWSER (*unable to get up, pulling at* PLUCK). Hey, you, sir, pass me bet . . .

KATE. Uncle, please . . . please, stop them making me the subject of a bet.

RALPH. Oh, my dear . . . It's done in a moment, and there's nothing in it . . . If the gentlemen insist —

SNOBB. One – minute!

> HAWK *comes and takes* KATE's *hand, and leads her back to the chaise.*

HAWK. I don't insist on it. That is, I don't insist that she denies, for even if I lose, it's worth it just to see her eyes, which seem to love the carpeting so much.

VERISOPHT. That's true. It's just too bad of you, Miss Nickleby.

PYKE. Too cruel.

PLUCK. Quite horrid cruel.

SNOBB. The lady can't deny that she was hoping for a gentleman to – um – within a minute . . .

> *45 second pause.*

HAWK. How goes it, Snobb?

SNOBB. Fifteen seconds left.

VERISOPHT. Won't you, for me, Miss Nickleby, just make one effort . . .

HAWK. Oh, not a chance, my lord. Miss Nickleby and I understand each other very well.

SNOBB. Six, five, four, three . . .

> KATE, *outraged, looks* SIR MULBERRY *straight in the eye. Pause. Then she breaks, stands, and runs to the side of the room.*

HAWK. Capital. That's a girl of spirit, and we'll drink to her health.

> HAWK *nods to the* FLUNKEY, *who passes round drinks as* HAWK *collects his winnings.*

PYKE. Oh, yes, we will.

PLUCK. Most definitely.

PYKE. Many times.

RALPH. But, perhaps, sirs, now the sport is over, you would care to drink it over dinner.

HAWK. Well, certainly.

> PYKE *and* PLUCK *dislodge* CHOWSER *from his chair.* LORD VERISOPHT *to* KATE.

VERISOPHT (*offering his arm*). Miss Nickleby . . .

KATE. No, no . . .

RALPH (*gesturing the company out*). I'm sure Miss Nickleby will join us in a moment. When she has, composed herself.

VERISOPHT. But, Nickleby —

RALPH. I'm sure she will be down directly. Please, please, gentlemen.
The COMPANY *leaves.* RALPH *is the last to go and* KATE
goes to him.

KATE. Please, uncle, don't —

RALPH. My dear. We are connected. And I can't afford . . . What
is it, after all? We all have challenges. And this is one of yours.

RALPH *goes out.* KATE *is left there. Enter a heavily edited
section of Act Three, Scene Five of Romeo and Juliet,*
CRUMMLES *as* CAPULET, MRS CRUMMLES *as* LADY
CAPULET, MISS SNEVELLICCI *as* JULIET *and* MRS
GRUDDEN *as the* NURSE. *This scene is played around* KATE.

CAPULET.
How? Will she none? Does she not give us thanks?
Is she not proud? Doth she not count her blest,
Unworthy as she is, that we have wrought
So worthy a gentleman to be her bride?

JULIET.
Proud I can never be of what I hate.

CAPULET.
God's bread! It makes me mad.
Day, night; hour, tide, time; word, play;
Alone, in company, still my care hath been
To have her matched; and having now provided
A gentleman of noble parentage,
To answer "I'll not wed. I cannot love;
I am too young, I pray you pardon me."!
Graze where you will, you shall not house with me.
Nor what is mine shall never do thee good.
Exit CAPULET.

JULIET.
Is there no pity sitting in the clouds
That sees into the bottom of my grief?
Oh, sweet mother, cast me not away!

LADY CAPULET.
Talk not to me, for I'll not speak a word.
Exit LADY CAPULET, JULIET *and the* NURSE. *Re-enter*
HAWK.

HAWK. Yes, capital.

KATE. Oh, sir . . .

HAWK. What a delightful studiousness. Was it real, now, or only to display the eyelashes? Why did I speak and destroy such a pretty picture?

KATE. Then please, be silent, sir.

HAWK *goes and sits next to* KATE.

HAWK. No, don't. Upon my life, you musn't treat me like this, dear Miss Nickleby. I'm such a slave of yours.

KATE. I wish, sir . . . You must understand, that your behaviour . . .

HAWK. Come on, now, be more natural, Miss Nickleby, more natural, please . . .

KATE *looks at him. Then she stands quickly.* HAWK *catches her skirt.*

A bit more natural, eh?

KATE. Oh, sir. Please. Instantly! Please let me go at once.

HAWK. Not for the world, Miss Nickleby . . .

RALPH *has entered.*

RALPH. What's this?

HAWK *looks round. He sees* RALPH, *lets* KATE *go, sits down and crosses his legs.* KATE *gestures vaguely. To* HAWK, *gesturing towards the door.*

Your way lies there, sir.

Pause. RALPH *shaking.*

HAWK (*furious*). Do you *know* me, you madman?

RALPH. Well.

Pause.

KATE (*in tears*). Please, uncle. Let me go.

RALPH. Yes. Yes, of course. I'll take you to your carriage presently.

RALPH *takes* KATE's *arm.*

But just one word. I didn't know it would be so; it was impossible for me to foresee it.

KATE *looking at* RALPH. *Ralph looking over her shoulder at* HAWK.

You have done no wrong.

KATE *goes out.*

HAWK. Hm. You want the lord. Your pretty niece an "entertainment" for that drunken boy downstairs.

He turns to RALPH.

And if *he'd* come up here instead of me, you would have been a bit more blind, and deaf, and a deal less flourishing than you have been?

Pause.

Who brought him to you first? Without me, could you wind him in your net?

RALPH. That net's a large one, and it's rather full. Take care that it chokes no one in its meshes.

HAWK. Oh –

RALPH. I tell you this. That if I brought her here, as a matter of business –

HAWK. Oh, yes, well, that's the word —

RALPH (*interrupts*). Because I thought she might make some impression on the silly youth that you are leading into ruin, I knew, knowing him, that he'd respect her sex, and conduct. But I did not envisage I'd subject the girl to the licentiousness of a hand like you. And now we understand each other. Hm?

HAWK. Especially, of course, as there was nothing you could gain by it.

RALPH. Exactly so.

Enter LORD FREDERICK VERISOPHT.

VERISOPHT. So, there you are, the both of you. Now, are we not to dine? And do some business too?

RALPH (*deliberately*). Of course, my lord. We'll dine. But business first. Two months to pay. At interest of twenty-five per cent. Those are the terms, what sum had you in mind?

VERISOPHT. Oh, five – or ten?

HAWK. Say, ten.

RALPH. Ten thousands pounds. Now, gentlemen, I'll join you very soon.

HAWK *and* VERISOPHT *go out one way,* RALPH *another. Two Crummles stage-hands run in with flats, which they set up as if the prompt side wing of our theatre was the audience of the Portsmouth theatre.* NICHOLAS, *as* ROMEO, *walks on the*

"stage" – facing off our stage. In the Portsmouth "wings" are
MASTER CRUMMLES, *waiting to enter as* BALTHAZAR, *and*
SMIKE, *waiting to go on as the* APOTHECARY. SMIKE *is*
concentrating very hard, mumbling through his lines.

ROMEO.
   If I may trust the flattering truth of sleep,
   My dreams presage some joyful news at hand.

   "Enter" BALTHAZAR.

   News from Verona! How fares Juliet?
   For nothing can be ill if she be well.

BALTHAZAR.
   · Then she is well, and nothing can be ill.
   Her body sleeps in Capel's monument,
   And her immortal part with angels lives.

ROMEO.
   Is it e'en so? Then I defy you, stars!
   Thou knowest my lodgings. Get me ink and paper
   And hire post-horses. I'll be with you straight.

   Exit BALTHAZAR.

   Well, Juliet, I will lie with thee tonight.
   Let's see for means. O mischief, thou art swift
   To enter in the thoughts of desperate men!
   I do remember an apothecary,
   And hereabouts 'a dwells, which late I noted
   In tatt'red weeds, with overwhelming brows,
   Culling of simples. This should be the house.
   What, ho! Apothecary!

   Pause. SMIKE *has been concentrating so hard, he's missed his*
   cue. NICHOLAS *repeats.*

   What, ho! Apothecary!

   SMIKE *rushes on, and bellows out.*

APOTHECARY. WHO CALLS SO LOUD?

And NICHOLAS *leads him away, as* RALPH *brings* KATE
downstage.

KATE. And as the door of her carriage was closed, a comb fell
   from Kate's hair, close to her uncle's feet; and as he picked it
   up and returned it into her hand, the light from a neighbouring
   lamp shone upon her face.

RALPH. The lock of hair that had escaped and curled loosely over her brow, the traces of tears yet scarcely dry, the flushed cheek, the look of sorrow, all fired some dormant train of recollection in the old man's breast; and the face of his dead brother seemed present before him, with the very look it wore on some occasion of boyish grief, of which every minute circumstance flashed upon his mind, with the distinctness of a scene of yesterday.

NEWMAN NOGGS *appears.*

NOGGS. And Ralph Nickleby, who was proof against all appeals of blood and kindred — who was steeled against every tale of sorrow and distress — staggered while he looked, and reeled back into the house, as a man who had seen a spirit from a world beyond the grave.

Darkness.

Scene Eighteen

The stage of the Portsmouth Theatre. A tatty, Crummlesian set for the last scene of Romeo and Juliet. Downstage, MISS SNEVELLICCI — as JULIET — and MR LENVILLE — as TYBALT — lie on couches, as if dead. Upstage, a badly painted cut-out of two arches, and behind that, a backcloth of Verona.

A note on this scene: There is much opportunity here for making the point that the Crummles Company are a troupe of not-very-good actors and actresses who have to rehearse plays very quickly, and therefore do not always get everything sorted out beforehand. Enter MR BANE as PARIS and MISS BELVAWNEY as his PAGE.

PARIS.
Give me thy torch. Do as I bid thee, go.

PAGE *(aside).*
I am almost afraid to stand alone
Here in the churchyard; yet I will adventure.

PARIS.
Sweet flower, with flowers thy bridal bed I strew
Which with sweet water nightly I will dew;

The PAGE *whistles.*

The boy gives warning something doth approach.

PARIS *retires. Enter* NICHOLAS *as* ROMEO, *and* MASTER

CRUMMLES *as* BALTHAZAR, *with a mattock and a crow of iron.*

ROMEO.
Give me that mattock and the wrenching iron.
Give me the light. Therefore hence, be gone.
Live, and be prosperous, and farewell, good fellow.

BALTHAZAR (*aside*).
For all this same, I'll hide me hereabout.
His looks I fear, and his intents I doubt.

BALTHAZAR *retires.* ROMEO, *opening the tomb.*

ROMEO.
Thou detestable maw, thou womb of death,
Gorged with the dearest morsel of the earth.

PARIS *strides forward.*

PARIS.
Stop thy unhallowed toil, vile Montague!
Condemned villain, I do apprehend thee.

ROMEO.
Good gentle youth, tempt not a desperate man,
By urging me to fury. O, be gone!

PARIS.
I apprehend thee for a felon here.

ROMEO.
Wilt thou provoke me! Then, have at thee, boy!

PARIS' PAGE.
Oh, lord, they fight! I will go call the watch.

PARIS *falls.*

PARIS.
Oh, I am slain! If thou be merciful,
Open the tomb, and lay me with Juliet.

He shuts his eyes.

ROMEO.
In faith I will. Let me peruse thy face.
Mercutio's kinsman, noble County Paris!

Pulling PARIS' *body into the tomb.*

I'll bury thee in a triumphant grave.
A grave? Oh, no, a lanthorn, slaughtered youth.

Dropping PARIS' *body and running to* JULIET.

For here lies Juliet, and her beauty makes
This vault a feasting presence full of light.
Tybalt, liest thou there in thy bloody sheet?
Why art thou yet so fair? Shall I believe
That unsubstantial death is amorous.
For fear of that I still will stay with thee
With worms that are thy chambermaids. O, here
Will I set up my ever lasting rest.
Here's to my love! Thus with a kiss I die.

He drinks the poison and kisses JULIET. *Outside the tomb,*
enter MR FLUGGERS *as* FRIAR LAWRENCE. *He carries a*
crow and spade.

FRIAR.
St Francis be my speed! How now! Who's there!

BALTHAZAR.
Here's one, a friend, and one that knows you well.

FRIAR.
Alack, alack, what blood is this which stains
The stony entrance of this sepulchre?

BALTHAZAR.
Then what I took to be a dream is true,
And – further horror – I did hear him speak
Of some fell liquor that with venomous speed
Would him to death's black bosom swift despatch.

FRIAR.
Then all is lost! Juliet still sleeps –
What unkind hour is guilty of this chance!
The watch approaches, we must fast away;
Come, come, good friend, we dare no longer stay.

The FRIAR *and* BALTHAZAR *run out. In the tomb,* JULIET
wakes.

JULIET.
What's here? A cup, closed in my true love's hand?
Poison, I see, hath been his timeless end.
Oh, churl! Drunk all, and left no friendly drop
To help me after? What, and Paris too?

JULIET *goes to* PARIS's *body.*

Oh, County, that would take my maidenhead:
Lie there, thy dagger rests in Juliet's bed.

JULIET *about to stab herself with* PARIS's *dagger.* ROMEO *sits up.*

ROMEO.
Hold, hold! I live!

JULIET.
What, Romeo, not dead?

ROMEO.
The pothac's poison coursed throughout my veins
A dizzy drowsiness which I mistook
For that numb torpor which doth presage death,
But in an instant it has passed. What, Juliet?

JULIET.
Oh, Romeo, thou starts. I am not dead
For I too drank a draught of fluid that
Had longer but the same benign effect!

The WATCHMAN, *played by* MR PAILEY, *the comic countryman, appears.*

WATCHMAN.
What's there? Who's that within! What's there! What ho!
Come, lights! Come, malting hooks! Look! Here! Look, ho!

ROMEO.
We are approached.

Enter the PRINCE, *played by* MR WAGSTAFF, *the drunken, virtuous old man. Falling to his knee.*

WATCHMAN.
Good morrow, noble Prince.

PRINCE.
What calls our person from our morning rest?

He goes into the tomb. The WATCHMAN *stands. Enter* CRUMMLES *as* CAPULET.

CAPULET.
What should it be, that is so shrieked abroad?

He goes into the tomb. Enter MRS CRUMMLES *as* LADY CAPULET, *and* JULIET'S LITTLE BROTHER, *played by* MASTER P. CRUMMLES, *and* PETER, *played by* MR FOLAIR.

LADY CAPULET.
What fear is this which startles in our ears?

They go into the tomb.

PRINCE.
Ah, Romeo!

JULIET'S BROTHER.
Oh, sister!

LADY CAPULET.
Paris!

PETER.
Slain!

CAPULET.
What strange reversal hath this morning brought,
With Romeo returned —

LADY CAPULET.
He having fled,
Dead Juliet alive,

CAPULET.
Quick Paris dead.

PARIS *sits up*.

PARIS.
Not dead so much as stunned, for Romeo's blow
Deflected from my heart, did but a moment give
The appearance and accoutrements of death.

JULIET.
As with my potion!

ROMEO.
And the pothac's draught!

Enter the irascible MR BLIGHTEY *as* MONTAGUE, MRS
LENVILLE *as* LADY MONTAGUE, MISS GAZINGI *as an*
ATTENDANT, *and the* PHENOMENON *as* ROMEO'S
LITTLE SISTER.

MONTAGUE.
What's this? The people cry of blackest death,

LADY MONTAGUE.
Some others of deliverance divine,

MONTAGUE.
Talk both of grief and joy's on every breath:

Enter MISS LEDROOK *as* ROSALINE.

ROSALINE.
Oh Romeo!

ROMEO.
Good heavens.

To JULIET.

Rosaline.

Pause. MR WAGSTAFF's *attention has wandered.* MRS
GRUDDEN's *head appears from the prompt corner.*

MRS GRUDDEN. But mourning –

PRINCE.
But mourning flowers now adorn a festival,
And merry peals o'ertake the tolls of funeral.

ROMEO.
'Tis true, our joy demands a cheerful bell:
Oh, Mother, Father, Sister mine as well!

ROMEO *embraces his* LITTLE SISTER. *Pause. Someone nudges*
MR WAGSTAFF.

PRINCE.
Who's there?

Enter the FRIAR, *who throws himself to the ground before the*
PRINCE.

FRIAR.
Dread sovereign, in guilty flight
I did attempt to 'scape your wrathful judgement.
But conscience stayed my steps, and turned them round,
And, penitent, I here abase myself.

PRINCE.
What, penitent? There is no crime, stand, see!
All those in chains of death are unbound, free.

FRIAR.
What joy! Then further tidings I must tell,
For on my hurried passage, I did meet
Another whom the jaws of death let go:
See, here, Prince, is your kin, Mercutio!

Enter MR HETHERINGTON, *the swaggerer, as* MERCUTIO,
and MISS BRAVASSA, *dressed as a man, as* BENVOLIO.

CAPULET.
Mercutio! Recover'd!

MERCUTIO.
Ay, sirs, ay,

For though thought dead, and bourn for balming up
My friend Benvolio observed a breath
Of slight proportion on my countenance
And I was taken to a nearby town,
Where I was cured by surgeons of renown.

FRIAR.
And further news comes with him. Speak, Benvolio!

Pause. FOLAIR *shrugs to* MISS BRAVASSA, *who shrugs, and points at* MR WAGSTAFF.

MRS GRUDDEN (*appearing again.*) Yes, yes —

PRINCE.
Yes, yes, Benvolio, speak.

BENVOLIO.
I shall, my lord,
But 'tis a tale I fear will try thy patience,
But I swear 'tis true. My friends know, oft
In their society have I been told
In jest, I am too gentle for our revels,
And almost feminine in countenance,
With not a hair of manhood on my chin.
Oft has it been so said; and I have laughed,
And spoken gruff, and slapped my thigh, to counter it.
But now deception's o'er, and I confess
That from this same near town I once did flee,
Pursuant of a love that fate denied,
And so t'effect my passage, took myself
The form and outward clothing of that sex
To which my love but not myself belongs.

BENVOLIO *reaches up, takes off his cap, and lets fall her long hair.*

From nature let deceit no more disbar:
Benvolio become Benvolia!

PARIS.
Ah me.

CAPULET.
Ah?

LADY CAPULET.
You?

BENVOLIA.
　Ay, sirs, 'tis he,
　Who thus from fell disguise releases me.
PRINCE.
　So everything is done —
　Enter PARIS' PAGE, *followed by* BALTHAZAR *and the*
　APOTHECARY.
PAGE.
　What Paris? Oh!
　Hath sweet concord o'ertaken —
BALTHAZAR.
　Romeo!
　Upon the road, in flight, I did perchance
　To come upon this wizened, withered man,
　Who hobbling was along the way from Mantua,
　And asked where he might find a desperate man
　Who might have bought a deathly liquid from him.
　From your description I resolved it was
　That self-same wretch from whom you bought the dram
　Of poison in that self-same town. I asked
　What was his purpose, and he told me straight,
　The darkness, and his age, and dread infirmity,
　Had caused him to prepare not poison, but
　An harmless cordial, of sharp effect
　But of no lasting peril.
　BALTHAZAR notices everything else.
　Oh. What's this?
ROMEO.
　Good Balthazar, all matters are resolved,
　And good apothecary, thy mischance
　Has proved the most enduring, happy circumstance.
PRINCE.
　And now at last may tocsin loudly ring?
　And tabor sound? And minstrels sweetly sing?
ROMEO.
　Yes, yes. All's concluded. Everything is done.
　The COMPANY *is leaving the tomb, when* LADY CAPULET
　runs to the corpse of TYBALT, *and cradles it in her arms.*
LADY CAPULET.
　But what of Tybalt? Tybalt, still lies locked
　Within the dread embrace of dreader death.

CAPULET.
  Why, come, dear wife, a half an hour ago,
  We'd thought a half-a-dozen kin were slain.
  Let grievance cease, let Tybalt's bones remain.

LADY CAPULET.
  Yes, let it be.

  She drops TYBALT *back on the slab. This gesture hurts* MR
  LENVILLE's *head.*

  Let Tybalt lie there.
  And to a merry dance let us repair.

PRINCE.
  A blooming peace this morning with it brings,
  The sun for happiness shines forth his head,
  Go hence, to have more talk of happy things,
  All shall be pardoned, and none punished.
  For never was a story better set
  Than this of Romeo and his Juliet.

  Blackout. The CRUMMLES COMPANY *form up for their
  curtain call, except for* MRS CRUMMLES, *and – if they are in
  the* COMPANY – *the actors who play* SQUEERS, YOUNG
  WACKFORD *and* BROOKER. *The lights come up, for the*
  COMPANY's *curtain call. Then they go down again, and* MRS
  CRUMMLES *enters as* BRITANNIA, *with helment and union
  flag. The lights come up, and with them, the music of the
  Crummles' closing song.*

MRS CRUMMLES.
  England, arise:
  Join in the new chorus!
  It is a new-made song you should be singing.
  See in the skies,
  Fluttering before us,
  What the bright bird of peace is bringing.

CRUMMLES COMPANY.
  See upon our smiling land,
  Where the wealths of nations stand,
  Where Prosperity and Industry walk ever hand in hand.
  Where so many blessings crowd,
  'Tis our duty to be proud:
  Up and answer, English yeomen, sing it joyfully aloud!
  Evermore upon our country,

God will pour his rich increase:
And victorious in war shall be made glorious in peace.

*And the Crummles' closing song becomes our closing song, and
the rest of our* COMPANY *enter:* KATE, MRS NICKLEBY,
MR *and* MRS LILLYVICK; SQUEERS, YOUNG WACKFORD
and one or more DOTHEBOYS HALL BOYS; THE
MANTALINIS; *available* KENWIGS; SIR MATTHEW
PUPKER, HAWK, VERISOPHT *and* RALPH, *representing High
Society;* MR CROWL, NOGGS *and the ragged beggar*
BROOKER *representing the low. And in the middle,*
NICHOLAS *and* SMIKE *triumphant; as the Song moves to its
climax.*

WHOLE COMPANY.
See each one do what he can
To further God's almighty plan:
The beneficence of heaven help the skilfulness of man.

Every garner filled with grain,
Every meadow blest with rain,
Rich and fertile is the golden corn that bears and bears again.

Where so many blessings crowd,
Tis our duty to be proud:
Up and answer, English yeomen, sing it joyfully aloud!

Evermore upon our country
God will pour his rich increase:
And victorious in war shall be made glorious in peace.

END OF PART ONE.

The Life and Adventures of Nicholas Nickleby

from the novel by Charles Dickens

PART TWO

ACT ONE

Scene One

The whole COMPANY *assembles on stage. A* NARRATOR *steps forward, to start the re-cap of the story of Part One.*

NARRATOR. The story so far. There once lived, in a sequestered part of the county of Devonshire,

MISS NICKLEBY. A mother,

KATE. And a daughter,

NICHOLAS. And a son,

NARRATORS.
 Who, recently bereaved, were forced to journey up to London,

 And to throw themselves upon the mercy of their only living relative, Ralph Nickleby.

RALPH. All three of 'em in London, damn 'em.

NOGGS. He'd growled to his clerk,

RALPH. And you, sir? You're prepared to work?

NARRATORS.
 He'd demanded of his nephew,

 And receiving the firm answer

NICHOLAS. Yes!

NARRATORS. Ralph took Young Nicholas and found him a position in a school in Yorkshire run by

SQUEERS. Mr Wackford Squeers.

NICHOLAS. Well, thank you, uncle. I will not forget this kindness.

NARRATOR. And arriving at the school, he met with

MRS SQUEERS. Mrs Squeers,

FANNY. Their daughter Fanny,

YOUNG WACKFORD. Their son young Wackford,

NARRATOR. And their poor drudge:

MRS SQUEERS. Smike!

NARRATORS.
 And forty boys,

 With pale and haggard faces,

Lank and bony figures,

Children with the countenances of old men,

All darkened with the scowl of sullen, dogged suffering.

SQUEERS. So – what d'you say?

BOYS. For what we have received, may the Lord make us truly thankful.

NARRATORS.
Meanwhile, in London,

Nicholas' sister Kate

Was found employment by her uncle

MISS KNAG. At the millinery establishment,

MADAME MANTALINI. Of Mr Mantalini,

MANTALINI. And his demned, engaging, captivating little Venus

MILLINER. Of a wife.

NARRATOR. She and her mother were taken from their lodgings in the Strand

MISS LA CREEVY. And from their friend and landlady, the portrait painter Miss La Creevy

NARRATOR. To a grim and meagre house nearby the Thames.

NOGGS. I'm sure, although it looks a little gloomy, that it can be made, quite –

KATE. Yes.

NARRATOR. While, up in Yorkshire, Nicholas took tea with Fanny Squeers

TILDA. Her best friend Tilda Price

JOHN. And her bluff beau John Browdie

NARRATOR. And tried to make it absolutely plain to everyone that his supposed affection for Miss Squeers

NICHOLAS. Is the grossest and most wild delusion that a human being ever laboured under or committed.

NARRATOR. A statement which did not improve his status at the school –

FANNY. Oh, sir, I pity you –

NARRATOR. Any more than did his firm resolve to stop the thrashing of the poor drudge Smike –

NICHOLAS. Uh – this must stop.

NARRATOR. His beating of the schoolmaster himself –

MRS SQUEERS. Get off him! Off him, monster!

NARRATOR. Or his and poor Smike's escape with the assistance of John Browdie,

JOHN. Eh? What? Beat the schoolmaster?

NARRATORS.
    To London,
    Where their new friend Newman Noggs

NOGGS. Was making up the number and the punch

    At a party given by the Kenwigses downstairs.

KENWIGS. That's Mr –

MRS KENWIGS. Mrs –

MR LILLYVICK. And the latter's uncle, Mr Lillyvick, the collector of the water-rate –

NARRATOR. And the latter's uncle's fancy –

MISS PETOWKER. Miss Petowker of the Theatre Royal, Drury Lane.

NICHOLAS. Three friends.

NARRATOR. Said Nicholas,

NICHOLAS. Three friends, in all the world. That bluff young fellow up in Yorkshire, Smike; yourself; and Mr Noggs our benefactor. And it is enough. It is indeed.

KATE. I won't believe it,

NARRATOR. Kate cried to her uncle, who had heard of everything from Fanny Squeers.

NICHOLAS. It is untrue,

NARRATOR. Insisted Nicholas.

MRS NICKLEBY. I don't know what to think,

NARRATOR. Said Mrs Nickleby.

RALPH. Then I'll renounce you all –

NARRATORS.
    Announced their uncle.
    And Nicholas was forced to leave his family once again . . .

NICHOLAS. Or else . . . you're destitute.

NARRATOR. And he and Smike then journeyed south to Portsmouth, with the thought perhaps, of going on board ship, and little knowing what in fact did lie in store for them.

CRUMMLES. Yes, I am Vincent Crummles, and I am in the theatrical profession, my wife is in the theatrical profession, and my children are in the theatrical profession.

NICHOLAS. What?

CRUMMLES (*handing scripts to* NICHOLAS). And you can study Romeo, and Rover too, of course, you might as well, while you're about it, Cassio . . .

NARRATORS.
And also an array of histrionic talent
That has never been assembled in one place
And on one stage before!

OTHER NARRATORS. Or since.

SMIKE. The stage!

MRS GRUDDEN. Stand by!

We are now beginning to transform into the next scene.

KATE. And Kate,

NARRATOR. In London,

MISS KNAG. Lost her situation with the millinery establishment.

NARRATORS.
While Nicholas,
In Portsmouth,

MISS SNEVELLICCI. Found *his* increasingly congenial.

KATE. And Kate was invited by her uncle to a private party

RALPH. For some gentlemen with whom he was connected in a business matter.

NICHOLAS. While Nicholas was witness to the secret nuptials of Mr Lillyvick and Miss Petowker,

MISS PETOWKER. Lately – of the Theatre Royal, Drury Lane.

NICHOLAS *and* SMIKE *slip out.*

NARRATOR. And at her uncle's, poor Kate was subjected to attentions that were neither honourable nor welcome –

VERISOPHT. How d'ye do, Miss Nickleby.

HAWK. Oh, come on, now, be more natural, Miss Nickleby, more natural, please . . .

NARRATORS.
  While, back in Portsmouth,
  Nicholas and Smike
  Went on from strength to strength,
  And it seemed
  For at least that moment
  That their troubles and misfortunes were at last, behind them.

  SMIKE *enters in his Apothecary costume, with NICHOLAS, carrying his Romeo costume.*

SMIKE (*raptly*). Who calls so loud?

NICHOLAS. Who calls so loud.

  And we are in the next scene.

Scene Two

Portsmouth Theatre. Backstage. It is immediately after the Crummles' triumphant performance of Romeo and Juliet. MRS GRUDDEN *drags a clothes rail across the stage. The rest of the* COMPANY *are around, packing their costumes and props, preparing to go.*

MRS GRUDDEN. All called at ten. Theatre now closing. Have you no homes to go to?

  SMIKE *happily lopes off to give his costume to* MRS GRUDDEN. LENVILLE, *who is clearly in some passion, is haranguing a doubtful-looking* FOLAIR, *as* MISS SNEVELLICCI *glides over to* NICHOLAS.

MISS SNEVELLICCI. Well, Mr Johnson.

NICHOLAS. Ah, Miss Snevellicci.

MISS SNEVELLICCI. Mr Johnson, I have asked some members of the company, to come to supper, Sunday. My father, and my dear mama, are to visit me in Portsmouth, and I am sure will be dying to behold you.

NICHOLAS. Well, I'm sure I –

MISS SNEVELLICCI. And the Lillyvicks have now returned from honeymoon, and are so keen to see you once again.

NICHOLAS. Dear Miss Snevellicci, I can require no possible inducement, beyond your invitation.

MISS SNEVELLICCI. Oh, Mr Johnson. How you — how you talk.

The MISSES BRAVASSA *and* GAZINGI *cross the stage, as* MISS SNEVELLICCI *graciously withdraws and* FOLAIR, *leaving* LENVILLE *drifts over to* NICHOLAS.

MISS BRAVASSA. So I said to Mr Crummles, that it's him or me —

MISS GAZINGI. Well, I said, if he does that trip again, once more, I'll kill him.

FOLAIR. Well, Johnson. Yet another great performance.

NICHOLAS (*thinking he was referring to* MISS SNEVELLICCI). Was it?

Realising he isn't.

Oh. You think so?

FOLAIR. Yes. Oh, yes. And Mr Digby. After all the pains you took, with his rehearsal.

SMIKE *is having a whale of a time, in conversation with* MR BLIGHTEY *and* MISS LEDROOK.

NICHOLAS. Well, he deserves all the help and kindness I can give him.

FOLAIR. He is a little — odd, though, isn't he?

NICHOLAS. He is, God help him.

FOLAIR. And devilish close. Nobody can get anything out of him.

NICHOLAS. What *should* they get?

FOLAIR. Zooks, Johnson! I'm only talking of natural curiosity. Of who you are, and who he is, and if indeed your name is really Mr Johnson, and if Digby's Digby, and if not —

NICHOLAS. Whose — natural curiosity?

FOLAIR. Oh, Johnson, it's just jealousy, you know, theatricals, I tell them, after all, what if you had, escaped from gaol or something of that sort, or —

LENVILLE *is now standing watching* FOLAIR *and* NICHOLAS, *surrounded by other men.*

LENVILLE. Well, Tommy, have you told him?

FOLAIR. Oh.

Slight pause.

NICHOLAS. Um — told me what?

FOLAIR (*whispering*). Oh, it's just that, since you joined, you see, old Lenville never gets the rounds he used to, and you get a couple every scene . . .

LENVILLE. Well, Tommy?

FOLAIR (*still whispering*). And then the final insult, Tybalt, after all . . .

NICHOLAS. Go on.

FOLAIR. Go on.

Breathes deeply.

Now, Mr Johnson, I'm to tell you, Mr Lenville's ire will not be brooked.

NICHOLAS. That's Mr Lenville's what?

FOLAIR. He naturally, presents his compliments, via me, and informs you that it's his intention –

To LENVILLE.

Now?

MR LENVILLE *nods.*

Intention, now to pull your nose in front of all the company.

NICHOLAS. To pull my nose?

FOLAIR. That's right.

NICHOLAS. Folair, I've half a mind to pull your nose for saying so.

FOLAIR (*whispering*). Now, come on, Johnson –

LENVILLE *strides forward.*

LENVILLE. Right.

He takes a step or two towards NICHOLAS, *and then strikes a pose.*

Object of my scorn and hatred. I hold you in the most rank contempt.

LENVILLE *adjusts his cuff, walks over, and is promptly knocked down by* NICHOLAS. MRS LENVILLE *utters a scream and runs to the prone* MR LENVILLE, *and falls on him.*

MRS LENVILLE. Lenville! Dear, my Lenville.

LENVILLE (*raising his head*). Do you see this, monster? Do you see this?

NICHOLAS (*walking over*). What? Oh, yes. Well, now, why don't you apologise for all this nonsense, and we'll say no more about it.

LENVILLE. Never!

MRS LENVILLE. Yes, yes, for my sake, Lenville, please, unless you'd see your wife a blasted corpse, dead at your feet!

LENVILLE. This is affecting. Yes, the ties of nature. The weak husband, and the father that is yet to be . . . relents.

NICHOLAS. Well, then, very good. And p'raps, sir, you'll be very careful, to what lengths your envy carries you another time, before you've ascertained your rival's temper.

And NICHOLAS *picks up* LENVILLE's *cane and breaks it across his knee, dusts his hands, and walks over to the exit, where he bumps into the entrance of* CRUMMLES, MRS CRUMMLES *and the* INFANT PHENOMENON.

MRS CRUMMLES. Mr Johnson. Pray, pray, what is going on?

NICHOLAS. Oh, Mrs Crummles. Well –

MRS CRUMMLES. It is past midnight.

MRS GRUDDEN *crossing*.

MRS GRUDDEN. Everybody out!

MRS CRUMMLES (*to everyone*). We have performances to give. Upon the morrow. We must be prepared. Have slept. And rested. Run through our lines. Mused on our dance steps. And rehearsed our songs. Resolved to act a little better. Sobered up.

Varied mumblings.

BLIGHTEY. Yes, well . . .

MISS BRAVASSA. Certainly . . .

MRS CRUMMLES (*sweeping all before her*). So, now, stand not upon the order of your going. Go. Be off. Be absent. Now. Begone.

The COMPANY *disappear, except for* CRUMMLES, SMIKE *and* NICHOLAS.

CRUMMLES. Ah, Johnson. What a woman.

NICHOLAS. Yes. I'm sorry, Mr Crummles –

CRUMMLES. No. No, no.

Pause.

Sometimes, I think, the strain, the running of a company . . . .
Sometimes, I think, we're not immortal, Johnson. Even Mrs
Crummles. Sometimes I think, to settle down, a plot of land, we
might bequeath to those who follow us . . .

Pause.

But, then. We're strolling players, Johnson. Outcasts. Rogues
and vagabonds. That is our lot. We carry on.

MRS CRUMMLES *reappears.*

MRS CRUMMLES. Well, Vincent?

CRUMMLES (*more cheerfully*). Yes. We carry on.

CRUMMLES *goes out with* MRS CRUMMLES.

SMIKE. Outcast.

NICHOLAS. No, Smike. Not any more.

Slight pause.

Oh, Smike. I wish that this was over.

SMIKE. What's the matter?

NICHOLAS. Smike, I'm worried. And I've written to our dear
friend Newman Noggs. To ask him of my mother and my sister.

SMIKE. Worried. Why?

NICHOLAS. Because . . . Because I have an enemy. He's rich and
powerful, and he's done me many wrongs.

SMIKE. What is his name?

NICHOLAS. He is my uncle. His name's Ralph Nickleby.

SMIKE. I'll learn that name by heart. Ralph Nickleby.

SMIKE *notices* LENVILLE's *stick and picks it up.*

You beat my enemy.

NICHOLAS. Oh, Smike. The time that we've spent dallying here.

MISS SNEVELLICCI *and* MISS LEDROOK, *in their street
clothes, stand there.*

MISS SNEVELLICCI. Oh, Mr Johnson.

NICHOLAS. Ah, Miss Snevellicci.

Slight pause.

Might I have the privilege . . . escort you home?

MISS SNEVELLICCI *puts out her arm.*

MISS SNEVELLICCI. With the very greatest pleasure, Mr Johnson.

NICHOLAS *takes* MISS SNEVELLICCI's *arm and leads her out.* SMIKE — *in imitation — takes the arm of* MISS LEDROOK *and leads her out too.*

Scene Three

Regent St., London. A sofa, on which SIR MULBERRY HAWK *and* LORD FREDERICK VERISOPHT *are asleep. Debris around them.* MR PLUCK *and* MR PYKE *explain.*

PYKE. The place:

PLUCK. A handsome suite of private apartments in Regent Street. The time:

PYKE. Three o'clock in the afternoon to the dull and plodding —

PLUCK. The first hour of the morning to the gay and spirited. The persons: one: Lord Frederick Verisopht.

PYKE. And two: his friend, the gay Sir Mulberry Hawk.

The two men note the debris.

PLUCK. Two billiard balls, all mud and dirt.

PYKE. A champagne bottle, with a soiled glove twisted round the neck,

PLUCK. To allow it to be grasped more firmly in its capacity as an offensive weapon. A broken cane —

PYKE. An empty purse —

PLUCK. A handful of silver, mingled with fragments of half-smoked cigars,

PYKE. All hinting at the nature of last night's gentlemanly frolics.

Pause. Then LORD VERISOPHT *wakes.*

VERISOPHT. What's that?

HAWK (*waking*). What's what?

VERISOPHT. What's that you said?

HAWK. I didn't.

VERISOPHT. Yes, you did. Last night. You said something. About, eight hours ago.

Slight pause.

And then I fell asleep.

HAWK. Perhaps . . . I do recall. Uh – Nickleby.

VERISOPHT. The moneylender or the niece?

HAWK. The niece, of course.

VERISOPHT. Ah, yes. The niece.

VERISOPHT sits up. Shortly.

You promised me you'd find her out.

HAWK. I did. But thinking of it. You should find her out yourself.

VERISOPHT. Who, me? Why? How?

HAWK (*sits up*). Just ask her uncle. Say to Nickleby, you must know where she lives, or else you'll cease to be his customer. That's if you're that concerned.

VERISOPHT. Oh, I am, that concerned. Upon my soul, Hawk, she's a perfect beauty, a – a picture. 'Pon my soul, she is.

HAWK. Well, if you think so –

VERISOPHT. You thought so. You were thick enough with her that night at Nickleby's.

HAWK. Oh, just enough for once. But hardly worth the trouble to be agreeable again.

Pause. He stands.

So. Shall we go?

VERISOPHT (*stands*). Let's go.

As they turn to go, the two men notice MR PLUCK and MR PYKE.

PLUCK. Good morning.

PYKE. Good morning.

HAWK. Good morning, Pyke.

VERISOPHT. Good morning, Mr Pluck.

VERISOPHT and HAWK walk out uneasily.

PYKE. And so Sir Mulberry accompanied his pupil, young Lord Verisopht,

PLUCK. to old Ralph Nickleby's at Golden Square.

Scene Four

A drawing room in Sloane St. A chaise longue, a small table with a bell, and two chairs. Enter KATE *and* MRS NICKLEBY.

KATE. As, meanwhile, Miss Kate Nickleby herself,

MISS NICKLEBY. And her mother Mrs Nickleby,

NARRATORS.

Set off from their mean lodgings in the East End for Cadogan Place, off Sloane St.

Cadogan Place:

With the air and semblances of loftiest rank,

But the realities of middle station;

Cadogan Place: the one great bond that joins two great extremes;

The link between the aristocratic pavements of Belgravia

And the barbarism of Chelsea.

Upon this doubtful ground lived Mrs Julia Wititterly,

Whose advertisement for a companion had been read that day by Mrs Nickleby,

MRS NICKLEBY. In a newspaper of the very first respectability.

MRS WITITTERLY, *a delicate woman in her late 30s, is reclining on the chaise longue,* MRS NICKLEBY *and* KATE *sit on the chairs, and the page,* ALPHONSE, *stands in attendance.* ALPHONSE *wears his wig and livery untidily. He doesn't much like being called Alphonse, either.*

MRS WITITTERLY. Now leave the room, Alphonse.

ALPHONSE. Or right.

ALPHONSE *goes.*

KATE. I have ventured to call, ma'am, from having seen your advertisement.

MRS WITITTERLY. Yes . . . One of my people put it in the paper.

Pause.

KATE. If you've already —

MRS WITITTERLY. Oh, dear, no. I am not so easily suited. Dear me, no. Well, I really don't know what to say. How is your temper?

KATE. Well, I hope it's good.

MRS WITITTERLY. You have a respectable reference for everything?

KATE. I have.

As she places a card on Mrs Wititterly's table, MRS WITITTERLY *glowers at her through her eyeglasses.*

Mr Ralph Nickleby. My uncle.

MRS WITITTERLY (*ringing her little bell*). I like, I do like your appearance.

Enter ALPHONSE.

Alphonse, request your master to come here.

ALPHONSE. *Please.*

A look from MRS WITITTERLY. ALPHONSE *goes.*

MRS WITITTERLY. Now, you have never actually been a companion before?

MRS NICKLEBY *can stay silent no longer.*

MRS NICKLEBY. No, not to any stranger, ma'am, but she has been a companion to me for some years. I am her mother, ma'am.

MRS WITITTERLY. Oh, yes. I apprehend you.

MRS NICKLEBY. I assure you, ma'am, that I very little thought at one time that it would be necessary for my daughter to go out into the world at all, for her poor dear papa was an independent gentleman, and would have been so now if he had listened to my entreaties –

KATE. Please, mama.

MRS NICKLEBY. My dear Kate, if you will allow me, I shall take the liberty –

She is interrupted by the entry of MR WITITTERLY.

MR WITITTERLY (*to* MRS WITITTERLY). Yes? My love?

MRS WITITTERLY (*with a vague gesture*). Companion. And her mother.

MR WITITTERLY. Oh, yes. Yes, this is a most important matter. For Mrs Wititterly is of a very excitable nature, very delicate, very fragile: one could describe, a hothouse plant; one could say, an exotic.

MRS WITITTERLY. Oh, now, Henry, dear.

MR WITITTERLY. You are, my love, you know you are. One breath and —

He blows, as if a feather.

Phoo, you're gone.

MRS WITITTERLY *sighs.*

Your soul is too large for your body. Your intellect wears you out, and all the doctors say so. "My dear doctor", said I to Sir Tumley Snuffim in this very room, "dear doctor, what's my wife's complaint? Please tell me, I can bear it." "My dear fellow", he replied, "be proud of her, that woman. Her complaint is soul."

MRS WITITTERLY. You make me out worse than I am, now, Henry.

MR WITITTERLY. I do not, Julia, do not: think, my dear, the night you danced with the baronet's nephew at the election ball at Exeter. It was tremendous!

MRS WITITTERLY (*to* KATE). Yes, I always suffer for these triumphs afterwards.

MR WITITTERLY. My wife is sought after by glittering crowds and brilliant circles. She's excited by the opera, the drama, the fine arts.

MRS WITITTERLY. Henry, hush —

MR WITITTERLY. I'll say no more. I merely mention it to demonstrate that you are not an ordinary person, that there is a constant friction going on between your mind and body, that you must be soothed and tended, and that you must have a companion, in whom there is gentleness, great sweetness, an excess of sympathy, and of course, complete repose.

MRS WITITTERLY. I am decided, Henry, that Miss Nickleby would be quite suitable. Now, I'm growing weary. Please . . .

MR WITITTERLY. Yes, of course.

To KATE.

So, can you start tomorrow?

KATE. Yes, that would be most convenient.

MR WITITTERLY. Then that is settled.

MRS WITITTERLY. And in the evening you will join us to the opera.

MR WITITTERLY. And Alphonse will appear to show you out.

MR WITITTERLY *leads out* MRS WITITTERLY.

MRS NICKLEBY. They are distinguished people, certainly.

KATE. You think so?

MRS NICKLEBY. She is pale, however, and looks much exhausted. I do hope she isn't . . . wearing herself out.

KATE. What do you mean?

MRS NICKLEBY. Oh, just . . . if suddenly the gentleman became a widower, and, after some appropriate elapse of time, decided to remarry, and, of course, with you engaged here –

KATE (*getting it*). Oh, mama! You are impossible.

ALPHONSE *enters to show the ladies out.*

ALPHONSE. This way.

Scene Five

Ralph's office and Noggs' room. RALPH sits at his desk, a watch to his ear. NOGGS is on his high stool.

NARRATOR. And at the very moment that they left Cadogan Place, in Golden Square, Kate's uncle Ralph sat in his office, being stared at through the little grubby window by his clerk,

RALPH *rings a little handbell on his desk.*

Who heard the bell, and went to answer it.

NOGGS *goes round into Ralph's office.*

RALPH. How now?

NOGGS (*turns to go*). I thought you rang. I'm sorry.

RALPH. Stop. I did ring.

NOGGS. Yes. What for?

RALPH. I called to say my watch had stopped.

NOGGS. I'm sorry.

RALPH. And to know the time.

NOGGS. It's half past three. Perhaps it isn't wound.

RALPH. It is.

NOGGS. Or overwound, then.

RALPH. That can't be.

NOGGS. Must be. It's stopped.

RALPH. Well, then. Perhaps it is.

HAWK, VERISOPHT, PLUCK and PYKE appear in Noggs' office. HAWK rings the bell.

That is the bell.

NOGGS. It is.

RALPH. Then answer it.

NOGGS goes out and is passed by HAWK, VERISOPHT, PLUCK and PYKE. There is some acidity between RALPH and HAWK.

RALPH. Gentlemen. Good afternoon.

HAWK. Is it?

RALPH. Ah. A late night. But, I trust, a pleasurable one.

VERISOPHT *(joking)*. Well, an expensive one, at any rate. I'm fearful, Nickleby. I shall be drawing on your generosity again.

A look from HAWK to RALPH.

RALPH. Oh, if . . .

VERISOPHT. And now, concerned with that, I'd like a word with you.

RALPH. Um . . . Certainly.

HAWK, PYKE and PLUCK withdraw a little.

What is it then, my lord?

VERISOPHT. Your niece, sir.

RALPH. So, what of her?

VERISOPHT. She's a devilish pretty girl. You can't deny it.

RALPH. I believe she is considered so.

VERISOPHT. Look, Nickleby, I want another peek at her. And you must tell me where she lives.

Slight pause.

RALPH. My lord —

VERISOPHT. Now, come on, Nickleby —

RALPH. My lord, she is a virtuous, country girl. She has been, well brought up. It's true, she's poor, and unprotected —

VERISOPHT. Nickleby, I only want to look at her.

Slight pause. Raising his voice.

Nickleby, you know you're making a small fortune out of me, and 'pon my soul —

RALPH (*interrupting, in case* HAWK *hears*). My lord, if I *did* tell you —

VERISOPHT. Yes?

RALPH (*with a nod towards* HAWK). You would, you'd have to keep it to yourself.

VERISOPHT. Oh, yes, of course I wouldn't —

Enter NOGGS.

NOGGS. Erm —

RALPH (*sharply*). What is it?

NOGGS. Mrs Nickleby.

HAWK *gestures to* VERISOPHT. *They withdraw a little — as do* PYKE *and* PLUCK *— so* MRS NICKLEBY *cannot immediately see them on her entrance.* MRS NICKLEBY *sails in.*

MRS NICKLEBY. Dear brother-in-law, I'm sorry to intrude, but I was sure you'd want to be the first to know that Kate is situated as companion with a Mrs Julia Wititterly —

Pause. RALPH *stops her with a gesture.* MRS NICKLEBY *notices the gentlemen.*

Oh, I'm sorry —

HAWK. Mrs Nickleby!

NOGGS *goes out.*

RALPH. Uh, sister-in-law, these gentlemen were leaving —

HAWK. Leaving? Nonsense. So, this is Mrs Nickleby, the mother of Miss Nickleby? But no. It can't be. No. This lady, is too young.

MRS NICKLEBY. I think, dear brother-in-law, you can tell the gentleman, that Kate Nickleby's my daughter.

HAWK (*to* VERISOPHT). Daughter, my lord, did you hear that? Daughter!

MRS NICKLEBY. Lord?

HAWK. Now, Nickleby, at once, please, you must introduce us.

RALPH. Mrs Nickleby: Lord Frederick Verisopht. Sir Mulberry Hawk. And, uh, Mr Pluck and Mr Pyke.

VERISOPHT. Upon my soul, this is a most delightful thing. Uh — how d'e do?

HAWK. I'm deeply charmed, dear lady.

PYKE. As am I.

PLUCK. And not to mention me.

MRS NICKLEBY (confused). Well, I don't — I'm quite overcome.

Pause. HAWK nods at VERISOPHT.

VERISOPHT. And, how's your daughter, Mrs Nickleby?

MRS NICKLEBY. Oh, she's quite well, I am obliged to you, my lord . . . Quite well. She *wasn't* well for some days after she dined here, and I can't help thinking, that she caught cold in that hackney coach coming home. Hackney coaches, my lord, are such nasty things. I once caught a severe cold, my lord, from riding in one. I think it was in eighteen hundred and seventeen, and I was sure I'd never get rid of it, and I was only cured at last by a remedy that I don't know if you've happened to hear of, my lord.

SIR MULBERRY HAWK nods to PYKE and PLUCK, who glide, as if on oiled rails, to either side of MRS NICKLEBY.

You heat a gallon of water as hot as you can possibly bear it, with a pound of salt and six pen'orth of the finest bran, and sit in it for twenty minutes every night, well, not all in it, obviously, but just your feet, and I tell you I used it on the first day after Christmas Day and by the end of April it had gone, the cold I mean, and I had had it since September. Now isn't that a miracle, my lord?

Pause. VERISOPHT doesn't know quite how to react. MRS NICKLEBY becomes aware of the presence of MR PLUCK and MR PYKE.

PYKE. What an affecting calamity.

PLUCK. It sounds quite — perfect horrid.

PYKE. But worth the pain of hearing, Pluck, to know that Mrs Nickleby recovered.

PLUCK. That's the circumstance which gives it such a thrilling interest, there's no doubt, Pyke.

MRS NICKLEBY. Oh, do you think so?

RALPH. Gentlemen . . .

HAWK. So. Your daughter has secured an attractive situation, ma'am?

MRS NICKLEBY. That's right, Sir Mulberry, as from tomorrow, when her first task is to escort her new employers to the opera.

HAWK *flashes a look at* PLUCK *and* PYKE. MRS NICKLEBY *misinterprets.*

And I knew you'd be so pleased, dear brother-in-law, I walked straight here to tell you so.

Another look from HAWK.

PYKE. But surely you don't intend walking home, Mrs Nickleby?

MRS NICKLEBY. Oh, no, Mr Pyke, I intend to go back in an omnibus.

PLUCK. Well, isn't that a strange coincidence.

MRS NICKLEBY. Is it?

PYKE. Seeing as how the omnibus lies quite directly on our route, Pluck, isn't that the case?

PLUCK. It is indeed, and as we were just going –

PYKE. At this very instant.

PLUCK. We can escort dear Mrs Nickleby.

MRS NICKLEBY (*overcome*). Well – I would be most grateful.

PLUCK (*ushering* MRS NICKLEBY *out*). Not half so grateful, Mrs Nickleby, as we.

MRS NICKLEBY *goes out with* PYKE *and* PLUCK. *A silence between* RALPH *and* HAWK *and* VERISOPHT. *The latter two bow and go out.* RALPH *alone.*

RALPH. Sometimes – I wish I had not done this.

Slight pause.

But still – she must take her chance.

Scene Six

A London street. Bare stage. Enter MRS NICKLEBY, PLUCK *and* PYKE.

MRS NICKLEBY. Well, Mr Pyke, and Mr Pluck, I must express my gratitude, a seventh time.

PYKE. Oh, please don't, Mrs Nickleby. A friend of Sir Mulberry Hawk, a friend of ours. Is that not so, Pluck?

PLUCK. Pyke, it's automatic. And, particularly, someone whom Sir Mulberry holds in such esteem.

MRS NICKLEBY. Oh, surely not –

PLUCK. Now, Pyke, is Sir Mulberry's esteem of Mrs Nickleby the highest?

PYKE. I should say the very highest, Pluck.

PLUCK. She cannot be in ignorance, of the immense impression that her daughter has –

PYKE. Pluck! Pluck, beware.

MRS NICKLEBY's *eyes popping. Pause.*

PLUCK. Pyke's right. I should not have mentioned it. Thanks, Pyke.

PYKE. Pluck, not at all.

MRS NICKLEBY. I'm sure that –

PLUCK. Mrs Nickleby should take no heed of what I said. It was imprudent, rash. And injudicious.

PYKE. *Very* injudicious.

MRS NICKLEBY. Now, you musn't –

PLUCK. But, to see such sweetness and such beauty on the one hand, and such ardour and devotion on the other – pardon me, I didn't mean to speak of it again. Please change the subject, Pyke.

PYKE. Consider it, Pluck, changed.

PLUCK. But to think that we may actually see your daughter, at the opera, tomorrow evening!

MRS NICKLEBY. What's that?

PLUCK. Oh, you didn't know?

PYKE. Of course she didn't, Pluck, how could she? It is just, dear Mrs Nickleby, as luck would have it, we – that is, Sir Mulberry, Lord Verisopht, myself and Pluck, are going to the opera tomorrow!

MRS NICKLEBY. You are!

PYKE. We are.

Pause. Elaborately, PLUCK *and* PYKE *snap their fingers, as if to indicate that they have here simultaneously realised the most obvious thing in the world.*

PLUCK. Pyke, are you thinking what I'm thinking?

PYKE. Pluck, I believe our minds must be as one. Mrs Nickleby.

MRS NICKLEBY. Yes?

PYKE. Would you care to join us, in our box, at the opera tomorrow?

PLUCK. When we are sure you would be more than welcome.

MRS NICKLEBY. But –

PLUCK. There's not a but in it, dear Mrs Nickleby, we'll send a carriage round, at twenty before seven.

PYKE. And, see, here is the omnibus.

Enter the Omnibus. MRS NICKLEBY boards it. Pluck and Pyke disappear. The PASSENGERS narrate.

PASSENGER. And Mrs Nickleby leant back in the furthest corner of the conveyance, and, closing her eyes, resigned herself to a host of most pleasing meditations.

MRS NICKLEBY. Oh, Lady Hawk!

PASSENGER. She thought,

MRS NICKLEBY. On Tuesday last, at St George's, Hanover Square! By the most Reverend the Bishop of Llandaff! To Catherine, the only daughter of the late Nicholas Nickleby, Esquire, of Devonshire!

PASSENGERS.
And then her thoughts flew back, to old meditations, and the times she'd said that Kate would marry better with no fortune than some other girls with thousands,

And as she pictured, with all the brightness of a mother's fancy, all the grace and beauty of the girl who'd struggled cheerfully with her new life of hardship,

Her heart grew too full, and tears began to trickle down her face.

Fade on MRS NICKLEBY.

Scene Seven

A London Opera House. Two boxes, represented by four chairs on either side of the stage, facing the actual stage of the opera house, on which a genuine, complete, three-minute Opera is

*presented, in Italian. It tells the story of two lovers, the father of
the female one of whom objects strongly to their secret love.
During this, the following things happen in dumb-show: A
BOX-KEEPER leads on MR PLUCK and MR PYKE, who in turn
are escorting MRS NICKLEBY. Much solicitation of the latter by
the two gentlemen. They are led into the first box, when the
BOX-KEEPER realises from the tickets he has made a mistake,
and leads them out again. As PLUCK leads MRS NICKLEBY into
the second box, MR PYKE clearly threatens the poor
BOX-KEEPER with great violence for his error; PLUCK seats
MRS NICKLEBY in the second box with great charm and
ceremony. PYKE joins them.*

*The BOX-KEEPER, having gone out, re-enters with SIR
MULBERRY HAWK and LORD FREDERICK VERISOPHT,
both dressed up to the nines, but a little unsteady. The
BOX-KEEPER, fearful of meeting up with PYKE again, points the
two men to the second box. HAWK and VERISOPHT enter, greet
PLUCK and PYKE, and, with much bowing and kissing of hands,
MRS NICKLEBY. MRS NICKLEBY looks round, as if expecting
someone else, but as no one is there, allows herself to be settled.*

*The BOX-KEEPER enters again, this time with KATE
NICKLEBY, JULIA WITITTERLY and HENRY WITITTERLY.
They are shown into the first box. Conversation about who
should take which chair is overheard by SIR MULBERRY
HAWK, who lays his finger on his lips – MRS NICKLEBY is
speaking – and summons VERISOPHT to the front of the box.
MRS NICKLEBY recognises her daughter's voice, stands, and
greets her.*

*MRS NICKLEBY indicates the other gentlemen in her box to
KATE who is clearly not best pleased. MRS NICKLEBY gestures
that she is coming round, and she – followed by the entire
population of the second box, ups, goes into the corridor – during
which KATE is explaining who these people are to the
WITITTERLIES, the male half of which rushes eagerly to welcome
all these lords and baronets. KATE stands there as MRS
NICKLEBY, HAWK, VERISOPHT, PYKE and PLUCK – the
latter two only just – enter the box.*

*MRS NICKLEBY gestures towards KATE to recognise SIR
MULBERRY. KATE turns away but SIR MULBERRY HAWK
comes forward with extended hand, and she is forced to shake it.
MRS NICKLEBY then gestures KATE – with some impatience, to*

recognise the others – VERISOPHT, PLUCK and PYKE – and then MRS NICKLEBY, unable to understand KATE's reticence, waves at her to indicate that she should introduce the party to the WITITTERLIES. KATE introduces VERISOPHT, PLUCK, PYKE and HAWK to MR and MRS WITITTERLY.

At the end of this ceremony, PLUCK suggests to HAWK that they should, perhaps adjourn, as this box is very full. "With so much skill were the preliminaries adjusted, that Kate, despite all she could do or say to the contrary, had no alternative but to be led away by Sir Mulberry Hawk". KATE and NARRATORS are joined in the second box by PLUCK, who occupies MRS NICKLEBY in conversation. Remaining in the first box are VERISOPHT, the WITITTERLIES and PYKE. The young lord is being fawned upon by JULIA WITITTERLY. MRS NICKLEBY is studiously avoiding interfering with the conversation between HAWK and her daughter.

Finally, HAWK's attentions become intolerable, and KATE stands, and makes to run into the corridor. HAWK follows and tries to kiss her. KATE pushes him away. VERISOPHT emerges, with PYKE, from the WITITTERLIES' box, and HAWK and PYKE escort VERISOPHT back into their box, so we are now back where we started, as the Opera finishes, and everyone there except KATE stands and applauds the PERFORMERS. Flowers are thrown as the chairs are whisked away.

Scene Eight

Ralph's office. RALPH at his desk. NOGGS admits KATE to her uncle.

RALPH. Well, well, my dear. What now?

   RALPH a sharp gesture. NOGGS withdraws, but we see he waits outside the room and listens. KATE too upset to say anything.

   Sit down, sit down. And tell me what's the matter.

   KATE sits. RALPH sits near her. "He was rather taken aback by the sudden firmness with which Kate looked up and answered him."

KATE. Uncle, I've been wronged. My feelings have been hurt, insulted, wounded, and by men who are your friends.

RALPH. What friends? I have no friends, girl.

KATE. By the men I saw here, then. And have been persecuting me. And if they're not your friends, and you know what they are – more shame on you for bringing me among them.

RALPH. There's something of your brother, in you, I can see.

KATE. I hope there is. I should be proud to know it. I will not bear these insults any longer.

RALPH. Insults? What d'you mean?

KATE. What do I mean? You ask me that? Remember, uncle, what took place in this house.

Pause. She stands, goes to RALPH, puts her hand on his shoulder.

I'm sorry, I don't mean to shout, be angry, violent. But you don't know what I have suffered. Oh, of course, you cannot tell what being a young woman feels like – how could I expect it? – but still, when I tell you that my heart is breaking, I am wretched, all I can ask is that you believe me.

RALPH *looking away.*

Uncle. I have had no counsellor, no one to help or to protect me. Mother thinks they're honourable men, distinguished, and that, sad delusion, is the only thing she has to make her happy, and how could I undeceive her? You're the only person left. My only friend at hand. Almost my only friend at all. I need your help.

RALPH. Help? How can I help you, girl?

KATE. By telling them to stop. To leave me be.

RALPH *looks up at KATE. Pause.*

So will you tell them, uncle?

Pause.

RALPH. No. They are my friends, in business. I cannot afford for them to be my enemies. Please understand.

He turns to her. A slight smile.

Some girls, would be quite proud, to have such, gallants at their feet.

Pause.

And even if, they are . . . it won't last long. Oh, soon enough, they'll find another entertainment.

Pause.

Surely, it is not too much to bear, just for a time?

KATE. Just for a time? I am to be wretched and degraded, and debased? Just for a time?

Pause.

Oh, uncle. You've been selling me.

She turns and runs out. RALPH motionless. Outside, KATE stops, and breaks. NOGGS steps towards her, puts his arm round her. She is too far gone to resist.

NOGGS. Oh, yes. Oh, yes. You're right to cry. But even righter, not to give way, back in there. Oh that was even righter. Now, cry, cry. I shall see you soon — and so will someone else.

KATE. Must — go. Bless you.

NOGGS. You too. Yes, yes, of course, must go.

NOGGS takes her towards the door.

Oh, you were right, in there, right not to let him see you cry.

KATE goes out. NOGGS returns to his desk. A determined look on his face. "Newman Noggs stood at a little distance from the door, with his face towards it. And, with the sleeves of his coat turned back at the wrists, was occupied in bestowing the most vigorous, scientific, and straightforward blows upon the empty air. At first sight, this would have appeared merely a wise precaution for a man of sedentary habits, with the view of opening the chest and strengthening the muscles of the arms. But the intense eagerness and joy depicted in the face of Newman Noggs, which was suffused with perspiration: the surprising energy with which he directed a constant succession of blows towards a particular panel about five feet eight from the ground, and still worked away in the most untiring and unpersevering manner, would have sufficiently explained to the attentive observer, that his imagination was thrashing, to within an inch of his life, his body's most active employer, Mr Ralph Nickleby." NOGGS recovers from his exertion. He goes to his desk. He finds a sheet of paper. He looks round, to doublecheck he is alone. He begins to write a letter.

NOGGS. My dear young man.

He crosses out.

Dear Nicholas.

Scene Nine

Portsmouth. Miss Snevellicci's apartments. The company is gathering for the party. At this point, not everyone is here: those not here appear in the next few moments. Downstage of the tables are, in three groups: NICHOLAS, SMIKE and FOLAIR; MR and MRS SNEVELLICCI; and MR and MRS LILLYVICK. MR SNEVELLICCI is red-faced, bombastic, irritable and on the way to being drunk.

FOLAIR. Well, there he is.

NICHOLAS. That's Mr Snevellicci?

FOLAIR. Yes, it is.

NICHOLAS. And he — he is theatrical as well?

FOLAIR. Oh, certainly. Been in the business since he first played the ten-year-old imps in the Christmas pantomime. He can sing a little, dance a little, fence a bit, and act, but not too much . . . And since he's took to so much rum and water, tends to play the military visitors and speechless noblemen, you know . . . Ah, dear Mr Snevellicci.

For MR SNEVELLICCI has come over to FOLAIR, with MISS SNEVELLICCI.

MISS SNEVELLICCI. Ah, mamma, papa, please do meet Mr Johnson.

MR SNEVELLICCI. Oh, a privilege, a privilege.

MRS SNEVELLICCI. Indeed.

NICHOLAS. The pleasure's mine.

MR SNEVELLICCI. And have to say, dear boy, that haven't seen a hit like that since my great, dear friend Mr Glavormelly played the Coburg.

FOLAIR *(drifting off)*. Glavormelly.

The rest of the COMPANY still arriving.

MR SNEVELLICCI. Ever see him, sir?

NICHOLAS. No, I'm afraid I never did.

MR SNEVELLICCI. What, never saw old Glavormelly? Not seen acting then, dear boy. If he had lived —

NICHOLAS. He's dead?

MR SNEVELLICCI. Oh, yes, completely. Pushing up the daisies now, the bourne from which no traveller, etcetera, and at least can hope the poor old boot's appreciated there. Ah, there he is. Old bricks and mortar. Go and do my stuff. Excuse us, sir.

And indeed, the CRUMMLES *family have entered, with the last of the* PERFORMERS, *and* MRS GRUDDEN. *As* MR SNEVELLICCI *goes over to greet him,* MRS SNEVELLICCI *takes the opportunity for a little word.*

MRS SNEVELLICCI. My daughter speaks, quite strongly of you, sir.

NICHOLAS. Oh, does she?

MRS SNEVELLICCI. Yes, she does. Quite, quite uncommon strong.

NICHOLAS. Well, I assure you –

MRS SNEVELLICCI. Yes, I know.

MRS SNEVELLICCI looks at NICHOLAS, *and gives a little wink and a smile, and goes off to join her husband.* NICHOLAS *turns to see* MR LILLYVICK, *whose wife is engaged in animated chatter with the other women.*

NICHOLAS. Well, Mr Lillyvick. And how are you?

LILLYVICK. Quite well, sir. There is nothing like the married state, depend on it.

NICHOLAS. Indeed!

LILLYVICK. How do you think she looks, sir? Mrs Lillyvick, tonight?

NICHOLAS. She looks as handsome as she ever did. You are a lucky man.

LILLYVICK. You're right there, sir, you're right. I often think, I couldn't have done better if I'd been a young man, could I? You could not have done much better, could you?

Jabbing NICHOLAS *with his elbow.*

Eh?

NICHOLAS. Oh, no, I –

He is interrupted by MR SNEVELLICCI, *who has finished greeting the* CRUMMLESES, *has had another drink, and feels it's time to get this jamboree on the road.*

MR SNEVELLICCI. Right then! Silence! Class to order.

The stragglers sit, including NICHOLAS, *whose closeness to* MISS SNEVELLICCI *is noticed by the others.*

Ladies! Gentlemen. All welcome. In particular, the first.

The LADIES *blush, the* GENTLEMEN *applaud.*

And so, raise glasses. To the ladies. May God bless 'em. All of 'em. Unspliced and spliced, and those who are now in the former state, and who knows, very shortly, in the latter.

This is so obvious a reference to MISS SNEVELLICCI *and* NICHOLAS *that the actress reacts.*

MISS SNEVELLICCI. Oh, papa!

MR SNEVELLICCI. But then, who knows? I don't. Does anyone?

MISS SNEVELLICCI. Papa!

And MISS SNEVELLICCI *turns and runs, but is caught up with by the* LADIES, *who cluster round her, covering her confusion.*

MR SNEVELLICCI. What's this?

MISS LEDROOK *runs from the cluster to* MR SNEVELLICCI.

MISS LEDROOK. Oh, don't take any notice of it, sir. Say, that she exerts herself too much.

MR SNEVELLICCI. She whats?

MRS LILLYVICK (*approaching*). She's only weak, and nervous. She has been so since this morning.

MR SNEVELLICCI. Weak?

MRS SNEVELLICCI. They mean – don't make a fuss of it, my dear.

MR SNEVELLICCI. A fuss? What do you mean?

MISS SNEVELLICCI, *recovered, comes over from the dispersing cluster.*

What? I'm to be instructed? Given marching orders? Told what I may do and say?

MISS SNEVELLICCI. Oh, pa, please don't –

MR SNEVELLICCI. Don't what?

MISS SNEVELLICCI. Talk in that manner –

MR SNEVELLICCI. Manner? Talk in any manner that I please.

MISS SNEVELLICCI *and* MRS SNEVELLICCI *look at each other.*

I'm not ashamed. The name is Snevellicci. Found in Broad Court, Bow Street, when in town. If out, inquire at the stage door. Look, dammit, had me portrait in cigar shops round the corner. Mentioned in the papers. Tell you what, if I found any chap was tampering, affections of me daughter, wouldn't talk. I would astonish him. In silence. That's my way. That is – my manner.

He downs his drink.

Hmph. What was I saying?

MRS CRUMMLES. You were toasting everyone.

MR SNEVELLICCI (*remembering*). Oh, yes. The ladies. All of 'em. I love 'em, every one.

All the MEN, *for the sake of getting it over with, raise their glasses.* MR LILLYVICK *has been growing agitated for some little time.*

THE MEN. The la –

LILLYVICK. Not all of them, sir, surely?

MR SNEVELLICCI. Oh, yes. Every one.

THE MEN. The la –

LILLYVICK. But that includes the married ladies, sir.

MR SNEVELLICCI. Oh course! The memsahibs, certainly.

THE MEN. The –

MR LILLYVICK. What, including Mrs Lillyvick?

MR SNEVELLICCI (*impatiently*). Why, yes, of course, including Mrs Lillyvick. If I may say so, Mrs L. especially.

And MR SNEVELLICCI *winks at* MRS LILLYVICK. *Then he blows her a kiss.*

Eh, what?

MRS LILLYVICK *blushes.* MR LILLYVICK *strikes* MR SNEVELLICCI *on the nose.*

Hey, what this? Fisticuffs?

The COMPANY *reacts as* MR SNEVELLICCI *tries to hit* MR LILLYVICK.

You strike me, sir?

LILLYVICK. I do.

NICHOLAS, SMIKE, *one or two other actors rush in to separate them.*

MISS BRAVASSA. What's this?

MISS GAZINGI. What's happening?

MRS LILLYVICK. Oh, lor.

LILLYVICK (*still struggling*). You see that, sir? Here's purity and elegance combined, whose feelings have been violated —

MRS LILLYVICK. Lor, what nonsense, Lillyvick. He ain't said nothing to me.

Pause. The men let LILLYVICK *go. He turns to* MRS LILLYVICK.

LILLYVICK. Said, Henrietta? It was how he looked —

MRS LILLYVICK. Well, d'you suppose that nobody is ever going to *look* at me again? A pretty thing, it would be, to be married, if that was the law!

LILLYVICK. You didn't mind it?

MRS LILLYVICK. Mind it? What I minded was . . . You know, you ought to go down on your knees, I tell you, Lillyvick, and beg for everybody's pardon, that you ought.

LILLYVICK. Pardon, my dear?

MRS LILLYVICK. Yes, and mine first. Do you suppose I ain't the best judge of what's proper and what's improper.

Pause.

MISS BRAVASSA. Well, to be sure.

MISS LEDROOK. We'd notice.

MISS GAZINGI. If there'd been anything that needed to be taken notice of.

MR SNEVELLICCI. Hm. Absolutely right. Spot on. There. So now that's settled — charge your glasses, one and all.

And MR SNEVELLICCI *goes round the ladies, starting with* MRS LILLYVICK, *giving them kisses.* LILLYVICK, *broken, stumbles to the side.*

MRS GRUDDEN (*hiccups*). Beg pardon.

We realise that MRS GRUDDEN *is slightly inebriated. She reaches into her reticule for a handkerchief and finds a letter.*

Oh. Mr Johnson.

NICHOLAS. Yes?

MRS GRUDDEN. There's a letter for you. Sorry, it completely slipped my mind.

MRS GRUDDEN *a little giggle.* NICHOLAS *a quizzical look, takes the letter. Increasingly worried look.* MR SNEVELLICCI *has finished kissing all the ladies.*

MR SNEVELLICCI. So — a toast.

MRS GRUDDEN. Toast.

MR SNEVELLICCI. To — to the brightest, male, star in your, way blue yonder — Mr Johnson.

EVERYONE. Mr Johnson.

FOLAIR. Speech! Speech!

MRS GRUDDEN. Speech.

Applause. NICHOLAS *steps forward.*

NICHOLAS. My dear friends, I am very sorry.

CRUMMLES. Sorry?

NICHOLAS. That I must — in a nutshell, I must leave your company.

Pause.

MISS SNEVELLICCI. What? Leave?

MRS GRUDDEN. Oh, hoity-toity.

FOLAIR. Stuff.

NICHOLAS. There are some — circumstances, that call me away.

CRUMMLES. But to return, sir, surely?

NICHOLAS. No.

CRUMMLES (*quietly*). Not even if, your salary was —

NICHOLAS. No.

Pause. Everyone looks at MRS CRUMMLES, *who has been building up to her reaction.*

MRS CRUMMLES. This is Astounding.

NICHOLAS. I am sorry that I could not have prepared you for it, Mrs Crummles.

MRS CRUMMLES. So am I.

Pause.

CRUMMLES. Well, then . . . Well then . . . We will announce it. Monday. Positively last appearance. Posters, first thing in the morning.

NICHOLAS. Sir, I'm —

MRS CRUMMLES. Yes, of course. And then, on Tuesday, re-engagement for just one night more, and then on Wednesday, Thursday, yielding to the wishes of our numerous and influential patrons –

NICHOLAS. Ma'am, I must be off tonight.

MRS CRUMMLES. Tonight?

NICHOLAS. Immediately. At once.

MRS CRUMMLES. No positively last appearance?

NICHOLAS. No.

MRS CRUMMLES. Not one night more, by popular demand?

NICHOLAS. No, sorry.

MRS CRUMMLES. There's nothing we can do or say, to move you from this awesome pass? There's nothing I can do or say, to melt your stern, unyielding heart?

NICHOLAS. There isn't, I'm afraid.

MRS CRUMMLES. Then – there's, no more to say.

She turns. Turns back.

Except – farewell.

CRUMMLES. Farewell, my noble, lion-hearted boy!

CRUMMLES *embraces* NICHOLAS. *The* PHENOMENON *bursts into tears. Others dab their eyes with handkerchiefs.*

MR HETHERINGTON. Farewell.

MISS BELVAWNEY. Farewell.

MR BANE. Farewell.

CRUMMLES. If nothing can detain you with us . . .

MISS SNEVELLICCI. Nothing?

CRUMMLES. Then –

MRS CRUMMLES (*embracing* NICHOLAS). Farewell.

The Great Embrace is still occurring when MRS GRUDDEN *makes an annoucement.*

MRS GRUDDEN. I shall. Now sing. A song.

Consternation.

I shall require. A player at the pianofort.

More consternation.

To sing it.

MRS CRUMMLES. Mrs Grudden, what is going on?

MRS GRUDDEN. I am.

To the musicians.

Thank you.

NICHOLAS *collars* SMIKE.

NICHOLAS. Come, Smike, let's go –

SMIKE (*fascinated*). But – look –

MRS GRUDDEN *is getting her note. She begins to sing an extraordinarily sentimental ballad. During it, various members of the* COMPANY *come to* NICHOLAS *and shake his hand.* LENVILLE's *shake is reconciliatory, but he is clearly delighted. The penultimate shaker is* MISS SNEVELLICCI. *As they finish shaking, the Company members join* MRS GRUDDEN's *song, or burst into tears, or something.*

MRS GRUDDEN & COMPANY – SONG
O stay but for an hour;
If any power I have in pleading,
No way but only this to yield a kiss
And feel my death succeeding,
O how can I be strong
As you would have me be
Though duty calls I long to keep you here with me,
But no, go, and hold this memory

Farewell, my dear, farewell,
For ever let us part:
But don't, I pray you, tell the news to my aching heart.
Be kind, my dear, be kind: Though hope at last be gone,
And even my love be blind,
O let it go hoping on.

During the next verse as the attention has completely transferred, NICHOLAS *taps* SMIKE's *arm, and nods regretfully, and* SMIKE *realises they have to go.* NICHOLAS *is nearly out when he is confronted by* MR LILLYVICK.

LILLYVICK. Sir. I can – I can see nothing.

NICHOLAS. What?

LILLYVICK. I can see nothing, more, in Mrs Lillyvick. Of Miss Petowker.

Pause.

NICHOLAS. I'm – so sorry.

NICHOLAS *and* SMIKE *leave. The song reaches a tumultuous climax.*

MRS GRUDDEN & COMPANY.
Farewell, my dear, farewell.
For ever we must part
But don't I pray you, tell the news to my aching heart.
Be kind, my dear, be kind:
Though hope at last be gone,
And even my love be blind,
O let it go hoping on.
Farewell, my dear, farewell,
For ever we must part:
But don't, I pray you, tell the news to my aching heart.
Be kind, my dear, be kind:
Though hope at last be gone,
And even my love be blind,
O let it go hoping on.

Scene Ten

The Wititterlies'. The chaise-longue, and one chair. Enter KATE *and* MRS WITITTERLY.

MRS WITITTERLY. Now, child, you must tell me how you came to know Lord Frederick, and all those other charming gentlemen.

KATE. Oh, I met them at my uncle's.

MRS WITITTERLY. I was so glad – if surprised – at the opportunity which that respectable person, your dear mother, gave us of being known to them.

KATE. Yes, I, too, was surprised.

MRS WITITTERLY. Though, of course, we have been nearly introduced a dozen times.

A bell.

Ah, that will be them now. Alphonse!

ALPHONSE *goes out.* KATE *agitated.*

I naturally told them they could call. Miss Nickleby . . . You cannot think of going.

KATE. You are very good. But —

MRS WITITTERLY. Please, please don't upset me, make me speak so loud, Miss Nickleby, I beg —

Enter ALPHONSE.

ALPHONSE. Uh, Mr Hawk, Lord Mulberry Pyke, Sir Frederick Pluck, and Mr Verisopht. Or something.

Enter the above-named.

MRS WITITTERLY. Gentlemen, I am delighted, I am sure. Please, gentlemen, my lord, sit down.

As they do so:

HAWK. And how are you today, Mrs Wititterly?

MRS WITITTERLY. Well, I must own, Sir Mulberry, that I am still quite torn to pieces.

HAWK (*with a look at* KATE). Mm?

MRS WITITTERLY (*to* VERISOPHT). I am always ill after drama, my lord, and after the opera I can scarcely exist for several days.

VERISOPHT. Yes . . . I'm the same.

MR WITITTERLY bursts in.

MR WITITTERLY (*to* LORD FREDERICK VERISOPHT). My lord, I am delighted, honoured, proud. I am indeed, most proud.

To MRS WITITTERLY.

My soul, you'll suffer for this thrill tomorrow.

MR WITITTERLY. Suffer?

HAWK. Pray, whatever for?

MR WITITTERLY. Oh, the reaction, sir this violent strain upon the nervous system, what ensues? A sinking, a depression, lowness, lassitude, debility. My lord, if Sir Tumley Snuffim were to see that frail creature at this moment, he'd not give a —

With a toss of snuff.

this, for her continued life!

MRS WITITTERLY *sighs.*

PYKE. It's obvious that Mrs Wititterly's a martyr.

MR WITITTERLY. Oh, she is.

PLUCK. Perhaps, in fact . . . the other room, in order to escape the draught . . .?

MRS WITITTERLY (*less faintly*). What draught?

PYKE *and* PLUCK *leading* MRS WITITTERLY *to the "other room".*

PYKE. A constitution like a flower, just the slightest puff of wind, it's clear —

MRS WITITTERLY (*vaguely*). Sir Mulberry, my lord . . .

HAWK *gestures to* VERISOPHT *that they must follow.* VERISOPHT *stands, annoyed, and follows* MRS WITITTERLY, *her husband,* PLUCK *and* PYKE. KATE *is trying to follow too, when* HAWK *turns, and stands in her way. This during:*

MR WITITTERLY. You're right, sir, you're so right. If anybody will produce to me a greater martyr than my wife . . .

And, as MRS WITITTERLY *is fussed round,* KATE *is in the first room alone with* SIR MULBERRY HAWK.

HAWK. Don't hurry, now, don't hurry —

KATE *tries to pass,* HAWK *prevents her.*

Now then, stay —

KATE. You'd better not detain me, sir.

HAWK. Why not? Oh, my dear creature, why d'you keep up this show of anger with me, eh?

KATE. Show? Show? How dare you, to presume to speak to me, sir — to address me —

HAWK. You look pretty in a passion, dear Miss Nickleby.

KATE. I hold you, I must tell you, in the bitterest detestation and contempt. If you find looks of, disgust, aversion, if you find such looks attractive — let me go, sir, let me join —

HAWK. Oh, I will let you join, Miss Nickleby, I promise you.

KATE, *speechless, looks at* SIR MULBERRY HAWK.

And I will see you very often, we're invited here, whenever and however we — desire.

KATE *makes another attempt to get past* HAWK, *who tries, roughly, to embrace her. Meanwhile, both* MRS WITITTERLY *and* LORD VERISOPHT *have realised the device that has been used on them.* MRS WITITTERLY *is insisting to her husband on going back into the first room.* KATE *pulls herself back from* HAWK. *He decides to leave it there.*

I will be joining you, Miss Nickleby.

KATE *turns to go. Then, she decides to turn back, to speak to* HAWK. *During this,* MRS WITITTERLY *appears in between the two rooms, followed by* VERISOPHT, PLUCK, PYKE *and* MR WITITTERLY.

Now, my lord. We should not outstay our welcome.

VERISOPHT. No.

Pause.

We shouldn't.

HAWK. We hope, Mrs Wititterly, to find you soon in better health. Don't we?

PLUCK. Certainly we do.

PYKE. Indubitably.

Enter ALPHONSE.

MR WITITTERLY. My lord, Sir Mulberry, I trust that you will –

HAWK. Oh, yes. Very soon.

MR WITITTERLY, *who doesn't understand the atmosphere, fusses round as* VERISOPHT, HAWK, PYKE *and* PLUCK *depart. Then* MR WITITTERLY *moves towards his wife, who has not moved. She dismisses him with a gesture.* MR WITITTERLY *goes out.* MRS WITITTERLY *takes a step towards* KATE.

MRS WITITTERLY. Miss Nickleby, I wish to speak to you. I'm sorry, but you leave me no alternative.

KATE *says nothing.*

Your – this behaviour, is so very far from pleasing me . . . I'm very anxious that you should do well, Miss Nickleby, but you will not, if you go on as, as you do.

KATE *turns away.* MRS WITITTERLY *stridently.*

And you needn't think that looking at me in that way, Miss Nickleby, will stop me saying what I'm going to say, which I regard as a religious duty. You will not look at me, in that, that manner. I am not Sir Mulberry, no, nor Lord Frederick Verisopht, Miss Nickleby; nor am I Mr Pluck, nor Mr Pyke. If such things had been done when I was a young girl – I don't suppose it would have been believed.

KATE. I don't –

MRS WITITTERLY. Please, I will not be answered! I will not, Miss Nickleby. D'you hear?

KATE. I hear you, ma'am.

MRS WITITTERLY. And I must tell you, once, for all, I must insist upon your altering your forward manner with those gentlemen, who visit at this house. It's not becoming. It's improper. It's – unchaste.

KATE. Oh. Is not this, too cruel, too hard to bear? It's not enough, that I should suffer as I do, from contact with these, people, but I am exposed to this unjust and most unfounded charge!

MRS WITITTERLY. You'll have the goodness to recall, Miss Nickleby, that when you use such terms as "unjust" and "unfounded", you are implying, in effect, that I am stating that which is untrue.

KATE. I do. I say that. It is vilely, grossly, wilfully untrue. Oh, is it possible! That someone of my own sex can sit by, and not have seen the misery those libertines have caused me! Is it possible that you can't see the disrespect, contempt they hold for both of us? And can I not expect from you, another woman, and so much my senior, a little – female aid and sympathy? I can't believe it.

MRS WITITTERLY. What? Disrespect? Contempt? What, senior?

MR WITITTERLY *and* ALPHONSE *run into the room.*

MR WITITTERLY. What's the matter? Heavens, Julia! Look up, my life, look up!

MRS WITITTERLY. Sir Tumley! Get Sir Tumley!

MR WITITTERLY (*to* ALPHONSE). Run, run quickly – fetch Sir Tumley. Go!

ALPHONSE *scuttles out. To* KATE.

I knew it, knew, Miss Nickleby. All that society, it's been too much for her. This is, this is all soul, you know, soul, every bit of it. Come, help, to get her to her room.

KATE *to the aid of* MR WITITTERLY. MRS WITITTERLY *looks up at* KATE.

MRS WITITTERLY. Please, take your hands off me.

MR WITITTERLY *looks surprised and confused. He picks up*

his wife and carries her out. KATE *left alone. Enter* SIR
MULBERRY HAWK. KATE *sees him. He picks up a cane that
he has left behind.*

HAWK. Oh, poor Miss Nickleby. Where can you look, now, for
protection?

Scene Eleven

The streets of London. Bare stage. NARRATORS *burst on to the
stage. Amidst them are* SMIKE *and* NICHOLAS.

NICHOLAS. London at last!

NARRATORS.

And there they were in the noisy, bustling, crowded streets of
London,

Now displaying long double-rows of brightly-burning lamps,
and illuminated besides with the brilliant flood that streamed
from the windows of the shops.

Streams of people apparently without end poured on and on,
jostling each other in the crowd, and hurrying forward, scarcely
seeming to notice the riches that surrounded them on every side;

Emporia of splendid dresses, the materials brought from every
corner of the world;

Vessels of burnished gold and silver, wrought into every
exquisite form of vase, and dish, and goblet;

Screws and irons for the crooked, clothes for the newly-born,
drugs for the sick, coffins for the dead, and churchyards for the
buried –

Pale and pinched-up faces hovered about the windows where
was tempting food,

Hungry eyes wandered over the profusion guarded by one thin
sheet of brittle glass –

Life and death went hand in hand –

Wealth and poverty stood side by side –

Repletion and starvation laid them down together –

But, still –

It was –

London!

The music changes. More urgent, darker. The streets more threatening than gaudy, as NICHOLAS *and* SMIKE *rush through them, to knock on a door.* CROWL *appears above?*

NICHOLAS. Oh, Mr Crowl. Is Newman here.

CROWL. Oh, no. But you're expected. Laid out food and drink as well.

NICHOLAS. D'you know when he'll be home?

CROWL. A troublesome affair of business, keeps him. Not be home, he says, till twelve o'clock.

NICHOLAS. Then, sir, look after this young man for me? And see he's fed and rested?

CROWL. Of, of course I will. Make sure he's fed, and warmed.

Music again, and NICHOLAS *runs round through the ever-darkening streets, to another front door. He knocks.*
HANNAH – *Miss La Creevy's maid – appears above.*

NICHOLAS. Oh, Hannah. Is your mistress in?

HANNAH. Who? Miss La Creevy?

NICHOLAS. Of course.

HANNAH. Oh, no. She's out.

NICHOLAS. Where out?

HANNAH. Out at the theatre.

NICHOLAS. Which? And when will she return?

HANNAH. Dunno.

And NICHOLAS *runs off again, till finally he comes to another door and beats on it.*

NICHOLAS (*banging on the door*). Hey, mother! Mother! Kate! Kate, are you there?

He leans against the door, exhausted.

What *is* this? Where *are* they? *All* of them!

NARRATORS.
And then Nicholas suddenly recalled, from Newman's letter, that his sister's new employers lived in Chelsea,

And with the firm resolve to leave no stone unturned, he set his course to Sloane Street,

And such was his state, confused and tired and desperate,

He hardly saw, outside the fashionable coffee-house, the cabriolet that juddered to a halt before him.

Scene Twelve

Inside and outside a fashionable coffee-house. Three tables, two with customers dining, being served by two WAITERS and a SERVING-GIRL, improbably called WALTER, WILBUR and WANDA. But, for the moment, our attention is on NICHOLAS, downstage, as HAWK, VERISOPHT, PLUCK and PYKE enter, on their way to the coffee-house. We imagine that the door to the coffee-house is behind NICHOLAS, and the entering Revellers need to pass round him to get to it.

HAWK. Now, gentlemen, another pint or two of wine?

VERISOPHT. Why not? Another toast?

PLUCK. Oh, yes.

PYKE. Indeed.

PYKE is already in the coffee-house, PLUCK following. VERISOPHT needs to be kept upright by HAWK.

PLUCK. Hey, waiter, magnum!

HAWK. To whom, my lord?

VERISOPHT. Who else? The lady we've been drinking to all evening. That damned, enchanting little . . .

HAWK (*promptly*). Kate.

VERISOPHT. Kate Nickleby.

HAWK and VERISOPHT enter the coffee-house. NICHOLAS follows.

HAWK. Hey, waiter! Magnum!

PLUCK. Where is that girl? Girl with the magnums? Is there no service here?

WANDA hurries in with the bottles on a tray. WALTER hurries up with a corkscrew. HAWK, who is sitting on the edge of the empty table with LORD VERISOPHT, grabs the screw.

HAWK. I'll do it myself, dammit. Doubtless you'll take half-and-hour, and break the cork.

To WANDA.

You — glasses!

WALTER bows obsequiously, and nods to WANDA, who hurries out, having her bottom pinched by HAWK on the way. NICHOLAS has entered. The place is rather richer than he is used to patronising, and he is aware that he is dusty and travel-stained.

PYKE (*to a terrified* CUSTOMER). Excuse me, sir, but could I –

Taking glasses from the table.

Thank you ever so.

HAWK (*opening the magnum and spilling its contents*). The thing, is my dear lord, about this little Nickleby, is that she is, in fact, quite similar to that old crow, her uncle.

HAWK *pours wine into the glasses which* PYKE *and* PLUCK *have liberated from the other Customers.*

VERISOPHT. Damned sight prettier.

WANDA *enters with the glasses. The party raise their glasses to her. She looks to* WALTER, *who nods at her, and she goes out, having her bottom pinched by* MR PLUCK. *One of the other customers gestures to* WALTER, *and they whisper about the intrusion.*

HAWK. Indeed. But, nonetheless, in essence, quite the same. You need something from her in the way of – interest, she holds back, to be more sought after – as he does; and when she/he relents, at last, the bargain's doubly hard, but the, advance, is more than doubly welcome.

PLUCK. The advance.

PYKE. Let's have some oysters, dammit!

WALTER *has gone to* NICHOLAS.

WALTER. Yes, can I help you?

NICHOLAS. No.

And NICHOLAS *marches over to* SIR MULBERRY HAWK. HAWK *looks up at* NICHOLAS.

Sir, may I have a word with you?

HAWK. With me?

NICHOLAS. That's what I said.

The rest of the coffee-house becoming aware of what's going on.

HAWK. Well. A mysterious intruder.

NICHOLAS. Will you step apart with me, or d'you refuse?

HAWK. Sir, name your business, and then go away.

WANDA *coming in with a tray of food.* NICHOLAS *takes a card from his pocket and throws it on the table.*

NICHOLAS. There, sir. My business you will guess.

WANDA stops in her tracks, turns to go, WALTER gestures to her, and she puts down the tray as far as possible from the hostilities, and goes out.

Now, sir. Your name, and your address.

HAWK. Sir, I will give you neither.

The CUSTOMER who has paid his bill gets up and leaves.

NICHOLAS. Then – if there's – one gentleman, among this party, he will tell me who you are, and where you live.

NICHOLAS is talking too loudly.

I am the brother of the lady who has been the subject of this conversation. I demand – some satisfaction.

PLUCK and PYKE a step towards NICHOLAS.

HAWK. Oh, no, let the fellow talk. I've nothing serious to say to a boy of his station, and his pretty sister shall save him a broken head, at least.

NICHOLAS. I'll follow you. All night, if need be. I will know you.

HAWK (*laughs*). Hm.

HAWK pours another drink. Another CUSTOMER gestures to WILBUR, who goes and takes his money. NICHOLAS to WALTER.

NICHOLAS. Do you know this person's name?

WALTER. This gentlemen? No, sir, I don't, sir.

HAWK (*to WALTER*). Do you know *this* person's name?

WALTER. I don't know anyone.

HAWK (*tossing NICHOLAS's card to WALTER*). Then you will find his name, there, sir. And when you've mastered it, then you can burn it.

WALTER. Burn it. Right.

WALTER picks up the card and withdraws. WALTER, WILBUR and WANDA now in a little huddle by the kitchen door.

HAWK (*to NICHOLAS*). You are an errand boy, for all I know. And now, be off with you.

HAWK turns to his friends.

NICHOLAS. I am the son of a country gentleman. Your equal in birth and education, and your superior, I trust, in everything besides.

HAWK *laughs.*

(Blurted.) Miss Nickleby's my sister, sir! I will not leave.

The last CUSTOMER *hurries out.*

HAWK. Well, then, we'll go.

NICHOLAS. I'll follow you.

HAWK. Well, then, we'll stay.

Long pause.

VERISOPHT. I think, perhaps, I will go. It's very late.

HAWK. Oh, is it? Very well, my lord.

PLUCK. Perhaps my lord would like a travelling companion.

PYKE. Or two.

HAWK. Then all of you – do go.

Slight pause. VERISOPHT *goes to* WALTER, *and signs the instantly proffered bill.*

VERISOPHT. Good night, then.

VERISOPHT, PLUCK *and* PYKE *go out.* HAWK *picks up the magnum, goes to another table. He sits and drinks.* NICHOLAS *is watching* HAWK *like a hawk. A very long pause. A clock chimes.* WALTER, WILBUR *and* WANDA *look at the clock and at each other. Another long pause.* HAWK *finishes his wine.*

HAWK. Waiter – my cane.

He stands. WILBUR *brings* HAWK's *cane.* HAWK *takes it, and throws some coins on the table.*

NICHOLAS. So, will you make yourself known to me, sir?

Pause.

HAWK. No.

HAWK *goes,* NICHOLAS *follows.* WALTER, WILBUR *and* WANDA *walk forward and deliver their lines out front, as the chairs and tables of the coffee-room disappear, and the cabriolet is set up in the darkness.*

WILBUR. And there was a private cabriolet in waiting,

WANDA. And the groom opened the apron,

WALTER. And jumped out to the horse's head,

WILBUR. Who was a thoroughbred,

WANDA. And consequently Very Highly Strung.

Now we can see the cabriolet; or, at least, only HAWK, NICHOLAS *and the head of the "horse".*

WALTER. And the young man walked up to the older gentleman,

WILBUR. And grasped his arm, and spoke:

NICHOLAS, *as if on the footboard of the carriage.*

NICHOLAS. So, will you make yourself known to me?

HAWK. No, damn you.

To his COACHMAN.

Barton!

NICHOLAS. I'll hang on the footboard.

HAWK. You will be horsewhipped if you do. Barton, let go her head.

NICHOLAS (*clinging on to* HAWK). You shall not – shall not go – I swear – till you have told me –

HAWK. Now! Leave go!

The "horse" plunges and rears.

Will you let go?

NICHOLAS. Will you tell me who you are?

HAWK. No!

NICHOLAS. No!

HAWK *strikes* NICHOLAS *with his whip.* NICHOLAS *grabs the whip and strikes* HAWK. *The "horse" is rearing wildly. Screams of passers-by.* NICHOLAS *strikes* HAWK *again. The "horse" "bolts".* NICHOLAS *reels away. A huge crash and darkness.*

Scene Thirteen

Noggs' garret and the Nicklebys' house in Thames Street. Early morning. NOGGS *and* SMIKE *enter one side,* NICHOLAS *the other. He is bleeding.*

NICHOLAS. Don't be alarmed. There's no harm done, beyond what a basin of water will repair.

NOGGS. No harm! What have you been doing?

NICHOLAS. I know everything. I have heard a part, and guessed the rest. But now we must go and see them. You see, I am collected. Now, good friend.

NOGGS. Your clothes are torn. You're walking lame. Please, let me see to you.

NICHOLAS. No. No, I must go to them.

Pause. NOGGS *nods to* SMIKE, *who is looking upset by* NICHOLAS's *appearance.* To SMIKE.

Smike, we're going to my home.

SMIKE. We – home? Your home?

NICHOLAS. Our home.

And NICHOLAS *takes* SMIKE's *hand, leading him, to* KATE. NOGGS *goes out. We are now in the Nicklebys' house in Thames Street.*

NICHOLAS. So Kate, this is my faithful friend and fellow-traveller

KATE (*going to* SMIKE). Dear Smike. I've been so looking forward, after all my brother's told me. And to thank you, for the comfort you have been to him.

SMIKE. I'm – very pleased to meet you. Uh – he's my only friend. I would lay down my life, to help him.

Enter MRS NICKLEBY, *and* MISS LA CREEVY, *with luggage.*

MRS NICKLEBY. Well, Lord bless my life. To think that Sir Mulberry Hawk should be such an abandoned wretch; when I was congratulating myself every day on his being an admirer of our dear Kate's . . .

MISS LA CREEVY. Now, come, dear Mrs Nickleby, please try to cheer up, do.

MRS NICKLEBY. Oh, I dare say, dear Miss La Creevy, that it's very easy to instruct someone to cheer up, but if you had had as many reasons to cheer down as I have – and, oh mercy, think of Mr Pyke and Mr Pluck, two of the perfectest true gentlemen that ever lived . . .

KATE. But come now, mother, there's a coach outside, to take us to the Strand. To Miss La Creevy's.

MISS LA CREEVY. Everything is ready, and a hearty welcome too. Now let me go with you downstairs.

MISS LA CREEVY *and* MRS NICKLEBY *turn to go and see* SMIKE.

MRS NICKLEBY. Oh, uh — uh, Nicholas —

NICHOLAS. Oh, mother, Miss La Creevy. This is Smike. My friend — who came with me from Yorkshire. You remember?

MRS NICKLEBY. Smike.

NICHOLAS. That's right.

SMIKE. I'm very —

MRS NICKLEBY. Oh, dear . . .

KATE. Uh, mother —

MRS NICKLEBY. Oh, it's so like Pyke. I shall be better presently.

She makes to go. Then turns back, trying hard to be a good hostess.

I don't suppose, that, while in Yorkshire, Mr Smike, you might have taken dinner with the Grimbles, of Grimble Hall?

SMIKE. The Grimbles.

MRS NICKLEBY. A most proud man, Sir — Sir Hadley Grimble — with six quite lovely daughters, and the finest park in the North Riding.

NICHOLAS. Oh, mother. D'you suppose that this — unfortunate poor outcast would receive an invitation to the finest house in the North Riding?

MRS NICKLEBY. Finest park, dear. The house was not, I think . . .

MISS LA CREEVY. Now, please come, Mrs Nickleby.

MRS NICKLEBY *a last look, and then she goes out.* MISS LA CREEVY *realises that brother and sister wish to talk to each other, so:*

MISS LA CREEVY. And, Mr Smike?

She takes SMIKE's *hand.*

SMIKE. New home.

MISS LA CREEVY *takes* SMIKE *out.* NICHOLAS *and* KATE *left together.*

NICHOLAS. I'd thought, to run away would help you. Thought, if I stayed here, you'd be without protection.

Pause. KATE *runs and embraces* NICHOLAS.

KATE. Oh, I've been so unhappy.

NICHOLAS. Oh, my darling girl.

KATE. Don't leave me any more. You promise me?

NICHOLAS. Of course. I'll never leave you.

Slight pause.

Tell me — tell me that I acted for the best.

KATE. Why should I tell you what we know so well?

They part to go out. NICHOLAS *stops her.*

NICHOLAS. I will write to him. I will tell him we renounce him, and will not be beholden to him any more.

Pause.

KATE. We are just beholden to each other.

SMIKE *enters to picks up the last of the luggage.*

SMIKE. I'm very pleased to meet you, Kate. Kate Nickleby.

KATE *and* NICHOLAS, *smiling, lead* SMIKE *out.*

Scene Fourteen

The apartments of Sir Mulberry Hawk. VERISOPHT *tending to the broken form of* SIR MULBERRY, *who lies on a couch, "with a shattered limb, a body severely bruised, a face disfigured with half-healed scars, and pallid from the exhaustion of recent pain and fever." Enter* PLUCK *and* PYKE, *with newspapers.*

HAWK. Well, then?

PLUCK. It is — it's noised abroad in all directions.

PYKE. Every club and gaming room has rung with it.

PLUCK. There's even been a song composed, we hear, and printed too —

PYKE. With most — unfunny lyrics, wouldn't you agree, Pluck?

PLUCK. Yes, Pyke, in the very worst of taste.

HAWK. When I, am off, this cursed bed — I will have, such revenge, as never man had yet. By God, I will. He's — this damned accident — has marked me for a week or two, but I'll put such a mark on him that he will carry to his grave. I'll slit his nose and ears — I'll flog him — maim him —

VERISOPHT (*nervously*). Yes, you might. Might try. But if you did – I should try to prevent you.

HAWK. What?

VERISOPHT. I have – been thinking.

Slight pause.

And – It is my view, in fact – that you – you should have told him who you were. And given him your card. For as it is – you did wrong. I did too. Because I didn't interfere. What happened afterwards was more your fault than his, and it should not, shall not, be cruelly visited upon him. It shall not, indeed.

HAWK. You pale, green boy, you parsonage, what's this?

VERISOPHT. I do believe, too, on my honour, that the sister is as virtuous and modest a young lady as she is a handsome one: and, of the brother, I say that he acted as a brother should. And I wish, with all my heart and soul, that any one of us came out of this – thing, half as well as he does.

Exit LORD FREDERICK VERISOPHT.

HAWK. Well, well, there's a thing. Well, there's a turnaround.

He turns, and screams as PLUCK *and* PYKE, *who have been notably silent and unsupportive over the last few moments.*

Don't you agree?

PYKE. Don't you agree that there's a turnaround, then, Pluck?

PLUCK. Pyke, don't you think that there's a – thing?

HAWK *looks at his lieutenants. They look at each other. They go out.*

Scene Fifteen

The street. Bare stage. Enter NICHOLAS.

NICHOLAS. And the next morning, Nicholas went once more to the General Agency Office, in search of a position.

NICHOLAS *goes downstage, looking in the window of an employment exchange.*

The office looked just the same as when he had left it last,

NARRATORS.

And indeed, with one or two exceptions, there seemed to be the very same placards in the window that he has seen before.

They are joined, looking at the placards, by a short elderly
GENTLEMAN, *dressed in a somewhat untidy, old-fashioned,
comfortable style.*

There were the same unimpeachable masters and mistresses in
want of virtuous servants,

And the same virtuous servants in want of unimpeachable
masters and mistresses.

And the same magnificent estates for the investment of capital,

And the same enormous quantities of capital to be invested in
estates,

And in short, the same opportunities of all sorts of people who
wanted to make their fortunes.

The NARRATORS *disperse. The old* GENTLEMAN, *who is
smiling, and even chuckling a little at the placards, is still there.
His name is* MR CHARLES CHEERYBLE.

LAST NARRATOR. And a most extraordinary proof it was of the
national prosperity, that people had not been found to avail
themselves of such advantages long ago.

NICHOLAS *and* MR CHARLES *looking at the cards, and,
occasionally, when they think the other isn't, at each other. This
pantomime carries on for a few moments, when* MR CHARLES
turns to go, and NICHOLAS *catches his eye, and stammers out,
in embarrassment.*

NICHOLAS. Oh, I'm sorry, I –

MR CHARLES (*who is Welsh*). Oh, no offence. Oh, no offence,
at all.

They both smile. NICHOLAS *waves at the cards.*

NICHOLAS. A great many opportunities here, sir.

MR CHARLES. A great many people, willing and anxious to be
employed, have thought so very often, I dare say.

Pause. They both smile again.

NICHOLAS. Yes, I, um –

MR CHARLES. Yes you um what, young sir?

NICHOLAS (*at a rush*). I merely hoped, or thought, I mean to say
– you had some object in consulting these advertisements?

MR CHARLES. You mean, you thought that I was seeking a
position? Eh? Hm? Eh?

NICHOLAS. Uh – no.

MR CHARLES. A very natural thought. Whatever. A highly comprehensible opinion. And, in fact, you'll split your sides at this, young sir, I thought the same of you.

NICHOLAS. Well, sir, if you had, you'd not be too far from the truth.

MR CHARLES. Eh? What? Dear me. No, no. A well-behaved young gentleman, reduced to such necessities. Can such things be?

NICHOLAS (*turning to go*). I'm sorry, but they are, in my case; you'll forgive me.

MR CHARLES. Stay. What do you mean, forgive you? What in heaven's name should I forgive you for?

NICHOLAS *turns back.*

NICHOLAS. Oh, merely that your face and manner – both so unlike any I have seen – tempted me into an avowal, which to any other stranger in this wilderness of London, I should not have dreamt of making.

Slight pause.

MR CHARLES. Now, that's very good. That is most aptly put. Yes, yes, a wilderness. As it was once to me.

NICHOLAS. It was?

MR CHARLES (*sticking out a foot*). Bare feet.

NICHOLAS. I beg your pardon?

MR CHARLES. Came here. They did. Bare and naked. I remember to this day. So what brings you to London?

NICHOLAS. Well, my father –

MR CHARLES. Died? And left a widowed mother?

NICHOLAS. Yes.

MR CHARLES. And little brothers, sisters?

NICHOLAS. Sister. One.

MR CHARLES. And you a scholar too, I dare say?

NICHOLAS. Well, I have been tolerably educated –

MR CHARLES (*looking at his watch*). Oh, a great thing, education. I have often wished that I'd more of it myself. So, shall we go?

NICHOLAS. Go?

MR CHARLES. Yes.

NICHOLAS. Go now?

MR CHARLES. That's right.

NICHOLAS. Go where?

MR CHARLES. Why, dear young man, go to the omnibus. And while we're travelling, you can be telling me the story of your life.

He is striding out. NICHOLAS stops. MR CHARLES turns back.

NICHOLAS. Please, sir. I must ask one question.

MR CHARLES. Ask away.

NICHOLAS. Who are you, sir?

MR CHARLES. My name's Charles Cheeryble.

NICHOLAS. Charles Cheeryble.

MR CHARLES. That's right. Now, please, sir, not another word.

Scene Sixteen

Ralph's office. RALPH sits at his desk, alone.

RALPH. I am not a man – the world knows – to be moved by a pretty face. I look and work beneath the surface, and I see the grinning skull beneath.

Pause.

And yet . . . And yet, I almost like the girl. If she had been less proud, less squeamishly brought up . . . And if the mother died . . . Who knows. This house might be her home.

He stands.

It is a splendid house. The rooms are costly. Glorious. But yet – a little still. And rather cold.

Pause.

A young girl's voice. Her laughter. And, when she's not there, a hundred little tokens of her presence. To remind . . .

RALPH *sits.*

But still. The world knows. That I know it. And myself.

Enter NOGGS.

Yes? What?

NOGGS. You in?

RALPH. To whom?

NOGGS. To him.

RALPH. Who's him?

NOGGS. He is.

NOGGS turns to go. Turns back, correcting himself.

They are.

He turns to go. Turns back.

And there's a letter come for you. Marked urgent.

RALPH. Give it here. And then get out.

NOGGS gives RALPH the letter.

NOGGS. See? Urgent.

NOGGS potters out. He is given an odd look by the entering SQUEERS and YOUNG WACKFORD.

RALPH. Well, this is a surprise. I should know your face, Mr Squeers.

SQUEERS. Ah, and you'd know it better, sir, if it hadn't been for all I've been a-going through.

RALPH. Ah, yes, sir, I trust you are now fully recovered from my nephew's scoundrelly attack?

SQUEERS. Well, if I am, it's only just, sir. I was one blessed bruise, sir, right from here to there. Vinegar and brown paper, sir, from morning till night. As I lay there, all of a heap in the kitchen, you might have thought I was a large brown paper parcel, chock full of nothing but groans. Did I groan loud, Wackford, or did I groan soft?

WACKFORD. Loud.

RALPH a quizzical look at the boy.

SQUEERS. My son, sir, little Wackford. I've brought him up, on purpose, to show the parents and guardians. I've put him in the advertisement this time, too: Look at a boy — himself a pupil. So, what do you think, sir?

RALPH. Think of what?

SQUEERS. Of him, sir, for a specimen of our feeding? Ain't he fit to burst right out of his clothes, and start the seams, and make the very buttons fly off with his fatness?

Poking and pinching WACKFORD.

Ooh, here's flesh, here's firmness, and here's solidness. Why, you can hardly get enough of him between your finger and your thumb to pinch him anywheres.

WACKFORD. Ow!

SQUEERS. Oh, well, been a long time since he had his breakfast. ooh, but look, sir, at those tears. There's oiliness!

RALPH. He certainly looks fit and well.

SQUEERS. In fact . . . D'you have such a thing as twopence, Mr Nickleby?

RALPH. I – think I have.

RALPH *produces "after much rummaging in an old drawer, a penny, a half-penny, and two farthings".*

SQUEERS. I thankee.

He gives the money to WACKFORD. RALPH *looking at the letter* NOGGS *brought him.*

Now, you go and buy a tart – and mind you buy a rich one. What d'you say?

WACKFORD. Yes, thank you, father.

WACKFORD *goes out.*

SQUEERS. Pastry makes his flesh gleam a good deal, and parents think that's a healthy sign.

Turning back to RALPH.

So, Mr Nickleby.

RALPH *still immersed in the letter.*

Um – Mr Nickleby?

RALPH *looks up, darkly. Something in the letter has made him angry.*

RALPH. Sit down. Attend to me.

SQUEERS *sits.*

I am not to suppose, that you are dolt enough to have forgotten or forgiven very readily the violence that was committed on you?

SQUEERS. Never.

RALPH. Or to lose the chance to pay it back, with interest.

SQUEERS. Try me.

RALPH. And maybe, it was some such object brought you here?

SQUEERS. Well . . . I had thought, perhaps, some compensation –

RALPH. Who's the boy? The boy that he took with him?

SQUEERS. Name of Smike.

RALPH. And is he old, young, healthy, sickly, tractable, rebellious?

SQUEERS. Well, wasn't young. Young for a boy, that is.

RALPH. That is, he's not a boy.

SQUEERS. I think, 'bout twenty. But – a little wanting, here,
Taps forehead.
like, nobody at home.

RALPH. How did he come to you?

SQUEERS. Oh, fourteen years ago, a strange man brought him to my place, and left him there. The money came some six or seven years. But then it stopped. I kept him, out of –

RALPH. Charity?

SQUEERS. That is the word. Though he's been useful, in the recent years.

RALPH. Yes, yes. Now, Mr Squeers, we'll talk of this again, when I've had time to think about it. So, where are you staying?

SQUEERS (*presenting a card*). With a Mr Snawley, Somers Town. I've got two lads of his, and he's that pleased with how they're being treated, that –

RALPH (*stands*). We are alone, sir. There's no need to advertise to me.
A thought.
This Snawley got two boys, you say, with you?

SQUEERS. That's right. Remarried, wife's two sons, you know.

RALPH. I do.

NOGGS *brings in* WACKFORD, *stuffing his face with a tart.*
SQUEERS *stands.*

SQUEERS. Ah, Wackford. He's a fine boy, ain't he, Mr –

NOGGS. Very.

SQUEERS. Pretty swelled out, eh? The fatness, twenty boys.

NOGGS. Oh, yes, he has. The fatness – twenty, thirty even. More. He's got it all. Ha! Ha! Oh, Lord.

SQUEERS (*to* RALPH). Is this man drunk? Or mad?

RALPH *shrugs.* NOGGS *cracking his knuckles.*

We'll speak then, Mr Nickleby.

SQUEERS *and* WACKFORD *go out.*

NOGGS. God help the others.

RALPH. What? Get out.

NOGGS. Get out.

NOGGS *goes out.* RALPH *alone, furious, with the letter.*

RALPH. Yes. Yes. To wound him through his own affections.
Yes. To strike him, through this boy.

Scene Seventeen

*The offices of the Brothers Cheeryble. The upstage area represents
the counting-house of the Cheerybles'; their old, round,
white-haired clerk* TIM LINKINWATER *sits at his high desk
working: above him hangs a birdcage with a blackbird inside. At
another desk* MR NED CHEERYBLE *sits, facing upstage, and,
upstage of him, a beautiful, if distressed,* YOUNG WOMAN.
CHARLES CHEERYBLE *enters Tim's area of the office, with his
new friend* NICHOLAS NICKLEBY.

MR CHARLES. Ah, Tim, you knave, God bless you. Is my
brother in?

TIM. Yes, he is, sir, but someone's with him.

MR CHARLES. Then we will not disturb him for the moment.
Tim. This young man is called Mr Nicholas Nickleby.

NICHOLAS. I'm pleased to meet you, sir.

TIM. And you. Hm, sir.

MR CHARLES. And, this, dear Nicholas, is Mr Tim Linkinwater,
possibly the most ferocious lion in the general region of
Threadneedle St. Am I not right, Tim Linkinwater? Hm?

TIM *shrugs and allows himself a little smile.*

MR CHARLES (*to* NICHOLAS). Note, sir, at first, the order.
Paper, pens, ink, ruler, sealing wax, Tim's hat, Tim's gloves,
Tim's other coat, Tim's blackbird and Tim himself; and you
shift any one of them, without a by-your-leave or even with it,
and you do so at your peril. Isn't that correct?

MR NED CHEERYBLE *opens his door. To let his visitor out.*
MR NED *looks exactly the same as his brother* MR CHARLES.
NICHOLAS *double-takes.*

MR NED. Ah, dear brother Charles. And how are you?

MR CHARLES. I am in quite outrageous health, dear brother
Ned. And how are you?

MR NED. I am in precisely the same condition, brother Charles.

MR CHARLES. Now, brother –

MR NED *puts his finger to his lips. The beautiful* YOUNG
WOMAN *comes out of the office.*

MR CHARLES. My dear Miss Madeline. Has Brother Ned
explained to you our view – has he expressed our most sincere
entreaty?

YOUNG WOMAN. Yes, he has. But my opinion is, and must
remain, the same. Your generosity, your kindness, is quite
unsurpassable. But still – I cannot do what you would have me
do. I cannot . . . For reasons that I know you understand.

MR CHARLES. Of course . . . Of course, we understand.

MR NED *guides the* YOUNG WOMAN *to the door. She goes
out.* NICHOLAS *following her with his eyes.* MR NED *turns
back to his brother.*

Now, Brother Ned, are you busy, or can you spare time for a
word or two with me?

MR NED. Brother Charles, my dear fellow, don't ask me such a
question.

MR CHARLES *notices that* NICHOLAS *is still looking after
the* YOUNG LADY.

MR CHARLES. Um – Mr Nickleby –

NICHOLAS. I'm sorry.

MR CHARLES. P'raps you'd grant us the inestimable privilege of
entering my room.

NICHOLAS. Of course.

They go into MR CHARLES' *office, which is downstage.*

MR CHARLES. Now, brother Ned, here is a young friend of
mine we must assist. You will wish, of course, to have his
statements, made to me, repeated, and then –

MR NED. Brother Charles, it is enough that you say he should be assisted. When you say that, no more statements are required. It would be churlish to demand them. Assisted he shall be. What are his needs, and what does he require? Where is Tim Linkinwater?

MR NED *is striding back towards the working* TIM LINKINWATER.

MR CHARLES. Stop, dear brother, stop. Before we – um, involve Tim Linkinwater – who, as I have said, dear sir, is quite a veritable tiger – I've a plan to put to you.

MR NED. Then put it, brother Charles.

MR CHARLES. I shall, dear brother Ned. Now, Tim is getting old, and Tim has been a faithful servant, and I don't think pensioning his mother and his sister and the buying of a little tomb when his poor brother died, was a sufficient recompense for all his services.

MR NED. Sufficient! It was miserly.

MR CHARLES. Exactly, so if we could somehow lighten old Tim's duties –

MR NED (*to* NICHOLAS). Parsimonious.

MR CHARLES. Prevail on him to go into the country now and then, and sleep in the fresh air –

MR NED. Cheeseparing.

MR CHARLES. And then come in, an hour later in the morning –

MR NED. Niggardly.

MR CHARLES. Then who knows, he'd grow young again in time.

MR NED. He would indeed. I'll go and tell him so.

MR NED *strides upstage and confers with* TIM LINKINWATER *as* MR CHARLES *talks to* NICHOLAS.

MR CHARLES. If Brother Ned, whom I hold dearer than I hold myself, has but a fault, it is an eagerness, enthusiasm, quickness of response, that sometimes edges close to the impulsive. Now, sir, what I had in mind was taking you on as a clerk, assistant to Tim Linkinwater, at a salary of one hundred and twenty pounds a year, which pennypinching churliness will without a doubt provoke you to depart my presence at an instant. So, good morning, sir.

NICHOLAS. Oh, sir.

MR CHARLES. What's this? Not gone?

NICHOLAS. Sir, I do not know how I can begin to thank you.

TIM *and* MR NED *enter* CHARLES' *room.*

MR CHARLES. Start by keeping quiet. Now, Tim Linkinwater, do you understand that we intend to take this gentleman into the Counting-Room?

TIM. Hm. Yes. I do.

TIM. Subject of course, to your inspection and investigation and interrogation.

TIM. Hm. So I should think.

MR CHARLES. And what is your opinion of this course of action?

TIM. Hm. Not coming in an hour later in the morning, that's for sure. Not going to sleep out in the fresh air, or be packed off to the country. Hm! A pretty thing to make a man do, at my time of life. The country. Phoo.

MR CHARLES. What's this?

MR NED. Phoo?

MR CHARLES. Damn your obstinancy, Tim.

MR NED. What do you mean, sir?

TIM. It is three and thirty, next May, since I first kept the books of the brothers Cheeryble. There ain't – I've said it again and again – such a square as this in all the world. There's not such a spring in England as the pump under the archway. There's not such a view in England as the view out of my window. I have slept in that room for three and thirty years, and if it isn't inconvenient, and doesn't interfere with the business, I shall request leave to die there.

MR CHARLES. Damn you, Tim Linkinwater.

MR NED. How dare you talk of dying? Do you hear that, Brother Charles?

TIM. That's all I've got to say. It's not the first time, Brother Edwin, Brother Charles you've talked of superannuating me; but I'd appreciate it if it was the last.

TIM LINKINWATER *goes back to his desk. Pause.*

MR CHARLES. He must be done something with, dear Brother Ned.

MR NED. That's true, dear Charles;

MR CHARLES. We must disregard his old scruples.

MR NED. They cannot be tolerated. He must be made a partner, Brother Charles.

MR CHARLES. And if he won't submit to it peaceably:

MR NED. We must have recourse to violence.

MR CHARLES. Quite right. Quite right, dear brother. If he won't listen to reason, we must do it against his will, and show him that we are determined to exert our full authority. We'll quarrel with him, Brother Ned.

MR NED. We'll quarrel with him now.

MR NED *is striding out, as* MR CHARLES *is giving a look to* NICHOLAS, *as if to say: "Impulsive!"* MR NED *bumps into the re-entering* TIM LINKINWATER.

Now, then Tim Linkinwater, curse you –

TIM. I've been thinking.

MR CHARLES. Yes?

TIM. That if the young man measures up –

MR NED. He will, of course he will –

TIM. Then it's all right. As long –

MR CHARLES. Yes, what's – as long?

TIM. As there's No Country.

MR NED (*pumping* TIM's *hand*). Well, then, Tim Linkinwater, devil take you sir, God bless you.

MR CHARLES (*to* NICHOLAS). Sir, you are approved.

MR CHARLES *takes* TIM *back into the counting-room as* MR NED *takes* NICHOLAS's *arm.*

MR NED. Now would it be beyond the bounds of the conceivable, for you to suffer the intolerable inconvenience of starting work on Monday?

Pause.

NICHOLAS. Sir, sir, I – Yes.

MR NED *goes after his brother,* NICHOLAS *turns out front.*

And Nicholas' heart was so full up with gratitude, that he could hardly speak, and he felt, more than at any time since he had come to London, truly happy.

NARRATOR. But his heart was even fuller, with a matter he

could not reveal, still less show thanks for to his benefactors.
For, since he had seen her, he had found it hard to think of
anything except the dark-eyed lady who had walked so sadly
through the counting-room.

NICHOLAS. I would, he thought, I would . . . I'd know her in
ten thousand.

Scene Eighteen

NICHOLAS *remains, as* RALPH *strides on.* NICHOLAS *is
quoting from the letter* RALPH *is reading.*

RALPH. So, this is it. He's loose again.

NICHOLAS. Your brother's widow and her orphan children
spurn the shelter of your roof, and shun you with disgust and
loathing.

RALPH. So, I'm to be defied, am I? And held up in the worst and
most repulsive colours?

NICHOLAS. We, your kindred, now renounce you, and your
riches –

RALPH. And, of course, she will be taught to hate me, and to feel
there is infection in my touch and taint in my companion-
ship . . .

NICHOLAS. Let them corrupt and rot you, we'll be free of their
infection –

RALPH. And always. Always. When my brother was like him, the
first comparisons were made; he, open, liberal, galiant; and I
cold and cunning, with no spirit but the thirst for gain:

NICHOLAS. I know you.

RALPH. Well, let it be so. If he, if they both, affect to despise the
power of money, I must show them what it is.

RALPH *goes out, as* NICHOLAS, *rapt:*

NICHOLAS. I would, he thought, I would: I'd know her in ten
thousand . . .

Scene Nineteen

The streets of the city of London. Just after dark. SMIKE *is
wandering round. There are sellers of everything, and buyers of it*

*too: There are Street-hands, and Balladeers, and Buskers. SMIKE
is entranced. "He had been gazing for a long time through a
Jeweller's window, wishing he could take some of the beautiful
trinkets home as a present, and imagining what delight they would
afford if he could, when the clocks struck three quarters past
eight. Roused by the sound, he hurried on at a very quick pace,
and was crossing the corner of a bye-street when he was violently
brought to, with a jerk so sudden that he was obliged to cling to a
lamppost to save himself from falling". SMIKE has been collared
by MR SQUEERS and YOUNG WACKFORD.*

WACKFORD. Oh, father, father –

SQUEERS. Well. Well, here's a go! Here's a quite delicious go.

*Onlookers are looking on. MR SNAWLEY, who has been with
the Squeerses, but has become detached in the hubbub, hurries
up.*

SNAWLEY. What's happening? Who's this?

SQUEERS. This is the boy I told you of, dear Snawley, one that
ran away. Hey, Wackford, fetch a hackney coach!

WACKFORD. A coach!

WACKFORD runs out.

A LABOURER. Hey. What's this lad been a-doing of?

RALPH. What doing of? Why, everything! Like running off, and
joining in bloodthirsty attacks upon his master – oh, there's
nothing he ain't done. Oh, what a most delicious go!

Hitting SMIKE.

SMIKE. I must –

SQUEERS. Yes, sir? What must you?

SMIKE. Must go home.

SQUEERS. Oh, will. You'll go home very soon. A week, locked
up, our lodgings, eh Snawley, and then to that delightful village,
Dotheboys, in Yorkshire. That's your home.

SMIKE. Go home.

Re-enter WACKFORD.

WACKFORD. I've found a coach! I've found one, father!

SQUEERS. Right.

He is dragging SMIKE out when SNAWLEY speaks.

SNAWLEY. Hard-heartedness and evil-doing never prosper, sir.

SQUEERS. That's true. That's very true.

SMIKE. Home!

SQUEERS. What a go! What a delicious go!

SMIKE *is dragged out by* SQUEERS. SNAWLEY *and* WACKFORD *follow.*

Scene Twenty

The garden of the Nicklebys' new home at Miss La Creevy's. A wall. Enter KATE *and* MRS NICKLEBY. *It's afternoon.*

MRS NICKLEBY. No, Kate, before your dear papa and I, and even after, for a while, we met at least, I was besieged by suitors. Quite besieged, and it was certainly a matter of some comment and occasionally a little jealousy.

KATE. Well, I am convinced of it, mama.

MRS NICKLEBY. It must have been, suitors I mean – at least a dozen.

KATE. Oh, mother, surely not!

MRS NICKLEBY. Well, yes, indeed, my dear, and that is not including your papa, or the young gentleman who used to go to the same dancing school and would send round gold watches to our house in gilt-edged paper – all returned, of course – and who, unfortunately, was sent out to Botany Bay, in a convict ship, and then escaped into a bush and started killing sheep – I don't know how they got there – and was going to be hung, until he accidentally choked himself, and so they pardoned him. No, there was Lukin –

A bunch of radishes flies over the wall. KATE *astounded.*

Mogley –

A cabbage.

Tipslark –

A turnip.

Cabbery –

A bunch of carrots.

Young Smifser –

KATE. Uh – mama –

MRS NICKLEBY. Good heavens. What can all these be?

KATE. They're vegetables, ma'am.

MRS NICKLEBY. Well, so they are indeed. They must be from the gentleman.

KATE. What gentleman?

MRS NICKLEBY. The one next door. It appears to be his custom, to communicate his feelings in this – charmingly eccentric way.

KATE. So this intrusion has occurred before?

MRS NICKLEBY. Oh yes, why, certainly. The cucumbers we ate at dinner yesterday –

A VOICE. A-hem!

KATE. That's him?

MRS NICKLEBY. Yes, yes, it must be, but I wouldn't say intrusion, dear, in fact, you will recall the cucumbers were excellent and I am seriously considering pickling the rest for winter, and –

THE VOICE. A-hem!

KATE. Mama, he's –

MRS NICKLEBY. Now, don't be alarmed, my dear. It's not intended to scare anyone; we must give everyone their due –

KATE. What do you mean, mama?

The GENTLEMAN NEXT DOOR *has climbed up a ladder behind the wall and appears above it. He is quite old, and wears a nightcap. He looks – and is – crazy.*

KATE. Now, mother. We are going to stand up and very calmly walk back to the house.

MRS NICKLEBY. Oh, Kate, you're such a coward.

To the GENTLEMAN.

Sir, what do you want? How dare you look into this garden?

THE GENTLEMAN. Queen of my soul. This goblet – sip.

He empties a basket of more vegetables into the garden.

MRS NICKLEBY. Nonsense, sir.

THE GENTLEMAN. Won't you sip the goblet? Oh, do sip the goblet.

MRS NICKLEBY. Go away, sir!

THE GENTLEMAN. Go away? Go quite away?

MRS NICKLEBY. Yes, certainly.

THE GENTLEMAN. Go now?

MRS NICKLEBY. Exactly now!

THE GENTLEMAN. Without the chance of asking you one question?

MRS NICKLEBY. Well –

KATE. Mama!

MRS NICKLEBY. One must be civil, dear.

THE GENTLEMAN. The question is – are you a princess?

MRS NICKLEBY. Sir, you mock me.

THE GENTLEMAN. No, but really.

MRS NICKLEBY. I am not sir. Obviously.

THE GENTLEMAN. Then are you a relation to the Archbishop of Canterbury? Or the Pope of Rome? Or the Speaker of the House of Commons? Forgive if I err, but I was told you were the niece to the Commissioner of Paving, which would account for your relationship to all three.

MRS NICKLEBY. Whoever has spread such reports has taken a great liberty, and one which I am sure my son, were he aware of it, would not allow one instant. The idea! Niece to the Commissioner of Paving.

THE GENTLEMAN. Beautiful madame –

KATE. Now, mother. Come away.

MRS NICKLEBY. Be quiet, dear.

THE GENTLEMAN. I am no youth, ma'am, but I venture to presume that we are fitted for each other.

MRS NICKLEBY. Oh, dear, Kate –

THE GENTLEMAN. I have estates, ma'am – jewels, lighthouses, fishponds, and a whalery of my own in the North Sea, and several oyster-beds of great profit in the Pacific Ocean. But I've enemies about me, ma'am – the Messrs. Gog and Magog – who would poison me and steal my property. But if you bless me with your hand and heart, we'll have the Lord Chancellor call out the military, and so clear the house before the service is performed. Then, bliss and rapture! Bliss and rapture! Love, be mine, be mine!
Pause.

MRS NICKLEBY (*to* KATE). I don't know what to say.

KATE. Surely, mama, you need only say one word.

MRS NICKLEBY. Sir, just one word. While I acknowledge that peroration – if only to a small extent – is quite agreeable –

KATE. Mama, inside.

MRS NICKLEBY. I have made up my mind to stay a widow, and devote myself to my two children. It's a painful thing, of course, rejecting a proposal – but –

KATE. Now!

MRS NICKLEBY. As I'm, somewhat rudely, summoned, sir, good day.

The GENTLEMAN *slumps suddenly, as if the ladder had been pulled. He looks down.*

KEEPER. Oi!

THE GENTLEMAN. Oh. You.

The voice of the GENTLEMAN'S KEEPER.

KEEPER. That's right.

THE GENTLEMAN. How's the Emperor of Tartary?

KEEPER. Oh, much the same as usual.

THE GENTLEMAN. In that case. Perhaps I'd best descend.

KEEPER. Well, yes. Perhaps you had.

The GENTLEMAN *descends. His* KEEPER *then appears.*

KEEPER. Ah. Beg your pardon, ladies. Has this gentleman been making love to either of you?

KATE. Yes.

KEEPER. Oh, dear. He always will, you know. There's nothing will prevent him making love.

KATE. Out of His Mind?

KEEPER. Way out.

KATE. A long time?

KEEPER. Very long.

KATE. And there's no hope for him?

KEEPER. No, none at all. And don't deserve to be. I tell you, he's a great deal pleasanter without his wits than with 'em.

Pause.

Well. So sorry you've been troubled, ladies. Afternoon.

And he climbs down the ladder out of view.

KATE (*firmly*). Out of his mind.

MRS NICKLEBY *picking up all the vegetables except one cucumber.*

MRS NICKLEBY. Oh, Kate! You don't think – you don't believe the gentleman is mad?

KATE. Of course I do. You heard –

MRS NICKLEBY. Oh, yes, I heard. Oh, yes, dear, I heard everything.

MRS NICKLEBY *sails into the house.*

KATE. Mama!

KATE, *in frustration, picks up the cucumber and throws it back over the wall.* NICHOLAS *stands there.*

NICHOLAS. Kate, what are you doing?

KATE. Oh, Nicholas –

NICHOLAS. Kate, do you know where Smike is?

KATE. Why, isn't he – I thought he'd gone to meet you.

NICHOLAS. No. Well, at all events . . . *Kate.*

NICHOLAS *suddenly panics, and runs into the house.* KATE *follows. The rumble of thunder.*

Scene Twenty-one

Outside the Saracen's Head. Enter TILDA *and* JOHN BROWDIE. JOHN *is carrying an immense amount of luggage, which he puts down.*

JOHN. So did tha see that, Tilda? See that Post-Office? Ecod, if that's a Post-Office, I'd like to see the house of the Lord Mayor of Lunnon. Wouldn't tha?

TILDA. I would indeed, John.

JOHN (*shouts off*). Come on, Fanny! Raise thissen! We're here!

And FANNY SQUEERS *shuffles on. She looks as if it's been a very long journey.*

Eee, lass, tha looks like summat that's been dragged from

Yorkshire, 'stead of coming on a big clean coach. Ee, don't tha think so, Tilda?

FANNY. Tilda. How you have been kicking me throughout this blessed night.

TILDA. Well, I like that! When you had nearly the whole coach to yourself.

Enter WILLIAM *the waiter.*

FANNY. No, don't deny it, Tilda, for it's true, although of course you won't have noticed it, as being fast asleep, but I've not closed my eyes a single wink, and so I think I am to be believed.

WILLIAM. Good morning, ladies. Sir. Welcome to the Saracen's Head.

JOHN. Eh. I were right. I said that it were Sarah, Sarah Summat.

FANNY. What.

JOHN. Sarah-son's head. I told 'ee, Fanny.

FANNY (*clocking* WILLIAM). Tilda, dear, please stop him, we'll be taken for I don't know what.

JOHN. Oh, let 'em take us how they find us. I'm a married man. Here be the wedding party: bride and bridesmaid, and the groom, and we've not come to Lunnon for another purpose but to 'joy oursens, now have we?

FANNY *looks at* JOHN. JOHN *elbows* FANNY.

Have we, Fanny. Eh?

FANNY (*to* WILLIAM). I wonder, sir, if you could tell me if my father's in.

WILLIAM. Your father? Who may that be, Miss?

FANNY (*impatiently*). It's Mr Wackford Squeers. He should be stopping − staying − in this here establishment.

WILLIAM. Oh, him. Oh, he's not stopping here, Miss. Stopping somewhere else, entirely, with some friends of his, to save on the expense, I would imagine. But he comes in every day. I'll go and tell him he's been asked for.

Enter SQUEERS.

SQUEERS. Eh. Fanny. Mr Browdie. Tilda Price. Well, who'd have thought of this?

Exit WILLIAM.

TILDA. It's Tilda Browdie now, sir. John and I are wed.

JOHN. And come down for our honeymoon.

SQUEERS. Well, Fanny, here's a thing. It's your turn to be married now. You must make haste.

FANNY. Oh, I am in no hurry, dear papa.

TILDA. No, Fanny?

FANNY. No, dear Tilda. I can wait.

TILDA. So can the young men, it appears.

FANNY. Oh, *Tilda*.

SQUEERS. Eh. Eh, Fanny. Who do you suppose we laid our hands on yesterday?

FANNY. Oh, pa! Not Mr Nick –

SQUEERS. No. But just about next door.

FANNY. You can't mean, Smike?

SQUEERS. I can. I do. I've got him hard and fast.

JOHN. What's that? You got that poor, damned scoundrel? Where?

SQUEERS. Why, at the top back room, my lodging. Him on the one side and a great key the other.

JOHN (*greatly amused*). At tha lodging! Got him at the lodging! Eh, I'm damned, but I must shake tha hand for that.

He pumps SQUEERS' *hand.*

Eh. Got him at tha lodging.

He punches SQUEERS *merrily on the chest.*

SQUEERS. Yes. That's right. My lodging. Thankee – and please don't do that again.

FANNY. Where are your lodgings, father?

SQUEERS. Oh, a place called Somers Town. It's quite a way but you must come to tea and meet the Snawleys, Fanny.

JOHN. 'Course we will. We'd come if it were 20 mile. Eh. Tilda?

TILDA, *a shruggy smile.*

SQUEERS. Uh –

JOHN (*picking up the baggage*). We can go and see the sights, tomorrow, can't we?

TILDA. Uh, John –

JOHN. Oh, certainly. We'll be there. Now. Where is that fellow?

He turns back. He is still amused

Be there. At tha lodging. Come on, Tilda!

He takes the bags out. FANNY *and* SQUEERS *look at* TILDA.

TILDA (*nervously*). I think – perhaps he's sickening for something. I have seen him – just the same. When he's been sickening.

She goes out.

SQUEERS. I think he's lost his wits.

FANNY. Poor Tilda.

SQUEERS *looks at his daughter. Thunder rumbles again, and they run indoors.*

Scene Twenty-two

A park. Thunder. RALPH *runs on, his collar up against the rain. He stops centre stage, looks up. We imagine he's under a tree. A beggar passes. The beggar turns back, looks at* RALPH. *Then he speaks. It's* BROOKER.

BROOKER. Oh, you. At last.

Pause.

RALPH. What's that?

BROOKER. At last, I've found you.

RALPH. What do you want?

BROOKER. What do I want? You see me. I'm a miserable and wretched outcast, nearly sixty years of age, and destitute and helpless, wanting even one dry crust of bread. So, what'd you think I want?

RALPH. I'm sixty, and neither destitute nor helpless. Work, sir, work. Don't beg for bread, but earn it.

RALPH *makes to go.*

BROOKER. Do you not know me?

RALPH *turns back.*

RALPH. No. Why, should I?

BROOKER. Do you not remember, 30 years ago, a man you threw in jail for owing you some paltry sum of money?

RALPH. Well, I've had many debtors in my time, and have arrested many, too.

BROOKER. But the one who you released – and took into your service? As a clerk, who wasn't overnice, and knew a little of the trade you drove?

Pause.

RALPH. Oh, yes. Perhaps I do remember.

BROOKER. And how I served you always faithfully?

RALPH. Well, yes. You had your wages, and you did your work. You owed me money, and you owe it still. Now, tell me what you want.

BROOKER. I've been looking for you, now, two days.

RALPH. Well, now you've found me. What d'you want?

BROOKER. I want to pay you back.

RALPH. Oh, yes? What with?

BROOKER. With interest. With something – that will interest you.

RALPH. Yes? What?

BROOKER. I know, there's something that I know. I took advantage of my place, with you. There's something that I did, to get at you. And you would, you'd give half of what you own to know it.

RALPH. Would I, now.

BROOKER (*forcefully*). I've been a convict now, for seven years. For some small trickery that lay outside the law, a nothing to the trickery you money-makers do within it. I have now returned, the broken creature that you see before you.

Slight pause.

I haven't come to beg. I've come to sell. My expectations are not monstrous, but I have to live.

Pause.

RALPH. Well, Mr – I don't know the name to call you.

BROOKER. By my old one. I don't care.

RALPH. Then hear this, Mr Brooker. You have claimed you have a hold on me. My answer is: you keep it, or publish it, for *I* won't care.

BROOKER. That wouldn't serve me.

RALPH. Sir, I know the world, the world knows me. Whatever

sin of mine you've gleaned, the world knows it already. You could tell it nothing that would shock it about me. I am reviled and threatened every day.

BROOKER. You're proud of that.

RALPH. Indifferent. For all the rank contempt in which I'm held, things roll on just the same, and I grow richer by them. So, now, go.

BROOKER. I won't.

RALPH. Then I will.

BROOKER. Then I tell you – you will hear from me again.

RALPH. Then I tell *you*, that if I do, and you so much as notice me by one small begging gesture, you shall see the inside of a jail once more, and contemplate your hold on me in there! That is my answer to your trash. So, take it!

RALPH strides off.

BROOKER. Oh, you'll hear from me again.

"The man remained upon the same spot with his eyes fixed upon the retreating figure until it was lost to his view, and then drawing his arms about his chest, as if the damp and lack of food struck coldly to him, lingered with slouching steps by the wayside, and begged of those who passed along".

Scene Twenty-three

The top back room of the Snawley's house in Somers Town. SMIKE is there, locked up. A rattle of keys, and JOHN BROWDIE enters. SMIKE shrinks in terror. JOHN grabs SMIKE, and puts his hand over SMIKE's mouth.

JOHN. My name is Browdie. I'm from Yorkshire. I'm a friend of your friend, lad who beat the schoolmaster. Don't say a word.

Pause. SMIKE nods. JOHN lets him go and takes a screwdriver from his pocket.

I've snuck up, making out I'm poorly. When you gone, I'm going to prise the lock off, make it look as how you did it.

SMIKE. Go where?

JOHN. Where? Go away. Go home.

SMIKE looking confused.

JOHN. Escape. Do you understand?

SMIKE. Yes, yes, I understand.

SMIKE *is beginning to go. Then he suddenly grabs* JOHN.

He brought me back, before. He'll do again. I know he will.

JOHN. He won't. Now, come on, quickly, off with 'ee.

SMIKE *can't move.*

Oh, th'art a broken-down old chap. I shouldn't shout at thee. Go down the stair, go quiet past the door t'where they are, s'tight shut, I swear they'll never hear thee.

SMIKE *releases* JOHN.

SMIKE. Now?

JOHN. Yes, now. One more thing. Just tell young master, when tha sees him, as I'm spliced to Tilda now, and staying at the Saracen's. Tha can remember that?

SMIKE. Yes, yes. Spliced to Tilda.

JOHN. Now, go, go.

SMIKE *a look at* JOHN, *then he goes.* JOHN *with his screwdriver, goes to prise off the door lock. But something is preventing him holding it steady. He is shaking, as if in a strong convulsion. It gradually becomes apparent that* JOHN BROWDIE *is even more vastly amused than he has ever been vastly amused before.*

Scene Twenty-four

The roads to and from the country. Enter SMIKE, *desperately running on the spot.*

NARRATOR. And without pausing for a moment to reflect upon the course he was taking, he fled with surprising swiftness, borne upon such wings as only fear can wear.

SMIKE *is in a spot running. Behind him, through the darkness, we see, as a fantasy, a nightmare vision of Dotheboys Hall:* MRS SQUEERS, *ringing her bell,* MR SQUEERS *with his cane,* WACKFORD *laughing,* FANNY, *the* BOYS. *We hear lines too, echoed and distorted:* "And a pretty thing it is". "O.U.T.C.A.S.T.". "Forsaken". "Homeless". "In here, you haven't finished". "I'll flog you within an inch of your life". *And gradually, the noises coalesce, and become the swishes of a cane, growing louder and louder.* SMIKE *puts his hands to his ears. The sounds grow even louder: they're inside his head. Finally, the nightmare fades,* SMIKE *stops, takes his hands from his ears, and there is silence. An owl hoots. Silence.*

NARRATORS. And it was not until the darkness and quiet of a country road recalled him to the world outside himself,

And the starry sky above him warned of the rapid flight of time,

That, covered with dust and panting for breath, he stopped to listen and look about him.

All was still and silent.

A glare of light in the distance, casting a warm glow upon the sky, marked where the huge city lay.

It was late now.

He turned back, and taking the open road, made again for London.

SMIKE *turns and walks. Passers-by cross the stage, and continue the Narration.*

NARRATORS. And by the time he re-entered it at the western extremity, the greater part of the shops were closed. Of the throngs of people who had been tempted abroad after the heat of the day, but few remained.

Suddenly, out of the passers-by leaps NEWMAN NOGGS, *who grabs* SMIKE. SMIKE *nearly jumps out of his skin.*

NOGGS. Dear fellow; oh, dear fellow.

SMIKE. Uh – uh –

NOGGS. Smike, it's only me.

SMIKE. Oh, Mr Noggs –

NOGGS. Where have you been? They've been half mad about you.

SMIKE. Who have?

NOGGS (*obviously*). Mr Nicholas. His mother. And Miss Nickleby. And I must take you home at once.

SMIKE. Yes. Yes.

NOGGS *is striding off.* SMIKE *not.* NOGGS *turns back, looks, questioningly.*

Miss Nickleby.

NOGGS. That's right.

SMIKE. Miss Nickleby . . . Half mad about me too?

Pause. NOGGS *a little nod, goes and takes* SMIKE's *arm. They go out together.*

END OF ACT ONE.

ACT TWO

Scene One

The coffee-room of the Saracen's Head. NICHOLAS sits at a table with a white cloth. Two other chairs. Enter JOHN BROWDIE, TILDA and WILLIAM the waiter.

JOHN. A gentleman? What gentleman?

Sees NICHOLAS.

Eh! Schoolmaster's assistant.

NICHOLAS. Mr Browdie.

JOHN (*to* WILLIAM). Well, din't stand there – gentleman has come to see us. Fetch some food, some pies, some cuts of beef, a tongue or two, a fowl, some ale. Come on, sir, bustle.

TILDA. John, we have just had dinner – and, p'raps, Mr Nickleby as well – ?

JOHN. What? Call that dinner? Come now, bustle, bustle.

WILLIAM. Yes, sir, certainly.

WILLIAM goes out.

JOHN. Well, then.

NICHOLAS. Sir, I have come here with three purposes. The first is to express my heartfelt thanks to you, releasing that poor lad, at such a risk –

JOHN. Oh, weren't no risk.

NICHOLAS. Well, I am sure that's not the case, but still. The second, naturally, is to express my most sincere congratulations on your recent nuptials.

JOHN. Oh, ay.

NICHOLAS. And trusting that I'll be allowed to take the usual license, Mr Browdie.

JOHN. Oh, ay – take whatever – dinner's coming soon.

NICHOLAS. I thank you. Mrs Browdie.

NICHOLAS kisses TILDA.

TILDA. Mr Nickleby!

JOHN. Oh, I see. Do, do make thaself at home.

NICHOLAS. I shall, of course – on one condition.

JOHN. Ay, what's that?

NICHOLAS. That when you have occasion for one, you'll make me a godfather.

TILDA. Oh, Mr Nickleby.

JOHN (*hugely tickled*). Wha's that? A godfather? Oh, ay. Oh, don't say another word. Tha'll not beat that. A godfather. Eh, Tilda, hast tha ever heard the like? Wha's going on?

And indeed, during the last few moments, we have become aware of a disturbance.

TILDA. I don't know, John.

Enter a gaggle of people, including an ANGRY FELLOW *with a bleeding nose and torn collar,* WILLIAM, *a* YOUNG MAN, *rolling up his sleeves, and a number of* CUSTOMERS *and* WAITRESSES.

ANGRY FELLOW (*to* WILLIAM). Police! I want the police.

Pointing to the YOUNG MAN.

I want that man arrested.

1st CUSTOMER. Right, so he should be.

1st WAITRESS. What a thing to do!

WILLIAM. Now, sir, please, if we could just keep calm about this –

ANGRY FELLOW. Calm? He asks me to be calm!

2nd CUSTOMER (*to* 1st WAITRESS). He asks him to be calm.

ANGRY FELLOW. The police, sir! Now!

JOHN. What's going on here, then?

ANGRY FELLOW. I'll tell you, sir, what's going on, that if a fellow sitting quietly with a drink, conversing with his friends, is liable to be assaulted by a perfect stranger –

2nd WAITRESS. Well, it's certainly a scandal.

ANGRY FELLOW. Sitting, quietly, doing nothing but conversing –

1st CUSTOMER. Nothing else.

ANGRY FELLOW. And then to have some great young lout come up to him, and tear his collar, punch him on the nose –

NICHOLAS. Could one inquire – what is the explanation of the gentleman concerned?

ANGRY FELLOW. Well – do you hear that! "Gentleman". "An explanation". Hmph!

2nd CUSTOMER. "Could one inquire".

1st WAITRESS. "The gentleman concerned".

The YOUNG MAN *steps forward. He is Welsh.*

YOUNG MAN. One could inquire, sir, and I would be pleased to give an explanation. I have just returned, sir, from a journey of some distance, and was sitting in the coach-house with a pint of wine, when I could not but overhear that person, choosing to express himself in very disrespectful and familiar terms, of a young lady. I informed him, with considerable civility, that I was sure he was mistaken in his vile conjectures, which were of a most offensive nature, and demanded he withdraw them unconditionally. This he refused to do, and so I took his collar and I punched him on the nose.

Pause.

NICHOLAS. I see. Well – that does sound, it seems you did have cause, sir, certainly – you know the lady, I presume?

YOUNG MAN. Oh, no, I never heard of her.

NICHOLAS. But, um –

YOUNG MAN. But it would be a pretty state of things, if names of ladies could be bandied round the town, without a let or hindrance, merely for the want of some acquaintance of the bandied person being present to defend their honour. Wouldn't it?

1st WAITRESS. Well, now –

2nd WAITRESS. That certainly sounds reasonable.

1st CUSTOMER. If not, I mean, uh –

1st WAITRESS. Where would be the end of it?

YOUNG MAN. My view entirely.

To the ANGRY FELLOW.

Now, sir, I'd suggest we both allow our tempers to cool down. I can be contacted, at this address.

He hands the ANGRY FELLOW *a card.*

If you wish to bring a charge. But now, I'd seriously advocate, that everyone proceeds about their business with no more ado.

1st CUSTOMER. Right, then.

2nd WAITRESS. Yes, back to business.

1st CUSTOMER. What an excellent idea.

They have all gone, except for the ANGRY FELLOW.

YOUNG MAN. Good evening, sir.

The ANGRY FELLOW *goes out. To* NICHOLAS.

Well, I must thank you for your intervention, sir, and ask to know where I may find you to express my formal gratitude. Here is my card. Good evening, sir.

NICHOLAS *gives the* YOUNG MAN *his card, as he accepts the* YOUNG MAN's.

NICHOLAS. Good heavens. You're a Cheeryble.

FRANK CHEERYBLE (*for it is he*). That's right, sir.

TILDA (*to* JOHN). What's a Cheeryble?

NICHOLAS. But surely not – that Cheeryble, who's nephew to the other Cheerybles, who has been for the last four years establishing an agency in Lancashire, and is expected back tomorrow?

FRANK. Yes, I am that Cheeryble, indeed, sir. And may I presume to ask if you are that same Mr Nickleby whom I have learnt was recently employed by my two uncles, and of whom I've heard, by letter and by wire, the most complete and constant good report?

NICHOLAS. Well, of the good report, I cannot speak. But I am Mr Nickleby.

FRANK. Well, there's a thing.

NICHOLAS. Yes, isn't it.

FRANK. You, Mr Nickleby. Do call me Frank.

NICHOLAS. You, Mr Cheeryble. Please call me Nicholas.

JOHN (*to* TILDA). D'you s'pose the dinner'll have come?

NICHOLAS (*suddenly*). Oh, Mr Browdie. I said I had come with a threefold purpose, and I did not complete my mission. Would you and Mrs Browdie do us the great honour of calling on us tomorrow night. And if you would forgive me making one addition to the party, I would hope that Mr Cheeryble might join us too.

FRANK. I would be most delighted.

TILDA. So would we.

NICHOLAS. Right, then. That's settled.

Enter WILLIAM.

WILLIAM (*to* JOHN). Sir, I have laid out what you ordered in your room. I would point out, though, that I didn't realise your party was — of only four. There is enough for twice or thrice that number, sir.

JOHN. In that case. It'll do.

Scene Two

The Kenwigs' front room. Chairs, tables, a clothes-horse with towels hanging. Downstage, kettles and teapots. At least three MARRIED LADIES, MRS CUTLER, MISS GREEN *and* MORLEENA, *who is nursing* LITTLE LILLYVICK, *the baby.* MR KENWIGS *himself is standing looking nervous, for* MRS KENWIGS, *offstage, is having another baby.*

NARRATORS.

And after a substantial supper with the Browdies,

Nicholas walked on to Golden Square,

And to the house of Newman Noggs,

Not knowing that downstairs from his old friend,

There had been an addition to the family of the Kenwigs,

An event which half the neighbourhood had come to witness and to celebrate.

Enter a NURSE *from Mrs Kenwigs' room of confinement. All the* LADIES *eagerly move towards her. The* NURSE *looks quickly round to select the most suitable people for the tasks in hand. Behind her enters* DR LUMBEY, *the doctor, whose task is completed, and is rolling down his sleeves.*

NURSE. Morleena. Fetch your ma a cup of something hot. And — Madam, will you fetch more salts.

KENWIGS *stepping forward.*

No, not yet, Mr Kenwigs!

The NURSE *goes back into the other room.* MORLEENA *puts* LITTLE LILLYVICK *in his crib, goes to the hob, pours a hot drink, and takes it in.* DR LUMBEY *talks to* KENWIGS *and goes to pick up the abandoned* LITTLE LILLYVICK.

DR LUMBEY. It's a fine boy, Mr Kenwigs, there's no doubt about it.

KENWIGS. Oh, Dr Lumbey, do you think so?

DR LUMBEY. Now this is —

KENWIGS. Little Lillyvick.

Enter the NURSE.

NURSE. Please, madam, put more water on to boil. And —

To MISS GREEN.

Miss, please run down down to the corner shop and get a bottle of sal volatile. In a few moments, Mr Kenwigs!

MISS GREEN *goes out to the shop.*

KENWIGS (*to* DR LUMBEY). Morleena was a fine child as well.

DR LUMBEY. Oh, they all were, sir.

To the BABY.

Goo goo goo goo.

KENWIGS. She'll be a treasure to the man she marries. Did you ever see her dance?

DR LUMBEY. No, I haven't had that privilege.

To the BABY.

Gob gob gob gob.

KENWIGS. Not to speak of course, about her expectations.

2nd MARRIED LADY. What, expectations?

MRS CUTLER. Mm.

KENWIGS. Well, ma'am; it's not perhaps for me to say. It's not for me to boast of any family with which I have the honour to be linked — but shall we say, my children might come into a small matter of a hundred pounds-a-piece. Perhaps. P'raps more; but certainly that much.

1st MARRIED LADY. A very pretty little fortune.

KENWIGS. I will make mention of no names, but many of my friends have met a relative of Mrs Kenwigs in this very room, as would give dignity to any company, that's all.

MRS CUTLER. I've met him. In this very room.

KENWIGS. And it's naturally most gratifying —

Enter the NURSE.

NURSE. Morleena, dear, the kettle.

KENWIGS. To my feelings as a father —

NURSE (*to* KENWIGS). You — stay there!

NURSE *goes out.* MORLEENA *goes and fills a teapot from the kettle.*

KENWIGS. To see a man like Mrs Kenwigs' uncle, Mr Lillyvick, a man like that a-kissing and a-taking notice of my —

Enter MISS GREEN.

MISS GREEN. Well, now, Mr Kenwigs, look who I found, coming up the stairs.

KENWIGS (*irritated*). Who is it?

Enter NICHOLAS. *He is slightly breathless.*

Why, Mr Johnson! What a privilege.

NICHOLAS. I fear, sir, that in fact my purpose was to Mr Noggs and must be, very soon, but having heard about your circumstance —

KENWIGS. Ah, yes. My circumstance. And, as I was saying, it is naturally very gratifying to my feelings as a husband and a father, to consider how dear Mr Lillyvick, how he will feel when he is made acquainted with this — happy circumstance.

NICHOLAS. Uh — Mr Lillyvick.

KENWIGS. That's right.

To 1st MARRIED LADY.

The Collector of the Water-Rate.

NICHOLAS. I wonder — if you've heard from him at all.

KENWIGS. No, not for several weeks. Oh, a week or two.

To 2nd MARRIED LADY.

And Mrs Kenwigs' uncle.

NICHOLAS. Or had a message.

KENWIGS. Why? Is there a cause for one?

NICHOLAS. Well . . .

KENWIGS. Well what?

Pause.

NICHOLAS. Sir, you remember Miss Petowker?

KENWIGS. Yes, of course I do.

NICHOLAS. He's married her.

Long pause.

KENWIGS. He's married Miss Petowker.

NICHOLAS. Yes, that's right. In Portsmouth.

KENWIGS. Portsmouth. Mr Lillyvick has married Miss Petowker.

NICHOLAS. That's correct.

Pause. MORLEENA *drops the kettle.*

KENWIGS. My children! My defrauded, swindled infants!

1st MARRIED LADY. What's this?

MORLEENA *goes rigid and starts screaming.*

NICHOLAS. Um –

KENWIGS. Villain! Cur! And traitor!

2nd MARRIED LADY. Hmph!

Enter the NURSE *and the* 3rd MARRIED LADY.

NURSE. What's all this? What's going on? What is this noise?

KENWIGS. Be silent, woman!

NURSE. You be silent, sir. Have you no feelings for the baby?

KENWIGS. No!

EVERYONE. Oh! Oh!

NURSE. Then, shame on you. Unnatural monster!

KENWIGS. Let him die! He has no expectations, and no property to come into. We want no babies here – take 'em away! Take all of them – off to the Foundling!

MORLEENA *screaming.* DR LUMBEY *trying to attend to* MORLEENA.

MRS CUTLER. Mr Kenwigs!

KENWIGS. Oh, the attention. The attention, that I've shown that man. The oysters he has eaten, and the pints of ale he's drunk, here in this house –

MRS CUTLER. Now, Mr Kenwigs, naturally, it's most upsetting –

KENWIGS. The presents that I've given him. The pipes, the snuff-boxes, a pair of india-rubber galoshes, costing six-and-sixpence – and then, for this – for this – Be quiet, Morleena!

MORLEENA *stops screaming.*

MORLEENA. Sorry, Pa.

NURSE. Oh, drat the stupid man!

The NURSE *goes out.*

KENWIGS. That man! His wild and careless passion – it has ruined us.

He goes out, dramatically.

NICHOLAS. Uh, I appear to be . . . the bearer of bad tidings. Please – excuse me.

NICHOLAS *goes out.*

1st MARRIED LADY. *Well.*

MRS CUTLER. What a performance.

2nd MARRIED LADY. What a vulgar man.

DR LUMBEY. Goo goo. Goo goo.

Scene Three

NOGGS' *garret. He's pottering round.* NICHOLAS *bursts in.*

NICHOLAS. Newman, I've come to thank you.

NOGGS. What?

NICHOLAS. For finding him, and bringing him to us.

NOGGS. Oh, don't, please don't.

NICHOLAS. And Newman, and to tell you something. Something I've been bursting with for days and cannot tell another living soul.

NOGGS. What's that?

NICHOLAS. It is – it is – oh, Newman, if you'd only seen her!

NOGGS. Seen her? Who?

NICHOLAS. Her lips, her eyes, her hair –

NOGGS. Uh – it's a lady?

NICHOLAS. Yes, of course, it is a lady. And, oh, what a lady. And – I had to tell you.

Pause.

There.

Pause.

NOGGS. Uh – tell me all about her.

NICHOLAS. I know nothing of her.

NOGGS. Nothing?

NICHOLAS. No. Except her first name. Which is Madeline. But now, I must – oh, if you saw her, Newman!

He runs out.

NOGGS. If.

Slight pause.

Oh, Nick.

Pause.

In Love. With lips and eyes and hair. With Madeline.

Scene Four

The Cheerybles' offices, upstage, and Ralph's downstage.
Narration, as NOGGS enters and sits at his desk.

NARRATORS.

The next morning, in his little office

And on the top of his little stool,

Newman Noggs heard the chime of a neighbouring church clock,

Looked up,

And clicked his tongue,

And soliloquised.

NOGGS. Three quarters past! My dinner is at two. And him not back. And told to wait. Three quarters of an hour.

Pause.

It's done on purpose. Just like him.

Pause.

I don't believe he has an appetite. Except for pounds, shillings and pence. I should like to have him made to swallow one of every English coin.

Pause. NOGGS relishes the idea.

The penny.

He laughs.

Ha – two shillings.

He laughs.

And – the crown!

NARRATORS.

His humour being in some degrees restored, Newman brought forth a little bottle,

Shook it,

Opened it,

And drank,

And restored it even more.

MR CHARLES, MR NED *and* NICHOLAS *assembling.*

While at the same time,

At the offices of the Brothers Cheeryble,

Nicholas was asked by Mr Charles and Mr Ned

If they could beg the quite immeasurable delight

Of having one quick word with them

In the privacy of their room.

NICHOLAS. Well, yes. Of course. Indeed.

NICHOLAS, MR CHARLES *and* MR NED *sit.*

NARRATOR. While Newman, having put away his bottle, heard the door, and voices –

The NARRATORS *withdraw.*

NOGGS. Well, that's it. There's someone with him. It'll be – "Stop till this gentleman has gone." Well, I won't do it, and that's flat.

NOGGS *hides and* RALPH *enters with* ARTHUR GRIDE, *an old, wizened miser.*

RALPH. Noggs! where are you, Noggs?

To GRIDE.

He must have gone to dinner. Hm.

GRIDE *shrugs and grins.* NOGGS *a look out of his closet. He sees the two men aren't going.*

Well, we'll use his room. It's cool and in the shade.

Another look from NOGGS. *He realises he's stuck.* GRIDE *shrugs and grins.*

So, sit down, Mr Gride, and tell me what's your business.

GRIDE *sits on the low stool,* RALPH *on the high one.* GRIDE *laughs.*

Hm. What's this?

GRIDE. Oh, you're a bold and deep one, Mr Nickleby.

Transfer focus to CHEERYBLES.

MR CHARLES. Now, sir, we would like to employ you, on a confidential and delicate mission.

MR NED. The object of the mission is a – um, young lady.

MR CHARLES. Nay, a very beautiful young lady, whom, I think you caught sight of in these very offices the first day you came here.

NICHOLAS. Ah, yes, I do remember, certainly.

Transfer to RALPH *and* GRIDE.

RALPH. So, then?

GRIDE. I'm going to be married.

RALPH. Hm. Some old hag with a fortune?

GRIDE. No, a pretty, dainty and bewitching little creature, of not yet nineteen. Do you remember Walter Bray?

RALPH. Oh, yes, indeed. The man about town, for whom the town became beyond his means. He owes me money. As I recall, nine hundred and ten pounds, four and – something.

GRIDE. Yes. And he owes me money too. A little more. And he is dying. And he has a daughter.

Transfer to CHEERYBLES.

MR CHARLES. The lady's father, sir, was married to a friend of ours. He was a wastrel and a profligate.

MR NED. His wife died, oh, about a year ago. He was committed to the King's Bench Prison.

NICHOLAS. So – she is destitute.

MR CHARLES. She is.

NICHOLAS. Can such a – is this possible?

MR NED. Well, yes, Mr Nickleby, I'm afraid it is.

Transfer to RALPH *and* GRIDE.

RALPH. So what you plan is this. You offer to release Bray from his debts, perhaps you give him an allowance, so he can live out his dying days in reasonable comfort, and, in exchange, you have his dainty daughter for your wife.

GRIDE. That's right.

RALPH. And as I'm the other creditor, you come here to ask me what I would accept.

GRIDE. Just so. I'd thought, nine shillings in the pound . . .

RALPH. Gride, tell me the whole story.

GRIDE. What?

Pause.

Oh, well . . .

Transfer to CHEERYBLES.

MR NED. And so, good brother Charles and I considered, and debated, and resolved, that we must undertake a harmless subterfuge.

MR CHARLES. That someone, feigning to be dealing in small ornaments and drawings and the like, should go to her and purchase what she makes for cash.

NICHOLAS. Uh — someone?

MR NED. So, then, there being no time like the present, can you go there now?

NICHOLAS (*going quickly to the door*). Yes, yes. At once, without delay.

He runs out. Transfer to RALPH's.

GRIDE. Oh. well. Supposing I was in possession of a deed, concerning some small property to which this pretty lady was entitled, of which nobody knows anything, except for me, and which her husband would lay claim to, would that, p'raps, account for —

RALPH. For the whole proceeding. Yes. You have the deed about you?

GRIDE. Oh, very well. If I'm to have my bride.

He hands over the deed. RALPH *reads it.*

My dainty bride.

RALPH *reads.*

Her eyelashes, and lips, and hair the fingers itch to play with . . .

RALPH. I've little eyes for beauty, I'm afraid. But if you choose to think you're buying her for love, then I can't stop you.

GRIDE. Buying her.

RALPH. Oh, Mr Gride, you have your dainty creature, Bray has his debts paid off, and I *my* debt, the full amount, and my share of your inheritance.

GRIDE *looks up in alarm.*

And so we're all content. Now, shall we go?

GRIDE *and* RALPH *go.* NOGGS *emerges.*

NOGGS. I think . . . I think I've lost my appetite.

Transfer to CHEERYBLES. NICHOLAS *bursts back in.*

NICHOLAS. Oh – Mr Charles.

MR CHARLES. What, back so soon?

NICHOLAS. You haven't told me where she lives. Or who she is. Or anything.

MR NED. Oh, please forgive us.

Handing over a slip of paper and an envelope.

Here is the address; the money; and the order. The young lady's name is Madeline. Her father's name is Walter Bray.

As the scene disperses:

NICHOLAS. And Nicholas, repressing every feeling that he should perhaps have stated his emotions with regard to the young lady, turned and left the chambers of the Brothers Cheeryble, and set a sprightly pace for the King's Bench Prison, and the meagre debtors' houses that surround it.

Scene Five

Near the King's Bench Prison. Bare stage, but full of beggars, criminals, the poor and the mad. For the first time, we are seeing the lowest of the low of London's poor. As NICHOLAS *walks through, he is grabbed and begged. Into the middle comes* MADELINE, *pushing her father* WALTER BRAY *in his wheelchair. The beggars and criminals withdraw, but their presence remains with us for this and the next scene.*

BRAY. Madeline, what's this? Who told a stranger that we could be seen? Who is it?

MADELINE. I believe –

BRAY. Oh, yes, you always do, believe. What is it?

NICHOLAS. Sir, I've called with a commission. For a pair of handscreens, and some painted velvet for an ottoman. I have a sum here, as deposit, of five pounds.

He hands the envelope to MADELINE.

BRAY. Hm. See it's right then, Madeline.

MADELINE. I'm sure it's absolutely right, papa.

BRAY. You're sure? How can you be? "I'm sure".

MADELINE *takes a five pound note out of the envelope.*

MADELINE. Well, I was right to be, papa.

BRAY. Now, go and get a newspaper, some apples, and two bottles of that port I had last week, and – and – I can't remember half of what I want. Well, you can always go out twice. And you can go too, sir, as soon as you've had your receipt.

NICHOLAS. It is no matter, sir.

BRAY. No matter? What d'you mean, sir? Do you think you bring your paltry money as a gift? It's business, sir, return for value given. Damn you, sir, d'you know that you are talking to a gentleman, who at one time could buy up fifty of such men as you, and all you have?

NICHOLAS. I merely meant that as I shall have many dealings with this lady, I'll not trouble her with forms.

BRAY. Well, we will have all the forms we need. My daughter, sir, requires no charity, and will not be the object of your pity. Business, sir! Now, Madeline, receipt!

MADELINE *writing a receipt.*

NICHOLAS (*to* MADELINE). When shall – when shall I call again?

BRAY. When you're requested, sir, and not before.

MADELINE. Oh, not for three or four weeks, sir. It is not necessary, I can do without.

BRAY. What? Not for three or four weeks, Madeline?

MADELINE. Then, sooner – sooner, if you please.

NICHOLAS. A week?

MADELINE (*giving* NICHOLAS *the receipt*). Yes, then, a week. Here's your receipt, sir.

NICHOLAS. Thank you. In a week's time, then. Goodbye.

He goes out. MADELINE, *after a moment, following.*

BRAY. Where are you going, my dear?

MADELINE. Oh, he's left his –

BRAY. What?

MADELINE. I – I'll be a moment, father –

BRAY (*unable to move without assistance*). What has he left?

MADELINE *catches up with* NICHOLAS.

MADELINE. Oh, sir, I don't know if I'm doing right, but pray – don't mention to your masters what has happened here this morning. He has suffered much. Today he's very bad. I beg you, sir.

NICHOLAS. You only have to hint a wish, and I would risk my life to gratify it.

MADELINE *turns away*.

Oh, I speak the truth. I can't disguise my heart from you. I'd – I would die to serve you. What else can I say?

MADELINE. Say nothing.

She goes out.

NICHOLAS. A week. How can I stand a week.

Scene Six

The same, a little later. BRAY *has been joined by* RALPH *and* ARTHUR GRIDE. NICHOLAS *and* MADELINE *have gone.*

RALPH. It must be in a week, sir. And we must know in five days.

Pause.

Now, sir, it's Mr Arthur Gride. An offer any father would be proud of! Think what a haul it is.

BRAY *looks at* GRIDE.

Come, sir. Mr Gride has money but no youth. Miss Madeline has youth and beauty but no money. Tit for tat. A deal of heaven's making. Hm?

GRIDE. Matches are made in heaven, so they say.

RALPH. So, what do you reply?

Pause.

BRAY. It's not for me to say. It's for my daughter.

RALPH. Yes, of course. But you have still the power to advise.

BRAY. Hm. Hm. Advise. I tell you, Nickleby, there were times when my will carried against everyone: her mother's family and friends, whole pack of 'em. With power and wealth on their side, and just will on mine.

RALPH. Well, there we are. Your wish is her command, I'm sure. But if it isn't . . .

BRAY *looks miserably at* GRIDE. RALPH *nods to* GRIDE, *who withdraws a little.*

BRAY. What? If I can't convince her?

RALPH. Well, shall we say . . . I see two pictures. One of Walter Bray, the fashionable fellow, as he once was, shining in society, in freer air, and under brighter skies, who knows, in France, but certainly in luxury. Another lease of life.

Moving closer.

Or else, another picture. In a churchyard, with a gravestone and a date. Perhaps two years, perhaps a little less, not more. Now, is it really not for you to say? It's really for your daughter to decide?

Pause.

You'll have cheated nature, Mr Bray.

Pause.

BRAY. But, Nickleby. Is this not cruel?

RALPH. Cruel. If he were younger, yes. But think, how long is it before your daughter is a widow?

BRAY. Yes, but still –

RALPH. By this, she is made rich. And you'll be young, and bright, and blazing once again.

BRAY. Yes, yes.

Pause.

You're right. It is for her, as well as me.

RALPH *gestures* GRIDE *back.*

RALPH. Exactly. And she'll live to thank you.

Sound of MADELINE *returning.*

BRAY. Hush. It's her.

Enter MADELINE *with apples, two bottles of port, and a newspaper.*

Ah, Madeline. Here are two gentlemen.

MADELINE. I see them, father.

BRAY (*trying to make a joke*). Huh. She used to say, Gride, that the very sight of you would make me worse. Well, p'raps she'll change her mind on that point; girls can change their minds, you know — you look so tired, my dear.

MADELINE. I'm not, indeed.

BRAY. Oh, yes, you are, you do too much.

MADELINE. I wish I could do more.

BRAY. I know. But still you overtax yourself, this wretched life, my love, it's more than you can bear, I'm sure of it . . .

Pause.

It's more than I can bear.

Slight pause. MADELINE goes and kisses her father.

RALPH. Five days, then, Mr Bray.

BRAY. Yes, very well. Five days.

RALPH *turns to go.* GRIDE *trying to take* MADELINE's *hand to kiss it.*

GRIDE. And if the lady . . . if the lady condescends . . .

MADELINE *shrinks from* GRIDE. GRIDE *looks to* RALPH, *who gestures him to go.* RALPH *and* GRIDE *leave* BRAY *and* MADELINE. GRIDE *a feeble grin to* RALPH *before scuttling off.*

RALPH. Oh Lord, how do people dupe themselves.

NOGGS *is there. The* BRAYS *have gone.*

They're here?

NOGGS. They've been here half an hour.

RALPH. Two men? One Mr Squeers?

NOGGS. That's right. In your room now.

RALPH. Good. Get a coach.

NOGGS. A coach? Whatever for?

RALPH. To ride in. To the Strand.

RALPH *goes upstage. We can see him greet* SNAWLEY *and* SQUEERS. NOGGS *gesturing vaguely.*

NOGGS. A coach. The Strand. Coach! The Strand! The Nicklebys. Oh, I should follow — but he'd see me.

He waves, agitatedly. We see BROOKER *groping along.*

Coach! Oh, the Strand, there's mischief in it. There must be!

He spots BROOKER.

Are you a coach?

BROOKER. No.

NOGGS (*searching in his pocket*). Uh –

BROOKER. Are you the clerk of Mr Nickleby?

NOGGS. Oh – no. Mean – yes.

BROOKER. Get him his coach. And see him off in it. And then, I want a word with you.

NOGGS. Coach!

Scene Seven

The Nicklebys' rooms in the Strand. A party. MRS NICKLEBY, KATE, NICHOLAS, SMIKE, MISS LA CREEVY, JOHN *and* TILDA BROWDIE, FRANK CHEERYBLE *and* TIM LINKINWATER. *A rug on the floor. Narration as the scene is set up:*

NARRATORS.
   And meanwhile, at the Strand,

   At Miss La Creevy's,

   The evening party was well under way,

   And it was universally agreed by all the guests,

   That they could not remember when they had had such a time,

   And, in particular, John and Tilda Browdie wished it to be known by one and all that they

JOHN. Would not have missed it for the world.

   The NARRATORS *withdraw.*

MISS LA CREEVY. Well, thank you *so* much, Mr Browdie, as it happens, I can't think –

MRS NICKLEBY. Well, yes, indeed, it's very good of you, dear Mrs Browdie too, because of course you come to see us in a very plain and homely manner. As I said to Kate –

MISS LA CREEVY. I just can't think of when I've had a better –

MRS NICKLEBY. As I said "Kate, dearest, you will only make the Browdies feel uncomfortable, if we indulge in great display, and how very inconsiderate that would be". But that is not to say –

MISS LA CREEVY. Of when I've had a better time myself.

MRS NICKLEBY. To say, of course, that we have no experience of high society, Kate, d'you recall those parties at Peltiroguses? They used to live about a mile from us, not straight you understand, but turning sharp left by the turnpike at the point the Plymouth mail ran over someone's donkey, Kate, you do recall those parties at the Peltiroguses?

KATE (*very firmly*). Mama. I entertain of them the most distinct and vivid memory.

Slight pause.

But also, I recall that earlier this evening Mr Browdie promised us that he would sing a song, and I am sure we are all most impatient that he should redeem his promise, and I'm certain that it will afford you much more pleasure and amusement than it's possible to think of.

MISS LA CREEVY. Oh, now, what a treat.

MRS NICKLEBY. Sing a song?

KATE. That's right, mama. Now, Mr Browdie?

JOHN. Oh, well, uh –

TIM. Oh, yes.

MISS LA CREEVY. Oh, Mr Browdie, please –

JOHN. Well, um –

To TILDA.

Sam Tansey's Fancy?

TILDA. No, John.

JOHN. Ballad of John Barleycorn?

TILDA. I think that's better.

JOHN. Right.

He stands, clears his throat.

Aye, right.

He sings

There came three men from out the west
Their victory to try –

A very loud knocking.

TILDA. What's that?

NICHOLAS. Must be some mistake. There's no one who would come here at this hour.

MRS NICKLEBY. Perhaps it's — some —

KATE. I'll answer it.

NICHOLAS *going to stop* KATE, *for fear that it's some malefactor, but* KATE *has got there, and* RALPH NICKLEBY *walks in.*

Oh, uncle.

MRS NICKLEBY. Brother-in-law. Why, what on earth —

RALPH. Now, stay, before that boy speaks, you will hear me, ma'am.

NICHOLAS. You won't, mama. Don't hear him. I will not have it. I do not know that man.

JOHN (*restraining* NICHOLAS). Come now, come now.

NICHOLAS. I cannot bear his presence, it's an insult to my sister, and I will not —

KATE. Oh, please, Nicholas —

NICHOLAS. This is my house, am I a child? Oh, this will drive me mad!

FRANK. Who is this man?

MISS LA CREEVY. It's Nicholas' uncle. Calls himself Ralph Nickleby.

SMIKE. Ralph Nickleby.

Pause.

RALPH. Ah. So this is the boy.

He goes and speaks outside.

Please come in, gentlemen. And Miss.

SMIKE. Ralph Nickleby!

Enter SQUEERS, SNAWLEY *and* FANNY.

JOHN. Eh, school master!

JOHN. Oh, Fanny!

SMIKE (*clinging to* MISS LA CREEVY). Huh. The enemies.

NICHOLAS. Am I to stand here and allow this? To allow my house to be invaded by these people?

RALPH. It will not last long, sir. I have come here on a simple mission, to restore a child to his parent —

NICHOLAS. What!

RALPH. — his son, sir, kidnapped and waylaid by you, with the base design of robbing him some day of any little wretched pittance which he might inherit.

SQUEERS. Oh, I bet you didn't think of this, eh? Got a father, has he?

RALPH. And as a proof, this is the father. Mr Snawley, there's your son.

Pause.

KATE. Oh, no.

SNAWLEY. Oh, yes. Yes, there he is. My son! My flesh and blood!

JOHN. Not that much flesh.

SNAWLEY. Come to me, boy.

Pause. SMIKE *rigid with terror.*

MISS LA CREEVY. Stay here.

RALPH. Then it is clear we must have further proof. You had a son by your first marriage, Mr Snawley?

SNAWLEY. Yes, I did, and there he stands.

RALPH. You and your wife were separated, and then you heard after a year or two, the boy had died.

SNAWLEY. Yes, I did. And now, the joy of —

RALPH. Whereas, in fact, you have discovered that your son's death was an invention by your former wife, to wound you, and in fact the boy had lived but was of an imperfect mind, and she had sent him to the school of Mr Squeers. Is that not so?

SNAWLEY. You talk like a good book, sir, that's got nothing inside but the truth.

NICHOLAS. I am expected to believe this fantasy?

RALPH *producing documents from a case.*

RALPH. Certificates of marriage, birth, the letters of the wife, and other documents. Perhaps you'd like to read them, sir.

NICHOLAS. Frank, Tim, please help me look at these.

FRANK, TIM *and* NICHOLAS *put documents on the table and read them.* RALPH *sits.*

SQUEERS. Well, sir, it seems you're reunited with your child. Oh, what a blessed moment!

SNAWLEY. Sir, I knew the very moment when you brought him to my house. I felt – at once – a tingling, a burning, and a palpitation.

SQUEERS. That's parental instinct, sir.

SNAWLEY. That's what it was, no doubt about it. My heart yearned.

SQUEERS. It only shows what nature is, sir. She's a rum one, nature.

SNAWLEY. She's a holy thing.

TIM, NICHOLAS *and* FRANK *have finished.*

FRANK. I'm afraid there's little doubt about it. Everything's in order.

TIM. It's a shame to say it, but it's so.

KATE. Oh, Nicholas, this can't be true.

NICHOLAS *shrugs.* RALPH *goes to the table and collects the documents.*

KATE (*quickly, to* SNAWLEY.) Sir, if you are the father of this boy, then look, sir, at the wreck he has become, and tell us if you plan to send him back to that vile den my brother took him from.

SQUEERS. Vile den! You hear that, Mr Nickleby?

RALPH. Now, there's a carriage waiting. Everything is proved. Let's take young Master Snawley and begone.

Pause.

NICHOLAS. There is – the documents speak clearly. If our pleas won't move this man, there's nothing to be done.

SNAWLEY. They won't indeed. Hmph! Have a father to abandon his own child?

SNAWLEY *goes and and takes* SMIKE's *arm.*

Come, son. The coach is waiting.

MISS LA CREEVY *looks away as* SMIKE *walks halfway towards* SNAWLEY. *He stops.*

SMIKE. O.U.T.C.A.S.T. A noun. Substantive.

SNAWLEY *looks bemused. He turns to* SQUEERS *who shrugs*

and smiles, as if to imply that SMIKE *is delirious.* NICHOLAS *turns away.*

SMIKE. Cast. Out. Home. Less. No!

He runs back to MISS LA CREEVY.

I won't. Won't go away again.

KATE. You hear that? Smike has chosen for himself.

SNAWLEY. Oh, this is cruel. Do parents bring children into the world for this?

JOHN (*nods to* SQUEERS.) Do they bring 'em into the world for *that*?

SQUEERS. Now, come on, blockhead, clear the way, and let him take his boy.

RALPH. Yes, sir, you have all blustered long enough.

JOHN. What, blockhead! Bluster? Well, I tell 'ee – I've released this poor chap from your clutches once – and I'll not stand by and see 'im going back to 'em again.

FANNY. Oh, Father, it was him! It was him let Smike go!

JOHN. Ay, 'twere, Fanny, and I tell 'ee – Get tha hands off me!

For SQUEERS *has been trying to get past* JOHN *and at* SMIKE. JOHN *elbows* SQUEERS *in the chest.*

I've had enough of this. The lot of you, get out, and leave the poor chap be.

And he starts pushing SQUEERS *and* SNAWLEY *to the door.*

SQUEERS. I tell you, sir –

JOHN. I'm telling you! Out! Out!

FANNY. Oh, Tilda! Stop him!

TILDA. Stop him what?

FANNY. He's beating up my father. Stop him!

TILDA. How?

SNAWLEY. I want my son! Ungrateful boy!

SQUEERS. Oh, he always was sir – he never loved me, never loved our Wackford, who is next door to a cherubim –

JOHN. Out, now, out!

SQUEERS. I warn you, sir –

But JOHN *has got* SQUEERS *and* SNAWLEY *out.*

JOHN. Well, done for two of 'em —

To RALPH.

You'd best get to your carriage, too, sir. And you, Fanny.

FANNY. Tilda.

SQUEERS. Eh, Fanny, s'got me hat!

TILDA *shrugs*.

FANNY. Tilda, I renounce you. I — I throw you off, for ever, I — I wouldn't have a child named Tilda — not to save it from its grave.

JOHN. Come on, now, Fanny —

FANNY. Don't you meddle with my Christian name. Don't you —

SQUEERS. Eh, me hat, or else he'll steal it!

FANNY (*to* TILDA). Viper! False friend! Vixen! Artful — vulgar — myrmidon!

TILDA. Oh, don't be silly, Fanny.

NICHOLAS. Yes, Miss Squeers, your father's gone —

SQUEERS. Not going. Not without me hat, I'm not.

FANNY. Oh, don't you speak to me.

FANNY *runs out.* SQUEERS *runs back in, grabs his hat.*

SQUEERS. I'll have you, Knuckleboy!

And JOHN *ejects him once again.*

RALPH. Well, sir. If reason and good feeling fail you, it will have to be the law.

Slight pause.

But one thing can be said. I take it your romance about this boy has been destroyed. No unknown, lost descendant of a man of high degree; but the weak, imbecilic son of some poor tradesman.

NICHOLAS. Sir. Now. Leave this house!

RALPH. I know you, sir. At least, do not delude yourself. I know your nature. Ma'am, goodnight.

RALPH *goes out. Pause.*

TIM. Well, what a business.

MRS NICKLEBY. I don't know — he's right of course, we should be reasonable. If only it was possible to settle it in a friendly manner – say, if Mr Snawley would agree to furnish something certain for Smike's board and lodging . . . wouldn't it be very satisfactory and pleasant for all parties?

KATE. No, mama. It wouldn't. You don't understand.

Slight pause.

MRS NICKLEBY. No, well – perhaps I don't. Perhaps I do – from time to time – find things a little hard to understand.

Pause. A hiatus. Then SMIKE runs to KATE and embraces her. Pause. MISS LA CREEVY goes to SMIKE.

MISS LA CREEVY. Now, Mr Smike, it's very late, and with all that excitement – shouldn't you be off to bed?

She takes SMIKE's hand and leads him towards the door. SMIKE turns back, to JOHN BROWDIE.

SMIKE. I am so grateful. Everything went black. I couldn't see.

He turns and goes out with MISS LA CREEVY.

JOHN. Well, now, don't this call for a celebration? Come on, gentlemen . . .

The MEN pouring drinks for everyone.

NICHOLAS. Well, yes, indeed, Frank.

FRANK. Now, Mrs Browdie –

The rug begins to move.

TILDA. What's that?

FRANK. What's what.

The rug is beginning to stand up.

TILDA. Oh, just, I thought I – oh, I did?

TIM. It's – under –

KATE. Oh, it's – from the cellar –

MRS NICKLEBY. From the –

The rug stands up. Under it is the GENTLEMAN FROM NEXT DOOR.

Oh, good heavens.

FRANK. What's this?

TIM. An intruder!

MRS NICKLEBY. Oh, it's him!

NICHOLAS. Mama, you know this person?

THE GENTLEMAN (*revealing himself*). Oh maid! Oh maid, I thee entwine!

He presents MRS NICKLEBY *with a cucumber.*

KATE. Oh, it's the man – the madman from next door!

MRS NICKLEBY. Now, Kate, I won't have that.

KATE. You won't?

MRS NICKLEBY. No, not at all. And I'm surprised at you. This is a most unfortunate and persecuted gentleman, in my view, to be aided rather than abused.

THE GENTLEMAN. That's excellent. So, bring the bottled lightning, one clean tumbler, and a corkscrew. Fetch the thunder sandwiches!

No-one fetches the thunder sandwiches. Enter MISS LA CREEVY.

MISS LA CREEVY. What's going on?

KATE. Oh, Miss La Creevy, it's –

THE GENTLEMAN. Ah, she is come!

MRS NICKLEBY. What's this?

THE GENTLEMAN. She's come! Take all three graces, all nine muses, melt 'em down with fourteen of the biscuit-baker's daughters of Oxford Street and make a woman half as lovely. Phoo! I defy you!

"After uttering this rhapsody, the old gentleman subsided into an ecstatic contemplation of Miss La Creevy's charms." He takes the cucumber from MRS NICKLEBY *and gives it to* MISS LA CREEVY.

FRANK. He seems to, um . . . have changed his mind.

MRS NICKLEBY. Oh, nonsense. He's mistaken me, that's all. It's often so. I am mistaken, frequently, for Kate. Now, sir –

THE GENTLEMAN (*to* MRS NICKLEBY). Avaunt ye, cat.

MRS NICKLEBY. I beg your pardon?

The MEN *move in to eject the* GENTLEMAN.

JOHN. Right now, that's enough.

THE GENTLEMAN. Cat! Puss!

MRS NICKLEBY *faints quite away.*

THE GENTLEMAN. Tit! Kit! Grimalkin!

FRANK. Or we may use force upon you.

THE GENTLEMAN. Tabby! Brindle! Whoosh!

As he departs, to MISS LA CREEVY.

Miss Milky Way – I am your puppet and your slave.

The GENTLEMAN *and the* MEN *have gone.*

MISS LA CREEVY. Well.

MRS NICKLEBY (*reviving*). Kate. Is he gone?

KATE. He is, mama.

MRS NICKLEBY. Oh, Kate, how dreadful.

KATE. It is that.

MRS NICKLEBY. I do believe the gentleman has lost his mind.

KATE. You do?

MRS NICKLEBY. And I am the unhappy cause.

KATE. You are?

MRS NICKLEBY. Of course. You saw him, just the other day,
you see what he is now. You've heard the dreadful nonsense he
has talked this evening, oh, can anybody doubt that he has gone
quite mad and it is my refusal of him that has made him so.

Exit MRS NICKLEBY. *The* MEN *returning.*

KATE. And with this, Mrs Nickleby turned tail, and, apologising
to her guests, went off to bed.

NICHOLAS. And soon the gentlemen came back, the old man
having been returned to his custodian.

TILDA. And John and Tilda, having to depart tomorrow morning,
took their leave, with many thanks, and invitations to the
company, if ever in North Yorkshire, to drop by.

ALL. North Yorkshire.

Exit JOHN *and* TILDA.

NICHOLAS. And although it was past midnight, Frank and Tim
remained a moment more.

TIM. Dear Miss La Creevy, please assure me you've recovered
from your terrible ordeal.

MISS LA CREEVY. Oh, yes. Certainly, dear Mr Linkinwater.

FRANK. Dear Miss Nickleby, I trust all those violent altercations
have not too disturbed your constitution.

KATE. No, I assure you, Mr Cheeryble.

And as the lights fade, we see SMIKE, behind them, looking fixedly at KATE and FRANK CHEERYBLE.

Scene Eight

The house of Arthur Gride. GRIDE enters, dragging an old, battered, metal trunk. He is singing "the fag end of some forgotten song."

GRIDE.
Tarantarantoo
Throw the old shoe
And may the wedding be lucky . . .

He opens the trunk, and takes out a bottle-green jacket.

Young, loving and fair . . .
Oh, what happiness there . . .

He looks at the jacket.

The bottle green? Now, that's a famous suit, for when I bought it at the pawnbroker, there was a tarnished shilling in the waistcoat pocket. So, it's a lucky suit . . . I'll marry in the bottle green.

He calls.

Peg!

Pause.

Peg! Peg! Peg Sliderskew!

"This call, loudly repeated, twice or thrice, brought into the apartment a short, thin, sweasen, blear-eyed old woman, palsy-stricken and hideously ugly." It is Gride's deaf housekeeper, PEG SLIDERSKEW. She is Scottish.

PEG. Wha's that?

GRIDE. Ah, there you are, Peg. I've decided. I'll –

PEG. Wha's that you calling?

GRIDE. Yes, of course, I wanted –

PEG. Or was't just the clock? It must ha' been one or the other – nothing else stirs in *this* house, that's for –

GRIDE (*tapping his chest*). Me, Peg, me.

PEG. Oh, you. What do you want?

GRIDE. I want, Peg, to be married in the bottle green.

PEG. Huh?

Slight pause.

What's this, dress up to be married? Why, what's wrong with what you usually wear?

GRIDE. But look my best, Peg, look my best.

PEG. What for? I tell ye, master, she's as handsome as you say, she won't look much at you, whatever you'se decked up in: bottle-green, sky-blue or tartan-plaid, won't make a fig of difference.

GRIDE. Now, Peg, I've told you, I've decided –

PEG. Och, I know –

GRIDE. And after, there'll be only she and me, and you, and we can live, the three of us, as cheap as you and I have always done . . .

PEG. Oh, is that so?

GRIDE. So take up the loose stitches in the bottle-green, Peg, best black silk, and put new buttons on the coat, you'll do this for me, Peg? My wedding day?

Pause.

PEG. Och, aye. I'll do't.

She takes the coat. The bell rings. PEG laughs.

Och, who'd have thought.

GRIDE. The bell, Peg.

PEG. That old Arthur Gride –

Bell rings.

GRIDE. The bell. Peg.

PEG (*still laughing*). Falling for a wee –

GRIDE. The bell!

Slight pause.

PEG. You what?

GRIDE. Go to it!

PEG. Go to what? What's wrong, me stopping here?

GRIDE (*gesturing a ringing bell*). It Is The Bell.

Slight pause.

PEG. Och. Aye. Well – I'll go answer it.

PEG goes out.

GRIDE. Hm. Half a witch that woman, I believe. But very frugal, very deaf, her living costs me next to nothing. Oh, she'll do, she'll do.

Calls.

Who is it, Peg?

PEG leads in NOGGS.

PEG. It's him.

GRIDE. Ah, Mr Noggs, my good friend, so what news d'you bring for me?

Exit PEG.

NOGGS (*handing over a letter*). No news. A letter. Mr Nickleby. The bearer waits.

GRIDE (*opening it eagerly*). A letter? Then it's news.

Quickly reading.

Oh, yes, and good news, too. The very best there could be.

NOGGS. The bearer waits.

GRIDE. And will not wait much longer – a verbal answer. Tell him: "Yes".

NOGGS. Just "Yes"?

GRIDE. That's right. He'll understand.

NOGGS (*turning to go*). I'm sure he will.

NOGGS going.

GRIDE. Oh – Mr Noggs?

NOGGS. Got the answer. "Yes."

GRIDE. I wondered –

NOGGS. Yes?

GRIDE. If you would like to join me in a little drop. To celebrate.

Pause.

NOGGS. Oh, well . . .

GRIDE. I know you're partial. Mr Noggs.

NOGGS. Oh. Very well.

GRIDE *opens the trunk to find a bottle and two small glasses. The hand which holds the letter is on the top of the trunk so* NOGGS *can read it.*

NOGGS. Poor girl. Poor girl.

GRIDE *has got the bottle and glasses, and suddenly shuts the trunk.* NOGGS, *to cover, stares "at the wall with an intensity so remarkable that Arthur was quite alarmed".*

GRIDE. Oh. Do you see anything in particular, Mr Noggs?

NOGGS. Only a cobweb.

GRIDE. Oh. Is that all?

NOGGS. No. There's a fly in it.

GRIDE. There's a good many cobwebs here.

NOGGS. So there are in our place. And flies too.

"Newman appeared to derive great entertainment from this repartee, and to the great discomposure of Arthur Gride's nerves, produced a series of sharp cracks from his finger-joints, resembling the noise of a distant discharge of small artillery." Then:

Sorry.

He looks balefully at the bottle. GRIDE's *grin reappears.*

GRIDE. I tell you, you have never tasted anything like this, I swear. Called eau d'or. It means "golden water". Water — turned to gold. I tell you, it's a sin to drink it.

GRIDE *looks at* NOGGS, *who looks balefully at him.*

Still.

He pours two small measures. NOGGS *picks up his glass.*

Oh, wait a minute, Mr Noggs. Don't drink it yet. I've had this bottle twenty years. And when I take a little taste, and that's not often, I do like to look at it. And think about it. For a moment. Tease myself.

Pause.

NOGGS. Uh —

GRIDE. Yes?

NOGGS. Uh — bearer waits.

GRIDE. Well, then. We'll drink it. Drink a toast. We'll drink it — to a lady.

NOGGS. To the ladies?

GRIDE. No – a lady. Little Madeline.

Slight pause.

NOGGS. What's that?

GRIDE. What's that? Oh, Mr Noggs, that is the prettiest, and daintiest, and –

NOGGS. Madeline?

GRIDE. That's right. With eyelashes, and –

NOGGS (*suddenly*). Bearer waits. Your hea –, her health. To Little Madeline.

He knocks the drink back in one.

I pray it can't be – But I fear it is. Good night.

He runs out, bumping into PEG as she comes in.

PEG. So. Who's that lunatic?

GRIDE. He's Nickleby's.

PEG. He's who's?

GRIDE. Oh, doesn't matter.

GRIDE gestures with Noggs' glass, to indicate NOGGS is a tippler.

PEG. Oh. I see.

GRIDE. Peg. Peg. It's Wednesday. Two days' time.

PEG. What is?

GRIDE. My wedding day.

Pause.

PEG. It's time for bed.

PEG shuffles off.

GRIDE. Huh. There's a change come over you, Mrs Peg. I don't know what it means. But if it lasts, shan't be together long. You're turning crazy, Mrs Peg, and if you do, I'll turn you out. All's one to me.

He comes across a document in the trunk.

Oh, here it is. Oh, here it is, my little beauty. "To Madeline." "To come of age or marry." Oh, my darling, dainty little deed.

He kisses the document and puts it away. Locking up.

Young, loving and fair,
Oh, what happiness there.
The wedding is sure to be happy.

GRIDE *goes out. We are aware that, in the gloom,* PEG *stands there. She has, if not overheard, at least overseen,* GRIDE *with the document. She potters forward.*

PEG. Huh – huh. A wedding, eh? A precious wedding. Huh.

Pause.

Wants someone better than this old Peg, eh? Take care of him.

Pause.

And wha's he said? So many times. Keep me content wi' short food, little wages and no fire? "My will, Peg, Peg, I've nobody, but you. Just think – my will."

Pause.

And now it's a new mistress, is it? Baby-faced young chit.

Pause.

She won't come in my way. Says you. Well, no she won't. I tell ye, Arthur, boy. She won't. But you – you don't know why.

Pause.

You're stuck to me, old Arthur Gride. You'll never throw out old Peg Slider.

Slight pause.

'Cos she's stuck to you.

Fade.

Scene Nine.

A street. Enter NICHOLAS, *followed by* NOGGS.

NICHOLAS. Tomorrow!

NOGGS. Yes – I didn't – never told me what her second name was –

NICHOLAS. But – *tomorrow* –

NOGGS. Had no way to know, you see; now, we must think –

NOGGS. I will go straight to Bray's. I'll see this man. And if there's one – small feeling of humanity, still lingering –

NOGGS. I doubt it.

NICHOLAS. Then what am I to do? You are my best friend, Newman, and I must confess I don't know what to do.

NOGGS. The greater need, then, for a cool head, reason and consideration. Thought.

NICHOLAS. There's only one thing. I can go to her. And try to reason with her, and point out the horrors she is hastening to.

NOGGS. Yes, yes, that's right! You see? That's bravely spoken.

NICHOLAS. Entreat her, even now, at least to pause. To pause!

NICHOLAS *runs out*.

NOGGS. He is a violent man. He has a violent streak. But still – I like him for it. There is cause enough.

NOGGS *potters out*.

Scene Ten

The King's Bench prison area. Beggars and criminals. MADELINE *wheels in* BRAY. NICHOLAS *arrives*.

NICHOLAS. Sir. Miss Madeline.

BRAY. Well, sir, what do you want?

NICHOLAS. I, um – I have come to –

BRAY. Hm. I s'pose you think you can burst in on us without a with-your-leave, because without the – paltry sums you bring, we'd starve?

NICHOLAS. My business, sir, is with the lady –

BRAY. With the daughter of a gentleman! Your business, sir! We didn't look to see your face again till Thursday, at the earliest.

NICHOLAS (*with a piece of paper*). Yes, but . . . My employers would appreciate, Miss Madeline, if you could undertake –

BRAY. Oh, I see, you have brought more orders, sir?

BRAY *takes the paper from* NICHOLAS.

NICHOLAS. That's not the term I would prefer to use. Commissions, yes.

BRAY. Well, you can tell your master that they won't be undertaken; you can tell him that my daughter – Miss Madeline Bray – condescends no longer, that we don't need his money, and that this is my acknowledgement of your "orders", sir!

He tears the paper.

So, unless you've any further "orders", sir . . .

NICHOLAS. No, I have none. Except . . .

BRAY. Yes, what?

NICHOLAS. I do have fears. And I must state them: fears, that you are consigning that young lady to something worse, worse even than to work herself to death. Those are my fears, sir.

BRAY *furious, hitting the side of his chair.*

MADELINE. For heaven's sake, sir, please remember that he's ill –

BRAY. I am not ill! Out, out! I will not see his face a moment longer. Take me out of here! Please.

Slight pause.

Please, Madeline.

MADELINE *wheels* BRAY *out. She returns to* NICHOLAS.

MADELINE. If you are charged with some commission to me, please don't press it now. The day after tomorrow – come here then.

NICHOLAS. It will be too late, then, for what I have to say, and you will not be here. Please listen to me.

MADELINE. No, I can't, I won't.

NICHOLAS. You will. You must. I must beseech you, contemplate again this fearful course to which you've been impelled.

MADELINE. What's this? What course?

NICHOLAS. This marriage. Yours. Fixed for tomorrow, by two men who have never faltered in a bad intent, and who have wound a web around you, and betrayed you, and bought you for gold.

MADELINE. I will not hear this.

NICHOLAS. But you must, you must. I know you don't know half of what this evil man has done – Think of the mockery of pledging yourself to this man, at the altar – solemn words, against which nature must rebel – and, think, too, of the days and days with him that stretch before you . . . Oh, believe me, that the most degraded poverty is better than the misery you'd undergo as wife to such a man as this. Believe me, Madeline.

MADELINE *looks at* NICHOLAS.

MADELINE. Believe me, sir. This evil, if it is an evil, is of my own seeking. I'm impelled by nobody, but follow this course of my own free will. It is my choice.

NICHOLAS. How *can* you say this?

MADELINE. Because it is true.

Slight pause.

I can't disguise – although perhaps I ought to – that I've undergone great pain of mind, since you were last here. No, I do not love this gentleman. He knows that, and still offers me his hand. Please don't think of me I can feign a love that I don't feel. Do not report this of me, for I couldn't bear it. He's content to have me, as I am. And I am happy for that. And I will grow happier.

NICHOLAS. You're crying with your happiness. Oh, just one week, postpone this marriage, for a few days, even just a day –

MADELINE. Before you came here, my father was talking, of the new life that he would lead, the freedom that will come tomorrow. And he smiled – a smile I haven't seen for – he was smiling, laughing at the thought of open air, and freshness, and his eyes grew bright, his face lit up – I'll not defer it for an hour.

NICHOLAS. These are – just tricks to urge you on –

MADELINE. It is no trick, my father's dying, sir. By doing this, I can release him not just from this place, but from the jaws of death itself. How *can* you tell me to act otherwise?

Pause.

BRAY (*off*). Hey! Madeline!

NICHOLAS. There's nothing I can say that will convince you.

MADELINE. Nothing.

NICHOLAS. Even if I – knew a plot, that you might, be entitled to a fortune that would do all that this marriage can accomplish? More?

BRAY (*off*). Where are you Madeline?

MADELINE. He's calling. What you say's a childish fantasy.

NICHOLAS. If I could prove to you the things I know –

MADELINE. It would mean nothing. I am happy in the prospect of what I'll achieve so easily.

BRAY (off). Come, Madeline!

MADELINE. Now, I must go to him.

NICHOLAS. We'll never meet again?

MADELINE. No. No. Of course not.

She goes, turns back.

Sir, the time may come when to remember this interview might drive me mad.

Slight pause.

Please tell them I looked happy.

BRAY (off). Madeline!

Exit MADELINE. NICHOLAS goes out.

Scene Eleven

A gambling house. At once, lights, music. Smoke, laughter. Upstage, a crowd of people, and a CROUPIER, upstage of them. We hear the rattle of a roulette wheel. At a table sits VERISOPHT, PLUCK, PYKE and a CAPTAIN ADAMS, with Ladies of Leisure and bottles of wine. The crowd upstage includes Men of Pleasure and Ladies of Leisure, and, in particular, a rival of Sir Mulberry Hawk called HANDSAW, and a couple of his young male friends. As the scene assembles:

CROUPIER. The wheel of fortune, gentlemen. Place your bets on red or black, or odd or even, or a number. Double with a colour, gentlemen, and much, much more, if the wheel points to your number. How do you do, sir, can I take your bet? Bets till the wheel spins, gentlemen – and then it's just waiting till we see who's won. All bets in now. The wheel's about to spin. Your bets please, gentlemen!

But the CROUPIER stops, as he, and shortly everyone else, has noticed the entrance of SIR MULBERRY HAWK, attended by MR WESTWOOD. HAWK gives his cape to an attendant. The PROPRIETOR goes over to him.

PROPRIETOR. Why, Sir Mulberry. Good evening. This is – a great pleasure. Please, sir, let me escort you to a table.

VERISOPHT looks at HAWK, but HAWK goes to an empty table, with WESTWOOD, and sits. We see HAWK still has a slight limp. VERISOPHT whispers to the waitress, who takes a bottle to HAWK. The PROPRIETOR nods to the CROUPIER.

CROUPIER. Last bets, gentlemen. And let the wheel of fortune spin!

Noise back in, as the wheel is spun, and the betters watch and shout eagerly.

Number 27! Red! Red 27, gentlemen!

The CROUPIER *pays out as* HANDSAW *comes over to Hawk. He has a couple of young men in tow.*

HANDSAW. Well, Hawk, and how are you, sir?

VERISOPHT *stands and goes over to* HAWK's *table as:*

HAWK. Well. I am very well.

HANDSAW. Still limping, I observe.

HAWK. But very nearly mended, I assure you.

HANDSAW. Yes, but still a little, ah, my lord, a little pulled down, rather, still, out of condition, eh?

VERISOPHT. I'd say, still in very good condition. I'd say, nothing much the matter. Actually.

HANDSAW. Upon my soul, I'm glad to hear it. And to see, of course, your good friend back, so soon, into society. It's bold, it's game: To withdraw just long enough for people to get curious, but not for men to have forgotten that, unpleasant — tell me, Hawk, I've never understood why you didn't give the lie to all those damned reports they printed in the papers . . . looked there every day —

HAWK. Look in the papers, then, tomorrow, or the next day.

CROUPIER. Place bets. Place your bets, gentlemen!

HANDSAW. Oh. What will I find there?

HAWK. Something that will interest you, I'm sure.

HANDSAW. What's that?

HAWK gestures towards the "wheel". HANDSAW bows and he and his acolytes leave HAWK and VERISOPHT.

VERISOPHT. Good evening, Hawk.

HAWK. My lord.

He waves his glass.

My thanks to you.

VERISOPHT. What should he look for in the papers?

HAWK. Oh . . . well, it won't be a murder. But, still, something near. If whipcord cuts and bludgeons bruise.

VERISOPHT. Bruise who?

HAWK. Who do you think?

CROUPIER. Last bets! Last bets please, gentlemen!

HAWK *stands, to go and place a bet.* VERISOPHT *stops him.*

VERISOPHT. I'd hoped – that after all this time, you would have reconsidered.

HAWK. Well, sir, I have not. So, there is your answer.

VERISOPHT. Then I hope you will remember what I said. That if you were to take this course, I would try to prevent you.

HAWK. I'd mind your business, if I was you, and leave me to mind mine.

VERISOPHT. It *is* my business. I shall make it so. It's mine already. I'm more compromised by all this than I ought to be.

HAWK *turns to go, but turns back to* VERISOPHT.

HAWK. My lord, I will be straight with you. I am dependent on you, as you know. But, if that's so, then your dependence upon me is ten times greater. Do not interfere with me in this proceeding, I warn you; or else you'll force me to destroy you. And I will.

CROUPIER. Come on, now, gentlemen. Last bets. Last bets before the spinning of the wheel.

HAWK *turns and quickly goes to join the crowd round the wheel and places a bet.*

Ah, Sir Mulberry. Most privileged. A bet, sir? Thank you. And let the wheel of fortune spin –

VERISOPHT *pauses, then goes to his table. His party bobbing to their feet, when* VERISOPHT, *on a sudden impulse, turns, strides over to* HAWK *and, as the wheel is spun, grabs his shoulder and pulls him round.*

HAWK. What? What's this?

VERISOPHT. I will not have it, Hawk. I cannot have it.

HAWK. Let me go, boy.

VERISOPHT. No.

HAWK *tries to push* VERISOPHT *away.* VERISOPHT *hits*

HAWK *across the face. Everyone's attention suddenly focussed.*
WESTWOOD *stands. The wheel clatters to a stop un-heeded.*

HAWK. He struck me.

Pause.

Do you hear? He struck me! Have I not a friend here?
Westwood!

WESTWOOD *to* HAWK.

WESTWOOD. I hear, sir. Come away, now, for tonight.

HAWK. No, I will not, by God. A dozen men here saw the blow.

WESTWOOD. Tomorrow will be ample time.

HAWK. No it will not. Tonight – at once – here.

VERISOPHT (*turning to* ADAMS, *who has joined the group
round the wheel*). Captain Adams. I say, let this quarrel be
adjusted now.

WESTWOOD *whispering to* HAWK.

ADAMS. My lord, an hour or so, at least.

VERISOPHT. Then, very well. An hour.

He walks aside.

HAWK (*shouts, at the company*). No more.

HAWK *marches out.* WESTWOOD *to* ADAMS. ADAMS *nods,
to say, "In a moment". He goes to* VERISOPHT.

WESTWOOD. Captain Adams.

ADAMS. You will not –

VERISOPHT. Only if he will retract. The things he said.

ADAMS *shrugs.*

ADAMS. He is a splendid shot, my lord.

VERISOPHT. So I have heard.

Slight pause. VERISOPHT *laughs.* ADAMS *looks at him oddly.*

Oh, so I've heard. Are you a married man, dear Captain?

ADAMS. No, I'm not.

VERISOPHT (*still laughing*). Well, nor am I. Oh, nor am I.

He stops laughing.

I'll see you in an hour, then.

VERISOPHT *goes out. The* PROPRIETOR *nods to the*
CROUPIER.

CROUPIER. Uh – place your bets. Your bets, please, gentlemen.

ADAMS *to* WESTWOOD. *They talk. The* PROPRIETOR *whispers to the* CROUPIER. *The* CROUPIER, *with more enthusiasm.*

Sir Mulberry, this side! Lord Frederick, the other – place your bets now, gentlemen!

PLUCK *and* PYKE *move in to place their bets. The wheel and the* GENTLEMEN *disappear.* VERISOPHT *is there alone.*

VERISOPHT. It was daybreak. And as they walked towards the place agreed, he saw the trees, and the fields, and gardens, and they all looked very beautiful, as if he'd never noticed them before. And young Lord Verisopht felt little fear; but more a sense of something like regret, that it should come to this.

Scene Twelve

Dawn. By the river. Enter ADAMS *to* VERISOPHT.

ADAMS. So here we are, my lord. My lord, you're shivering.

VERISOPHT. I'm cold.

ADAMS. It does strike cool, to come out of hot rooms. Do you want my cloak?

VERISOPHT. No, no.

HAWK, WESTWOOD, *the* GENTLEMAN *acting as* UMPIRE, *a* SURGEON, *one or two other* GENTLEMEN, *come in. Among the group, too, at the back, unnoticed, are* MR PLUCK *and* MR PYKE.

Well, here they are.

He laughs.

ADAMS. My lord?

VERISOPHT. It's nothing.

ADAMS *goes to* WESTWOOD *and they talk.* VERISOPHT *jumpy, laughing to himself, light-headed.* ADAMS *returns to him.*

ADAMS. My lord. They're ready.

VERISOPHT. Ready.

As the UMPIRE *opens the box of pistols,* VERISOPHT *comes over to him and* HAWK.

VERISOPHT. Uh – Hawk.

HAWK (*gruffly*). My lord?

VERISOPHT. Hawk, just one word.

HAWK. Yes? What? Speak, quickly.

VERISOPHT. I – you know, I owe Ralph Nickleby £10,000.

Pause. Everyone looking edgy.

HAWK. I know.

Pause.

VERISOPHT. I am not married.

HAWK. That is true. Can we begin?

Slight pause.

VERISOPHT. And being in that state, my debts die with me.

Pause.

HAWK. What?

VERISOPHT. I don't mean . . . We must settle this, of course.
But, just to let you know.

Slight pause. He looks at the pistols.

The terms. My father's will. I die unmarried – and I die a
pauper. And my creditors live, paupers, too.

A slight laugh. He takes a pistol from the case. Pause.

HAWK. What's this?

VERISOPHT. So. Either way, Hawk, I'll destroy you. Won't I.

VERISOPHT *laughs.*

Won't I. Eh?

Pause. HAWK *takes a pistol from the case.* VERISOPHT *turns
his back to* HAWK. HAWK *turns his back on* VERISOPHT.

HAWK (*to the umpire*). Begin.

UMPIRE. Yes. Yes. Sir Mulberry. My lord. Proceed. One, two,
three, four, five, six, seven, eight, nine, ten.

HAWK *and* VERISOPHT *take ten paces. They turn and fire.*
VERISOPHT *falls. The* SURGEON *to* VERISOPHT. *He finds
that* VERISOPHT *is dead. He nods. Quickly:* ADAMS *takes*
VERISOPHT's *pistol, and* WESTWOOD *gives it to* HAWK,
who shakes his head and pockets his pistol; the UMPIRE *and
the other* GENTLEMEN *depart. Only, still at a distance,*
PLUCK *and* PYKE *are left.*

WESTWOOD. Now, Hawk, there's not a moment to be lost. We must leave here immediately — for Brighton, and then France.

Pause. HAWK *impassive.*

Come, Hawk. This is a dreadful business, and delay will make it worse.

HAWK. An hour. Meet you at the stage-coach: in an hour.

Striding out.

WESTWOOD. But — but, Hawk —

HAWK. An hour!

Exit HAWK. WESTWOOD *looks at* ADAMS, *shrugs and goes out.* ADAMS *nods to* PLUCK *and* PYKE. *They come forward.*

PLUCK. Well. Is this a bad business, Pyke?

PYKE. Is this a dreadful business, Pluck?

ADAMS. You both know what to do.

ADAMS *goes out.* PYKE *and* PLUCK *take* VERISOPHT's *watch, rings and all valuables. Then they pick him up by the arms and drag his body out.*

Scene Thirteen

London. Dawn. NICHOLAS *enters, on a bare stage.* KATE *stands to the side. During the following, we hear the hiss of gas lights, and a* LAMPMAN *slowly crosses the stage with a long pole. He mimes shutting off the gas at the top of an imaginary street lamp. Then, slowly, the stage fills with the* POOR *of London, at dawn: maids scrubbing doorsteps, blind men begging, street-sweepers sweeping, prostitutes soliciting, and pimps watching. There are mothers and fathers with babies and children, too. Gradually, the naturalistic evocation of a London morning turns into a Chorus: the* POOR *move forward into a phalanx around* NICHOLAS, *eventually surrounding and obscuring him.*

NICHOLAS. And at the same daybreak, Nicholas arose,

KATE. And softly left the house,

NICHOLAS. And wandered into London. And as he paced the streets and listlessly looked round on the gradually increasing bustle of the day, everything appeared to yield him some new occasion for despondency. Last night, the sacrifice of a young, affectionate and beautiful creature to such a wretch had seemed a thing too monstrous to succeed. But, now, when he thought how regularly things went on:

POOR PEOPLE.
From day to day
In the same unvarying way
How crafty avarice grew rich, and manly honest hearts were poor and sad
How few they were who tenanted the stately homes,
And how many those who lay in foul and rancid tenements,
Or even
Lived
And died
Father
and son,
Mother,
and child,

HALF. Race upon race,

ALL. And generation upon generation, without a home to shelter them.

PROSTITUTE. How in seeking, not a luxurious and splendid life, but the bare means of a most wretched and inadequate subsistence,

ALL. Subsistence.

PROSTITUTE. There were women and children in that one town, divided into classes,

PIMP. And reared from infancy to drive most criminal and dreadful trades –

YOUTHS AND CHILDREN. How ignorance was punished and never taught –

PROSTITUTES AND THIEVES. How jail-door gaped and gallows loomed for thousands.

ALL. How many died in soul, and had no chance of life –

NICHOLAS. How many who could scarcely go astray, turned haughtily from those who could scarce do otherwise,

ONE THIRD. How much injustice,

TWO THIRDS. Misery,

ALL. And wrong there was,

NICHOLAS *now surrounded and is obscured as:*

NICHOLAS. And yet how the world rolled on from year to year, alike careless and indifferent, and no man seeking to remedy or redress it: – when he thought of all this, and selected from the mass the one slight case on which his thoughts were bent, he felt indeed that there was little ground for hope, and little cause or reason why it should not form an atom in the huge aggregate of distress and sorrow, and add one small and unimportant unit to the great amount.

The POOR *look at us. And then they split and melt away.* NICHOLAS *is left alone.* NOGGS *appears.*

NICHOLAS. Oh, Newman. Legal right, the power of money, everything is on their side. And I can't save her.

NOGGS. Don't say that.

NICHOLAS *looks at* NOGGS.

Oh, don't say it, Nick. Never lose hope, never leave off it, it don't answer. *I* know that. If nothing else, I have learnt that.

Pause.

Don't leave a stone unturned. At least you know you've done the most you could. Or else – how could you bear to live with it?

Pause.

NICHOLAS *looks at* NOGGS. NICHOLAS *goes out.*

Hope. Always hope.

NOGGS *goes out, too.*

Scene Fourteen

Ralph's house. A room, set up for a wedding ceremony. Two chairs, on one of which sits MADELINE, *Bray's wheelchair behind.* BRAY *looks very ill; he is dressed up in uncomfortable finery. A* MINISTER *stands waiting.* GRIDE *enters, and is met by* RALPH.

RALPH. Well, good day, Mr Gride. Congratulations, on your wedding morning.

GRIDE. Nickleby. Is everything prepared?

RALPH. It is. Your bride waits to receive you, sir.

GRIDE. And, how is she?

RALPH. Bray says that she accepts it. She is calm. She may be safely trusted, now. It won't be long.

GRIDE. What won't be?

RALPH (*with a nod at* BRAY). Paying his annuity. You have the devil's luck in bargains, Gride.

He turns to go to the ceremony.

GRIDE. Uh, Nickleby —

RALPH. Yes? What?

GRIDE *takes two crushed carnations from his pocket.*

What's this?

GRIDE. To wear. Your buttonhole. It is a wedding day.

Slight pause. RALPH *shrugs. The two men put on their buttonholes. Then they go to the* MINISTER. RALPH *nods at the* MINISTER. GRIDE *sits next to* MADELINE. *The* MINISTER *begins the service.*

MINISTER. Dearly beloved, we are gathered together here in the sight of God and in the face of this congregation to join together this man and this woman in Holy Matrimony, which is an honourable estate, instituted of God in the time of man's innocency, signifying unto us the mystical union that is between Christ and his church which holy estate Christ adorned and beautified —

RALPH *gestures to the* MINISTER *to hurry it along. The* MINISTER *turns the page.*

I require and charge you both, as ye will answer at the dreadful day of judgement, when the secrets of all hearts shall be disclosed, that if either of you know any impediment, why ye may not be lawfully joined together in matrimony, ye do now confess it.

NICHOLAS' *voice, from off.*

NICHOLAS. Won't you? Won't you confess it, Madeline?

GRIDE. What's this? What, Nickleby?

BRAY. It's him — him, Madeline —

MADELINE. Oh — sir —

NICHOLAS *and* KATE *are in the room,* RALPH *to them.*

RALPH. I don't believe it.

GRIDE. Who is this man? This girl? Why have they come here?

NICHOLAS. We know everything. We've come to stop this marriage. And we won't go till we have.

RALPH. Gride. This is my niece. And this, her brother. I'm ashamed to say, my brother's son.

NICHOLAS. Oh, *you're* ashamed –

KATE. Nicholas –

RALPH. Now you, my dear, retire. We can use force on him, aned will if need be, but I would not hurt you if it could be helped.
Slight pause.
Retire!

KATE. I won't, and you misjudge me if you think I will. You may use force on me – and it would be most like you if you did; but I will not go till we've done what we have come to do.

NICHOLAS. Well said.

RALPH. Oh, yes. I see. This fellow here – he brings with him, you note, his sister, as protection. I shouldn't be surprised, in fact, Gride, if he doesn't have a mind to marry Madeline himself.

GRIDE. What's that?

RALPH. Well, why d'you think he's here? Philanthropy?

NICHOLAS. I tell you, both of you, that there has been no word of love, no contract, no engagement –

RALPH. Certainly, there's no engagement. This young lady is engaged already. And about to be a bride.

GRIDE. My bride!

NICHOLAS. And we demand to speak with her.

GRIDE. And how we'll laugh together, she and me, at how this little boy was jilted –

NICHOLAS. Will you let me speak with her?

GRIDE. And I wonder, is there anything of mine he'd like besides? He wants my bride, perhaps he'd like his debts paid, and his house refurnished, and a few banknotes for shaving paper, if he shaves at all?

NICHOLAS *tries to push past* GRIDE. KATE *is between* RALPH *and* NICHOLAS, *and* RALPH, *to get to* NICHOLAS, *clasps her arm.* NICHOLAS *turns and takes* RALPH's *collar, when they are all interrupted by the entrance of* SIR MULBERRY HAWK.

HAWK. Well, look at this. A family reunion.

RALPH *pulls himself free from* NICHOLAS.

And – a wedding, too? Well, I'm sorry, Nickleby, to interrupt, but I have urgent news about an opposite affair.

RALPH. What's that?

HAWK. A funeral.

RALPH. Whose funeral?

HAWK. Lord Frederick Verisopht's.

KATE *a step forward. Pause.* HAWK *takes out his pistol.*

He struck me – as a consequence of something I had said – concerned with a young lady. And her brother. So . . . I had my answer.

There is something strange about the face of WALTER BRAY, MADELINE *wheels her father a little further apart, and looks at him, and loosens his collar. The* MINISTER, *seeing that no one is noticing him, slips out.*

RALPH. But –

HAWK. Oh, yes. You know. For you know everything. Unmarried. And his bills, and mine on his account, all guaranteed by you, all over town. What would you say? Ten thousand pounds?

RALPH *looking blank.*

You do – you understand?

RALPH. I understand.

NICHOLAS (*laughs*). Oh, yes. At last you understand.

HAWK *quickly to* NICHOLAS, *with the pistol.*

HAWK. I tell you. That this should have been for you.

MADELINE *has left* BRAY. *She looks at* HAWK, *bemused.*

I'm sorry, ma'am. To frighten you.

He is going.

MADELINE. He's dead.

It sounds almost like a question. Hawk doesn't understand.

HAWK. Oh, yes. He's dead. Indeed.

HAWK *goes out. The penny drops for* RALPH, GRIDE, KATE *and* NICHOLAS, *as they see* BRAY, *slumped in his chair.*

MADELINE. He looked at me. And whispered that he couldn't bear to see – And shut his eyes. And wouldn't open them again.

RALPH. What's this you say?

RALPH *and* GRIDE *rush to the body of* BRAY. KATE *to* MADELINE.

KATE. Oh, I'm so sorry.

GRIDE *trying to get to* MADELINE.

GRIDE. Oh, Madeline. My pretty little Madeline.

NICHOLAS. Oh, no. Her obligation to you's ended, now.

RALPH. This man – she's still his wife-to-be. And he shall have her.

GRIDE. Oh, she still shall be my wife, my dainty – now – with no one, she will need me, won't she – precious –

MADELINE. No. Of course not. You said you would save him. And you've killed him.

GRIDE. What is this? What, me, my chick?

MADELINE. Yes. Indeed. That's what he meant. He couldn't bear to see me married to you.

Suddenly, furiously to GRIDE.

How *can* you think that I could bear it, now?

NICHOLAS. Kate, downstairs.

KATE *taking* MADELINE's *arm.*

RALPH. You will not take her, girl.

KATE. Uncle, I will.

RALPH. You have no right to do this –

KATE. I have more right to do this, uncle, much more right, than you had to allow what happened to me here.

She makes to lead MADELINE *out.* MADELINE *to* NICHOLAS.

MADELINE. Please, sir – I want him taken from here.

NICHOLAS *nods.* KATE *takes* MADELINE *out.* NICHOLAS *to the wheelchair.*

RALPH. Just one word.

NICHOLAS. Not even one. Your bills are now waste paper. Your debts will not be paid — save this — the one great debt of nature.

He takes out the body of WALTER BRAY. *Long pause.*

GRIDE. It's not my fault.

RALPH. Who said it was?

GRIDE. You look as if you thought I was to blame.

RALPH. I don't. I blame him. Bray.

GRIDE. What for?

RALPH. For not — for not living an hour longer.

Pause.

Now, go Gride.

To himself.

Ten thousand pounds.

GRIDE *turns to go. He is suddenly aware of something in the movement. He pats his coat, outside a pocket. He feels inside the pocket. Nothing there. He feels in the other pockets. He rips his coat off, searching desperately for something.*

What are you doing, Gride?

GRIDE. Lost something.

RALPH. Something? What.

GRIDE. It's gone.

RALPH. What is?

GRIDE. The deed. She's taken it.

RALPH. Who has?

GRIDE. Peg Sliderskew. Old, mad and deaf Peg Slider. She has robbed me of the deed!

He waves his coat.

I had it in my pocket. And it's gone!

RALPH. Now, come, Gride, first go home —

GRIDE. Oh, Nickleby. I shouldn't have it. It's not mine. Someone will read it for her. And she'll take it to the police. And then — and then — I'm done for.

RALPH. Gride. At least go home, and see you didn't drop it somewhere. See it isn't locked up where you left it.

GRIDE. I tell you Nickleby. I know it's gone. And I tell you something else. You said you'd help me to be married. And it's been prevented, by your flesh and blood. I tell you, if I go down with this business, then you're going too.

Pause.

RALPH. All right, Gride. Yes. Now, tell me all about it. And we'll try and get it back.

And they go out together.

Scene Fifteen

The Nicklebys' garden. SMIKE *is tending pot plants in a tray downstage, helped by* KATE *who wears gardening gloves. Enter* NICHOLAS.

NICHOLAS. How's Madeline?

KATE. She's sleeping.

NICHOLAS. But is she –

KATE. She's exhausted, nothing more.

Enter MRS NICKLEBY.

MRS NICKLEBY. Well, now, Nicholas, perhaps you can explain all this to me.

NICHOLAS. Mother, I thought we'd —

MRS NICKLEBY. Well, you did, indeed, at length, but still I can't see why, in the name of wonder, Nicholas should go about the world forbidding people's banns?

NICHOLAS *flapping with frustration.*

KATE. I don't think, mother, you quite understand.

MRS NICKLEBY. Not understand? I have been married myself, Kate, and have seen other people married, frequently, and as to this Miss Magdalen marrying a man that's older than herself, I would remind you of Jane Dibabs, who –

KATE. Jane Dibabs!

MRS NICKLEBY. Yes, that's right, who used to live in that attractive little cottage past the lunatic asylum, and she married someone twenty or so years above her, and who was so honourable and excellent, that she was blissfully content about the whole arrangement, and remains so to this day.

Pause. KATE, *very patiently.*

KATE. Mama, the husband in this case is greatly older; he is not her own choice; his character is quite the opposite of that which you've described; mama, don't you see a broad distinction between the two cases?

MRS NICKLEBY. Well, I daresay, I'm very stupid, Kate –

KATE. Mama!

KATE *runs to* SMIKE, *and helps him with the garden, to cover her anger and frustration.*

MRS NICKLEBY. Well, I don't know what that's about, I'm sure.

NICHOLAS *about to join his sister when enter* HANNAH.

MRS NICKLEBY. Yes, Hannah, dear?

HANNAH. There are three gentlemen without.

MRS NICKLEBY. Now, Hannah, dear, what gentlemen?

HANNAH. Uh . . .

Enter MR NED CHEERYBLE, MR CHARLES CHEERYBLE *and* FRANK CHEERYBLE. HANNAH *goes out.*

FRANK. Mrs Nickleby.

MR CHARLES. Oh, my dear young man, my dear young man. Miss Madeline is safe?

NICHOLAS. Yes, she is safe.

KATE *comes to the* CHEERYBLES, *followed by* SMIKE.

MR NED. And you, sir, we have had the scantiest of reports, have sustained no injury?

NICHOLAS. I am completely well.

FRANK. And your dear sister, sir, we hear that she too was involved in this heroic enterprise –

FRANK *has moved to* KATE.

KATE. And have survived my humble part in it, sir, I assure you.

MR NED. May we inquire – if it is possible to see the lady?

KATE *smiles and goes out, followed by* MRS NICKLEBY. MR CHARLES *to* NICHOLAS.

MR CHARLES. We cannot express, sir, our full admiration of your actions on this day. We will, sir, at the earliest opportunity, relieve you of the burden of her upkeep.

Slight pause.

NICHOLAS. Well . . .

Re-enter KATE.

KATE. Miss Bray's awake – and would be most delighted to speak with you, gentlemen.

FRANK (*taking KATE's arm*). Now, Kate, please tell me everything . . . I wish for every detail . . .

The BROTHERS, followed by FRANK and KATE, go out. NICHOLAS looks at FRANK and KATE together. He stands a moment, and then goes into the garden. SMIKE is sitting clutching his knees, looking miserable.

NICHOLAS. Well, Smike. And how are you today?

SMIKE doesn't reply.

How are you feeling?

SMIKE doesn't reply.

Smike, please answer me.

SMIKE looks at NICHOLAS.

Smike, what's the matter?

SMIKE. It's my heart. It is so very full. I cannot tell you why. You cannot tell how full it is.

NICHOLAS. Come on, now, Smike. It's growing chilly. Stand up, and let's go in.

Pause.

SMIKE. I can't. I feel so ill.

NICHOLAS *looks at SMIKE. Suddenly, he calls.*

NICHOLAS. Frank! Kate!

FRANK and KATE appear to help NICHOLAS with SMIKE.

Scene Sixteen

The same. As KATE and FRANK arrive, five NARRATORS emerge from the darkness at the back of the stage. They walk forward together, obscuring SMIKE. BROOKER enters behind them, and stands, staring at SMIKE, now dressed for travelling.

NARRATORS.

There is a dread disease which so prepares its victim, as it were for death

In which the struggle between soul and body is so gradual, quiet and solemn,

That day by day

And grain by grain

The mortal part wastes and withers, and the spirit part grows light and sanguine with its lightening load,

A disease which medicine never cured, wealth warded off, or poverty could boast exemption from – which sometimes moves in giant's strides, and sometimes at a tardy, sluggish pace, but slow or quick.

Is ever sure and certain.

The NARRATORS *disappear.* SMIKE *looks at* BROOKER.

BROOKER. I know you. Do you know me?

SMIKE. I – know you.

BROOKER *hears something and scuttles away.* KATE *and* NICHOLAS, *dressed for travelling, enter, with* MRS NICKLEBY, MISS LA CREEVY *and* HANNAH.

NICHOLAS. Come, Smike. It's all right. Time to go.

SMIKE. To Devon.

SMIKE *looks at* MISS LA CREEVY *and* MRS NICKLEBY.

MISS LA CREEVY. Oh, Mr Smike. To your return.

MRS NICKLEBY. Yes. Yes, dear Mr Smike. Please. Soon.

NICHOLAS *and* KATE *help* SMIKE *to his feet. They leave with him, the other* WOMEN *waving.*

END OF ACT TWO

ACT THREE

Scene One

Upstage, the Kenwigs' front room. MR and MRS KENWIGS eating a meal at the table. The crying of the new baby. MR LILLYVICK appears downstage. He looks nervous. He knocks.

MRS KENWIGS. Morleena! Morleena!

MORLEENA (*off*). Yes, Ma!

MRS KENWIGS. Door, Morleena!

MORLEENA (*off*). What, Ma?

MRS KENWIGS. Door!

    MORLEENA *runs on as baby cries.*

    Shh, shh. Hush, baby.

    MORLEENA *sees* MR LILLYVICK.

MORLEENA. Uh?

LILLYVICK. Morleena.

MORLEENA. Oh, it's – Uncle Lillyvick!

LILLYVICK. It is. It is.

    Pause.

    Morleena, tell me – did your mother have the child?

MORLEENA. Oh, yes. She did. A boy. That's him.

LILLYVICK. And was it – she said – that she hoped that he would look like me.

MORLEENA. Oh, yes. He does. I s'pose. At least.

LILLYVICK. I would like someone, looked like me.

    Pause.

MORLEENA. Oh, Uncle. Heard about your wedding, Uncle. Made Ma cry. And Pa got very low as well. And I was ill, too. But I'm better now. Oh, Uncle.

    Pause.

LILLYVICK. Would you – give your uncle – just one kiss, Morleena?

    Pause.

MORLEENA. Yes. I would. But not Aunt Lillyvick. I won't kiss her. She is no aunt of mine.

MRS KENWIGS. Who is it at the door, Morleena?

LILLYVICK. Take me to them. Take me up, Morleena.

MORLEENA *takes* LILLYVICK *to the* KENWIGS *as:*

MRS KENWIGS. Morleena!

KENWIGS. Now, don't shout, dear.

MRS KENWIGS. Suppertime, Morleena!

KENWIGS. Please don't shout, dear.

MRS KENWIGS. Oh, I do declare.

KENWIGS. Yes, what do you declare, dear?

MRS KENWIGS (*pouring herself a drink*). That there's nobody, in all the world, as tried as I am. Nobody. That's all.

MORLEENA. Uh — ma —

KENWIGS. Oh. Mr Lillyvick.

LILLYVICK. Kenwigs, shake hands.

KENWIGS (*standing*). Oh, sir, the time has been when I was proud to shake hands with the kind of man that now surveys me. Oh, the time has been, sir, when a visit from that man's excited in my and my family's bosoms feelings both uplifting and awakening. But now I look at him, and ask, where is his human nature?

Pause.

LILLYVICK. Susan Kenwigs, will you speak to me?

KENWIGS. She is not equal to it, sir. What with the nursing of her child, and the reflecting on your cruel behaviour, four pints of malt liquor, daily, has proved insufficient to sustain her.

MR KENWIGS *looks away.*

Oh, I remember thinking, all the time it was expected, if the child's a boy, what will its uncle say? Will it be Pompey, he will ask it to be called; or Alexander, or Diogenes; and when I look at him, a precious, helpless, cut-off child . . . Was it the money that we cared for, Susan?

MRS KENWIGS. No, it was not. I scorn it.

KENWIGS. Then what was it, Susan?

MRS KENWIGS. It was seeing your back turned upon us, Uncle. It was feelings — mine have been quite lancerated.

KENWIGS. Poor Morleena's pined, the infant has been rendered most uncomfortable and fractious —

MRS KENWIGS. I forgive all that, and with you, Uncle, we can never quarrel. But I won't receive her, Uncle. Never ask me. For I will not. No, I won't, I won't, I won't —

KENWIGS *ministering to his wife when* LILLYVICK *intervenes.*

LILLYVICK. You will not need to. Susan. Kenwigs. For a week ago last Thursday, she eloped.

KENWIGS. Eloped?

LILLYVICK. That's right. With three sovereigns of mine, eight silver teaspoons, and the proprietor of a travelling circus.

Slight pause.

With moustaches. And a bottle nose.

Slight pause.

'Twas in this room — this very room — I first set sight on Miss Petowker. It is in this room I cast her off for ever.

Pause.

KENWIGS. Oh, Mr Lillyvick. What suffering have you endured.

MRS KENWIGS. Oh, Uncle. You'll forgive our harshness, please.

KENWIGS. And furthermore, the fact that we have nurtured in our bosom that — that —

MRS KENWIGS. Viper.

KENWIGS. Yes, and —

MRS KENWIGS. Adder.

KENWIGS. Absolutely, and that —

MRS KENWIGS. Serpent, snake and crocodile.

KENWIGS. Indeed. And all we pray now is that you, dear Mr Lillyvick, won't give way to unprevailing grief, but seek for consolation in the bosom of this family, whose arms and hearts are ever open to you.

Bursting into tears.

MORLEENA. Yes.

She runs and puts her arms round MR LILLYVICK.

Yes, yes.

KENWIGS. Morleena, leave your uncle be.

MORLEENA *leaves* LILLYVICK.

LILLYVICK. I gave her everything she asked for. Humoured her in every whim. Those teaspoons, for but one example.

Slight pause.

I feel I'll never knock a double-knock again, upon my rounds. I can't see how I'll manage it.

Slight pause.

But still. Important matters. Kenwigs. Susan. First thing in the morning, I shall settle on your children all these moneys I once planned to leave them in my will. Don't argue, don't protest – that's my decision.

KENWIGS. Mr Lillyvick!

MRS KENWIGS. Morleena – quickly, kiss your uncle, beg his blessing, fall down on your knees.

LILLYVICK. Yes, yes. Let her approach.

KENWIGS. This is a happening on which the Gods themselves look down!

Scene Two

Ralph's house. Bare stage. Enter RALPH.

RALPH. Ten. Thousand. Pounds. How many years of scrimping, scraping, calculating. For ten thousand pounds. And what I would have done with it. How many proud dames would have fawned and smiled. How many spendthrift nobles would have cringed and begged. How many smooth-tongued speeches, courteous looks, and pleading letters. And how many mean and paltry lies would have been told, not by the money-lender, but by his debtors . . . all your thoughtless, generous, liberal, dashing folk, who wouldn't be so mean as to save a sixpence for the world!

Pause.

Ten – thousand – pounds.

Pause. NOGGS *and* SQUEERS *appearing.*

But now. I'm firm. I must be. Come what may.

NOGGS *coughs.* RALPH *turns.*

RALPH. Ah, Mr Squeers.

SQUEERS. You sent a letter.

RALPH. Yes, indeed.

SQUEERS. First, let me say –

RALPH. First, let *me* say, Noggs.

NOGGS. Yes? What?

RALPH. Go to your dinner.

NOGGS. But it isn't time.

RALPH. Your time is mine, and I say it is.

NOGGS. You change it every day. It isn't fair.

RALPH. Begone.

NOGGS *withdraws*.

Now. What?

SQUEERS. I'm worried about Snawley.

RALPH. Why? Where is the risk?

SQUEERS. You know the risk as well as I do.

RALPH. No, I don't. There is no risk. The certificates are genuine, he *has* been married twice, his former wife *is* dead, and the only lie is Snawley's, and he'll stick to it, why should he not? He tells the truth, and he's in gaol for perjury. So where's *your* risk in this conspiracy!

SQUEERS. I say, don't call it that — just as a favour, don't.

RALPH. But now, attend to me. The purpose of the fabrication of this tale was to cause hurt and pain to someone who half-cudgelled you to death. Now, is that so?

SQUEERS. It is.

RALPH. And are your bruises at his hands forgotten and forgiven?

SQUEERS. They are not.

RALPH. So. There's an opportunity to hurt him once again. There is a deed — a will. If it is found by him, then it will make a girl he wants to marry very rich. If it is found by us, and then destroyed, then all his expectations crumble.

SQUEERS. Well. Go on.

RALPH. Together, we are going to find the person with the will. You're going to take it from this person, and I'm going to give you fifty pounds in gold.

SQUEERS *scratches his ear*.

A hundred pounds.

SQUEERS. Well, in that case . . . I suppose, as you're a friend . . .

RALPH. Attend to me.

SQUEERS *is led out by* RALPH. *In the shadows,* NOGGS *follows.*

Scene Three

Devon. Bare stage. Dappled light. KATE, NICHOLAS *and* SMIKE *enter.*

NARRATOR. Dividing the distance into two days' journey, in order that their charge might sustain the less exhaustion and fatigue from travelling so far, Nicholas and Kate found themselves at the end of the second day back in the village where they had grown up together.

NICHOLAS. Look, there's our garden, Smike. That's where we used to play, and run, and hide.

SMIKE. You used to hide?

NICHOLAS. Yes, Smike, you know, the game.

KATE. And Nicholas would climb that tree: that big one, over there, to look at young birds in their nests – and he'd shout down, look Kate, how high I've climbed.

NICHOLAS. And you'd be frightened, and you'd tell me to come down.

KATE. And you, you wouldn't come down. But climb even higher, waving all the time.

SMIKE. You climbed up there.

NICHOLAS. And that's the house, Smike, where we used to live, that was Kate's room, behind that tiny window.

KATE. I remember still, the way the sun would stream in, every morning.

SMIKE. Every morning? Winter too?

KATE. I think . . . I can't remember.

NICHOLAS. I suspect that it was always summer here.

SMIKE *has been looking at "the tree".*

SMIKE. Is it the same? As when. Is it the same?

KATE *and* NICHOLAS *look at each other.*

NICHOLAS. Things look a little different, Smike. The tree looks smaller. And the garden has become a little overgrown. But still – it is the same.

SMIKE *goes towards the tree.*

SMIKE. You climbed up there.

KATE, NICHOLAS *and* SMIKE *move round the stage.*

NARRATOR. And from the house they walked on to the churchyard, where their father lay, and where Kate and her brother used to run and loiter in the days before they knew what death was, let alone its meaning.

NICHOLAS. Once, Smike, Kate was lost, and we searched for an hour, and we couldn't find her, and at last we found her here, beneath that weeping willow, fast asleep. And so our father, who was very fond of her, picked up her sleeping body in his arms, and said that when he died he wanted to be buried here, where his dear, little child had lain her head. Do you remember, Kate?

KATE. I've heard it told so often, I don't know.

SMIKE. You lay down here?

KATE (*smiling*). Yes. So they say.

KATE *wanders a little away.* SMIKE *takes* NICHOLAS's *hand.*

SMIKE. Please promise me.

NICHOLAS. What promise? If I can, you know I will.

SMIKE. Please, if I can, may I be buried near — as near as possible — to underneath that tree?

NICHOLAS. Of course. Yes, yes, you will.

KATE *turns back from her wander. She puts out her arms and spins round.*

NARRATORS.
And in a fortnight, Smike became too ill to move about. And he would lie upon an old couch, near the open doors that led into a little orchard.

Two actors set a couch upstage.

And Nicholas and Kate would sit with him and talk for hours and hours together.

Till the sun went down, and Smike would fall asleep.

SMIKE *on the couch. It's sunset.* KATE *and* NICHOLAS *leave* SMIKE *and walk downstage. During the scene, it grows darker, and we can no longer see* SMIKE *through the dusk.*

KATE. Nicholas.

NICHOLAS. Yes, what?

KATE. What is it?

NICHOLAS. I was thinking about those we left behind.

KATE. One person, in particular?

Pause. NICHOLAS *turns to* KATE.

NICHOLAS. It is, I suppose . . . I love her, Kate.

KATE. I know. Your feelings are as obvious to me, as mine must be to you.

Pause.

NICHOLAS. Oh, Kate. Oh, both of us. Has he –

KATE. He has proposed.

NICHOLAS. What did you say?

KATE. I said – that it was very painful for me, very difficult. But, still, I had to tell him, no.

NICHOLAS. And why?

KATE. Because – you know why.

NICHOLAS. Tell me, Kate.

KATE. Because – of all the kindness of the brothers, to you, and to all of us. Because – Frank's rich, and we are poor, and it would look as if, we'd taken gross advantage of . . .

NICHOLAS. There's my brave Kate.

Pause.

You've no idea, how much your strength in making your, this sacrifice, will help me making mine.

KATE. But Nicholas, it's not the same.

NICHOLAS. It is the same. For Madeline is bound to our two benefactors with ties just as strong – and she too has a fortune.

Pause.

KATE. So – we shall stay together.

NICHOLAS. Yes. And when we're staid old folk, we will look back, on these times, and wonder that these things could move us so. And, even, who knows, we might thank the trials which bound us to each other, and which turned our lives into a current of such peace and calm.

Pause.

We'll always be the same.

KATE. Oh, Nicholas. I cannot tell you how, how happy I am, that I've acted as you would have had me.

NICHOLAS. And you don't, at all, regret . . .

KATE. I don't regret. At least. Perhaps . . . No, no. I don't regret.

Slight pause.

And, yes, I hope and pray we'll never change.

SMIKE *stands there.*

SMIKE. Who calls? Who calls so loud?

NICHOLAS *and* KATE *look at* SMIKE. KATE *to go towards* SMIKE, *but* NICHOLAS *stops her with a touch.* SMIKE, *insistent.*

Who calls so loud?

NICHOLAS *a step towards* SMIKE.

NICHOLAS. Come hither, man. I see that thou art poor. Hold, there is forty ducats. Let me have –

SMIKE. Such mortal drugs I have, but Mantua's law

Is – is –

NICHOLAS. Oh, Smike –

SMIKE. Is death to any he that utters them.

Prompting.

Art thou so bare – ?

NICHOLAS.
Art thou so bare and full of wretchedness,
And fearest to die? Famine is in thy cheeks,
Need and oppression starveth in thy eyes.
Contempt and –

SMIKE. No. No, I don't fear to die. My will consents.

NICHOLAS *turns to embrace* SMIKE, *who throws his arms round* NICHOLAS' *neck to stop himself collapsing.*

You know, I think, that if I could rise up again, completely well, I wouldn't want to, now.

SMIKE *looking over* NICHOLAS' *shoulder at* KATE.

For nothing – can be ill, if she be well.

NICHOLAS. Then she is well, and nothing can be ill.

Pause.

Her body sleeps in Capel's monument.

Pause.

But her immortal part with angels lives.

NICHOLAS *lifts* SMIKE *up into his arms.*

SMIKE. Is it. E'en so. I see a garden. Trees and happy children's faces. And her body sleeps. Light on the faces. Living with the angels. Dreamt my lady came and found me dead. Such happy dreams.

He pulls himself up to whisper in NICHOLAS' *ear. Then, out loud, to* KATE:

I'm going home. Who calls. Who calls so loud?

SMIKE *is still.* NICHOLAS *realises he is dead. He turns to* KATE. *He is crying.*

NICHOLAS. He said – I think you know.

Pause. KATE *can say nothing.*

And then he said he was in Eden.

Scene Four

Lambeth. Two adjacent attic rooms, represented simply by the people in them. On one side, SQUEERS *sits, on a wooden box, with a candle, drinking. On the other side – presently in darkness – PEG SLIDERSKEW *sits, surrounded by rubbish.*

NARRATORS.

It was a dark, wet, gloomy night in autumn –

An obscure street in Lambeth, muddy, dirty and deserted –

A mean and miserable house –

A bare and wretched attic chamber –

And a grotesque, one-eyed man.

SQUEERS. Well. Here's a pretty go. Uncommon pretty. Here have I been – what is it – six weeks – a-following up this blessed old dowager – and the Academy run regular to seed the while. Hm. It's the worst of getting in with an audacious chap like Nickleby. You never know when he's done with you. You go in for a penny, find that you're in for a pound.

Slight pause. He grins.

A hundred pounds.

He takes another drink.

I never saw a file like that old Nickleby. To see how sly and cunning he grubbed on, day after day, a-worming and a-plodding and a-tracing and a-turning, and a-twining of himself about, until he found out where this precious Mrs Peg was hid, and cleared the ground for me to work upon – creeping and crawling, gliding – out of everybody's depth, he is.

Slight pause.

Well. So.

He looks at a letter.

The pigs is well. The cows is well. The boys is bobbish. Young Mobbs has been a-winking, has he? Well, I'll wink him when I'm back. and Cobbey would persist in sniffing while he was a-eating of his dinner, saying that the beef was so strong as it made him. Well, then, Cobbey, see if we can't make you sniff a little without beef. Oh, and Pitcher was took with another fever – so he would be – and fetched by friends, he died the moment he got home. Of course he did, to aggravate us. An't another chap in all the school but that boy would arrange to die exactly at the quarter's end. If that's not spite and malice, then I do not know what is.

He puts the letter away. Standing.

Well, so. It's pretty nigh to time, to wait on the old woman. Pretty sure, that if I'm to succeed at all, I shall succeed tonight. So one quick glass to wish myself success, and put myself in spirits.

He pours the drink and raises it.

Mrs Squeers. Young Wackford. Fanny. Here's your health.

SQUEERS *drinks. Then he turns and goes out of his room and into the other room.*

Well, my Slider!

PEG. Huh? That you?

SQUEERS. It is. It's me. And me's first person singular, the nominative case, agreeing with the verb "its," governed by "Squeers" understood. And if it isn't, you don't know any better.

PEG. Wha? What's that?

SQUEERS (*coming over to her*). This. Is a bottle, Peg. You see?

PEG. O' course I see.

SQUEERS. And this here is a glass. And see, I fill the glass, and I say "Your health, Slider" and I empty it —

He does so.

I fill it once again, and hand the glass to you.

PEG (*takes the glass and drinks*). Your health.

SQUEERS. That's right, that's right. You understand that, anyways. Now, Peg, how's the rheumatics?

SQUEERS filling PEG's glass.

PEG. Ooh, they're better. Ooh, much better, thank'ee, sir.

She drinks.

SQUEERS. You look a great deal better, Peg, than when I first came here.

PEG. Och, well . . . you frightened me.

SQUEERS. I did?

PEG. Och, aye? You knew me name. And where I'd ganged from, and the reason why I'se hiding here.

Slight pause.

Nae wonder. I was frightened. Eh?

SQUEERS pouring PEG another drink.

SQUEERS. Oh, well, Peg, yes, I understand. But see, there's nothing of that kind takes place that I don't know about. See, I'm a sort of lawyer, Peg, of first rate standing, and of understanding, too; I'm the intimate and confidential friend of nearly everyone as has got themselves into a difficulty by being a bit nimble with their fingers. See, I'm a — what's the matter, Peg?

For PEG has been chuckling for a few moments, and is now cackling.

PEG. So he weren't married after all.

SQUEERS. No, Peg. He wasn't. No.

PEG. And some wee lover came and carried off the bride, eh? From beneath his very nose.

SQUEERS. That's right, Peg, yes.

PEG becoming very affectionate with SQUEERS.

PEG. So. Tell me it again? Will ye? Tell it me again, beginning at the beginning, now, as if you'd never told me. Tell it again, and then, who knows, I might show you the paper, you'se so keen to see.

Pause.

SQUEERS. Oh, might you, Slider?

PEG. Och, I might. But only if you tell me how the old goat lost his dainty bride.

Pause. PEG *caressing* SQUEERS.

Go on.

SQUEERS. Well, certainly, I will. But after you've shown me the paper, Peg.

He pours her another drink.

And then, we'll drink the health of Arthur Gride.

PEG *cackles with pleasure, and stands, and potters off into the gloom.*

PEG. Och, aye, then. But only if you tell me the tale. If you promise. Will you?

SQUEERS. Of course I will, Peg, course I will.

PEG *comes back with the deed.*

PEG. Then here you'se are. Right!

SQUEERS *eagerly opens the deed.*

He said it was his beauty. Well, he's lost his beauty, now. Lost both of 'em.

SQUEERS *reading.*

PEG. So, then. What's it say?

SQUEERS. 'To Madeline'. 'To come of age or marry'. 'The said Madeline . . .' That's it. This is the go!

SQUEERS *stands, to go out.*

PEG. Uh? Where you'se going?

SQUEERS (*too quietly for* PEG *to hear*). Out. I've finished with you, Peg.

PEG. Wha's tha' you're saying? I can't hear.

SQUEERS (*shouts*). I'm going, Mrs Sliderskew!

PEG *hobbling across the room after him*

PEG. But wha' about the tale! And toasting Arthur Gride! You canna just up an' leave me! Hey!

SQUEERS *gets to the "door", and finds two* OFFICERS,
FRANK CHEERYBLE *and* NEWMAN NOGGS.

SQUEERS. What's this?

NOGGS. That's him.

OFFICER. You're Mr Squeers?

PEG (*stumbling to the door*). Hey!

NOGGS. And that's her.

SQUEERS. What's this? What's going on?

OFFICER. I have a warrant, issued on advice from these two
gentlemen.

Slight pause. NEIGHBOURS, *including a* YOUNG WOMAN
appear.

PEG. The polis?

SQUEERS. Yes, Peg, yes.

NOGGS. That's right.

PEG. Hey — it's the lunatic!

SQUEERS. Huh — so it is.

The OFFICERS *grabbing at* PEG, *who waves the bottle wildly.*

PEG. Hey! Get your hands off me!

The attention of the OFFICERS *on* PEG, *as* SQUEERS *makes a
run for it.* FRANK *notices.*

FRANK. Hey, stop! Stop that man!

Many NEIGHBOURS *now watching, as* FRANK *and an*
OFFICER *chase* SQUEERS. *Finally,* SQUEERS *finds a little
hiding place and his pursuers rush past him. He attempts to
sneak off unnoticed.* NEWMAN NOGGS, *however, has spotted
him, and brings a metal tray down firmly on his head.*
SQUEERS *collapses.*

NOGGS. Hey, not so much of the lunatic! Not so much, Mr
Squeers and Mrs Sliderskew! Eh! Eh?

FRANK (*putting his hand on* NOGGS' *arm*). Now, Mr Noggs, we
must go home, and tell my uncles what has happened.

The OFFICERS *take out* SQUEERS *and* SLIDERSKEW.
NOGGS *and* FRANK, *with the deed, follow.*

Scene Five

Ralph's room; and his run round London. A large number of NARRATORS *round* RALPH NICKLEBY.

NARRATOR. And on the next day, half-way through the morning, Ralph Nickleby sat alone, in the solitary room where he was accustomed to take his meals.

RALPH. What is this, that hangs over me, and I can't shake it off? I'm never ill, I've never moped, and pined – but what can any man do without rest?

Slight pause. The sound of a bell.

Night after night goes by, I have no rest. I sleep, and I'm disturbed by constant dreams. I wake, I'm haunted by this heavy shadow of – I don't know what.

Slight pause. The sound of a bell.

One night's unbroken rest, and I should be a man again.

RALPH *suddenly aware that the bell has been ringing.*

Noggs! Noggs!

Silence. He picks up his watch.

What? Noon? Where is he? Noggs!

No answer. The bell. RALPH *turns.*

Yes? Who are you?

MESSENGER. Is this the residence of Mr Nickleby?

RALPH. I am that man.

MESSENGER. A letter, sir.

He takes the letter.

RALPH. Thank you.

RALPH *turns back downstage. He reads the letter.*

What is this? "It's most urgent", "Matters come to light". We will explain it". "Dreadful news". What, are the old fools mad? Or is this, from its wildness, just another waking nightmare? Sent to haunt me?

NARRATORS.
And like a haunted man, without his hat or coat, Ralph stumbled through the door, into the street.

At first he drifted aimlessly, a sleepwalker, but then his pace grew brisker, and he almost ran . . .

The streets and people swirled around him, and the sounds of London merged into a single roar, as Ralph sped on, he scarcely could tell why, towards a house in Somers Town.

RALPH *bangs on the floor.*

RALPH. Door! Door! Where are you, Snawley? Door!

SNAWLEY'S WIFE *appears.*

MRS SNAWLEY. Who – oh –

RALPH. I wish to see your husband, ma'am.

MRS SNAWLEY. He's not in. Gone away.

RALPH. Do you know who I am?

MRS SNAWLEY. Oh, yes, I know, but still, he's gone away.

RALPH. Tell him I saw him, through the window-blind above. Tell him that I must speak to him, most urgently.

MRS SNAWLEY. There's nothing that he wants to say to you. Except that, wasn't him that forged the letter. You or schoolmaster did that, so don't you try to lay it at this door.

RALPH. He sets me at defiance, does he?

MRS SNAWLEY. Yes, he does. And so, sir, so do I.

And she withdraws, and the "door" closes behind her.

NARRATORS.
And so Ralph turned again, and hurried back,

Through different streets across the city,

To another house,

Whose windows were closed shut,

Whose blinds were drawn,

All silent, melancholy and deserted.

RALPH. Gride! Gride!

GRIDE, *as if at an upper window.*

GRIDE. What? Who's that?

RALPH. Gride, let me in.

GRIDE. Hush. Hush, no. Go away.

RALPH. Come down!

GRIDE. I won't. Don't speak to me, don't knock . . . Don't call attention to the house – Just go away.

RALPH. I'll knock, I'll shout, I'll sweat, till I have all your neighbours up in arms, if you don't tell me what you mean by lurking there!

GRIDE. I mean – I mean – it isn't safe. Please, please, don't talk to me. Just go away.

GRIDE *disappears*.

RALPH. How is this? They all fall from me and shun me like the plague! How have they changed! These men who used to lick the dust at my feet. I *will* know what it is. I must, at any cost.

NARRATORS.

And so Ralph set off once again,

And crossed the river,

And determined now to hazard everything, came to the meagre house in Lambeth where his tried auxiliary the schoolmaster had lately lodged.

A YOUNG WOMAN – *clearly a Prostitute – appears*.

YOUNG WOMAN. Hallo. What can I do for you?

RALPH (*breathless*). Old woman. Old, and wizened. Deaf. Top floor.

YOUNG WOMAN. You what?

RALPH. And a man. Short, stunted. With a leer. One eye.

YOUNG WOMAN. Oh, yur. I know them people. What d'you want?

RALPH. I want to know where they are now.

YOUNG WOMAN. They're gone.

RALPH. Gone where?

YOUNG WOMAN. Gone with the constables. The Police-Office, I think.

RALPH. Where is the police office?

YOUNG WOMAN (*with a shrug*). Now that — I know.

RALPH *takes the* YOUNG WOMAN's *arm and hurries her upstage*.

Scene Six

The Lambeth Police Office. WACKFORD SQUEERS, *sitting on a bench, with a bandaged head. He is drunk.*

NARRATORS.
And in the Lambeth Police Office there was a kind of waiting room, and Ralph was shown to it, and told to wait:

And shortly afterwards an officer admitted him to Mr Wackford Squeers.

RALPH *comes to* SQUEERS.

SQUEERS. Hm. I say, young feller, you have been and done it now.

RALPH. You have been drinking.

SQUEERS. Hm. Well, not *your* health, I can assure you, my old codger.

RALPH. Why did you not send for me?

SQUEERS *sits. Not answering the question.*

SQUEERS. With me locked up here hard and fast, and you all loose and comfortable.

RALPH. It's only for a few days. They will give you bail. They cannot hurt you, man.

SQUEERS. Well. S'pose that's right. If I explain it all.

Slight pause.

"Prisoner", he says, the powdered head, "You have been found in company with this old woman; as you were apprehended in possession of this document. In absence of a satisfactory account, I shall detain you."

Slight pause.

Well, then, what I say now is, that I *can* give a satisfactory account. I can hand in my card, and say, "I am the Wackford Squeers as is therein named, sir. Whatever's wrong's no fault of mine. I'm merely an employee of a friend – my friend Ralph Nickleby, of Golden Square."

RALPH. What documents?

SQUEERS. *The* document. The Madeline Whatsit document. The will.

RALPH. Whose will? How dated? Benefitting whom? To what extent?

SQUEERS. I can't remember. In her favour, all I know.

Pause.

RALPH. I tell you once again. That they can't hurt you. We'll devise a story for you; if you need a thousand pounds security, you'll have it. All you have to do is keep your wits about you, and keep back the truth.

SQUEERS. Oh, that's it, is it? That's what I'm to do? Well, I tell 'ee, Mr Nickleby. That what I do, or say, is up to me, what serves me most, and if I find it serves me to reveal your part in this, then reveal it's what I'll do.

Slight pause.

My moral influence with them lads, is tottering to its basis.

Slight pause.

The images of Mrs Squeers, my daughter Fanny, and my son, all short of victuals, is perpetually before my eyes. All other thoughts just melts away and just vanishes in front of 'em.

Slight pause.

In short, the only number in arithmetic I knows of as a husband and a father, now, is Number One. In this most fatal go.

Pause.

A-double-L. All. Everything. A cobbler's weapon. U-P, up, an adjective, not down. S-Q-U-double-E-R-S. Squeers, noun substantive. An educator of youth

Pause.

In sum total. It's All Up With Squeers.

RALPH *turns away from* SQUEERS.

RALPH. So. This fellow turns on me as well. They are all struck with fear, while, yesterday, was all civility, compliance. But they shall not move me. I won't budge an inch.

NARRATORS.
And so, then, finally, with a reluctant, grudging step, Ralph Nickleby set course towards the City.
He had not eaten or drunk anything all day, he felt sick and exhausted, and his every sense was numb, except for one of weariness and desolation.

Scene Seven

The Cheerybles' house. A chair, beside a small table with a lamp on it. RALPH *approaches* MR CHARLES, MR NED *and* TIM LINKINWATER.

RALPH. So – which is Mr Charles?

MR CHARLES. I am.

RALPH. You sent me this, this morning, asking me – demanding that I come here to your house at half past seven o'clock. Well, it is only shortly after. I am here.

Slight pause:

As no one bids me to a seat, I'll take one for I am fatigued with walking.

RALPH *sits*.

And now, if you please, gentlemen, I wish to know, I demand to know, I have the right to know – what you have to say to me which justifies the tone you have employed.

Waving the letter.

MR CHARLES. Very well, sir. Brother Ned.

MR NED *goes out and returns with* NEWMAN NOGGS.

RALPH. Oh – this – this is a good beginning. Oh, yes, you are candid, honest, open-hearted and fair-dealing men! To tamper with a fellow such as this, who'd sell his soul for a drink, whose every word's a lie – oh, this is a beginning!

NOGGS. I will speak.

RALPH. Oh, yes, I'm sure you'll –

NOGGS. I *will* speak. And ask, who made me "a fellow such as this"?

Slight pause.

If I would sell my soul for a drink, why wasn't I a thief, a swindler, a robber of pence from the trays of blindmen's dogs, rather than your drudge and packhorse? If my every word was indeed a lie, why was I not a pet and favourite of yours! A liar! When did I ever fawn and cringe to you?

Slight pause.

I served you faithfully. You were talking just now about tampering. Who tampered with the Yorkshire schoolmaster? Who tampered with a jealous father, urging him to sell his daughter to old Arthur Gride, and tampered with Gride too, and did so in a little office *with a closet in the room*?

RALPH *a sharp gesture.*

Aha! You mind me now! And what first set the drudge to

listening at doors, and watching close and following? The master's cruel treatment of his flesh and blood, his vile designs upon a young girl, which made the miserable and drunken hack stay on in service, in the hope of doing her some good, when he might have otherwise relieved his feelings by pummelling his master soundly, and then going to the Devil. I'm here now because these gentlemen thought it best. When I sought them out — as I did, there's no tampering with me — I told them that I wanted to help to find you out, to track you down, to finish what I had begun, to help the right; and that when I'd done it I would burst into your room, and face you man to man, and — like a man. And now I've done it. Now I've had my say. Let anybody say theirs. I've done.

Pause.

At last.

Pause. A general gesture.

So — fire away!

RALPH. Hm.

Pause. A little wave.

Go on, go on.

MR CHARLES. It is, sir, simply told.

He waves to MR NED.

MR NED. We knew about the deed, and how Gride had acquired it, and we heard, from neighbours, of the great to-do Gride made when it was gone.

MR CHARLES. Our dear friend Mr Noggs acquainted us with Squeers' visit to you, and as you and he pursued Peg Sliderskew, we in our turn followed you, and then the schoolmaster, and found the house in Lambeth, and procured a warrant to arrest them for possession of a stolen document.

MR NED. Which then was done. The woman, and the schoolmaster, and most of all, the deed, are now in police possession.

MR CHARLES. Now, sir, you've heard it. How far you are implicated in this matter, you best know. But we would not — would not see an old man like you disgraced or punished.

RALPH. Sir, you have not the man to deal with that you think you have.

Pause.

MR NED. What's this?

RALPH. Oh, merely, that I have not heard a word of proof of any of these wild allegations; that I spit on your fair words and your false dealings; and that there is law, still, to be had, and I will call you to account. Take care, sir, you have said enough already. I'd advise you, say no more.

MR CHARLES. Then we've not said enough.

He looks at MR NED.

MR NED. No, no, indeed.

MR CHARLES. Sir, what would you say if we said that this man Snawley had confessed?

RALPH. Snawley? Then I'd reply that Snawley is a frightened coward, and that this "confession" was most likely forced from him.

MR CHARLES. And if we told you that the boy was dead?

Pause.

RALPH. You mean — the simpleton —

MR NED. Is dead, indeed.

Pause. RALPH *laughs.*

RALPH. Oh, gentlemen, then I forgive you everything. For this news, I am in your debt, and bound to you for life.

NOGGS. Oh, you. Oh, how can — it's unnatural.

MR CHARLES. It is.

He nods to MR NED *who goes out.*

RALPH. What's this? Another? Have you dredged my nephew up, to add to all these lies?

Re-enter MR NED *with* BROOKER.

What? Him? D'you know, this is a felon, a convicted criminal?

MR NED. You asked, sir, for our proof that broken boy was not the son of Snawley.

RALPH. Yes, I did. Well —

MR NED. Our proof is not concerned with papers, or confessions. It is that we know the poor boy was another's son.

RALPH. Another's? Whose?

BROOKER. Yours.

Pause. RALPH *presses the palms of his hands against his temples.*

RALPH. What?

Pause.

BROOKER. Do you remember? About, oh, what, a quarter of a century ago? A family in Leicestershire? A father and a daughter? A father that you'd wound into your net, you'd cheated, like you cheated me? But a daughter who had grown attached to you, because of, he was young, then, charming in his way, and she could not believe he was not their family's benefactor? And who fell in love with you, Ralph Nickleby. And married you.

Pause.

But, of course, it had to be a secret, from the father. He was rich. And if he'd known, the daughter would have lost a great inheritance. And that would never do. Oh, would it. So, a secret wedding. And a little secret son. Put out to nurse. A long way off. So not to interfere.

Pause.

And then, as time went on, began to see her less and less. Stayed up in London, making money. And your wife, a young girl, alone, in a dull old country house. And eventually, she couldn't bear it any more. Could she?

Pause.

And so she ran off? Didn't she?

Pause.

And you ordered me to fetch the boy, to keep him from her — didn't you?

Pause.

And you had used me ill. And cruelly. The boy was hidden in an attic, and neglect had made him sickly, and the doctor said that he must have a change of air or else he'd die. You went away. Six weeks. When you returned, I told you that the child was dead.

Pause.

And you — I think — realised — you missed him. When he'd gone. You missed someone who thought well of you. He brightened up your house, and made a little laughter in your halls. And you missed him. Didn't you?

Pause.

MR CHARLES. So the boy was not, then, dead.

BROOKER. Sirs, I offer no excuses for myself. You could say, I was harshly treated and driven from my real nature. But, I'm guilty.

Slight pause.

Yes, I stole the boy. And took him to a Yorkshire school. And paid his fees, for six years. And then went away.

Pause.

But then . . . came back. And went to look for him. I couldn't find him, there, he'd gone. So – came to London. And confronted him. No use. But then, a month, six weeks ago, I saw the boy. He was sitting in a garden. Knew his face. And he, I think, knew mine.

To RALPH.

The school was run by your friend, Mr Wackford Squeers. I gave the boy a name. Do I need to tell you?

RALPH. Smike.

Pause. Throughout BROOKER's *speech, it has been growing steadily darker. Now the only source of light is the lamp on a table near* RALPH.

MR NED. Unhappy man. Unhappy man.

MR CHARLES. But doubly, trebly, ten times more unhappy must *you* be, Ralph Nickleby.

Pause. Then, like a reptile's tongue, RALPH's *hand shoots out towards the lamp. It crashes and there is darkness.*

Scene Eight

Lights. RALPH *is running.*

NARRATORS.

Creeping from the house, and slinking like a thief . . .

Groping like a blind man . . .

Ralph Nickleby went from the city, and took the road to his own home.

RALPH *is stumbling, fearful of what follows him.*

And there was one black, gloomy mass that seemed to follow him,

Not hurrying in the wild chase with the others,

But lingering, sullenly, behind, and following him.

A line of people, at crazy angles, like bent and broken iron railings; in front, a pile of bodies, forming hideous shapes.

He passed a poor, mean burial ground,

A rank, unwholesome spot, where the very grass and weeds appeared to tell that they had sprung from paupers' bodies, and Ralph peered in through the iron railings . . .

The railings become a group of drunks, careering round in front of the bodies, one actor playing a pipe.

And then there came towards him, full of shouts and singing, a group of fellows full of drink, in high good humour,

And a member of their company, a little, weazen, hump-backed man, began to dance.

And indeed a little man does dance, to the music of the pipe, and RALPH joins in the clapping, until he is swallowed up and disappears. And suddenly, everything stops, and the NARRATORS stand there, still.

And Ralph came home.

He could hardly make up his mind to turn the key and open up the door.

And when he had —

And closed it, with a crash behind him —

He felt as if he had shut out the world.

The NARRATORS dispersing now. One NARRATOR appears, with a single chair.

There was no light. How dreary, cold and still it was.

He groped his way towards the stairs, and climbed, up to the very top —

To the front garret —

Which was now a lumber room.

RALPH appears. The last NARRATOR places the chair carefully.

LAST NARRATOR. Here Ralph remained.

The NARRATOR *goes.* RALPH *stands there. We see he is holding a piece of rope.*

RALPH. I know this room. This room was where he slept. I was his father. But he didn't die here. And he didn't die with me. He died – elsewhere.

Pause.

But if he hadn't . . . If he'd grown up here. Might we have been – a comfort to each other. And might I – have been a different man. A man more like my nephew. Or my brother. Nicholas.

He begins to tie the rope into a noose.

But now. To be held up in the most repulsive colours. And to know that he was taught to hate my very name. "Ralph Nickleby."

Pause.

"To wound him, through his own affections. Oh, to strike him through this boy . . ."

Pause.

"All love is cant and vanity".

A knocking on the door downstairs.

RALPH. What's that?

We hear TIM's *voice.*

TIM (*off*). Is that – Ralph Nickleby?

RALPH. What do you want from him?

TIM (*off*). I'm from the Brothers. They want to meet with you tomorrow.

RALPH. Yes, yes. Tell them, they can come tomorrow.

TIM (*off*). At what hour?

RALPH. At any hour! What time they like.

Pause.

All times will be alike to me.

RALPH *looks up.*

That hook. Big, black one, in the ceiling. Never noticed it before.

Slight pause.

Perhaps he noticed it. Perhaps it frightened him.

Slight pause.

It frightens me.

Slight pause.

But it would hold me.

He looks round the room where his son had slept.

Outcast. A noun. Cast out. And homeless.

Long pause.

Me.

RALPH *quickly puts the noose round his neck and raises it above him. Darkness. The thud of a body falling from a chair. A moment. Then light.* MR CHARLES, MR NED *and* TIM LINKINWATER.

MR CHARLES. And in the morning, they went round, and knocked, and knocked again.

MR NED. And eventually, they broke a window, and went in, and searched the house.

TIM. And they found the body of Ralph Nickleby, and cut it down.

Blackout.

Scene Nine.

The Cheerbyles' house. Two chairs.

NARRATORS.

And some weeks passed, and the first shock of these happenings subsided.

Madeline was living in the house of friends of the Mr Cheerybles;

Young Frank was absent;

And Nicholas and Kate were trying, in good earnest, to stifle their regrets, and to live for each other and their mother.

And there came one evening,

Per favour of Mr Linkinwater,

An invitation from the Brothers Cheeryble for dinner on the next day but one,

An invitation comprehending not just Nicholas, his mother and his sister

But their great friend Miss La Creevy, too —
Who much to the astonishment of Mrs Nickleby,
Was most particularly mentioned.

The NICKLEBYS *and* MISS LA CREEVY *are greeted by* MR CHARLES, MR NED *and* TIM LINKINWATER.

MR CHARLES. Now, we took the liberty, dear friends, of naming one hour before dinner, as we had a little business to discuss, which would occupy the interval. I wonder, Tim, if you would be so kind as to escort dear Mrs Nickleby and Miss La Creevy too — to show them something of the house, perhaps, and p'raps to tell them something too.

TIM. It would be my great pleasure. Ma'am. And Ma'am.

Pause. MRS NICKLEBY, KATE *and* NICHOLAS *in their different ways, looking bemused.*

MRS NICKLEBY. Well, certainly, I —

MR NED (*his finger to his lips*). Not another word.

With as much grace as she can muster, MRS NICKLEBY *allows herself to be escorted out by* TIM, MISS LA CREEVY *following, a little smile on her face.*

MR CHARLES. Now, Kate, my dear. Tell me. Have you seen Madeline since your return to London?

KATE. No, sir. And I have not heard from her.

MR CHARLES. Not heard from her? What do you think of that, Brother Ned? Is that not sad?

MR NED. Oh, very, Brother Charles. Yes, very sad. The whole thing's so upsetting, that you will forgive me if, for just a moment, I withdraw myself into another room.

Much winking between the BROTHERS: MR NED *withdraws.*

MR CHARLES. Poor Brother Ned, as I've remarked to you before, sir, often, always such a prey to his emotions. Now. We were engaged, I think, upon the topic of Miss Madeline, who, as you know, becomes entitled, on her marriage, to a certain sum of money.

NICHOLAS. Yes, we know that, sir.

MR CHARLES. In fact, a sum amounting to twelve thousand pounds, from the will of Madeline's maternal grandmother. One could say, quite a dowry. Hm?

Pause.

NICHOLAS. You did receive our letter, sir?

MR CHARLES. Yes, yes, we did. You both explained your feelings — yours for Miss Madeline, and Kate's for nephew Frank. You had resolved, despite those feelings, to reject all thought of love and matrimony — and to live, instead, just for each other.

NICHOLAS. Yes, sir. That is our resolve.

MR CHARLES. A noble sentiment. But still, perhaps, a selfish one.

NICHOLAS. What, selfish? Why?

MR CHARLES. Because of other people's feelings. For an instance, those of Brother Ned and I.

NICHOLAS. I'm sorry. I don't understand.

MR NED *has appeared. Behind him, unseen by* NICHOLAS *and* KATE, *are* FRANK *and* MADELINE.

MR NED. You don't? You don't see why *we* are offended? To have thought that we were such mean judges of two persons' characters. To think that we'd consider for a moment that your love for Madeline, or Kate's for Frank, had anything to do with money? Come, how could you think so!

KATE. We — we did not think so, sir.

MR CHARLES. And worse than that. Much worse. To think that you yourselves would be corrupted and debased, by marrying the people whom you've set your hearts upon?

NICHOLAS. Sirs, I had thought we'd made it plain. We have — my sister and I have — learnt nothing in our journeyings so strongly as we've learned what happens to the kindest, and the noblest and the gentlest people, when their souls are tainted by the touch of money.

KATE. We have seen our father, and our uncle, sirs, the one who was most dear to us, the other, one who should have been, destroyed; one in the want of money; and the other by the having it, and loving it too much.

FRANK. Oh, Kate. Oh, Nicholas. How can you be so blind? They stand in front of you!

MR NED. Now, Frank —

FRANK. No, no, you cannot say it, Uncle Ned, you cannot say it, Uncle Charles; but I can: that you see before you, Nicholas and

Kate, two men who walked barefoot to London, penniless and hungry, and who have made their fortune, and have they been tainted or debased? Have they been made ignoble, or ungentle, or unkind? You see them, Nicholas.

KATE. Frank. Back.

MR NED. Yes, yes, returned most unexpectedly, without so much as a presentiment.

MR CHARLES. As is his wont.

MR NED. And with him, someone else whose feelings, we might take into account.

NICHOLAS *sees* MADELINE.

NICHOLAS. Oh, Madeline. You've heard, all this?

MADELINE. Yes, yes. I've heard.

NICHOLAS. And you — they've told you, everything, I —

MADELINE. Yes they have.

NICHOLAS *is completely thrown.*

NICHOLAS. This is — I told you, sirs, in confidence, my feelings for Miss Madeline, I . . . I have no idea, of course, if they, if she — what feelings she has entertained, I — do you understand?

MADELINE. I understand what I have understood since we first met. And I understand that, since then, you have changed.

NICHOLAS. Oh, no —

MADELINE. And that you cannot see me any more, but only my inheritance.

Pause. MADELINE *takes* NICHOLAS's *hands.*

Oh, Nicholas. That someone who has been through what you've been through, who has striven as you've striven, who has learnt what you have learnt, could think that it is right to sacrifice our happiness for such a superstition, to believe that there are any barriers between us that we can't surmount.

NICHOLAS. Our happiness.

MADELINE. Oh, Nicholas. How could you ever think that I felt otherwise?

Pause. NICHOLAS *turns to* KATE.

NICHOLAS. We're over-ruled.

KATE *to* FRANK.

KATE. So it would seem.

MR CHARLES. And so it is.

MR NED. And so it is.

We hear MRS NICKLEBY *approaching.*

MRS NICKLEBY. Oh, Mr Linkinwater, this is too extraordinary.

MR NED. Quick, quick, everyone away . . . and talk among yourselves, if you've got anything to talk about . . .

MR CHARLES. Yes, hurry, all out, everyone –

NICHOLAS, MADELINE, KATE *and* FRANK *go apart as:*

MRS NICKLEBY (*approaching*). Now, of course, it's very pleasant, if it is true, but I assure you, if it isn't, it's a most cruel . . . Mr Cheeryble.

And MRS NICKLEBY, MISS LA CREEVY *and* TIM *are now back in the room.*

MR NED. Yes, Mrs Nickleby?

MRS NICKLEBY. Can this be true?

MR CHARLES. Not only can, but is.

Slight pause.

TIM. Hm. Didn't keep 'em in suspense as long as said you would. Impatient, what I call it.

MR CHARLES. What, d'you hear that, Brother Ned, from Tim, who has been wearying us from morning until night –

MR NED. It's true, Charles, it's all true, the man's a wild young fellow, he must sow his wild oats, and then perhaps he'll come in time to be a respectable and normal member of society –

The BROTHERS *taking the arms of* MRS NICKLEBY.

MR CHARLES. I'm sure that Mrs Nickleby agrees, dear brother –

The BROTHERS *leading* MRS NICKLEBY *out.*

MRS NICKLEBY (*with a desperate look back at* TIM *and* MISS LA CREEVY). Well, I . . . I mean, if I am asked my view . . . Uh – oh –

And they are gone. TIM *and* MISS LA CREEVY *left alone.* MISS LA CREEVY *sitting.* TIM *moves the other chair closer, and sits.*

TIM. Well, isn't it a pleasant thing. To people like us, to see young folks we are so fond of brought together.

MISS LA CREEVY. Yes, it is. Indeed.

TIM. Although – although it makes one feel, oneself, quite solitary. Almost cast away. I don't know, if you feel . . .

MISS LA CREEVY. Well, certainly, that's true; I mean, it's true, that I don't know.

TIM. It's . . . almost something that would make one think of getting wed oneself. Now isn't it.

MISS LA CREEVY. Oh, nonsense, Mr Linkinwater.

TIM. Now, is it? Is it nonsense? Really?

Pause. MISS LA CREEVY *holding her breath.*

MISS LA CREEVY. Now, Mr Linkinwater, you are mocking me.

TIM. No, no, I'm not.

MISS LA CREEVY. Why think – how we'd make people laugh.

TIM. Well, let 'em. We'll laugh back.

MISS LA CREEVY. And, think, as well: what would the brothers say?

TIM. Why, Miss La Creevy, bless your soul! You don't suppose I'd think of such a thing without their knowing it? Why, they left us here on purpose!

MISS LA CREEVY. Oh, I can never look them in the face again.

TIM. Now, come. Let's be a comfortable couple. We shall live in this old house; we'll sit and talk, or sit and sit, quite calm and perfectly contented. Oh, let's be a comfortable couple, let's, my dear.

MISS LA CREEVY. Oh, Mr Linkinwater, since you put it in that – most affecting fashion – yes.

They kiss. Then they look up to see, behind them, FRANK, KATE, MADELINE, NICHOLAS, MR CHARLES, MR NED *and* MRS NICKLEBY.

MRS NICKLEBY. Oh, Miss La Creevy!

TIM *stands up.*

TIM. There is not, I swear, another woman like her in the whole of London. I just *know* there ain't.

MRS NICKLEBY. And – Mr Linkinwater!

A knock at the outside door. MR NED *slips out, as:*

MR CHARLES. Mrs Nickleby, I wonder, might I be granted the incalculable pleasure of escorting you to dinner?

MRS NICKLEBY (*vaguely*). Yes, of course . . .

MR CHARLES. And, everyone, and everyone . . .

And MR CHARLES *and* MRS NICKLEBY, KATE *and* FRANK, TIM *and* MISS LA CREEVY, *followed by* NICHOLAS *and* MADELINE, *the last. As they are going, re-enter* MR NED, *followed by* NEWMAN NOGGS.

MR NED. Uh, Mr Nickleby. Forgive me.

MR NED *takes* MADELINE's *arm.*

NICHOLAS. Yes, of course, I –

NOGGS. Nick.

NICHOLAS *to* NOGGS, *as* MR NED *takes* MADELINE *out.* NOGGS *is "genteelly dressed in black".*

NICHOLAS. Oh, Newman. Newman.

NOGGS. Yes, it's your own Newman. Nick, my dear boy, I give you – everything. All health, all happiness, and every blessing. I can't bear it, it's too much – it makes a child of me!

NICHOLAS. Where have you been? How often have I asked for you, and been told that I should hear before long!

NOGGS. I know, I know. They wanted all the happiness to come together. I've been helping 'em. I – I – look at me, Nick, look at me!

NICHOLAS (*"in a tone of gentle reproach"*). You'd never let *me* buy you such a suit. I offered to.

NOGGS. I didn't mind, then. Couldn't have the heart to put on clothes like these. They'd have reminded me of old times, made me miserable. But now – I am another man, Nick – Oh, my dear boy, I can't speak, please don't do anything – you don't know what I feel today; you can't, and never will.

NICHOLAS. I can. I think I do. But, come, let's go to dinner.

And as NICHOLAS *takes* NOGGS' *arm,* MR NED, MR CHARLES *and* KATE *re-appear.*

MR NED. And never was there such a dinner since the world began.

MR CHARLES. And at the end of all the toasts and speeches, Nicholas took Kate apart –

NICHOLAS. And whispered to her that, in all his happiness, there was still one dark cloud, and that his joy could never be complete until it was dispelled.

And so the two of them set forth, the next afternoon, to book Nicholas a place on the coach for Greta Bridge in Yorkshire.

NARRATORS.
And on their way back to the Strand, as luck would have it, they passed by a little theatre,

On which was displayed a boldly-printed bill,

Announcing that tonight would be the positively last appearance of the celebrated company of Mr Vincent Crummles, and his wife and family.

Scene Ten

The stage door of a theatre. Enter CRUMMLES, *dressed as a Bandit, to* NICHOLAS *and* KATE.

CRUMMLES. My dear young man! My dear young man!

NICHOLAS. Oh, Mr Crummles. This is – a most happy chance. May I introduce my sister?

CRUMMLES (*pumping* KATE's *hand*). It's a pleasure. It's a double pleasure, meeting you, Miss Johnson.

KATE *a look to* NICHOLAS, *who shrugs.*

I'm delighted, sir, I'm quite delighted, with this chance to say goodbye.

NICHOLAS. Goodbye? Why, are you going? Where?

CRUMMLES. Oh, haven't you seen it, in the papers?

NICHOLAS. No.

CRUMMLES. Well, that's a wonder. It was there, in the varieties. Ah, look.

Producing a cutting.

I have it here.

NICHOLAS (*reads*). "The talented Vincent Crummles, long favourably known to fame as a country manager and an actor of no ordinary pretensions, is about to cross the Atlantic" – ! – "on a histrionic expedition. Crummles is to be accompanied, we hear by his wife and gifted family. Crummles is quite certain to succeed."

Handing the cutting back.

America!

CRUMMLES. That's right, sir.

NICHOLAS. With – with all the company?

CRUMMLES. Well – no. In fact, sir, I own our numbers have been much depleted since we saw you last. Finances, sir, the main cause – always, sir, finance. But there have been departures, too: old Fluggers joined the church, by reasons of his years of practising; and Tom Folair defected to a company that mounts spectaculars hard-by the bridge at Waterloo: attracted by the glitter, sir, and promises of quick and easy fame. Well, he'll find out, of course . . . and even, this may well upset you rather more, Miss Snevellicci left us –

NICHOLAS. Oh?

KATE. Miss Snevellicci.

CRUMMLES. Yes, to marry the good-looking young wax chandler who supplied the candles to the Portsmouth theatre . . . but apparently, deliriously happy.

KATE. Ah.

CRUMMLES. So, we thought . . . We have a fair start – The Americans are much devoted to grand gesture and the melodrama, and I've heard, on the best authority, that they'll pay anything . . . and then, who knows, we might buy that little plot of land, support ourselves in our old age . . .

NICHOLAS. I think, as always, you have acted wisely, sir.

CRUMMLES. But, see – it is herself approaching!

MRS CRUMMLES *sailing over, with the* MASTER CRUMMLESES *and the* INFANT PHENOMENON, *all in costume.*

MRS CRUMMLES. Mr Johnson! What an unexpected joy! And – Mrs Johnson?

KATE. Miss.

MRS CRUMMLES. Sir, here are two you know. And another.

NICHOLAS *is kissed by the* PHENOMENON. *He shakes hands with the* MASTER CRUMMLESES.

NICHOLAS. I'm very pleased to see you once again. I'm very pleased – to see – see everyone.

MRS CRUMMLES. So are you coming – to tonight's performance? It is positively, quite unalterably, the last –

NICHOLAS. I know. But sadly, I regret –

MRS CRUMMLES. Regret? That's all that I remember of you, Mr Johnson. All the time, regretting.

NICHOLAS. I have, unfortunately, to be up at dawn, for a journey of my own. And in fact – have such preparations to complete . . .

MRS CRUMMLES. And if not regretting, then farewelling, Mr Johnson.

Pause. Something in NICHOLAS's *tone has deflated the bombast.*

NICHOLAS. Yes, I am afraid . . .

A smile.

Yes, yes.

He shakes CRUMMLES's *hand.*

CRUMMLES. We were a happy little company, Johnson. You and I never had a word. I shall be very glad tomorrow morning to remember that I saw you once again, but now I almost wish you hadn't come.

Slight pause.

KATE (*out front*). And Mr Johnson submitted to another hug with even better grace than before, if that were possible; and waving his hat as cheerfully as he could, took farewell of the Vincent Crummleses.

Scene Eleven

The journey to Yorkshire; Dotheboys Hall. The NARRATORS, *as the stage grows darker and darker:*

NARRATORS. And the next morning, Nicholas began his journey. It was now cold, winter weather,

And sometimes, he would recognise some place which he had passed on his journey up to Yorkshire, or on the long walk back,

And as night fell, it began to snow, and everything became as he remembered it, and it was easy to believe that everything which had since happened had been but a dream, and that he and Smike were plodding wearily along the road to London, the world before them.

Very early morning gloom. We can hardly see. A scrape, a scuffle – someone running, others running after. Some of the boys are chasing YOUNG WACKFORD. *It is a slow, stumbling, dark kind of chase.*

JACKSON. Hey, Wackford, Wackford –

COATES. Where's your pa then, Wackford?

BOLDER. Where's he be?

Slight pause.

WACKFORD. Dunno.

A violent scuffle as the BOYS *follow* WACKFORD's *voice. Three or four boys find* WACKFORD *and pinion him against a wall.*

JACKSON. Dunno? Come on, now, Wackford. Summat's happened. We know that.

SNAWLEY SNR. We heard your mam cry, through the parlour window.

JACKSON. Heard your sister, screaming in the night.

JENNINGS. Tell us what happened, Wackford.

BOLDER. Or we'll . . .

JACKSON. There's no telling what we'll do.

WACKFORD. My ma –

JACKSON. Yuh? What?

WACKFORD. My ma said –

SNAWLEY SNR. Yuh?

WACKFORD. Pa's gonna be transported to Australia. And some old lady with him. And one man he worked for's going to jail. And another one's gone and hanged hisself. What else d'you want to know?

Slight pause.

JACKSON. Right, then.

The heavy noise of footfall. The BOYS *quickly push* WACKFORD *away. All the* BOYS *now on stage. Enter* MRS SQUEERS, FANNY, PHIB *and a small* BOY *who has become the* NEW SMIKE, *carrying the brimstone-and-treacle bowl.* MRS SQUEERS *carries the spoon.*

MRS SQUEERS. What's going on? Where's Wackford?

WACKFORD *hurries to his Mother, looking nervously at the* BOYS.

It's brimstone-and-treacle morning! Every boy on line. Quick! Quick! What are you thinking of? First boy!

The BOYS *get into line.*

TOMKINS. First boy. Tomkins. Twelve. A cripple.

COBBEY. Second boy. Cobbey. Thirteen. Another cripple.

PETERS. Third boy. Peters. Seven. Blind.

GREYMARSH. Fourth boy –

And he is interrupted by JACKSON, *who pushes himself forward, through the line, and past* JENNINGS.

JACKSON. Jackson.

MRS SQUEERS. What's this?

JACKSON (*grabbing the spoon*). Johnny Jackson.

BOLDER, *pushing his way through the line.*

MRS SQUEERS. Boy!

BOLDER. Fifth boy. Bolder.

He grabs the bowl from the NEW SMIKE.

MRS SQUEERS. Right, then, Bolder –

She lifts the cane. It is grabbed by COATES.

COATES. Sixth. Coates. Eat.

MRS SQUEERS. Have you gone mad!

JACKSON. Said – eat.

JACKSON, COATES *and* BOLDER *push* MRS SQUEERS *to her knees, helped by the others.* JACKSON *forces the spoon into* MRS SQUEERS' *mouth.*

JACKSON. Eat.

MRS SQUEERS. You – little –

But she is forced to eat the brimstone.

BOLDER. There. What now?

JACKSON. It's the end of term. It's break-up. So, let's break up. Break it all up. Break it all up – now.

And a few BOYS *start to chant. And the chant grows louder. And, as it grows, the* BIGGER BOYS, *followed by the*

SMALLER BOYS, *start to rush about, smashing everything they can see, pushing at* MRS SQUEERS *and* FANNY, *and dipping* WACKFORD's *head in the brimstone bowl.*

BOYS. Break-up. Break-up. Break-up. Break-up.

And in the general melee, MRS SQUEERS *manages to escape, pulling* WACKFORD *after her, but* FANNY *and* PHIB *are pinioned, pinched and prodded by groups of* BOYS, *while the others continue to smash up Dotheboys Hall. The chant louder and faster.*

BOYS. BREAK–UP. BREAK–UP. BREAK–UP. BREAK–UP. BREAK–UP.

And as the chant and the smashing-up build on, until they can grow no faster and louder, and JOHN BROWDIE, TILDA *and* NICHOLAS *burst in.*

JOHN. Stop! Stop! Hey, all of 'ee – ye lads – stop! STOP!

And everything stops.

What's happening? What's going on here, eh?

Pause. A little voice.

SNAWLEY SNR. Please sir. Squeers is in prison, sir, and going to be transported, sir, and –

COBBEY. And we're breaking out.

BOYS. Break-up – break-up.

JOHN. Well, I'll not stop ye. But – don't hurt the women, eh? Where's Mrs?

GREYMARSH. Run away, sir.

JOHN. Little fat one?

TOMKINS. Gone with her.

JOHN. And Fanny?

FANNY and PHIB are allowed to come to JOHN.

Right, then. So – that's it.

Pause.

BELLING. Can we – go now, sir?

NICHOLAS (*suddenly*). Yes. Yes, go. Go, run away. As far as possible. Don't hurt them, don't hurt anyone, but still – yes, break it all up, then go. Go! Go!

And cheering, the BOYS run out, some confidently, some

tearfully, some fast, some slowly, reluctantly, taking everything with them.

FANNY. Well, Mr Browdie. And your friend as well. Excited all our boys to run away. But we will pay you out for it, even if our pa's unfortunate, and trod down by his enemies, we'll pay you out, I promise, you, and him, and Tilda!

JOHN. No, tha won't. I tell thee, Fanny, that I'm glad the old man's been caught out at last, but you'll have enough to suffer from without me crowing. More than that, tha'll need a friend or two to help thee get away, and here we are, and ready to lend thee a hand. So, are tha coming?

FANNY *turns away, arms folded.*

TILDA. Come on, Fanny, please.

FANNY *turns back. She's crying.* TILDA *takes her arm, and she,* FANNY *and* PHIB *go out.* JOHN *and* NICHOLAS *left there for a moment.*

JOHN. Well, then. Bloodshed. Riot. Eh?

Pause.

NICHOLAS. Thank God — at least — it's over.

And as they go, NARRATORS:

NARRATORS.
And for some days afterwards, the neighbouring countryside was over-run with boys.
And some were found crying under hedges, frightened by the solitude;

We see a BOY *wandering on from some hiding place. He holds the brimstone bowl and spoon.*

One was discovered sleeping in a yard nearby the building;

We realise the BOY *is the* NEW SMIKE.

And another wandered twenty miles, lost courage, and lay down in the snow, and slept.

And the BOY *sits, at the very front of the stage.*

And in the course of time the Hall and its last breaking up began to be forgotten by the neighbours,
Or only spoken of as among things that had been.

And the stage is empty now, except for the NEW SMIKE, *sitting alone at the front of the stage.*

Scene Twelve

Devon at Christmas. The NEW SMIKE, *in the loneliness and silence, begins to sing what he can remember of a Christmas carol.*

NEW SMIKE. God – rest ye, merry gentlemen – Let – uh – uh – you, dis-play . . .

Pause.

For uh-uh-uh, our uh-uh-uh, Was born on, Christmas Day –

Pause.

To la-la-la from Satan's power When – uh, uh gone astray –

Pause.

Oh, oh, uh, uh, of comfort and joy –

Slight pause.

Comfort and joy . . .

Pause.

Oh, oh, tidings of comfort and joy.

And the NEW SMIKE *is still. And then, very faintly, we can hear the tune of the carol, being hummed. And more voices join, and we are in Devon, at Christmas. And the* FAMILIES *enter, to form a pleasant, almost photographic tableau:* NICHOLAS, KATE, MRS NICKLEBY, MADELINE, MR CHARLES, MR NED, FRANK, TIM, MISS LA CREEVY *and* NEWMAN NOGGS. *And during their final narration, the carol grows behind them.*

COMPANY.

God rest ye merry, gentlemen
Let nothing you dismay
For Jesus Christ our saviour
Was born upon this day
To save us all from Satan's power
When we were gone atray
O it's tidings of comfort and joy
Comfort and joy
O it's tidings of comfort and joy

From God that is our Father
The blessed angels came
Unto some certain shepherds
With tidings of the same;
That there was born in Bethelehem
The Son of God by name
And it's tidings of comfort and joy

Comfort and joy,
And it's tidings of comfort and joy.

Meanwhile

MADELINE. And when her term of mourning had expired, Madeline gave her hand and fortune to Nicholas.

KATE. And on the same day and at the same time, Kate became Mrs Frank Cheeryble.

MR CHARLES. And it had been expected that Tim Linkinwater and Miss La Creevy would have made a third couple on the occasion,

MISS LA CREEVY. But they declined,

TIM. And two or three weeks afterward went out together one morning before breakfast,

MR NED. And,

KATE. Coming back with merry faces,

MR CHARLES. Were found to have been quietly married that day.

NICHOLAS. And the money which Nicholas acquired in right of his wife he invested in the firm of the Cheeryble Brothers, in which Frank had become a partner.

FRANK. And before many years elapsed, the business began to be carried on in the names of "Cheeryble and Nickleby",

MRS NICKLEBY. So that Mrs Nickleby's prophetic anticipations were to be realised at last.

TIM. The twin brothers retired.

FRANK. Who needs to be told that they were happy?

KATE. They were surrounded by happiness of their own creation, and lived but to increase it.

NICHOLAS. The first act of Nicholas, when he became a rich and prosperous merchant, was to buy his father's old farm;

MADELINE. And soon, he and his wife were blessed with a group of lovely children.

FRANK. And within a stone's throw was another such retreat, enlivened by children's voices, too,

KATE. And here lived Kate, with many new cares and occupations,

NICHOLAS. But still, the same true loving creature and the same gentle sister, as in her girlish days.

MRS NICKLEBY. And Mrs Nickleby lived sometimes with her daughter and sometimes with her son,

MADELINE. And spent much time relating her experience,

MRS NICKLEBY. Especially on the matter of the management and bringing up of children,

KATE. With much importance and solemnity.

MR CHARLES. And there was one grey-haired,

MR NED. Quiet,

MR CHARLES. Harmless gentleman,

NOGGS. Who lived in a little cottage hard by Nicholas' house, and in his absence, attended to the supervision of affairs.

MADELINE. His chief delight and pleasure was the children,

NOGGS. With whom he became a child himself, and master of the revels. The little people could do nothing without dear, old Newman Noggs.

KATE. And, as time went on, the house in which young Nicholas and Kate had spent their childhood was enlarged and altered, to accommodate the growing family.

NICHOLAS. But no old rooms were ever pulled down,

KATE. No old tree was rooted up,

NICHOLAS. Nothing with which there was the least association of old, bygone times and childhood days was ever cut down,

KATE. Or removed,

NICHOLAS. Or even – changed.

And all the COMPANY *are singing now, and* JOHN *and* TILDA *run in to join the* FAMILIES, *who are shaking each others' hands, and talking and moving from person to person, and embracing: the happiest of Christmasses.*

COMPANY.
Now to the Lord Sing Praises
All you within this place,
Like we true loving brethren,
Each other to embrace.

And NICHOLAS, *a little apart, looks downstage, as if out of a window, and sees the* BOY, *sitting outside in the snow.*

For the merry time of Christmas
Is drawing on apace –

And, unnoticed, NICHOLAS *slips away, and trudges over to the still* BOY.

And it's tidings of comfort and joy,
Comfort and joy,
And it's tidings of comfort and joy.

NICHOLAS *has reached the* BOY. *He touches him. The* BOY *does not move.* KATE *and* MADELINE *notice that* NICHOLAS *has gone.*

God bless the ruler of this house
And send him long to reign,

NICHOLAS *turns back to the house. He sees his wife and his sister appear. They look at him. Upstage of them, the party is going on.*

And many a merry Christmas
May live to see again . . .

NICHOLAS *takes a step back towards the house. But he can't leave the boy. A despairing look at* KATE *and* MADELINE.
Among our friends and kindred
Let's sing with mickle main . . .

And, as the carol builds up to its climax, with descants and the organ coming in, NICHOLAS *turns back to the* BOY *and picks him up in his arms, looking at his wife and sister.*

O, it's tidings of comfort and joy,
Comfort and Joy —

And then he turns to us, and stands there, holding the boy in his arms.

O, it's tidings of comfort and joy,
Comfort and joy,
Comfort and joy.

Darkness.

THE END

Entertaining Strangers

a new version of
Entertaining Strangers:
A Play for Dorchester

Introduction

Although built round a 'core' of professionals (director, writer, stage manager, composer, designer), Ann Jellicoe's community plays arise out of the resources, interests and needs of the community for and by which they're created. Having accepted a commission to write a play for Dorchester, virtually my first act was to locate and set up a group of local historical researchers on whose diligent and imaginative labours much of the play is based.

In addition to this vital resource, *Entertaining Strangers* involved not only a cast of 180 (ranging in age from 85 to three) but also a gargantuan army of painters, carpenters, costume- and prop-makers, musicians, accountants, caterers, babysitters, drivers, publicists, printers, box-office helpers and ushers throughout the town and beyond. In reworking the play for the more modest resources on offer at the National Theatre, I was able to develop the relationships of the central characters, and to allow myself greater leeway with their history. But I realised early on that I would need to create some kind of metaphorical surrogate for the sheer power of Dorchester's numbers (and the emotional strength of the fact that the play was performed in a church established by one of the central characters, within a stone's throw of a brewery founded by the other).

In outline, *Entertaining Strangers* is about the attempt to impose two eminently Victorian values on an English county town in the process of transformation from an essentially rural to an urban society. Both sets of beliefs are found wanting in face of the older and more basic realities which emerge to challenge them during the course of the play. These realities – and the ancient mysteries that both acknowledge and confront them – are represented in the new version by fragments from a mummers' play, which is sometimes actually happening, but more often takes the form of a snatch or echo in the mind. The mummers' play itself is a compound of many, drawn from various styles and forms of the old art. But, as has always been true, the play is acted by performers with hidden faces, with a seriousness, if not a solemnity, appropriate to its ancient significance.

Entertaining Strangers was first performed on 18 November 1985, in St Mary's Church, Dorchester, as a community play presented in association with the Colway Theatre Trust, and directed by Ann Jellicoe.

A revised version of the play was first performed in the Cottesloe auditorium of the National Theatre on 9 October 1987.

This version incorporates some changes made for a radio adaptation of the play, directed by Hilary Norrish for the BBC World Service in 1994. The National Theatre cast included three characters (Sarah Albinia Eldridge, Benjamin Voss and Sarah Holland) who do not appear in the current version.

THE ELDRIDGE HOUSEHOLD

SARAH ELDRIDGE	Judi Dench
CHARLES ELDRIDGE	Michael Byrne
SOPHIE	Charlotte Coleman
EMILY	Helen Fitzgerald
CHARLES JNR	Nicholas Simpson/ Corin Helliwell
SARAH ALBINIA	Nadia Chambers
CHRISTIAN, maid	Sally Dexter
FANNY LOCK, maid	Shirley Henderson
JOHN JAMES BESANT	Michael Bottle
JOHN TIZARD	Peter Woodward

THE MOULE HOUSEHOLD

HENRY MOULE	Tim Pigott-Smith
MARY MOULE	Janet Whiteside
GEORGE	Patrick Brennan
HORACE	Garry Cooper
CHARLES	Simon Scott
HANDLEY JNR	Steven Mackintosh
HENRY JNR	Nicholas Simpson/ Corin Helliwell

GEORGE as a child	James Hillier Brook/ Ian Harris
ELLEN WRIGHT, nurse	Frances Quinn
HANNAH, maid	Joanne Lamb

COURT AND GENTRY

CAPT WILLIAM HENNING	John Bluthal
ANN HENNING	Sally Dexter
MARY FRAMPTON	Mary McLeod
HENRY FRAMPTON	Robert Arnold
ROBERT WILLIAMS	Basil Henson
LIEUTENANT VANDALEUR	Michael Bottle

PROFESSIONAL

THOMAS PATCH	Patrick Brennan
GEORGE ANDREWS	Michael Bottle
DR CHRISTOPHER ARDEN	Basil Henson

TRADE

JAMES BROOKS	Peter Gordon
ANN BESANT	Jenny Galloway
ALFRED MASON	Robert Arnold
GEORGE LODER	Richard Bonneville
JOHN GALPIN	Peter Gordon

LABOURING/AGRICULTURAL

JOHN LOCK	Richard Bonneville
MARTHA LOCK	Jenny Galloway
LOUISA LOCK	Laura McMahon/ Annabelle Ryan
JANE WHITING	Mary McLeod
MARTHA WHITING	Nadia Chambers
FIRST COMMUNICANT	Simon Scott
SECOND COMMUNICANT	Michael Bottle
THIRD COMMUNICANT	Garry Cooper

WILLIAM BARTLETT	John Bluthal
WILLIAM FUDGE	Robert Arnold
EDWARD FUDGE	Steven Mackintosh
NATTY SEALE	Basil Henson
JANE SIBLEY	Helen Fitzgerald
LIZZIE SIBLEY	Charlotte Coleman
ALBERT SIBLEY	James Hillier Brook/ Ian Harris
FLORENCE CHAFFLEY, child	Joanne Lamb
FLORENCE CHAFFLEY	Frances Quinn
BENJAMIN VOSS	Robert Arnold
SARAH HOLLAND	Frances Quinn

OUTSIDERS

CAPT AUGUSTUS HANDLEY	Peter Woodward
SERGEANT	Richard Bonneville
MR MACARTE	John Bluthal
MR HENGLER	Peter Woodward
MR TURNLEY	Simon Scott
YOUNG WARDER	Patrick Brennan

Mummers, congregations, race-goers, cholera victims, crowds and other parts were played by members of the company.

Directed by Peter Hall
Designed by William Dudley
Lighting by Gerry Jenkinson
Music by Dominic Muldowney
Director of the Mellstock Band David Townsend

Entertaining Strangers is based on original research by Bridget Bowen, Beth Brooke, Billie Brown, Terry Hearing, Joan Kimber and Jill Pope. Alan Chedzoy was dialect consultant for both versions.

ACT ONE

Scene One

1.1.1. The Mummers' Play: The Presentation. *The characters are the* PRESENTER, FATHER CHRISTMAS, *the* DRAGON *and* ST GEORGE. *Rhythmic knocking punctuates the speeches.*

PRESENTER.
> Make room! Make room for us to sport,
> For in this place we do resort.
> We have not come to laugh or jeer,
> But for a pocketful of money and a skinful of beer.
> And if you believe not what I say:
> Enter old Father Christmas! Clear the Way!

FATHER CHRISTMAS.
> I am Old Father Christmas,
> Welcome or welcome not.
> I hope Old Father Christmas
> Will never be forgot.
> And now if you will our sport to start:
> Come on, bold Dragon, play your part!

DRAGON. Who's he that seeks the Dragon's blood,
> Who calls so angry and so loud?
> With my long teeth and scurvy jaw,
> Of such I'll break up half a score.

But before ST GEORGE *can respond to the challenge, the knocking becomes less rhythmic and more urgent, and focus shifts to:*

1.1.2. The Green Dragon Inn, Dorchester, *towards the end of 1829. The room is in near darkness.* SARAH ELDRIDGE, 32, *the proprietor, has been roused from bed. She hurries through the room to answer the door.*

SARAH. Charles! Christian! Charles! Do *no one* but I hear the door?

She opens the door. A tall young clergyman stands there. He is HENRY MOULE, 28.

Why, parson.

MOULE. Madam, I am so sorry.

SARAH. Yes, well —

MOULE. I'm afraid it's very late, but I —

SARAH. What was it you were wan-

MOULE. — but when I saw the light above —

SARAH's *servant* CHRISTIAN, *still in her teens, hurries on, assembling her person.*

CHRISTIAN. Oh, ma'am, I'm sorry —

SARAH. Christian. Please to see if Sophie's woken, and then find your master.

CHRISTIAN. Yes, ma'am. Yes, directly.

She hurries out.

MOULE. It was — it seemed to be the only light in Dorchester.

SARAH. Well, as you say, 'tis very late. Please to come in.

MOULE *nods a bow and enters.* SARAH *closes the door.*

In fact, the light is in my malthouse. At advent time, my husband likes to watch the mummers practise there. Some folks do say that 'tis next-door to witchcraft, but we don't hold with that.

Slight pause.

Now, parson, I must tell you, that we run a simple alehouse, and it's not our custom to take guests —

Another knock, more of a rhetorical character. CHARLES ELDRIDGE *announces his entrance.*

CHARLES. I am St George! from England sprung!

SARAH *is delighted to see her 38-year-old husband.*

SARAH. Why, Charles . . .

CHARLES. My name through all the world is rung!

SARAH. Um, Charles —

CHARLES. And may I ask, inquire, implore: Who's this dark stranger by the door?

SARAH. Oh, Charles. It's, um — it's —

MOULE (*handing his card to* SARAH). Sir. Ma'am. Please accept my card.

SARAH. The reverend Henry —

MOULE. Yes, indeed, as such recently appointed to the cure of Fordington, which I think to be the adjacent parish to your own. As yet the vicarage is not vacated by my predecessor's widow. And the only inns where I could raise an answer at this hour were full.

Slight pause.

SARAH. Well, 'tis market day tomorrow. You should a-been here earlier.

MOULE. I would have been, had my trap not lost a wheel. It took me some time to remount it.

SARAH *looks at* MOULE — *she doesn't expect vicars to be able to change wheels.*

And I appreciate that you do not usually offer accommodation. But as a stranger to your town, I would appreciate it if you could make an exception in this case.

CHRISTIAN *rushes in.*

CHRISTIAN. Now, ma'am — Miss Sophie's fine, she didn't wake, but I can't find Mr —

SARAH. Now don't fuss, Christian, Mr Eldridge found us by himself. Now, could you put the kettle on, and then go make up the settle in the parlour as a bed for Reverend —

She glances at the card. Pronouncing MOULE *'mool'.*

— Moule, then make him up a bottle, for 'tis grown quite brisk
and the fire's been dead an hour, while maybe Charles could
stable up the parson's animal.

CHARLES. Why, yes, at once, my sweetheart. Dearest.

He kisses SARAH.

Angel.

CHRISTIAN *grins and scurries out.* CHARLES *goes too.*
SARAH *is embarrassed.*

SARAH. You will forgive my husband, Mr Moule. He's of a —
well, a somewhat expansive cast of character. And we were
married just a threemonth since. Now, no doubt your journey's
left you tired and thirsty. Would you like a brandy? Or indeed a
glass of beer?

MOULE. No, madam, I abstain.

SARAH. Oh, yes, of course. Well, I say 'of course', but 'tis by no
means universal. Indeed, there was common talk about your
predecessor . . . So, a cup of tea?

MOULE. No, nothing, thank you, ma'am.

A slightly heavy pause.

SARAH ⎫
⎬ (*simultaneously*).
MOULE ⎭

And so —
In fact —

They gesture each other to continue. SARAH *wins.*

MOULE. In fact, ma'am, it is 'Mole'.

SARAH *looks bemused.*

'Mool' is a mussel.

SARAH. Ah.

Another slightly heavy pause.

MOULE. And so, may *I* enquire —

SARAH. Of course. I'm sorry. Mrs Sarah Eldridge, the Green Dragon Inn.

MOULE. I see. How do you do.

SARAH *nods.*

And may I ask, who is the child?

Slight pause.

SARAH. I beg your pardon?

MOULE. 'Sophie'. If you were married 'but a threemonth since'.

Slight pause.

SARAH (*quite sharply*). Well, Mr Moule, my husband was a widower, left with a small baby. I was a widow, and my first marriage was not fruitful. We met up, and it seemed a most convenient arrangement.

CHARLES *has entered with* MOULE's *bags. He sets them down.*

CHARLES. Well, Mr Moule, you'll guess that 'met up's' not the half of it.

SARAH. Ah, Charles. In fact, it's 'Mole'. 'Mool' is by all accounts a mussel.

CHARLES. You see, afore we met up, I was a domestic steward, to the family of Mr Robert Williams of Little Bredy, of whom you may have heard –

CHRISTIAN *rushes in.*

CHRISTIAN. Bed be made up, ma'am –

SARAH. Well, thank you, Christian –

CHRISTIAN (*to* MOULE). – and the kettle's on –

MOULE. Please, there's no need –

CHARLES. – and Mrs Eldridge, or Mrs Balson, as she was then, called to try and interest me in purchasing her ales and beers, thus saving us the trouble –

SARAH. Charles, I'm sure that Mr Moule –

CHARLES. – and in fact, I was actually raising up a glass of her best brew, to test it like, outside the back door, when master and his guests arrived from riding.

SARAH. *Charles.*

CHARLES. But perhaps 'tis a little late for talespinning.

SARAH. Indeed that's so.

CHARLES. So if the kettle's –

CHRISTIAN. Oh, sir, *no.* (*To* MOULE.) Oh, 'tis the story of the way they met. 'Tis *beautiful.* I never wearies of it.

Pause.

Well, leastwise, while the *kettle* –

SARAH *shrugs.*

CHARLES. So, as I say, the quality arrives, and I'm there, raising up my glass, and as they're passing, Mrs Balson nods, as if to say 'good morning', not disrespectful, like –

CHRISTIAN. – but not *obsequious* –

CHARLES. – indeed, like she don't bow nor scrape nor curtsy. And quite the most superior of all the ladies turns, and whispers –

SARAH. – in the kind of whisper you can hear in Somerset –

CHARLES. To the effect that servants nowadays appear to think that they can stand around –

CHRISTIAN (*correcting*). Can *lounge* around –

CHARLES. – like as if they owned the place. And then, quick as a flash – well she can tell you what she said herself.

He turns to SARAH, *who resists for a moment. But, then:*

SARAH. Well, all I said was, something like, 'Excuse me, madam, but I think you are in error . . . because in fact I'm not in service, I'm in commerce, I'm an independent trading person, ma'am.'

CHRISTIAN. And you should'a seen her *face.*

SARAH (*to* MOULE). She wasn't there.

CHARLES. And then she say —

CHRISTIAN. This is the lady, see —

CHARLES. 'Yes, and I assure you that it's obvious enough what it is you trade in — '

CHRISTIAN (*to* MOULE). Like, a-smelling of the beer . . .

CHARLES. To which she says:

SARAH. 'Yes, that's right, madam, beer.'

Slight pause.

CHARLES. Go *on*.

SARAH. 'A beverage of malted barley, boiled with hops, fermented with the finest yeast. The pride of Dorsetshire. Retailed as far away as London, at the most select establishments.'

CHARLES (*prompting*). Trafalgar.

SARAH. Yes, 'Chosen to sustain our sailors at the battle of Trafalgar, and throughout the French wars, at Admiral Nelson's personal command.'

CHRISTIAN. His personal, *express* command —

SARAH. 'Yes, that's right. Dorset beer. And may I ask,'

CHRISTIAN. — she asks —

SARAH. 'What *you* do for a living?'

CHARLES, SARAH *and* CHRISTIAN *are vastly amused.* MOULE *is not, which* SARAH *is the first to notice.*

And off they go, and it's really not a very funny story, and I'm sure the parson wants —

CHRISTIAN. Oh, *no*. You're leaving out the best bit, ma'am. 'Cos then he, Mr Eldridge, he do take her hands, that's Mrs Balson's as she was, and say how he never come across a body nothing like what she is and how he do have this little baby who do need a mother, that's like little Sophie, and that's not to mention like his own need of a wife, and thereby and therefore she must wed with him at once, and she, that's Mrs Balson, she do say she could never be like married to a butler, on account of the obsequiousness required, but he that's Mr Eldridge he do say he think that he could be like married to a brewhouse keeper, he do think he has the head for that, and Mrs Balson she do say that she don't plan to be a brewhouse keeper all her life for she has got ambitions like to run a proper brewery or have charge of a coaching inn or something of that character, and that's at *least*, and Mr Eldridge he do say that that's all right with him, and he's about to take things a bit further if you take my drift when he that's Mr Robert Williams hisself, he come back out and he do taste the beer and say that she, that's — her, that she's no cause to feel 'ferior to anybody by way of her business or the product she do sell and may he be the first to wish them every happiness. (*Pause.*) And so, like — so he was.

Slight pause.

CHARLES. And so he was indeed.

SARAH. Well, yes, that's right, and that be how we met, and since then we've been wed and we do live here in my father's hostelry, we haven't got ourselves a coaching inn but I still live in hope, and that's our story top to tail and I'm convinced the parson don't want nothing better than to be a-bed.

MOULE. That is the case, ma'am.

SARAH. So, Christian, that kettle —

MOULE. But I must say something first.

SARAH. Yes? What?

MOULE. It is, that I have listened to your story with the greatest interest. But I must state nonetheless that I judge your business to be no more than a commerce of corruption, a trade in sin; and that your filial inheritance is gall. Sir, I am sorry to come upon you at this hour, I am most grateful for your hospitality, I need no further service and I would appreciate it if my bill could be prepared for settlement at half past seven at the latest. Goodnight, sir, and ma'am.

MOULE *picks up his bag and goes out.*

Pause.

SARAH. Well, I'll remember that.

CHARLES. He's for St George's? For St George's *Fordington*?

He looks to SARAH *and* CHRISTIAN.

CHRISTIAN. Be better biding here.

1.1.3. The Mummers' Play: *The focus shifts to* NARRATORS *below, and, in a moment, to a* MUMMER *aloft.*

NARRATIVE. And thus it was, in 1829, that Henry Moule,

hitherto curate of the church at Gillingham,

proceeded from the Dragon to the adjacent parish of St George's, Fordington,

which, as has often been remarked, embraces Dorchester as an egg enfolds its yolk,

and what was to prove from its first days a most eventful ministry.

The NARRATORS *look up at the* MUMMER *and we look up with them.* ST GEORGE *has his flag, the red cross on a white ground.*

ST GEORGE. I am Saint George, from England sprung,
My name throughout the world has rung.
I'll clip this Dragon's wings, he shall not fly:
I'll cut this wild worm down else I do die.
What mortal man would dare to stand
Afore Saint George with sword in hand?

Scene Two

1.2.1. St George's Church, Fordington. JOHN *and* MARTHA LOCK (20 *and* 30) *wait by the font, with their baby and* JANE WHITING, *a woman of indeterminate age, status and character. We are not yet aware of it, but the church* ORCHESTRA *is*

*assembling to practise aloft: its members are not in the first flush of
youth, and indeed its best friends could not describe its playing as
anything other than awful. The clerk, JAMES BROOKS, appears,
as does HENRY MOULE.*

BROOKS. Well, morning to you, Mr Moule.

MOULE. Ah. Mr Brooks.

BROOKS. Now, be you and Mrs Moule well cribbed down in the
vicarage?

MOULE. Yes, thank you, Mr Brooks. In fact –

BROOKS. Old parson, he do say, best thing about the parish, you
can lumper from the vestry to the vicarage, smoke half a pipe,
and be back afore they'm done the Jubilate Deo. Now, what
have we this morning. Ah. Baptising little Henry Lock. Good
morning John and Martha.

JOHN LOCK. Morning, Mr Brooks.

MARTHA LOCK. Morning, parson.

MOULE. Good morning. And is this . . . a godparent?

BROOKS. Ar. This be Miss Whiting.

JANE WHITING. How'st do.

BROOKS. And we'd a-had her, like, companion as t'other, but he
be took bad, and t'will have to be I if that do fay with all the
ordinances like.

   Pause.

MOULE. Well. Let us proceed. 'Dearly beloved, forasmuch as all
men are conceived and born in sin – ', um, Mr Clerk?

BROOKS. Sir?

MOULE. There is no water.

BROOKS. Water, sir?

MOULE. No water in the font.

   BROOKS *laughs. It's infectious – the* OTHERS *join in.*

MOULE. Why is this matter so diverting?

BROOKS. Lawks, sir, last parson bisn't bothering with no water for no christening. He just spit in his old hand, and anoints the babe with that.

Pause.

MOULE. Mr Clerk. In Mark, chapter one verse nine, I think you'll find, the Baptist speaks of this sacrament, and says, 'I indeed have baptised you with water; but He shall baptize you with the Holy Ghost' . . . And in, again I stand to be corrected, John three five, the Saviour tells us that except a man be born of water and the spirit, he cannot enter into God's kingdom. I note from the evangelists two references to water, one to the Spirit, and one, synonymically, to the Holy Ghost. I see no reference to spit. The service will recommence in five minutes time, when there will be water in the font.

MOULE *is turning to go. A horrible wail from the* ORCHESTRA: *it is beginning to rehearse.*

What – is – that – noise?

BROOKS. Why, sir, 'tis the orchestra. 'Tis Wednesday, so she be practising.

MOULE. I – see.

He goes out.

JOHN LOCK. Well.

JANE WHITING. Well, then.

BROOKS. Well, I daresen wager what he'll think to she come Sunday.

1.2.2. **The Vicarage, Fordington.** *Enter* MRS MOULE, CAPT WILLIAM HENNING, *35, and* MRS ANN HENNING, *26.* MARY MOULE *is the same age as her husband. Their maid* ELLEN WRIGHT, *in her late 30s, is in attendance.*

ANN HENNING. So Mrs Moule, you really can't imagine what delights you have in store . . .

HENNING. The spring, of course, particularly . . .

MRS MOULE. Well, yes, the natural beauty of the countryside is, well, manifest . . . But I must admit it does concern us that the very *size*, the parish's extraordinary *circumference* . . . must make it hard for many to attend the church with any regularity, particularly in winter . . .

HENNING. Well, in fact, yes, there are times . . .

MRS MOULE. And, further, Captain, we confess we find it strange, to say the least, that at his time of life the previous incumbent could have made even the most modest excursions through a large part of the benefice.

HENNING. Well, certainly . . .

ANN HENNING. I think, um, William, that Mrs Moule should know . . . that Mr Palmer, well, particularly in his latter years . . .

HENNING. Though of course a man much loved . . .

MOULE *has entered.*

MOULE. Well, yes, indeed, ma'am. I am growing daily more aware of the eccentricities of the latter years of Mr Palmer.

They look at him.

MRS MOULE. Henry, it is Captain, and . . .

HENNING. Henning. I'm pleased to meet you, Mr –

MOULE. Enquiring as I have this very morning of a woman put up for a sponsor – a regular attender I was told, and indeed compared to many of her class and quarter more or less a paragon – enquiring as I did of her what were the gospels and being told that she was certain there were two: St Peter's and St Paul's.

Pause.

ANN HENNING. Well, yes, indeed, there is of course much ignorance, for which no doubt Mr Palmer bears his share of the responsibility. But, Mr Moule, I must assure you that if not his teachings then his works, his acts of kindness and of simple charity –

MOULE. Madam, I am a vicar in the Church of Christ, and thus confess we are accounted righteous before God not by our own deservings, but by the gift of faith, and that without that gift, our 'works' avail us nothing.

HENNING. Um . . .

MOULE. It is a privilege to meet you, Captain, Mrs Henning.

  MOULE *goes quickly out. Pause.*

ANN HENNING. Um, Mrs Moule . . . I understand, your husband takes an interest in fossils. And — remains.

  Pause.

MRS MOULE. Yes. Yes, he does.

ANN HENNING. Because —

HENNING. Because it is clearly fortunate that in that sense, if in no other, Mr Moule has found a suitable appointment, ma'am.

1.2.3. **St George's Church, Fordington,** *on Sunday, with a full* CONGREGATION, *which sings the last verse of 'Now thank we all our God'. They do not sing it well, but then, they are accompanied by the St George's Church Orchestra. During the verse, three very old* COMMUNICANTS *assemble at the altar rail, and* MR BROOKS *and* HENRY MOULE *converse.*

CONGREGATION.
        All praise and thanks for God
        The Father now be given
        The Son, and him who reigns
        With them in highest heaven,
        The one eternal God,
        Whom earth and heaven adore,
        For thus it was, is now,
        And shall be ever more.

  Meanwhile:

MOULE. Tell me, Mr Clerk. Is the orchestra more than usually out of tune this morning?

BROOKS. Oh, no. I'd say that she be round middling, sir.

MOULE. I see. And may I ask, is it normal for there to be so few to take the sacrament on Communion Sunday?

BROOKS. Oh, I tell you sir, that's not too bad a number, for a morning, in the winter. Why, half the time, 'twixt Christmas Day and Candlemas, we be hard put to it to worret up any soul at all.

MOULE *looks at* BROOKS *before going to address the* COMMUNICANTS. *The hymn comes to an end.* MOULE *goes to the* FIRST COMMUNICANT.

MOULE. 'The body of our Lord Jesus Christ, which was given for thee, preserve thy body and soul unto everlasting life. Take and eat this in remembrance that Christ died for thee, and feed on him in thy heart by faith with thanksgiving.'

He gives the wafer to the FIRST COMMUNICANT.

FIRST COMMUNICANT. Well, thank 'ee, parson.

MOULE *gives a slight look, but carries on, presenting the cup to the* FIRST COMMUNICANT:

MOULE. 'The blood of our Lord Jesus Christ, which was shed for thee, preserve thy body and soul unto everlasting life. Drink this in remembrance that Christ's blood was shed for thee, and be thankful.'

FIRST COMMUNICANT (*taking the wine*). Best o'health, Jesus.

MOULE (*to the* SECOND COMMUNICANT). 'The body of our — ' what did you say?

FIRST COMMUNICANT. I said, 'best o'health, Jesus', sir. Be summat wrong?

MOULE. Is something wrong?

SECOND COMMUNICANT. Ees, sir. Bissen us drinking health of Our Lord Jesus?

MOULE. Drinking *what*?

FIRST COMMUNICANT. Ar. S'right. Old parson he do say hisself. Communion be drinking Jesus' health.

THIRD COMMUNICANT. Right. Your best o'health, Jesus.

SECOND COMMUNICANT. Cheers, lord.

MOULE *almost snatches the cup back from the* SECOND COMMUNICANT *and puts it on the table. He turns to* BROOKS, *in fury:*

MOULE. Well, Mr Brooks?

BROOKS. Well, beggars can't be choosers. Would you be wanting 'Glory be on high' now, Mr Moule?

As the ORCHESTRA *begins to play,* MOULE *climbs quickly into the pulpit.*

1.2.4. St George's, Fordington. MOULE *addresses the* CONGREGATION.

MOULE (*silencing the* ORCHESTRA). Thank *you*. May the words of my mouth, and the meditations of all our hearts, be now and forever acceptable in thy sight, O Lord, our strength and our Redeemer. Now.

He surveys the CONGREGATION.

Now, before I proceed to the main body of my sermon, I have a statement to make concerned with the proceedings of this church, and some changes which are in my opinion long overdue.

First of all, from now on, the font will be employed solely for the purpose of baptism — for which purpose water will be provided — and not as a receptacle for the headgear of the male members of the congregation.

Second. From this day forth, in addition to the morning Sunday service, there will be evening prayer on Sundays and on Wednesdays, and communion will be heard monthly. Further, communicants will not be paid sixpence or indeed any sum at all for taking the sacrament, and will do so in a manner and with words appropriate to its solemnity.

He clears his throat.

And finally . . . From today, I have decided that the orchestra will be suspended, and replaced by a, a seraphine, to be purchased by myself and played by Mrs Moule. My text today is taken from One Timothy: 'Let the elders that rule well be counted worthy of double honour, especially those who labour in the word and doctrine. Let as many servants as are under the yoke count their own masters worthy of all honour, that the name of God and doctrine be not blasphemed.'

A MUMMER *is seen.*

DRAGON. I say that you speak very bold
    To such a man as I.
    I'll cut you into eyelet holes
    And make the buttons fly!

1.2.5. The Vicarage. MRS MOULE *admits a delegation from the* ORCHESTRA. *The men carry instruments in green cases. They are* WILLIAM BARTLETT, *an old man,* WILLIAM FUDGE, *in his mid-40s, and his son* EDWARD, 17.

BARTLETT. Ah, Mrs Moule.

MRS MOULE. Why, Mr –

BARTLETT. Bartlett. And Mr William Fudge. And his young Edward. And we be wondering if we might see the parson.

MRS MOULE. Yes, I'm sure.

 MOULE *appears.*

MOULE. Ah, gentlemen. Forgive me, I was in the garden. Now, what can I do for you?

BARTLETT. Mr Moule, we've been a-considering of your announcement of last morning.

MOULE. Yes?

BARTLETT. And we hope that we might strike a bargain, like.

MOULE. A bargain?

BARTLETT. Mr William Fudge.

WILLIAM FUDGE. Mr Moule. Us do know that playing is uncommon rough, particular in wind, and 'tis true tidden fitting. Fact, we been a-trying to unwriggle old Bill Swyer from his serpent now for many a year.

BARTLETT. And fluster Joseph Normal off his flute.

WILLIAM FUDGE. That's right. So sir, our offer's this. We'll stop up her wind, and just be the strings.

Pause.

MOULE. Uh, well. I'm of course delighted that you have been considering matters with – consideration. But I'm afraid that I remain of the opinion that from now on the singing should be accompanied by seraphine.

Pause.

BARTLETT. Ar. Excuse us for one moment, if you would.

MOULE. Of course.

The MEN *go into a huddle, a little apart.* MOULE *looks at* MRS MOULE. MRS MOULE *gives a slight smile.* BARTLETT *turns back to* MOULE.

BARTLETT. Now, Mr Moule. We've a-been given theasan matters some further considering, and us have resolved –

WILLIAM FUDGE. Reluctantly –

BARTLETT. Ees, with reluctancy, to make a further proposal, like.

MOULE. Yes, what is it?

BARTLETT. Mr Fudge.

WILLIAM FUDGE. Our offer is, we do break up the orchestra, but us stay up in the gallery, leading the singing, as us always has.

Pause.

MOULE. Yes. But I'm afraid, still, I do feel that the whole congregation should be – and sing – in the body of the church. Together.

BARTLETT. Hm. Forgive us for one further moment, if you would.

MOULE. Indeed.

The same: the huddle of conference, and a smile from MRS MOULE. BARTLETT *leads his* MEN *back.*

BARTLETT. Now, sir. We do have to tell you, that we be unanimously resolved, that if the concluding of this business were to be as you might say *postponed* like –

MOULE. Look, I'm sorry, but I have considered this most carefully myself. I had hoped that what I heard at first was just an aberration. But it is clear, however, that the standards I have witnessed are the standards which obtain, and I must insist that the changes I have announced are implemented.

Pause.

BARTLETT. I do see.

MOULE. I'm glad.

WILLIAM FUDGE. These be your last words, then, like.

MOULE. Yes.

BARTLETT. Well, then. So be it.

WILLIAM FUDGE. You're certain –

MOULE. I'm absolutely certain.

BARTLETT. Well, we'll be a-wishing you a good day, then.

MOULE. Good day.

The delegation leaves. WILLIAM FUDGE *has left his violin case, but neither they nor the* MOULES *notice.* MRS MOULE *smiles.*

Well, there we are.

MRS MOULE. 'With *great* reluctance . . .'

MOULE. Yes, in fact, 'reluctancy . . .'

MOULE's *amused too. Neither notice the re-entrance of* EDWARD FUDGE.

EDWARD FUDGE. My father left his fiddle.

He picks up the green case.

He didn't like to come for she hisself.

MOULE. Please, I –

EDWARD FUDGE. I think, sir, if you'll excuse me saying, you will regret what you do say here this afternoon.

Slight pause.

MOULE. Oh, I assure you, Edward –

EDWARD FUDGE. Like it might be as you'll come to see things from a different angle, in the course of time.

MOULE. Well, Edward, I must say, I find it hard –

EDWARD FUDGE. Like the angle of an old man on eight shillen for a full week in the fields. And with the threat like hanging over he, that with the threshers and the winnowers and such, he'll lose his hire and house and end up God knows where.

Slight pause.

Like what a fiddle on a Sunday means to he. Good afternoon, then, reverend.

He turns and goes.

Scene Three

1.3.1. **Dorchester High St,** *from the Vicarage of Fordington, up High St East and High St West, to the Barracks at the*

Top'o'Town. This scene represents MOULE's *walk from the Vicarage to the Barracks, during which he passes representatives of most of the social classes of the borough: by the end, they will form both a geographical and social 'map' of the town.*

NARRATIVE. And such was the abrasive manner of the Reverend Henry Moule,

that by the time that he accepted a commission to preach weekly at the Barracks

there was hardly anyone who saw him on his brisk walk through the town

who did not know him as a man of the most unaccommodating creed,

if not an actual Methodist.

MOULE *appears from the Vicarage, to meet* NATTY SEALE, *a shepherd of indeterminate age, wearing a moleskin cap, smock, and leggings.* NATTY *is accompanied by his sheep* CAROLINE.

NATTY. Good morrow to you, parson.

MOULE. Morning, Mr –

NATTY. Seale. Name's Natty Seale. Tell Natty by he's hat. Bissen none in old Ford'n as don't know I, and me old friend Caroline.

Pause.

Say I a buggalug or gallypot, they do say. But I bissen.

He waves the tail of his hat at the sheep.

Tell by he.

MOULE. Well, church is at eleven, Mr Seale. I'll doubtless see you there.

NARRATIVE. And then left on to High St East where

MOULE *passes* INNKEEPERS, *including* ANN BESANT, *50, and* CHARLES *and* SARAH ELDRIDGE.

the widow Ann Besant, proprietor of the White Hart coaching inn, is testing her best Sunday brew.

ANN BESANT. Good health to you then, parson!

NARRATIVE. A barrel rolls in from the backyard to the Phoenix taproom —

LANDLORD. Morning!

NARRATIVE. And catching sight of no less a couple than the Eldridges,

SARAH. beerhouse keepers,

CHARLES (*reminding his wife*). but with eyes on higher things,

NARRATIVE. as they made their way into All Saints' Church for early service.

Just a moment between MOULE *and* SARAH: *a nod, a bob and they pass on. Now we are half way up the High St, at the point where East gives way to West, and* MOULE *passes the* PROFESSIONAL CLASSES, *including* MR PATCH *the Music Teacher,* CAPT *and* MRS HENNING, *the middle-aged* HENRY FRAMPTON *and his aunt* MRS MARY FRAMPTON.

NARRATIVE. Towards which place of worship came not only the professional classes,

surgeons,

and solicitors,

PATCH. and music teachers and the like,

MRS FRAMPTOM. but also Mrs Mary Frampton and her nephew Henry,

NARRATIVE. with their friends the Hennings;

who following their first and only call on Mr Moule,

ANN HENNING. had determined to transfer their spiritual custom

HENNING. to more congenial surroundings.

In the 'Barracks' itself, CAPT AUGUSTUS HANDLEY, 24, *sits proudly on a* HORSE. *We do not immediately notice he is fast asleep.*

NARRATIVE. And thence to Top'o'Town, and to the Barracks,

where Mr Moule said Morning Prayer and preached a sermon;

and, his congregation having been dismissed,

he picked up the guinea from the drumhead,

and turned to go.

1.3.2. The Barracks. AUGUSTUS HANDLEY *gives out a horrible groan.*

MOULE. Um – Captain –

HANDLEY. Uh . . .

MOULE. Can I help you, Captain?

CAPT HANDLEY *slides gently off the* HORSE *onto the floor. The* HORSE *neighs.* HANDLEY *looks up.*

HANDLEY. Ah. Padre. Morning.

He tries to stand. An error.

In the name of Christ –

He looks at MOULE.

I'm sorry.

MOULE. Oh, Captain, don't apologise to me. I cannot save your soul from everlasting fire, unless you honestly repent you of your blasphemy.

HANDLEY. Beg pardon?

MOULE. I know. It must seem hard. All you did was take the Lord's name in vain, and even then, not in a particularly outrageous fashion. But, in fact, sin has nothing to do with harm, or injury to other men. It is offending against God, by flouting His great law, and thus the lightest of profanities is on a level with the worst of murders. Quite literally, sin is sin, its wages death.

MOULE *smiles pleasantly.* HANDLEY *climbs to his feet.*

HANDLEY (*a little irritated*). Well, if it's of any comfort, padre, at this moment I feel very close to death, and –

MOULE. Oh, no comfort, Captain. For even if you at this very moment spurned all sin, it would be nothing worth, unless through faith and faith alone you do accept God's grace, without which, as Isaiah preaches, 'all our righteousness is but as filthy rags'.

Pause. HANDLEY *tries to go for lightness.*

HANDLEY. Well, certainly –

MOULE *has taken a penknife from his pocket, and thrusts it at* HANDLEY.

MOULE. Captain. This is my penknife. Take it.

HANDLEY. I'm sorry?

MOULE. I offer you my penknife. Do you accept it?

HANDLEY. No, of course I don't.

HANDLEY *looks at the vicar holding out a penknife to him.*

I mean . . . What do you mean?

MOULE. I mean . . . That from birth you are a child of wrath, from birth you run astray, choosing the company of strangers. And unless you are offered, and *accept* His grace, as I offer you this penknife, then you will remain, cursed, in that company for all eternity.

Pause.

HANDLEY. I mean . . . I can't.

Pause.

I mean . . . Forgive me, padre.

Scene Four

1.4.1. Outside St George's, Fordington. MOULE *joins* MRS
MOULE, *their servant* ELLEN WRIGHT, *and their two small
boys*, HENRY JNR, *nine, and* GEORGE, *six. Round the church
gate wait a number of* ROUGHS, *including* LIZZIE *and* JANE
SIBLEY (15 *and* 20). *Aside, watching, are* FLORENCE
CHAFFLEY, 11, JANE WHITING, NATTY SEALE *and*
MARTHA LOCK.

NARRATIVE. And so Henry Moule returned to East Fordington,
to collect his wife and family for Morning Prayer:

and to find himself confronted by another delegation.

MOULE *leading his* FAMILY *into church, through a gauntlet of
the* YOUNG ROUGHS.

YOUNG ROUGHS (*variously*).
Eh. Here they comes.
Who?
Parson. Parson's missus.
Ooh. Look at t'black face on'n.
Eh. And parson's lambs.
Baa baa.
Baa baa!

SOMEONE *grabs at* GEORGE's *cap*.

YOUNG ROUGH. Eh look 'is pretty cap.

LIZZIE SIBLEY *grabs at* HENRY JNR's *cap*.

LIZZIE SIBLEY. And this un's too.

They play catch.

JANE SIBLEY. Eh, here to I!

JANE WHITING. Here's to your best health parson!

YOUNG ROUGHS. Baa baa! Baa baa! Parson's lambs! Baa baa!

The MOULES *are through. Bravely, though from a distance,*
ELLEN WRIGHT *turns back and shouts:*

ELLEN WRIGHT. You be the devil's sheep you be!

Catcalls and laughter, as the ROUGHS *sing:*

YOUNG ROUGHS. Hokey, pokey, winkey, wum,
                       How d'ye like your teaties done?
                       All to pieces, that's the fun —
                       Can ye now just gie I one?

NARRATIVE. And even after Church, the protests were not over,

as the citizens of Fordington continued to display their dim opinion of the Reverend Moule:

from the landowners and gentry who declined to call,

to those who made their views known more directly.

1.4.2. **The Vicarage.** *Night.* MRS MOULE *appears to* MOULE, *her arms full of dead flowers and vegetables, ripped up by the roots.*

MOULE. Mary, what is it?

MRS MOULE. What do you think? They're flowers, from the garden. And the vegetables. Ripped up and scattered.

Pause.

And they pulled the railings up. And they broke into your shed, and smashed your specimens.

Pause.

MOULE. So, did you see them?

MRS MOULE. No. But I heard them. Heard them, clear as clear. 'Oh hokey pokey, winky wum. How do you want your taters done?'

MOULE *embraces* MRS MOULE.

MOULE. Oh, Mary, this will end.

MRS MOULE. I know. I know.

A cough. MARTHA LOCK *appears.*

MOULE. Who's there?

MARTHA LOCK. Uh — parson —

MOULE. I'm sorry? Mrs Lock?

MARTHA LOCK. Uh, parson. I just wanted – I did want to say
. . . As how it's not everyone as holds with they around the
church a-Sunday.

Slight pause.

And they do say it's being's they be so poor. But with that I can't
concur. For there's always summat left for spending in the public
house, or for betting at the races. And I may not be that regular
a churchgoer. But I do know sin is sin, its wages death. And
whatever be their circumstances, they will die and suffer
everlastingly. As it is written, Mr Moule.

MARTHA LOCK *hurries out.* MOULE *embraces his wife.*

MOULE. For everyone that asks receives. For everyone who seeks
shall find.

Scene Five

1.5.1. **The Green Dragon Parlour.** *It is 1833.* SARAH, *who is
carrying a baby, enters with a manuscript, followed by* CHARLES.
CHRISTIAN *their servant is filling jugs and mugs of beer, to take
them through to the public bar.* SARAH's *manuscript is the draft
of an advertisement.*

SARAH. Right. First of all: CHARLES ELDRIDGE. Big. In
capitals.

CHARLES. I see.

CHRISTIAN *is watching, open-mouthed, as* SARAH *reads the
advertisement: so much so that she allows a jug to overflow.*

SARAH. CHARLES ELDRIDGE has the honour to announce to
the nobility, the gentry, and all readers of the *Dorset County
Chronicle* oh do be *careful* Christian –

CHRISTIAN. Ooh. Ooh, sorry, ma'am.

She carries the tray off. A look shared between SARAH *and*
CHARLES. CHRISTIAN *will return for another load a little
later.*

SARAH. – that he is upon the 7th of November 1833 to enter upon proprietorship of the Antelope Hotel in Cornhill, Dorchester, and hopes that by sparing neither pains nor expense – that should be '*trusts* that' . . . by sparing neither la-di-da to render it one of the first houses in the West of England.

CHARLES (*as if that's it*). Very good. When does it –

SARAH. Mercy, I've not begun.

CHARLES. You've not?

SARAH. By no means. Carry on.

She hands the manuscript to him and he carries on reading.

CHARLES. As a FAMILY HOTEL,

SARAH. – in capitals,

CHARLES. – the Antelope possesses very superior accommodation . . .

This is not a universally accepted truth. CHARLES *looks dubiously at* SARAH.

Well –

SARAH. Read on.

CHARLES (*with increasing incredulity*). . . . having been utterly re-embellished and repaired and now possessing every requisite for comfort and convenience?

SARAH (*sweetly*). Five weeks.

CHARLES. The most complete accommodation is afforded to travellers by COACH from Bath and London and to Exeter and Weymouth . . . The STABLING is of a first-rate character, with experienced ostlers and the best of corn and hay –

SARAH reads over his shoulder as CHRISTIAN *carries a tray of mugs across – a nerve-racking spectacle.*

SARAH. The DINING ROOMS will be supplied with the finest production of the respective seasons.

CHARLES. While the TABLES will be served by active and steady waiting staff.

They look at CHRISTIAN, *then each other.*

SARAH. Well, yes, we may well have to let her go. So that's it. Well, thus far.

CHARLES. Thus far?

SARAH. Like, that's the first.

CHARLES. First? Of how many?

SARAH. Five. One a week. For five weeks. So that nobody in Dorchester won't know that Charles Eldridge, formerly steward to Mr Robert Williams of Little Bredy, do be appointed by that same Mr Robert Williams to manage his famed Coaching Inn the Antelope, of Cornhill, Dorchester.

The Antelope, the setting of no less lustrous an occasion than the Annual Race Meeting Steward's Ordinary Dinner.

That's Mr Williams, of 'May I be the first to wish you every happiness'.

SARAH's *eyes are blazing.* CHARLES *is caught up with her enthusiasm, and takes her in his arms.*

Oh, mercy, Charles. We've not begun.

1.5.2. Mrs Mary Frampton's house. MRS FRAMPTON *is in conversation with* HENRY MOULE.

MOULE. Madam, I speak what must be plain to you. These 'races' are a sport, or rather an amusement, which bring good to no one, but misery to many; which are a great promoter of both drunkenness and fornication, and whose very essence is gambling. How can it not be manifest, to a Christian woman –

MRS FRAMPTON. Mr Moule.

Pause.

Mr Moule. You have closed down your church orchestra, you have distressed one portion of your congregation, and you are an object of the rankest ridicule to the other, and now you wish me, in public association with your name, to withdraw my patronage from one of Dorchester's most popular festivities.

MOULE. Mrs Frampton, I must assure you, with the greatest possible sincerity, that popular or no —

MRS FRAMPTON. An event of which, this year, my son is steward.

MOULE. Yes, ma'am, I am aware of Captain Frampton's association with this year's event. Indeed, that is precisely why I have approached you.

MRS FRAMPTON. Yes. I see.

Pause.

Well, Mr Moule, I must assure you I am in no doubt of your sincerity. But I can go no further than to say that I will observe this year's race meeting with the utmost diligence. There's really nothing more to say.

Pause. MOULE gives a slight bow.

MOULE. Well, I — I thank you, ma'am.

He turns to go.

MRS FRAMPTON. Mr Moule, may I ask if you're aware of the extent of your unpopularity, even among the gentler classes?

MOULE. I am aware, ma'am. I cannot wholly understand it.

MRS FRAMPTON. Well —

MOULE. I have always striven to uphold legitimate authority. Indeed I believe that to be one of the sources of hostility towards me and my family.

MRS FRAMPTON. Well, yes, of course. But, nonetheless, your doctrine is a harsh and unforgiving one. It does not speak to men and women as they are. And they'll not thank you for assuring them that as they are, they're damned.

MOULE. Well, ma'am, I do not wish for thanks.

MRS FRAMPTON. Well, Mr Moule, I'm glad of that, for otherwise I fear you will be often disappointed.

Scene Six

1.6.1. Maiden Castle: Dorchester Races. *The races are held on the ancient earthwork just outside the town. It is September 1835.*

NARRATIVE. September 1835!

Maiden Castle!

Dorchester Races!

To the Music of the Regimental Band of the Seventh Lancers!

And suddenly, the RACES *are everywhere, and almost every character we have met – with the exception of the* MOULE *family – could be here. Certainly,* SPECTATORS *include* MRS FRAMPTON, HENRY FRAMPTON *and the* HENNINGS; CAPT AUGUSTUS HANDLEY; ANN BESANT, *who runs a beertent;* CHARLES ELDRIDGE, *who patronises it; and, from Fordington, at least* JANE *and* LIZZIE SIBLEY. *There is also much else happening, at many stalls, and some or all of the following could be going on, in addition to the* MUSICIANS, *from the* REGIMENTAL BAND *to* HURDYGURDYMEN *and* GYPSIES *playing on fiddles and spoons.*

FIRST BOOKIE. Come on then sonnies, come on then, what d'you know, here's evens on this good thing, I'm giving evens on Miss Careful and a bottle on Anticipation, sonnies, over here . . .

SECOND BOOKIE. Right I'm not giving evens I'm giving two to one the Jolly, Miss Careful the Jolly and I'm taking on six to four the Sultan, eleven to one outside Bacchanal . . .

ANN BESANT. Best beer here! Best Besant beer for three farthen! That's three farthen for a pint, and a ha'pence for a refill! Rum, whisky and the finest wines! As retailed at the famous White Hart Inn. Retailed right here exclusive!

MUMMIFIER. Form a line here, for the Egyptian mummy! After three thousand years clasped in the clammy grasp of death, to be revived and recalled to life for the very first time before your very eyes! Separate showings at three o'clock precisely, half past three, and each half hour thereafter! The price reduced by a full quarter so to place this novel treat within the reach of all!

PIGMAN. Line up here, gentlemen and ladies, for the greatest curiosity of this or any age, Toby, the world-famed Sapient Pig. Who will in front of you and with no aid of any kind read, spell, play cards, and cast accounts; tell any person what o'clock it is, and to the minute, and the age of any one in company!

TEST STRENGTH. So, gennlemen. So lads. Who'll test his strength against the notorious Tattooed Man of Tomboctoutu! A pound of baccy to the man holds out the longest, and a yellow capon to the boy! Roll up here, for the famous man of Tomboctoutu and his famous tattooed arm.

TATTOOED MAN. Not just me arm, mum, neither.

WAXWORKS. Ladies and gents! At vast expense, for your enlightenment, we present Signora Capelli's famed Waxwork Exhibition – containing as it does two Grecian Venuses – both utterly dissectable in all their parts – and a parade of British monarchs from the Conqueror unto the present day!

SECOND BOOKIE. . . . did I say six to four I now say two to one on Sultan, that's a bottle on the Sultan, evens for the Jolly, a shillen on the Sultan gets you two, and sixpence on the Bacchanal you're swimming . . .

FIRST BOOKIE. . . . what d'you know he's down on Sultan, I'm still showing you a bottle on Anticipation, a shillen'll get you two, come on then sonnies, show your silver evens on the jolly, get this good thing here . . .

NARRATIVE. And to the main event!

The high spot of the afternoon!

The Dorset Yeoman Stakes!

Ten sovereign each, with 25 added from the fund!

A handsome silver cup donated by the Steward!

And they're OFF!

And the ENTIRE ASSEMBLY *watches the race run around them, shrieking for their* HORSES, *until the race is won, betting slips fly in the air, the ASSEMBLY disperses, and only a carpet of paper is left.*

1.6.2. A Corner of the Racecourse. *On the nearly deserted earthwork, the 12-year-old FLORENCE CHAFFLEY is selling bits and pieces from a tray. A little apart, MRS FRAMPTON meets MOULE.*

MRS FRAMPTON. Well, Mr Moule. I have fulfilled my promise. But I must tell you honestly that I have seen nothing that can be readily complained of.

CHARLES ELDRIDGE, *who has had a vinous afternoon, approaches little FLORENCE.*

CHARLES. So, missie. What's this here?

FLORENCE. It's firewood, sir. And posies. Lemon balm.

CHARLES. Let's see your posies.

FLORENCE (*showing CHARLES*). They're a farden, sir.

CHARLES. Then I'll take three. And here's a penny for you.

FLORENCE. Thank 'ee, sir.

As he goes, CHARLES overhears MRS FRAMPTON and looks quizzically towards MOULE.

MRS FRAMPTON. And I therefore must inform you, in all conscience, and here upon this ancient site, I really cannot undertake to bring about the downfall of this harmless and traditional festivity.

CHARLES *steps forward.*

CHARLES. Well, if it baint our tall dark stranger.

MOULE. I beg your pardon?

CHARLES. Charles Eldridge, and your servant, sir. When we last meet, a brewhouse keeper. Now proprietor of the Antelope

Hotel. You might do me the honour, sir, of recalling the night as you sought shelter in our – under our, our roof.

MOULE. Why, yes.

Slight pause.

MRS FRAMPTON. Mr Eldridge. Does not the steward's dinner start at five o'clock.

CHARLES. Of course. My great respects, um, Mr Mole. Your humble servant, Mrs Frampton. Ma'am.

CHARLES *bows and leaves.*

MRS FRAMPTON. Nor, Mr Moule, can I withdraw my patronage from this event because one publican has drunk a glass too many.

Pause.

MOULE. You must do as your conscience guides you, Mrs Frampton.

He turns and goes. MRS FRAMPTON *turns to go in the opposite direction. Two* DRAGOONS *appear. One is* CAPT AUGUSTUS HANDLEY. *The other is a* SERGEANT. HANDLEY *is very much worse for wear. He stops.*

HANDLEY. Um – Sergeant.

SERGEANT. Sir.

HANDLEY. I am – I am waited for in Dorchester. For dinner.

SERGEANT. Is that so, sir.

HANDLEY. Yes.

The SERGEANT *looks quizzically at* HANDLEY, *who has shut his eyes.*

SERGEANT (*to himself*). Well, then. Bon appétit.

He walks on, leaving HANDLEY. *He comes to* FLORENCE. MRS FRAMPTON *still watches.*

FLORENCE. Uh – firewood, Captain? Mushrooms? Lemon balm?

SERGEANT. Well, maidy. And is that kindling that you're selling there?

FLORENCE. That's right, sir. It's three fardens, sir.

SERGEANT. And is kindling all you got on sale today?

FLORENCE. Sorry?

SERGEANT. 'Cos there's sixpence in it for you if it ain't.

Pause.

So what's your name?

FLORENCE. Be Florence. Florence Chaffley, sir. There's a place back of the waxworks we can go.

FLORENCE *goes off quickly with the* SERGEANT. MRS FRAMPTON, *horrified, hurries to* HANDLEY.

MRS FRAMPTON. Captain!

HANDLEY. Um – yes?

MRS FRAMPTON. Your sergeant, captain. And a girl. They went that way. And you must *stop them.* Instantly.

HANDLEY. Uh – when you say, a girl –

MRS FRAMPTON. She can be no more than twelve, sir!

HANDLEY *grasps the situation and hurries in the direction* MRS FRAMPTON *indicated. But he can see nothing. He turns back towards* MRS FRAMPTON.

HANDLEY. Um – Uh, I'm so sorry, I . . .

MRS FRAMPTON. Captain, you should be ashamed.

Scene Seven

1.7.1. The Antelope: Servery and Dining-Room. *A sudden burst of male noise from the dining-room establishes the Stewards'*

Ordinary Dinner, at which the diners include HENRY
FRAMPTON, CAPT HENNING, MR PATCH, *the elderly*
ROBERT WILLIAMS, *the young* LIEUT VANDALEUR, *and, by
the time we move into the dining-room,* CAPT HANDLEY. *At the
moment, we are in the servery, where* CHRISTIAN *is drawing
corks from claret bottles. Other* SERVANTS *bring through trays of
dirty plates from the dining-room, where the meal is just about
completed.* SARAH *enters the servery from the dining-room.*

SARAH. Now, Christian. Are the decanters in the market room?

CHRISTIAN. Yes, Mrs Eldridge.

SARAH. And the claret corks be drawn?

CHRISTIAN. Yes, ma'am.

SARAH. And do you see your master?

CHRISTIAN. Mr Eldridge? No, ma'am.

She picks up a tray of claret bottles.

Sorry.

SARAH (*briskly, taking the tray*). Well. No doubt before the
evening is quite over –

CHARLES *enters.* CHRISTIAN *sees him.*

CHRISTIAN. Uh – uh, ma'am –

SARAH *turns to see her husband.*

SARAH. Why, Charles.

Slight pause. CHRISTIAN *scuttles out.*

Charles, it be near to half past seven.

CHARLES. Ah. Is dinner served?

SARAH. And eaten. Charles, are you –

CHARLES. I'm sorry.

He takes the posies from behind his back and presents them to
SARAH.

Was I missed?

SARAH. Well, if I be absolutely honest with you, Charles, I'd have
to say that things have got on cheerfully enough without you. If
the truth be told.

A moment before ROBERT WILLIAMS *enters from the dining-
room.*

ROBERT WILLIAMS. Well, good evening, Charles.

CHARLES *takes the tray from* SARAH, *and proceeds past*
ROBERT WILLIAMS *to the dining-room.*

CHARLES. Good evening to you, Mr Williams.

SARAH (*half-whispered*). Charles . . .

But now ROBERT WILLIAMS *has reached her.*

ROBERT WILLIAMS. Mrs Eldridge. You must know, that your
table has surpassed all expectation.

SARAH. Well, Mr Williams, naturally, 'tis not for me to judge.

ROBERT WILLIAMS. Well, no. But nonetheless, we *are* judged, as
you know, throughout the town if not the county, as a most
extraordinary success.

SARAH. Well, certainly, if we've achieved . . .

ROBERT WILLIAMS. From every quarter, I receive most glowing
compliments. I nod, I smile. I bask, in your reflected glory.

CHRISTIAN *re-enters from the market room.*

SARAH. . . . then it must be down to you. Your generosity, and
faith in us.

ROBERT WILLIAMS. Indeed. My confidence that what is past is
past. A confidence most amply justified.

SARAH *is unsure of what* WILLIAMS *is implying. In the dining-room, there is a chant of 'cloth, cloth'.*

SARAH. Well, certainly —

ROBERT WILLIAMS. But hark. The cloth is called for. You'll forgive me, Mrs Eldridge.

He smiles and goes back into the dining-room. SARAH *looks perplexed.*

CHRISTIAN. So who's that, ma'am?

SARAH. That, Christian, be Mr Robert Williams. The owner of this here hotel.

CHRISTIAN. What, Mr Robert Williams of *Little Bredy*?

SARAH (*beginning to move*). Yes. That's it.

She goes into the dining-room as HENRY FRAMPTON *finally demands the cloth.*

FRAMPTON. Gentlemen. Gentlemen. The cloth.

There are cheers, and then an accelerating chant, as CHARLES *prepares to, and then does, whisk the cloth off the table, with an alarming flourish.*

THE GENTLEMEN. Cloth, cloth, cloth, cloth, cloth!

Applause. FRAMPTON *strikes his gavel for silence. He proposes the first toast.*

FRAMPTON. Gentlemen. His Majesty.

ALL. His Majesty.

HENNING. The continued glory of his Forces here and overseas.

ALL. Continued glory. Forces.

VANDALEUR. *Particularly* the Seventh Lancers.

ALL. *Particu*lancers.

PATCH. The prosperity of Dorchester, its professional, commercial and agricultural endeavours!

ALL. Prosperry Dorch and agrideavours!

FRAMPTON. And naturally — the races!

ALL. The races!

FRAMPTON. Now, Mr Patch?

ALL. Yes, Patch! Song! Mr Patch!

PATCH *stands with studied diffidence.*

PATCH. Um — Spotted Cow? Sheepcrook and Black Dog?

SOME (*variously*). Spotted Cow!
No, the Hawk! Grey Hawk!

The Grey Hawk has it. MR PATCH *clears his throat and begins. During the song* CHARLES *and* SERVANTS *pour wine for the* GENTLEMEN.

PATCH. Once I had a grey hawk,
      And a pretty grey hawk,
      A sweet little bird of my own,
      But she took a flight,
      She flew away quite,
      And nobody knows where she's gone,
        my brave boys,
      There's nobody knows where she's gone.

Once the song is established, WILLIAMS *whispers to* FRAMPTON, *who smiles and goes with him to* SARAH ELDRIDGE.

ROBERT WILLIAMS. Now, Mrs Eldridge. Let me introduce you to the Steward.

SARAH. Captain Frampton. It's the greatest honour.

FRAMPTON. Well, Mrs Eldridge, I must own, that after this — extraordinary display, the 'honour' is all mine —

ROBERT WILLIAMS *is returning to his seat, as there is a banging at the table, and the song begins to grind to a halt.*

Not that, I fear, that everyone is in a fit condition to appreciate —

Both he and the song are brought to a halt by the insistent banging of a mug on the table. To everyone's considerable surprise — if not horror — it appears that CHARLES ELDRIDGE has abandoned his hosterly duties, and has resolved to address the assembly.

What's this?

CHARLES. Gentlemen, gentlemen.

Silence.

Gennlemen.

VANDALEUR. Who's this?

HENNING. It's Eldridge. Landlord.

VANDALEUR. Should he, um —

CHARLES. Far be it from your humble host to interrupt an occasion of such — manifest convil — conviviality . . .

SARAH. Oh no.

CHARLES. But I view it as imperative, that everyone is made aware of the danger in which we are all — situated.

PEOPLE *look round, nervously.*

For even within half a mile, at the Parish Church of Fordington, St George, I say there lurks, a viper — snake in the grass — who has set himself the task and purpose to destroy, to cancel, to emil — eliminate, these races. These, our races.

Pause.

And this Ordinary.

Pause.

And with this fell purpose. And with this in mind. Has canvassed.

He's swaying. ROBERT WILLIAMS *stands.*

ROBERT WILLIAMS. Charles. For God's sake, sit down.

CHARLES. Or is that — canvassed?

He looks around. He realises where he is. He picks up the wine bottle and jug with which he's been serving the COMPANY, and tries to carry on where he left off. He slumps, virtually on VANDALEUR. It's obvious he's gone.

VANDALEUR. Give us a hand here, Captain.

HANDLEY. Yes, of course.

HANDLEY comes and helps. They get CHARLES up and out.

VANDALEUR. Now, all right, Mr Eldridge. Steady as she goes.

They've gone. SARAH, superhumanly:

SARAH. Now, gentlemen. May I suggest, there are spirits laid out in the market room . . .

The COMPANY disperses to the other room.

HENNING. Quite unbelievable.

PATCH. Well, certainly – most singular.

HENNING. Indeed.

FRAMPTON and ROBERT WILLIAMS remain.

FRAMPTON. Mrs Eldridge, I – I had been going to say . . . that I was sure that this would be the first of, first of many . . .

SARAH. Well, I'm not sure that's appropriate, now is it, Captain.

FRAMPTON. No. No, no.

He turns and goes. ROBERT WILLIAMS comes to SARAH.

ROBERT WILLIAMS. I'm very sorry.

SARAH. Yes. We will of course move out the instant you have found a replacement.

ROBERT WILLIAMS. Well, naturally, it would be in the interests of all parties . . .

SARAH. And then, I suppose, 'tis back to the old Dragon.

She tries a little smile.

ROBERT WILLIAMS. He did — when he left my service, Mrs Eldridge — he did *swear* to me —

SARAH. What, that 'the past' was past? Well, yes.

Half to herself, with bitterness:

'Well, Mrs Balson. I do think I have the head for that.' Well yes, indeed.

HANDLEY *has re-entered.*

HANDLEY. He'll be all right, now. He's asleep.

SARAH. Why, thank you, Captain.

ROBERT WILLIAMS *slips quietly out.*

HANDLEY. It does, if you'll forgive me saying, it does seem — a shame. It does just seem, to me, a terrible, great shame.

SARAH. Oh, 'tis just — what you might call a hazard of the occupation, Captain. Yes, that's all.

Slight pause. SARAH smiles weakly at HANDLEY. A moment between them. Then, HANDLEY makes to go into the market room, then changes his mind and goes out another way. SARAH sits, disconsolate. Enter CHRISTIAN.

CHRISTIAN. Oh, I'm sorry, ma'am.

SARAH *turns to CHRISTIAN.*

SARAH. Well, it's happened. And I suppose we do have to make the best of it.

CHRISTIAN. But, ma'am. With your contrivances and plans. Like, for the brewery, and all. It must be — well, a mortal let-down for you, ma'am.

SARAH. Oh, yes. 'Tis so.

Pause.

Oh, Christian. You know, they're going to build the railway line, to London. And to Bristol. And I think, you see, I think that in no time the world, the whole world will be moving like a rocket, at the most – tremendous speed. And it would – it just would a-been, so thrilling, to a-been a part of that. But still.

Pause. She makes to go.

CHRISTIAN. Ma'am, do you know what *I* do read, like in the paper?

SARAH. No?

CHRISTIAN. The comet, ma'am. The Halley comet. Like, I do reckon she do spin a sight faster even than the railway locomotive, wou'n you say?

SARAH takes CHRISTIAN by the shoulders. As she speaks, CHARLES comes back in, unnoticed.

SARAH. Let me tell you, Christian. We live, today, in the most thrilling times there's ever been. Because – we be that comet's children, Christian, you do hardly dare to snatch a peek at us, we fly so fast and beam so bright and dazzling in the sky.

And the only thing can stop us, Christian, is the weakness of our own imagination. Truthfully. Elsewise, there be no limit, to how far we can go.

She lets CHRISTIAN go. CHARLES stands there watching.

CHARLES. Well, you just wait. I'm right. You'll see.

SARAH looks at CHARLES.

About the vicar, trying to stop the races. You just wait.

SARAH says nothing.

CHARLES. That comet. Sounds a sight too bright for me.

A moment. Then he goes.

SARAH (*to herself*). Oh, yes. As far as far.

SONG (*from off*). And there's nobody knows where she's gone,
        my brave boys,
                No, there's nobody knows where she's gone.

1.7.2. The Vicarage. *First of all, a light on* MRS MARY FRAMPTON, *speaking the text of a letter she has written to* MOULE. *Then fade up light on the Vicarage, where* MOULE *is watching* MRS MOULE *reading the letter.*

MRS FRAMPTON. 'Well, Mr Moule. It seems that you were right and I was wrong. After our brief meeting, I was witness to a spectacle which underlined in fullest measure your worst fears, and I have to tell you that I shall indeed withdraw my patronage from next year's meeting, and will encourage all my friends to do the same. Remaining, then, your most sincere supporter in this matter . . .'

MRS MOULE. 'Mary Frampton.'

MRS MOULE *folds the letter.* MRS FRAMPTON *disappears.*

MRS MOULE (*to* MOULE). What did she see?

MOULE. I've no idea.

A knock at the door.

What is the time?

MRS MOULE (*moving to the door*). It's very late.

MOULE. Is Ellen . . .

Enter ELLEN WRIGHT.

ELLEN WRIGHT. Ma'am, 'tis a – military cast of gentleman.

MRS MOULE (*with a glance at* MOULE). Well, show him in.

ELLEN *admits* AUGUSTUS HANDLEY.

HANDLEY. Mr Moule, I doubt if you remember. My name's Augustus Handley.

MOULE. Why, yes, of course. Do, please . . .

HANDLEY. And I would like – I would consider it the greatest privilege . . . if you still possessed a penknife, Mr Moule . . .

Scene Eight

1.8.1. Dragon Inn and Brewery; Fordington Vicarage. *An antiphonal, narrative scene between the* ELDRIDGES *and the* MOULES.

NARRATIVE. And in the years that followed Sarah Eldridge set about to build what she resolved would be the biggest brewery in Dorsetshire . . .

SARAH *has entered with papers to* CHARLES.

SARAH. Now, Charles, first of all, I want to buy a mash-tun of decent size. Indeed, 'tis more important than a second copper, because I can use the one for water and for wort. Now, there be a coopering concern in Poole . . .

She sees his face.

I'm sorry. First of all, I suggest *we* buy a mash-tun of decent size . . .

NARRATIVE. And having built new premises behind the Dragon malthouse, was quickly in production of 30 barrels of best beer a day.

SARAH *is in conversation with* ANN BESANT.

SARAH. Now, my dear Mrs Besant, the thing is, not that your brew is not delicious, which 'tis . . . I do never countenance the view it's always dark and cloudy, that's certainly not *my* experience . . .

ANN BESANT. Well, I should think not, Mrs Eldridge.

SARAH. But rather that however light and clear and sharp it may be, on occasions, that I can readily provide you, without a moment's worry, with a guaranteed and regular supply of beers and ales at what I'm sure you will agree to be the most attractive prices.

ANN BESANT. Well, Mrs Eldridge, I would need convincing of –

SARAH. – thus leaving you the time both to maintain and who knows to improve your service to the coaching and soon enough no doubt the railway trade. The service for which your establishment is nationally renowned.

NARRATIVE. While in Fordington, the Reverend Moule addressed the pressing need for the construction of a church or mission in the western reaches of his parish.

MOULE *with* MRS MOULE.

MOULE. Friends, I must report that I have once again approached the Council of the Duchy of Cornwall, who are as you know the major landowner, but I have to say that they have as before informed us they can offer no assistance in these straitened times.

NARRATIVE. Until, in 1846, two events occurred:

First, and despite the parsimony of the Duchy, the consecration of Christ's Church, West Fordington, under the charge of the recently ordained Augustus Handley . . .

And second, the death of one Charles Eldridge, suddenly, of apoplexy, at the age of 55.

And now the two FAMILIES *have formed themselves into formal groups, like ceremonial photographs. On one side, in Fordington, are* MOULE, MRS MOULE *and* REV AUGUSTUS HANDLEY; *their teenage sons* GEORGE, HORACE *and* CHARLES; *and on the other, in Dorchester, the widowed* SARAH ELDRIDGE *and her children* SOPHIE, EMILY *and* CHARLES JNR. *At the time of their father's death, they were 20, 15 and 13 respectively, but for most of the subsequent action they are between four and eight years older. The two groups join in Psalm 90:*

PSALM. Lord, thou hast been our refuge: from one generation to another. Before the mountains were brought forth, or ever the earth and the world were made: thou art God from everlasting, and world without end. Thou turnest man to destruction: again thou sayest, come again, ye children of men.

During which:

NARRATIVE. And Henry Moule, now in his 46th year,

faced the continuing burdens of his ministry in the knowledge
that those burdens were now shared . . .

While Sarah Eldridge, approaching 49,

confronted for the second time a life of widowhood,

and the knowledge that responsibility to keep her family

now rested in her hands alone.

The scene disperses, as:

While Dorchester itself prepared to welcome the arrival

marked by the most extensive public decoration,

and accompanied by regimental music and a seven-gun salute,

of a most distinguished Royal Personage,

borne for the first time in the county on the wings of
locomotion, by the awesome and majestic power of steam . . .

*And through the rising steam we see the first railway locomotive,
bedecked with flags and accompanied by wild cheers from all
sides, arrive in Dorchester.*

Scene Nine

1.9.1. **The Dragon Brewery.** *It is 1850: the brewery is decked out
for a celebration.* CHARLES JNR *stands in the middle, looking
proudly around him.* CHRISTIAN *also stands there, beaming.*

CHRISTIAN. Well, Master Charles. Who would have thought it,
eh? So fast. So *far.*

CHARLES *smiles at* CHRISTIAN. *Enter* EMILY.

EMILY. Now, Christian. Surely, you have twenty things to do.

CHRISTIAN. Yes. Yes, I'm sorry, Miss Emily.

She goes out, but doesn't miss a grin from CHARLES. EMILY
looks at her brother.

EMILY. If we're to be even half-way ready, Charles.

CHARLES *looks suitably abashed and goes out one way,*
EMILY *another, as* SARAH *and* SOPHIE *appear, putting up
bunting.*

SARAH. John James? Ann's nephew? What? John James *Besant*?

SOPHIE. Mama, there's no need to affect such huge surprise. We
have been walking out for quite a time.

SARAH. And you do insist that your engagement is announced
tonight?

SOPHIE. Well, I never say '*insist*' –

SARAH. 'Neighbours and friends. I have brought you here to
celebrate a great new venture at the Dragon Brewery, the
harnessing of the great power of steam to the ancient art of beer-
making, oh and by the by my step-daughter Sophia's lost her
mind.'

SOPHIE. Oh, really now, mama!

CHRISTIAN *enters with a tray of pastries.*

SARAH. Ah, Christian.

CHRISTIAN. Ma'am?

SARAH. I don't see no bumpers. Could you bring some up?

CHRISTIAN. Yes, ma'am.

SARAH. Oh, and send Fanny to me, please.

CHRISTIAN. Yes, directly, ma'am.

SARAH. And – are those the pastries?

CHRISTIAN. Yes, ma'am.

SARAH *takes a pastry and eats it.*

Miss Emily was of the 'pinion I should lay 'em out in the
counting-room.

SARAH. Miss Emily was right.

CHRISTIAN *hurries on.*

Well, I suppose that if you are to marry this — this person, then tonight's as fine a time as any for me to seek the sympathy and comfort of my friends.

SOPHIE. Mama. What is amiss with John James? I mean, truly?

SARAH. Oh, nothing, nothing. Splendid fellow. The only brewer west of Salisbury who spends his leisure hours translating Ovid.

SOPHIE. Tacitus. Mama —

SARAH. Whereas, you know, your sister Emily —

SOPHIE. My sister Emily.

SARAH. — has been speaking most appreciatively of that young attorney whom we met in Melcombe Regis. Tizard, an old business family.

SOPHIE. Coal merchant.

SARAH. And the boy not 25, and already set upon a legal and political career.

FANNY LOCK *is the* ELDRIDGES' *second maid. She's in her mid-teens. She hurries in.*

Ah, Fanny.

FANNY. Yes, mm.

SARAH (*inspecting*). Now, do you have a clean bib for when the guests arrive?

FANNY. Of course, mm.

SARAH. Good girl. Now, do you please find Master Charles, and tell him that I want him to start up the engine now. Just to see that everything's in order. Right?

FANNY. Yes, mm.

FANNY *goes out.*

SARAH. While you on the other hand wish to attach yourself to this, to a sterling-silver gawk who's more or less in's dotage —

SOPHIE. Thirty-two!

SARAH. – who appears to enjoy a much more intimate
acquaintance with Thucydides and Cicero than with his relatives,
his business or indeed the contemporary world.

Enter CHRISTIAN *with the glasses.*

Ah, Christian. Tell Mr Mason Master Charles is firing up the
engine.

CHRISTIAN *makes to go in one direction.*

Mr Mason's somewhere in the brewery.

CHRISTIAN *makes to go in another direction.*

After the glasses, mind.

CHRISTIAN. Yes, Mrs Eldridge.

CHRISTIAN *moves off in a third direction.*

SARAH. Now –

SOPHIE. Mama, it's only that you don't share his opinions.

SARAH. Oh, yes, indeed. Well, I'd hoped that you'd a-learnt one
thing of me, but clearly not.

SOPHIE. What's that, mama?

SARAH. It is, that one should entertain the most acute suspicion of
a person spends more time a-worreting about *reform*,
a-wallowing in all the pressing troubles of *society*, than
bothering about the folks he actually knows, and things he might
do summat practical about. Don't trust utopians. That's always
been my policy.

SOPHIE. Mama!

SARAH. Because –

Screams from off.

Now, what?

Enter CHRISTIAN *in high alarm.*

CHRISTIAN. Oh, ma'am –

SARAH. Now, Christian, what –

CHRISTIAN. Oh, ma'am, it's Master Charles —

FANNY *runs through.*

SARAH. What's happened? Fanny?

CHRISTIAN. Oh, the blood!

SARAH. The *blood*?

Enter EMILY.

EMILY. What's going on?

SARAH. Oh, Emily, your brother —

CHRISTIAN. Oh, Miss Sophie, you d'ave no idea . . .

SARAH. I must —

SARAH *is rushing towards the exit when* ALFRED MASON *hurries in. He's* SARAH's *brewer, 29 years old.*

CHRISTIAN. You cass'n picture it —

SARAH. Now, Alfred —

ALFRED. Sarah, it's all right. He's cut his foot, that's all.

SARAH. His foot?

CHRISTIAN. Great pools of it.

EMILY. Oh, Christian, do calm down.

CHRISTIAN. Like spurting . . .

SARAH. But, is somebody —

ALFRED. I've sent the new girl for the bandages.

SARAH. What, Fanny?

CHRISTIAN. And a-gushing, like you never see —

ALFRED. And he will be all right.

Enter FANNY *with water and bandages.* SARAH *turns to look at her. She doesn't understand the intensity of* SARAH's *look.*

FANNY. Uh — bandages.

SARAH. Right, thank you, Fanny. Thank you very much.

She grabs the bandages and hurries out followed by ALFRED, SOPHIE and FANNY. CHRISTIAN is still whimpering.

EMILY. Oh, come on, Christian. Just a little blood.

EMILY goes out. GEORGE LODER enters. He's in his late 40s. He's in his best clothes, and carries a letter. He looks around.

CHRISTIAN. M'sorry, Miss Emily.

Ignoring LODER, CHRISTIAN hurries out.

GEORGE LODER. Um, 'scuse me . . . 'Scuse me . . .

He's alone. He looks round a little more. Enter SARAH.

SARAH. Christian! Christian, will you run for –

GEORGE LODER. Ah. Good evening. Mrs Eldridge?

SARAH. Yes, it is – Um, look, I'm sorry –

GEORGE LODER. Name be George Loder. I were sent this invitation.

SARAH. Yes, indeed. Now, Mr – Loder, you'll forgive me . . .

GEORGE LODER. From the Bull's Head.

SARAH. Bull's Head?

GEORGE LODER. Fordington.

SARAH. From *Fordington*. You're from the Bull's Head, *Fordington*.

GEORGE LODER. That's right.

SARAH. Well, Mr Loder. I'm delighted you could come. And first of all, I want to see you with a pint of Eldridge's best bitter in your hand. And then, I have a matter to discuss with you.

SOPHIE has entered.

SOPHIE. I think the bleeding's stopped, mama.

SARAH. Well, well. That's very good.

Pause.

That's excellent.

A moment. SOPHIE moves in and takes her mother's hands.

SOPHIE. Mama. That's what I calls you, but you know I'm not your daughter. You never knew my mother. Nor did I.

Slight pause.

But I still take heed of what you say. And I want to do what you think best.

Slight pause.

And I know that John James tends to irk you, 'cos he hasn't really got a head for commerce, like . . . But, still, I love him. Like you loved my father, too.

Pause.

SARAH. Sophie. Your father was a kind man. But a weak one. And he thought that everybody was the same as him. And that's not just bad for business. Why, in these times, be downright dangerous.

SOPHIE *looks hard at her mother.*

You see, I thought I couldn't have a baby. So I married him for you.

She becomes aware that GEORGE LODER *is still there. To him:*

Forgive me, Mr Loder. We've been having something of a family crisis. And now I must go and see a silly boy.

She is moving quickly towards the exit when she confronts a MUMMER.

FIRST MUMMER. Is there a doctor to be found
          All ready, near at hand,
          To cure this dread and deadly wound,
          And make the champion stand?

SARAH *turns back, her face full of fear. She sees another* MUMMER.

SECOND MUMMER. Oh, doctor, doctor, play thy part:
          My son be wounded to the heart.

SARAH *quickly runs out, as a* THIRD MUMMER *appears.*

THIRD MUMMER. Oh George Prince George what have you
          done?

You have slain your own beloved son.
You have cut him down like the evening
    sun.

1.9.2. Still the Brewery. *The bunting still up, but some detached,
hanging.* SARAH *stands. Around her are* SOPHIE, EMILY,
ALFRED MASON, JOHN TIZARD, 24, *and* JOHN JAMES
BESANT, 32.

SARAH. Who would have thought it. Just an itty-bitty little
    scratch. And nothing for a week. And then his throat swell.
    Mouth clamp shut. He arch up like a bow.

ALFRED. It's lockjaw, Sarah. Sometimes the blood's infected.
    Nothing can be done. And nobody to blame.

SARAH. Oh, isn't there?

SOPHIE. No. No, mama.

SARAH *looks up at* SOPHIE. *Then she looks to* EMILY *and*
JOHN, *then to* SOPHIE *and* JOHN JAMES.

SARAH. I want you to get married. Both of you. I want my
    grandchildren.

Pause.

Well, at least no change of wardrobe. I'm in black for Charles
already.

She looks at her daughters.

Like, having blinded both of them.

She goes out.

1.9.3. Dorchester High St. *The* CITIZENS *of the town, with
handbills, read of an important forthcoming attraction.*

CITIZENS. Oyez oyez.

Be it hereby known to all the patriotic citizens of Dorchester –

– and if there be any citizens of Dorchester who are not of the
most patriotic cast of mind particularly at this hour of national
peril we are yet to hear of them –

— that that most famous troupe, the Macarte Leviathan
Equestrian Extravaganza —

— will represent in Salisbury Fields on Thursday next at five
o'clock precisely —

— the heroic actions of our Turkish allies at the battle of the
Danube basin and Silistra —

— following a Grand Procession through the town!

Scene Ten

1.10.1. The Dragon Brewery: Parlour. *August 1854. Enter*
SARAH, EMILY *and* SOPHIE.

SARAH. The Crimea. Don't talk to me about the Crimea.

EMILY. Mother. No one is talking to you about the Crimea. We're
just reminding you that on Thursday John comes up to
Dorchester and that we could take the children to the grand
equestrian parade.

SARAH. Shall I tell you what this war means to your mother?
Ruin.

SOPHIE. Oh, mama. What do you mean?

SARAH. Well, first, of course, they march the soldiers off, and
then they do pack the barracks with the only class of person in
society denied my services —

EMILY. What is this?

SOPHIE. They're convicts, from the Millbank prison.

EMILY. Convicts?

SARAH. Yes. Yes, Fanny?

For FANNY LOCK *has entered.*

FANNY. Ma'am. It's the parson here to see you.

SARAH. Parson?

FANNY. Reverend Moule. From Fordington.

SARAH. Well, show him in . . .

FANNY *goes out.*

I'll see you two later.

EMILY *and* SOPHIE *go out as* FANNY *admits* MOULE.

Why, Mr Moule.

MOULE. Well, Mrs Eldridge.

SARAH. You'll know our Fanny, doubtless: Fanny Lock. Her family lives down Mill Street.

MOULE. Oh, yes, I think I —

SARAH. And I'm sure she pays the closest possible attention to everything you tell her from the pulpit, don't you, Fanny?

FANNY. Yes, o'course, ma'am.

SARAH. Off you go.

FANNY *goes out.*

As good as gold. But still a trifle shy and awkward. Now, Mr Moule, I'm at full stretch for the harvest-home, so you'll please forgive me if we get straight down to business.

MOULE. Madam, it is of your servant's birthplace I would speak to you. Of Mill Street. Back of Ansty. Cuckold's Row. You know the area?

SARAH. Well, by repute.

MOULE. It is an area of considerable degradation.

SARAH. So I am told.

MOULE. Its population comes in large part from the countryside, and is now crammed into that tiny freehold of my parish which is not part of the demesne of the Duke of Cornwall.

SARAH. Well, I am not Prince Albert, Mr Moule.

MOULE. In many of the homes there is no possibility of even the most basic privacy. Most of the households draw their water from the millstream, an open channel of the vilest effluent.

SARAH. Nor, I regret, a sanitary inspector.

MOULE. The quarter is I tell you a repository of all that is unwholesome and immoral.

SARAH. Nor do I sit upon the Board of Guardians.

MOULE. No, madam, but you are a publican.

Pause.

SARAH. Indeed.

MOULE. Whose business is expanding. Dorchester, Cerne Abbas, Weymouth and beyond.

SARAH. I have purchased leases in those boroughs, yes.

MOULE. And in addition I am told the freehold of a public house in Fordington. 'The Bull'.

SARAH. The Bull's Head. Yes. The landlord, Mr Loder, is a person of the utmost probity.

MOULE. I wonder, then, how he squares his conscience with his trade?

Pause.

SARAH. Mr Moule. Let me be plain with you. I am a business person, one of modest means, who has just been through a harsh and unrewarding winter, and who now faces the evacuation of the military. I have to tell you that those setbacks leave me little room for charitable contributions. And indeed I must confess my view that as a man sows, may he reap, and that his conditions – even in the circumstances you describe – are his responsibility not mine.

MOULE. Oh, Mrs Eldridge, then we are at one. I do not see the salvation of the darker quarters of my parish in philanthropy.

SARAH. Well, I'm glad of that.

MOULE. Nor, I assure you, do I share the fashionable and dangerous opinion that men are immanently virtuous, and that their vice is merely consequent on circumstance.

SARAH. No more do I, I'm sure.

MOULE. I am convinced my parish cries out not for social but for moral restitution.

SARAH. Well, then we are agreed.

MOULE. And as drink is such an obvious contributor to the phenomena I have described, I must plead with you to cease your operations there.

Pause.

SARAH. Mr Moule, are you suggesting that I cease to trade in Fordington?

MOULE. In intoxicating liquors, yes.

SARAH. That's what I manufacture.

MOULE. And for the consequences of that fact are thus responsible.

SARAH. Might I suggest, therefore – that your quarrel might not be with me, but rather with those who consume my devil's brew –

MOULE. Oh, I have addressed them, madam. In yours and many other hostelries. There is a publication I retail on such occasions. Perhaps you'd accept a complimentary copy.

SARAH (*taking a tract from* MOULE). Thank you. D'you do a brisk trade, Mr Moule?

MOULE. No, I do not.

SARAH. In fact, I'd guess you comes in for a fair amount of ridicule. If not abuse.

MOULE. I have been victim to a certain – boisterousness, from time to time.

SARAH. Yes. Yes, I'm sure.

Pause. Then SARAH *has an idea. She goes and calls:*

SARAH. Sophie! Emily! One of you, come here!

Enter SOPHIE.

SOPHIE. Yes, mama?

SARAH. Sophie, a glass of beer, please, for the vicar.

SOPHIE. Yes, at once.

She goes out.

MOULE. But, madam, I'm a —

SARAH. Yes. And if you choose not to accept my offer, I assure you, I won't be offended in the least. You see, I sell rope, Mr Moule. And people choose to buy it, or conversely not, and spend their money in another way. And once they've got it, they can use it to secure their property, or tow their vehicles, or for all I know hold up their britches.

Enter SOPHIE with a glass of beer.

They can keep it coiled up in the attic, or they can swing upon it from the rafters. But for the uses that they put it to, I am due neither compliment nor blame. Why thank you, Sophie.

She takes the beer and drinks.

Your best health, Mr Moule.

MOULE. So I must conclude that I am misinformed.

SARAH. Oh, what about?

MOULE. About the cause of the untimely death of Mr Eldridge, ma'am.

Pause.

SARAH. Mr Moule. My second husband — and my son — were both called to their maker's arms before their time. They are beyond the shadow of my judgement. And, if I may say so, yours.

MOULE. But not beyond that of that very maker, ma'am. And as I have repeated to those on the very rim of ruin, if a man destroys himself by dissipation, vice or drunkenness, he is as guilty as a suicide. And as Paul wrote to the Thessalonians, the punishment for that is everlasting exile from the presence of the Lord. There is, I must assure you, no reprieve.

Pause.

SARAH. Well, I'm sorry, but I can't believe that, Mr Moule.

MOULE. And I, too, am sorry, but it is really not a matter of what you 'can' or 'can't' believe. In all solemnity, I must ask you to consider the Epistle to the Hebrews, thirteen seven —

SARAH. No. No, thank you, Mr Moule —

SOPHIE. 'Remember them which have the rule over you, who have spoken unto you the word of God . . . Jesus Christ, the same yesterday, today and forever.'

MOULE. Yes.

SOPHIE. May *I* ask if you remember the first verses of that chapter?

MOULE. I —

SARAH. No *more*.

Pause.

Now, really. I do really think, that it is now appropriate, for you to go.

Pause. MOULE *gives a slight bow, turns to go, but then turns back. Urgently:*

MOULE. It is — it is the babies, Mrs Eldridge. As a mother you may understand. It is the babies, beaten by their fathers, or abandoned by their mothers, found left on doorsteps, or — or buried in back gardens, stuffed in ratholes by the river. There is a woman in my parish, now thankfully reformed and in at least a reasonably decent way of trade, who began to sell her body to the soldiers in the taverns and the beertents, at the age of hardly twelve. She'd lost three babies by the age of seventeen. And she will bear no more.

Slight pause.

As you say, you sell rope, Mrs Eldridge.

He goes out. SOPHIE *goes to her mother.*

SOPHIE. Now, mama . . .

SARAH. Well. Really. What a — nonsense. How, absurd.

Slight pause.

Have we no Poor Laws? Board for Public Health? I pay a ransom to the Borough . . .

Slight pause.

No, I will not be blamed. I won't be held responsible.

SOPHIE. Mama –

SARAH. No, *don't*. Don't touch me. Don't.

She is fighting hard.

SOPHIE. Mama. D'you ever see one? Do you ever come across a mother, down in Mill Street, with a baby she can't feed? With a child who if it isn't fed will die?

SARAH. No. No, I haven't.

SOPHIE. Then – then isn't that utopian of *you*, mama.

Pause.

SARAH. Your mother died when she had you.

SOPHIE. I know. I was a stranger. And you took me in.

SARAH. No, no. You weren't a stranger. You were his. So you be mine.

Pause.

That's right. There's nothing I can do. 'Cept waste time wallowing in silly sentiment, 'bout folks I don't know and I can't do nothing for.

She looks at SOPHIE.

I mean to say. The Reverend Moule, and Mill Street. Not our parish. Not our business or concern. So what be they to us?

She looks to EMILY.

Where's Fanny?

SARAH *goes out.*

1.10.2. **Clifftops** *above the sea.* FANNY *and* HORACE *sit there, looking down. They have a picnic.*

FANNY. Well, here we be. 'Tis the first time, this year, that I don't go to the harvesting.

HORACE. Is that where you're supposed to —

FANNY. Right enough.

She looks out over the cliff.

HORACE. It's supposed to be a good one. Bounteous. This year.

FANNY. Well, cass'n be worse than last year, cans't it?

HORACE *smiles.*

HORACE. I don't know. I was in Oxford.

FANNY. Oxford. Well.

She looks out, over the sea.

The sea. 'Tisn't often I set eyes on her.

HORACE (*looking down*). That's Lulworth Cove. Our father used to take us there when we were children.

Slight pause.

FANNY. Well, I wonder what he'd think to you today?

HORACE. I daren't imagine.

FANNY. Saw him, yesterday.

HORACE. My father? Why? ·

FANNY. Came to see my mistress.

HORACE. At the brewery? Why, whatever for?

FANNY. Well, I dunno. I didn't overhear.

Slight pause.

But I don't doubt he've a way of getting what he's after. Reverend Moule.

Slight pause. HORACE *looks out to sea.*

HORACE. You know, from here, and on a day like this, you could imagine you could see, not France, or Spain, or Italy . . . But Athens, Constantinople. Or . . . Jerusalem.

He turns and smiles at FANNY.

You know?

Pause. FANNY *smiles back.*

FANNY. Like father, like son, eh?

Scene Eleven

1.11.1. High St, Dorchester. *And now the great* PROCESSION *enters, headed by the showman* MR MACARTE *and his associate* MR HENGLER, *and passing – as it were – down the High St towards the White Hart Inn, where many* FORDINGTON RESIDENTS *wait to greet it, before it turns off towards Salisbury Fields. The* CROWD *includes many we have already met, with the exception of the* MOULES *and* SARAH ELDRIDGE. *The* PROCESSION *is headed by* RIDERS *representing the* OMAR PASHA, *a* BRITISH OFFICER, *a* FRENCH OFFICER, *a* RUSSIAN PRINCE, *and a* GERMAN MERCENARY.

HENGLER. See! See the noble Omar Pasha, Supreme Commander of the Turkish Force in the Crimea!

MACARTE. Observe as well those brave young Englishmen in the service of the Turkish cause!

HENGLER. Not to mention our heroic Gallic allies!

MACARTE. Attend as well to the enemy, Prince Gorchakov:

HENGLER. And the pitiless and cruel Prussian mercenary General Luders.

MACARTE. View the might of men and armour of the Imperial Guard, the Volkynia Regiment and the dreaded Georgian Cossacks!

Meanwhile, the CROWD:

CROWD. Look, they're a-coming!
　　　　　Is that they?

D'ye hear the band?
Mama, what's a Gallic ally?
Is that the Russians?
No, that's a Turk.
Hooray for Turkey!
It's the Pasha!
What's a Pasha?

And round about this point, the COMMENTARY *stops, and there is* NARRATIVE:

NARRATIVE. And, near the White Hart,

at the back of the crowd some people were aware

of some old man,

yes some old parson,

who was shouting something it was hard to hear . . .

And MOULE *is indeed there, trying to attract attention:*

MOULE. You must go home! You must leave this place!

NARRATIVE. But no one heard, or if they did, they ignored this odd old body —

MOULE. You must depart at once!

NARRATIVE. And so Henry Moule ran back towards the Green,

trying to think of some way he could stop the growing flood of people as it swept towards his parish . . .

And now the COMMENTARY *continues:*

HENGLER. Witness the Russian Army cross the River Pruth and advance into Moldavia!

MACARTE. Share plucky Turkey's heroic defence of Oltenitza against nine hundred thousand blood-hungry Muscovites!

HENGLER. And rejoice in fullest measure at the routing of the Slavic hordes at Giurgevo!

Meanwhile:

CROWD. Boo! Shame!
Hooray!

Death to the Tsar!
Look at the Cossacks!
What a wonderful display!

The PROCESSION *reaches the thickest point of the* CROWD. *Suddenly,* MOULE *appears, on a strange, erratic steed. As the* NARRATIVE *describes events, the* CROWD *begins to boo and shout insults, throwing streamers and missiles, so* MOULE *is garlanded.*

NARRATIVE. And suddenly,

in the path of the procession,

appeared the strangest spectacle:

a parson, on a kind of horse or mule or pony that he couldn't well control,

and shouting warnings that could not be heard . . .

And when they recognised the man as the notorious killjoy Henry Moule,

the merry crowd,

particularly the younger set,

responded to this ludicrous performance with catcalls, boos and laughter,

and in some cases, even, missiles . . .

The catcalling and jeering reaches a crescendo. Then silence.

Until suddenly the crowd fell silent.

And each person asked their neighbour if they could make out

what the almost voiceless vicar had been shouting.

And like a fire the news spread through the huge assembly:

MOULE. I say – there is a stranger in our midst. His name is Cholera.

SOME. Cholera.

ALL. Cholera.

Blackout.

ACT TWO

Scene One

2.1.1. **The Fields near Fordington.** FANNY LOCK *lies there in the sun. The* FOOL *and the* LADY, *from a Plough Play, dance around her.*

FOOL. Come write me down the power above
      The man that first created love
      I'll give you gold, I'll give you pearl,
      If you can fancy me my girl.

LADY. It's not your gold should me entice
      Leave of virtue to follow your advice,
      But stay young man and you may find
      That this proud prim dame may prove more kind
      That this proud prim dame may prove more kind . . .

The FOOL *and the* LADY *stay.* HORACE MOULE *has entered, with a spade and bag.*

HORACE. Well, so then, maidy. What's your name?

FANNY looks up.

FANNY. Be Fanny. And what's it to you?

HORACE. And where d'you work then, Fanny?

FANNY. I'm in service, up in Dorchester.

HORACE. And who might you be serving?

FANNY. Mrs Eldridge, of the Dragon Brewery. You're full enough of who's and why's and where's. So who d'you be?

Pause.

HORACE. My name's Horatio. Or – Horace. I'm the parson's son.

FANNY. Well well.

Slight pause.

So, Horatio or Horace. And what do we be doing, with our little bag and spade.

HORACE. We been a-digging for old pots and suchlike, with our little spade. And because it's thirsty work we've got a little bottle in our bag. And a bit of bread and cheese besides. And who knows, we might be looking out for somebody to share 'em.

FANNY. Oh, well. Might we now.

Long pause. Then FANNY *hops up, brushes herself down. As if that's settled:*

Well, what a summer, eh?

As they go off together.

FOOL. Now all my sorrows is come and past,
      For joy and bliss I've found at last . . .

LADY. So may all young ploughboys take their chance
      And lead their loves to the harvest dance:
      So lead me to the harvest dance.

NARRATORS *appear.*

NARRATIVE. For it was, and it had been, the most dazzling of summers,

and in the weeks before the harvest

they had strolled along the walks and through the fields,

had laid upon the beaches, run across the dunes and climbed the clifftops,

as if, like any dazzling summer, it would never end . . .

And suddenly, the FOOL *and the* LADY *take off their masks and speak to us.*

FOOL. And little knowing of the dread and deathly stranger who would come among them:

LADY. And little thinking of the poisoned seed so soon to sojourn in their midst.

2.1.2. Town Council meeting. MEMBERS *include* CAPT FRAMPTON, CAPT HENNING, *the iron-foundry owner* JOHN GALPIN, *41,* DR ARDEN, *65, and the* MAYOR, GEORGE ANDREWS, *37.* ANDREWS, *a solicitor, has only recently been elected, and has bad news to report. A buzz of conversation, silenced by* ANDREWS' *gavil.*

ANDREWS. Um, gentlemen. Please come to order. I declare this special session of the Dorchester Town Council in – um, session.

Quiet.

Members will be aware I know of the imminent arrival of our – unexpected visitors from London –

GALPIN. Convicts!

HENNING. Unexpected and unwanted.

ANDREWS. – well, yes, who are to be – appropriated to, or accommodated in the Barracks.

GALPIN. Dumped.

ANDREWS. Due to the infection raging in the Millbank prison.

Chunter.

Of which distemper we're assured these convicts are yet free.

GALPIN. Gammon!

ANDREWS. Accordingly, on your instructions, on last Thursday I proceeded up to London, to the Home Office, but was sadly not fortunate enough to find Lord Palmerston in –

Chunter.

However, I did speak to an Under-Secretary who informed me that the application was too late, as the Government had already determined upon it. And that the convicts would arrive – on Monday.

Heavy chunter.

Yes, Mr Galpin.

GALPIN. Mr Mayor, Under-Secretary or no Under-Secretary, this is not good enough at all.

ANDREWS. Well, no.

GALPIN. We must make every effort to prevent the affliction of this injury upon the town.

ANDREWS. Yes, but what –

GALPIN. We must draw up and send a petition the – to the Home Office – to Prince Albert – protesting in the strongest terms.

ANDREWS. Well, surely. Captain Frampton.

CAPT FRAMPTON. Mr Mayor, I am sure this matter has been considered by the Government –

Protests.

And although I naturally regret that the Barracks have been fixed upon –

GALPIN. Regret!

CAPT FRAMPTON. I shall myself decline to sign any petition or memorial against it.

Protests, but also some deferential hushes.

Not least as the convicts will presumably arrive, and we would be best occupied in resolving what to do about it when they do.

HENNING. Hear hear.

ANDREWS. Well, indeed. At which point, gentlemen, perhaps we should resolve ourselves into the Board of Health.

MEMBERS (*perfunctorily*). Aye, aye.

ANDREWS. And call upon Alderman Dr Arden to report.

ARDEN. Thank you, Mr Mayor. The Board will remember in July it considered the appointment, under the Health of Towns act, of an Inspector of Nuisances, Surveyor, Treasurer and Clerk. An appointment it was decided to postpone, on grounds of cost. This postponement following a motion, as I recollect, proposed by Mr Galpin.

Some hmming and hmphing.

GALPIN. So what the devil's that supposed to mean?

ARDEN. A decision which I pray the Board will not live to regret.

2.1.3. Fordington Vicarage. *In the sudden darkness, a spot picks out a young man, dressed in black, and reading the Bible. It is* GEORGE MOULE.

GEORGE. And after this I looked, and behold, a throne was set in heaven, and one sat upon the throne. And round about the throne were four and twenty seats: and upon the seats I saw four and twenty elders sitting, clothed in white raiment:

Gradually, lights are growing around GEORGE; *we discover we are in the vicarage, at evening prayers, and with* GEORGE *are* MOULE, MRS MOULE, CHARLES, HANDLEY JNR, ELLEN WRIGHT *and the maid* HANNAH, 14.

And out of the throne proceeded lightnings and thunderings and voices: and there were seven lamps of fire burning before the throne, which are the seven spirits of God.

GEORGE *closes the book.*

MOULE. Thank you. Now. Following our discussion of last evening, as to the nature of John's vision of this chapter of his Revelation, what further conclusions can we draw? George?

GEORGE. Well, father, does not the throne remind us of Jeremiah, and the 'glorious high throne' which 'from the beginning is the place of thy sanctuary'.

MOULE. Indeed. And – Charles?

CHARLES. We should note, father, should we not, that 'four and twenty elders' are prophesied as keepers of the Tabernacle in One Chronicles.

MOULE. Correct, and – Handley?

HANDLEY JNR. Um . . .

Pause.

GEORGE (*prompting*). The candlesticks . . .

HANDLEY JNR (*bit of a rush*). And are not the seven lamps of fire the seven candles of the self-same Tabernacle laid down in, Deuter –

MOULE. Exodus. So from all this we must conclude that the vision of St John is of the *actual* Holy Temple of Jerusalem. Indeed, the scripture can admit no other interpretation. The question remains, however –

He stops, seeing HORACE *enter quickly with his bag. The rest of the* FAMILY *turn to identify the intruder.*

HORACE. Good evening. Sorry.

HANNAH. Mr *Horace.*

MOULE (*firmly*). – to which we shall address ourselves tomorrow. So, the Grace of Our Lord Jesus Christ, the Love of God, and the Fellowship of the Holy Spirit, be with us all for ever more.

ALL. Amen.

MOULE. Now Hannah, and you, Handley, time for bed.

HANNAH. Yes, sir.

HANDLEY JNR. Yes, father. Goodnight, mother.

Slight pause.

Horace.

He goes out after HANNAH.

GEORGE. I think . . . that Charles and I will work a little further on our presentation to the Annual Meeting of the Society for the Conversion of the Jews.

They go out, followed by ELLEN.

HORACE. I'm sorry.

MRS MOULE. We did wait.

HORACE. Thank you.

MOULE. Until we could do so no longer.

Pause. MRS MOULE *hands* HORACE *a letter.*

MRS MOULE. This came for you.

HORACE. Thank you, mother.

He opens the letter, and reads.

Oh, splendid.

MRS MOULE. Is it –

HORACE. They will take me at Queens' College, Cambridge, father.

MRS MOULE. Oh, that is excellent.

MOULE. Indeed. Particularly as he so singularly failed to graduate at Oxford.

Pause.

No doubt he will find Cambridge more congenial. Where he can happily surround himself with antinomians and universalists.

HORACE. I'm sorry. *Universalists?*

MOULE. The heresy that all are ultimately graced, and that the immanence of sin and everlastingness of hell are morbid superstitions.

HORACE. Oh, I *see*. Well, there's an argument –

MOULE. What need has such an undemanding doctrine of the sustenance of prayer?

Pause.

HORACE. Father, I have been walking round your parish. The part down there. The iron foundry, Mill Street, Cuckold's Row. The area does not improve.

MOULE. No, it does not.

HORACE. But I suppose your argument would be that as they are so used to misery and torment in this life, they really won't mind if they're sentenced to the same in perpetuity.

MRS MOULE. Now, Horace, you must not —

HORACE. Because of course, it would be the rankest heresy even to consider the idea that paucity of spirit might be caused by poverty of circumstance —

MOULE. Oh, Horace.

His tone stops HORACE *in his tracks.*

Horace, I am full of fear. Fear and foreboding.

HORACE. Father, why?

MOULE. Because . . . Because John tells us there are seven angels, that are sent by God to pour the vials of his wrath upon the earth, and sea, and air. And for reason of man's disobedience and sin will sow upon the earth great plagues and pestilences. And who knows when the Day of Reaping will be come?

And in the distance, we hear the singing of a harvest hymn.

HARVESTERS. Hosanna say, hosanna sing,
              The groaning harvest bring we in.
              Hosanna sing, hosanna say,
              For the harvest-home we make today.
              Hosanna we sing, hosanna we say:
              For the harvest-home we make today.

Scene Two

2.2.1. **Mill Street.** RESIDENTS *sit round in the heat. They include* JANE SIBLEY, *now middle aged, and* MARTHA LOCK's *ten-year-old daughter* LOUISA. MOULE *stands a little apart. From* *off, a* WOMAN's *voice, loud. When we see her, we will recognise* LIZZIE SIBLEY, *now well into her 30s.*

LIZZIE SIBLEY (*off*). Hey, Martha! Martha Whiting! Just you bring that bonnet here!

JANE WHITING's *19-year-old daughter* MARTHA *runs on with a brightly coloured hat.*

MARTHA. So why *you'm* wanting it? What use be she to you?

LIZZIE SIBLEY *runs in after* MARTHA.

LIZZIE SIBLEY. I said you fetch that here. Elsewise I fetch your mother to 'ee.

MARTHA *stops, shrugs.*

You wants to feather yoursen out, you learns to pay for it.

MARTHA *hands over the hat.*

MARTHA. Ah, well. There's some as needs their plumage more than t'others, bain't there, Mrs Sibley.

LIZZIE *grabs the hat and goes, followed by* MARTHA. MRS LOCK *enters with a bucket from the mill stream.*

MARTHA LOCK. Why, good morning to you, parson.

She gives a cup of water from the bucket to LOUISA.

MOULE. Ah. Mrs Lock. And this I think — Maria?

MARTHA LOCK. No, Louisa. Twin. Maria's sick today.

MOULE. I'm sorry.

MARTHA LOCK. Oh, 'tin't uncommon. We bide that near the mill stream, 'tis hard to keep a body spry.

MOULE. Well, no. And how's your eldest daughter — ?

MARTHA. Fanny? Oh, she's in service, at the Eldridge brewery, in Dorchester. But I doubt that meets with your approval, parson.

MOULE. No.

MARTHA LOCK. But even so, maybe you do see, why I do prefer our Fanny going up to Dorchester, like even to a brewer's shop, than a-garnering the fruits of idleness round here.

From off, we hear the neigh of horses, and the voice of the publican, GEORGE LODER.

GEORGE LODER. Gee up!

GEORGE LODER *drives in his dray, on which is piled dirty washing. With him are* MR TURNLEY, *a prison warder, and another,* YOUNG WARDER.

TURNLEY. So, this is it?

LODER. Should be.

To JANE:

Hey, you! This Florence Chaffley's house?

JANE (*shrugs*). Were yesterday.

LODER. Whoa there!

LODER *and the* WARDERS *dismount.*

LODER. Right. Florence! Florence Chaffley!

FLORENCE CHAFFLEY, *now 30, calls from within:*

FLORENCE (*off*). Ar! Who wants her?

LODER. 'Tis Mr –

TURNLEY. Turnley.

LODER. Mr Turnley with the washing. From the Barracks.

MOULE, *about to leave, turns back.* JANE *and* LIZZIE *look at each other with interest.* JANE *whispers to* LIZZIE, *who goes.*

FLORENCE (*off*). Oh, right, then. Be with you directly.

TURNLEY *looks at* JANE, *who smiles.* FLORENCE *emerges, tying on an apron.*

FLORENCE. Well, then. Good morning, Mr Turnley. Hello, George Loder. And how be trade with you?

LODER. Well, I has to say he's looking summat more cheerful than a-were.

FLORENCE. Well, that's a mercy. Right, then, Mr Turnley. We should be getting this lot back to you – I'd say, by Thursday, certainly.

TURNLEY. Uh, Wednesday would be better.

FLORENCE. See what I can do. Now come on, Janie Sibley, do you give us a hand.

JANE, FLORENCE *and the two* WARDERS *unload the washing.* MOULE *approaches.*

MOULE. Miss Chaffley. May I, may I ask what all this is?

Pause. FLORENCE *for some reason seems guilty.*

FLORENCE. Why, parson. Where d'you spring from?

Slight pause.

'Tis just washing.

They carry on unloading. During the following, LIZZIE SIBLEY *returns with* MARTHA WHITING, *who stands apart as* LIZZIE *goes and whispers to* TURNLEY. TURNLEY *then has a word with the* YOUNG WARDER, *who nods.*

JANE. Gennlemen's unmentionables.

FLORENCE. That's it.

JANE. Or p'raps in this case, mind, more *un*gennlemen's unmentionables.

FLORENCE. Well, yes.

JANE. Seeing as how they be locked up in the Barracks, like, for all kinds of most ungennlemanly behaviour.

MOULE. What, you mean, the convicts – ?

FLORENCE. Yes. Well, that be around the length of it. But that don't mean their small-clothes don't get soiled, now do it? So let's have all this done.

FLORENCE *carries on working.*

TURNLEY. In fact, ma'am, I think we're going to have a draught of summat with this lady. On account of this uncommon heat.

FLORENCE. Well, there's nothing untoward in that.

TURNLEY. We'll be back in 20 minutes.

LIZZIE SIBLEY. Say an hour.

TURNLEY. An hour, then.

JANE (*leaving the washing*). Don't look like rain to me.

FLORENCE *and* LODER *share a glance, as* TURNLEY *and the* YOUNG WARDER *follow out* LIZZIE *and* JANE, *joined by* MARTHA, *to the door of* JANE WHITING's *house, where that lady appears to greet them. We see that* MARTHA LOCK *has returned and is watching* MOULE.

JANE WHITING. So in you do come, please, gentlemen. For a mug of summat, if you can be tempted in that way.

TURNLEY. Well, thank you, ma'am. A pleasure.

They are about to go in when JANE WHITING *spots* MOULE.

JANE WHITING. Well, if 'tisn't parson. Be it warm enough for 'ee?

MOULE. Yes, thank you. But I must, must warn you that there is a real risk —

JANE WHITING. Hey, parson. Do you ever meet my daughter Martha? Go on, Martha. Pay respects to Mr Moule.

MARTHA *curtsies, suggestively. All the* WOMEN *laugh. As they turn to go in:*

MOULE. 'And the heathen are sunk down into the cess-pit they have dug; and by the work of his own hands the wicked man is snared.'

EVERYONE *laughs again. The* SIBLEYS *start to sing — a mocking version of the old children's round song, but to the tune of the harvest song.*

SIBLEY SISTERS. Oh hokey, pokey, winky, wum
           How do you like your taters done
           Why all to pieces that's the fun
           And can ye now just gie I one?

Merging into the second verse of the Harvest Hymn:

HARVEST HYMN. No greater load e'er laid in store,
           No finer a harvest ever we saw.
           Now reapers may rest, their reaping
             done,
           The scythe to sheathe, corn carry
             home.
           Hosanna we say, hosanna we sing,
           And harvest bells all loudly ring.

2.2.2. **Cornhill, Dorchester.** *Narrative from the Councillors of Dorchester.*

HENNING. And within a day or two, it was reported in the *County Chronicle*

GALPIN. that the alarm created in the town by the arrival of the convicts had to a large degree subsided;

CAPT FRAMPTON. that the prospect of the Grand Equestrian Spectacular was now exciting the most keen anticipation, and

ANDREWS. that the splendid weather was expected to produce a harvest of the most munificent proportions.

2.2.3. **St George's Church, Fordington.** MOULE *is setting out fruit and vegetables for the harvest thanksgiving service.* AUGUSTUS HANDLEY *has entered.*

HANDLEY. Loder. George Loder. Publican.

MOULE. I think so. Yes.

HANDLEY. He'd lent his dray. Or – hired it, I'd imagine, for the washing.

MOULE. There was certainly a dray. What's happened, then, Augustus?

HANDLEY. He has developed colic. Headache. A little diarrhoea. As yet.

Pause.

MOULE. I see.

The crash of the church door.

Now, what on earth –

JANE WHITING *runs in.*

JANE WHITING. Parson! Where's parson?

MOULE. Mrs – Whiting?

JANE WHITING. There! There he be. The murderer! Assassin!

HANDLEY. Mrs Whiting, what is this?

JANE WHITING *starts attacking the harvest display.*

JANE WHITING. He puts a spell on her. 'Cos she do show lewd to he. And he do curse her with his talk of pits and snares and wickedness, and now she be dead –

HANDLEY *is trying to restrain her.*

HANDLEY. Please – please calm down . . .

JANE WHITING. Why he – why he –

HANDLEY. Your daughter's dead?

MOULE. Mrs Whiting, please –

JANE WHITING. Course. Course she be. First she'm all tired. Then her voice be hoarse. Now she do plim up like a bladder, and water stuff do come out of her, all yellow, and her nose do go pointy and her chin all blue . . . and she smell like – like I cass'n say . . .

HANDLEY. There is no question, I'm afraid –

Enter CHARLES *and* HANDLEY JNR. *They see the fruit and vegetables flung around.*

CHARLES. Father, what is this?

JANE WHITING *has begun to cry.*

JANE WHITING. Baa. Baa baa.

HANDLEY. The symptoms, undeniably —

MOULE *hears something:*

MOULE. What's that?

HANDLEY. First Loder. Now this woman's child —

JANE WHITING. Baa. Baa. You be . . .

MOULE. That noise — What is that noise?

HANDLEY JNR. It's music. It's the band. With the Equestrian parade.

MOULE. Parade?

JANE WHITING (*whimpering to herself*). Baa baa. You be the parson's lambs you be.

Scene Three

2.3.1. Fordington and Dorchester. *And now at last the Harvest-home appears before us, a magnificent tableau of* LABOURERS *and* FARMERS, *their sheafs of produce held before them, and the* CHILD *of the Harvest held aloft.*

HARVEST SONG. So pray God's bounty never shall
                        cease,
                    His providence shall e'er increase.
                    See what a burden bring we home,
                    When our next reaping shall be
                        done —

And we hear MOULE *calling:*

MOULE. You must go home! You must leave this place! I say — there is a stranger in our midst . . .

And the hymn finishes:

HARVEST SONG. What Hosanna hear, what Hosanna see:
When the harvest comes that is yet
to be.

And suddenly the tableau splits, and we see the CITIZENS *of Dorchester — including some of the* COUNCIL MEMBERS — *frozen in horror at the climax of the Equestrian Parade. A moment or two of silence, then they too split, dispersing quickly in all directions.* CAPTAIN HENNING *stands in the middle of it all, biting his lip. He makes a decision, looks round, sees* JOHN GALPIN, *and chases after him.*

HENNING. Galpin.

JOHN GALPIN. Yes, Captain Henning?

HENNING. Look. You know Moule.

JOHN GALPIN. Of course. Most of my foundryhands are his parishioners. Not that he's very popular.

HENNING. I know. But he has this, this vast family . . . And between us, we could accommodate them away from the worst of it. At least until the worst is over. As an act of, Christian . . .

Pause.

JOHN GALPIN. You mean, as a good work, Captain Henning.

HENNING. Well, I wouldn't actually, if I were you, I wouldn't mention good works, Mr Galpin.

2.3.2. **The Vicarage, Fordington.** *Open chests stand in the room.* GEORGE, CHARLES, *and* HANDLEY JNR *are bringing in piles of clothes and dumping them in the chests, assisted by* HANNAH *and* ELLEN WRIGHT. MRS MOULE *is bringing in bottles of liquids and putting them on a table. Everything is very busy.*

MRS MOULE. Charles, have you been through all the servants'
linen?

CHARLES. Yes, mother.

MRS MOULE. George, we must pack up all the winter underwear
. . . Where's Hannah?

HANNAH. Here, ma'am.

MRS MOULE. Please help Mr Charles.

MOULE *has entered with* HENNING, ANN HENNING *and*
JOHN GALPIN. *The business continues with the* SONS *coming
in and out with more clothes, as the conversation progresses.*

HENNING. Mr Moule, I appreciate that we have not seen eye to
eye. But this is an offer from our hearts. We have our coach, and
Mr Galpin's cabriolet outside. You are *all* most welcome to
come with us.

HANDLEY JNR. I've looked in the back attic, mother. Nothing.

MOULE. I am of course most grateful for your offer –

ANN HENNING. Mr Moule. In times like these, disputes,
misunderstandings, surely fade away and we can see each other
as we are, God's creatures –

GEORGE. Mama, I can't find the winter clothes!

MOULE. But I'm afraid I cannot –

MRS MOULE. Back hall closet!

JOHN GALPIN. Look, reverend. Let's not beat about the bush.
You have a country parson's living. There are – what, ten people
here? Where are you going? Where will you be accommodated?

MRS MOULE. There must be more shirts somewhere, Charles.

MOULE. Going? I am going nowhere.

HENNING. Sorry?

MOULE. That is what I have been trying to explain. My parish has been struck by cholera. My place is here.

ANN HENNING. You mean – you mean to stay?

MOULE. That is my meaning quite precisely.

JOHN GALPIN (*pointing at the baggage*). So what's all this?

MOULE. These are the garments of this household we can spare, to clothe those whose own raiment is infected by the pestilence.

JOHN GALPIN. But surely, Mr Moule, your wife, your children and your staff –

MOULE. Mary, would you like to accept this kind offer, from this lady and these gentlemen?

MRS MOULE. I thank them for it. But, no, I will stay here.

MOULE. And what is the view of our children?

MRS MOULE. They will stay.

MOULE. Have you asked our servants?

MRS MOULE. Yes. They too.

MOULE. Well, then. It does appear . . .

Pause.

HENNING. We have made our offer in good faith. There's nothing more to say.

He turns to go, followed by ANN HENNING. *But* JOHN GALPIN *has one last try.*

JOHN GALPIN. Look, Moule. There's something that you ought to know.

MOULE. What's that?

JOHN GALPIN. I've been talking to a fellow at the Barracks. And he says, in London, nobody is safe.

MOULE. I'm sorry?

JOHN GALPIN. Don't you understand? It isn't like before. It's not just in the slums, among the feckless and the miserable. It's taking tradesmen. And professional people. Gentry, even.

MOULE. Well, in that case, Mr Galpin, you must pray our efforts to restrict its spread succeed. Or otherwise, who knows who might be stricken.

Pause. ANN HENNING runs out.

JOHN GALPIN. Well. Have it your way, reverend.

He turns and goes, followed by HENNING.

MRS MOULE. We are well provided with the chlorides and the aromatics. We must take care however not to run out of laudanum. And —

MOULE. Indeed. George! Handley!

Enter GEORGE followed by HANDLEY JNR.

GEORGE. Father?

Re-enter ANN HENNING with a bag of clothes. She puts it on the table with the others.

ANN HENNING. For your — parishioners.

She's going, as MOULE looks in the bag.

MOULE. But, madam . . . these are silks, brocades . . .

ANN HENNING. Mr Moule, you will not make us guilty. You will not.

She goes out.

MOULE. We must take the kitchen copper set to Mill Street. Augustus is already there. We must get a fire going, boil the victims' clothes. Except the ones we need to burn.

The SONS go. MOULE follows. MRS MOULE, alone, falls to her knees. Very intense, very fast, very pained:

MRS MOULE. Oh Lord I thank Thee that in judgement Thou dost thus remember mercy. Keep me ready for Thy call should it please Thee to take me to Thyself by this fearful disease. It makes the flesh terrible; fix mine eyes on Jesus and it shall have no terror . . .

A MUMMER *appears.*

MUMMER. So in come I Beelzebub
On my shoulder I carries a club
In my hand a dripping-pan,
Don't you think I'm a funny old man?

2.3.3. The Dragon Brewery. SARAH *enters, briskly, followed by* EMILY, SOPHIE *and* ALFRED MASON.

EMILY. Mama, why not?

SARAH. Why not? Is this a brewery?

ALFRED. But just to *Weymouth.* For a week.

SARAH. Alfred, you may of course desert your post at any time –

ALFRED. Oh, Sarah . . .

SARAH. But I – I will not go.

SOPHIE. Then none of us will go.

SARAH. Good. Settled. We'll all stay.

FANNY LOCK *enters with a letter.*

FANNY. A letter, ma'am.

SARAH *opens the letter.*

SARAH. Aha. An order. For eight barrels of dark ale. For the Bridge and Railway Inns, in Bridport, Monday next. I think we can complete that order, Alfred?

ALFRED. Yes, of course.

He goes.

SARAH. For it won't spread. For 'tis a – a disease of – the afflicted. The already wretched, sickly and debased.

FANNY *runs out*.

What's that?

SOPHIE. Mama. Her family lives there. In the midst of 'the afflicted and debased'.

Pause.

SARAH. Well, then, I'd say she be best out of it. Here safe and sound with us.

Slight pause.

It will not touch us, Emily.

Scene Four

2.4.1. Mill Street. REV HANDLEY, GEORGE *and* CHARLES *working round a copper, boiling over a fire.* FORDINGTON PEOPLE *bring them clothes in wheelbarrows; they put them in the copper and boil them, then remove them and lay them out. A group of* CHILDREN *play nearby. They're singing:*

CHILDREN. Eena meena mino mo
        Kewska leena lina lo
        Eggs butter cheese and bread
        Stick stock stone dead
        And out goes SHE.

2.4.2. The Locks' House. MARTHA LOCK *is almost hysterical.* MOULE *is with her.*

MOULE. Now, Mrs Lock, please, let us make rice water . . .

MARTHA LOCK. Oh, sir, oh, Mr Moule, just the sight of him, I cass'n

MOULE. Now, why not sit down, for a moment, why –

MARTHA LOCK. I mean, the colour of's face, the stuff comes out of en –

MOULE. Just for a moment, so you can –

MARTHA LOCK. See, 'tis not like anything I d'ever see. 'Tis like a
– flood, a bursting blather. I could never fancy so much do come
out of one frame so fast. And I cass'n touch 'en.

Slight pause.

That's what 'tis. For all them years, I held 'en. Now he'm a-
dying. And I cass'n bear to touch my son.

MOULE. Mrs Lock. You will not have to for too long.

MARTHA LOCK (*crying*). But even so . . .

Pause.

MOULE. Now, ma'am, where is your husband?

MARTHA LOCK. In the fields.

MOULE. Can he be sent for?

MARTHA LOCK. Sent for? No.

MOULE. Why not? Your little girl . . .

MARTHA LOCK (*obvious*). He be a-working, sir.

MOULE. But – but –

MARTHA LOCK. I mean, he cass'n afford to take a holiday. If so
be Henry . . . still we've seven mouths to feed. He be able
bodied; like Parish don't give him no relief.

MOULE. Mrs Lock. Did you say that you have *seven* of your
family living here?

MARTHA LOCK. That's it. Since our Fanny went to service. Like,
we eat and live in here, this room, while we do sleep in t'other.

Enter LOUISA LOCK. She's covered in ordure, her face white.

LOUISA. Mother. He be gone.

A pause. MARTHA LOCK looks at MOULE.

MARTHA LOCK. So. D'you keep a Bible 'bout you, Mr Moule?

MOULE. Why, yes, indeed . . .

He finds his Bible and hands it to her. She opens it arbitrarily, and hands it back.

MARTHA LOCK. Then find me consolation.

A MUMMER appears.

MUMMER. Here come I old Poor and Mean
      Hardly worthy to be seen,
      Half be starved and t'other half blind
      With a well-ricked back and a broken mind.

2.4.3. **The Dragon Brewery.** SARAH, EMILY *and* SOPHIE *enter.*

SOPHIE. How is she?

EMILY. Hard to tell.

SARAH. Well, she's always been a one to keep her counsel to herself.

EMILY. Yes. But in fact –

FANNY enters with a tray of pewters on the way to the bar.

SARAH. Ah, Fanny. Very sorry, 'bout your – your sad news.

FANNY. Yes, ma'am.

SARAH. Your brother was – 19?

FANNY. Yes, right enough. So I be eldest now.

EMILY. Fanny, you know, if you wanted to go home, to help your mother –

FANNY drops the tray.

FANNY. Oh, ma'am, beg pardon –

SOPHIE. Fanny, it's all right –

FANNY. I – I'll be –

EMILY. It doesn't matter.

FANNY. I'll be fetching up a cloth to mop it up.

FANNY rushes out.

SARAH. Well, obviously –

EMILY. In fact, she's been distract for days. I mean, before this business started. I asked Christian to try and find out what it was, but she didn't know.

SOPHIE. This 'business'.

EMILY. All right, then. The cholera.

Slight pause.

SOPHIE. They say they've got the farmers to let loose the hatches.

SARAH. What?

EMILY. To flood the meadows, sluice the, you know, from the land.

SARAH. Sounds sensible.

SOPHIE. And he – and they, his sons, are working in the most afflicted streets. To boil and disinfect the clothing. In their kitchen copper.

SARAH. Are they now.

Pause.

Oh – don't – you – *dare.*

And away, we can hear the cry of GEORGE *and* HORACE *as they ride through the farmers' fields:*

GEORGE. Farmers! Open your locks! Let forth the waters!

HORACE. Raise your hatches! Farmers! Open your locks!

And we hear the CHILDREN *singing.*

CHILDREN. Hokey pokey wangery tum
　　　　　Plokery, hockery, bulum, kum
　　　　　Wingery, fungery, wingery wum
　　　　　King of the Cannibal Islands . . .

2.4.4. The Fudge Home. EDWARD FUDGE, *now 41, his father* WILLIAM, *now 69, kneeling beside his dead wife* SUZANNAH. MOULE *is there.*

EDWARD FUDGE. Well, parson. D'you see, I got meself a family.

MOULE. Mr Fudge, in this your time of desperate grief —

EDWARD FUDGE. And I scrimp and save and p'raps I starve a bit, to keep father and mother in their last years.

MOULE. Mr Fudge, I pray, you must not —

EDWARD FUDGE. And now we be rewarded for our husbandry. My Ann, my Johnathan. Now my mother, his Suzannah. So do you reckon, that's our just deserving?

MOULE. Edward. Please tell me, why you came here, to this place.

EDWARD FUDGE. Oh, that. That's easy. Being as how my father caught pneumonia one winter, and squire squot his house. And being as I tells squire he should leave poor father in his place, there bain't no work for I. So we ups, like all of us. And we comes here, to Mill Street. Is that your answer, Mr Moule?

Pause.

MOULE. I can — I have — there's nothing I can say.

He goes upstage to WILLIAM FUDGE. *But* EDWARD, *insistent, grabs him by the shoulder.*

EDWARD FUDGE. And maybe now at last you'm sorry for what you do say to 'e?

Enter CHARLES MOULE.

CHARLES (*breathless*). Ah. Father. Mr Handley asks: can you call on Mrs Sibley. Jane. In Ansty Street.

MOULE *prepares to go.*

MOULE. Yes. Yes, of course. What's that?

He's hearing the CHILDREN *singing.*

CHARLES. It's children. Singing plague-songs. From the Middle Ages. 'Out goes she.'

Slight pause.

MOULE. They hear the beatings of the wings of Azrael.

CHARLES. Azrael?

MOULE. Death's angel. Who lurks unseen in every open privy. Every drain. But who need not. And who *should* not, in a country groaning with the bounty of God's providence and plenty . . .

Pause.

And the Corporation tells me they can find me no more laudanum. And that they cannot find me three – or even *one*, more copper for the clothes.

Pause.

But I am informed that they will close the *pigsties*.

He looks into the eyes of EDWARD FUDGE.

CHILDREN. One a zoll, zen a zoll
            Zig a zoll zan
            Bobtail vinegar tittle toll tan
            Harum Scarum Virgin Marum
            YOU

2.4.5. **The Sibley Home, Ansty Street.** LIZZIE SIBLEY *with her child* ALBERT, *ten, and a crib.* MOULE *appears from an inner room.*

MOULE. Well, Mrs Sibley, I'm afraid your sister's dead.

LIZZIE SIBLEY. Um, do she –

MOULE. No. She did not regain consciousness. She did not repent her of her sin, before the end. I'm sorry.

LIZZIE *doesn't want him to go.*

LIZZIE SIBLEY. Parson.

MOULE. Yes, Mrs –

LIZZIE SIBLEY. Miss, if I be honest, parson.

MOULE. Yes. I see.

Slight pause.

LIZZIE SIBLEY. Parson, us used – that's Jane and me, oh, twenty years back, us did shout and us did bawl at you. Athwart the

Lych Gate. And I do very well mind your old maid a-shouting back: 'You be the devil's sheep you be'.

Pause.

And I guess now she be right. Don't you?

MOULE. Now, Mrs – Mrs –

LIZZIE SIBLEY. But still. Whatever she done. And whatever I done, cass'n deserve all this. Now can we?

Pause.

MOULE. Miss Sibley. I must tell you, it is my belief, that this dreadful sickness is a visitation of God's just and wrathful judgement on His sinful and forgetful children. For . . . as was said to me, by someone living in this very quarter: sin is an abomination, there is no excuse, and no reprieve. And its child is cursed for all eternity.

He turns and leaves quickly.

2.4.6. **Ansty Street.** MOULE *emerges into the street, and meets* MARTHA LOCK.

MARTHA LOCK. Well, Mr Moule. And here you be.

MOULE. Why, Mrs Lock. There's not –

MARTHA LOCK. Oh, no.

Pause.

No, 'tis about our Fanny, who's in service in the town, and we did have great hopes for.

MOULE. I trust –

MARTHA LOCK. And it be a comfort, like in all of this, she's safe and sound up there in Dorchester, even though it's in a brewery.

MOULE. Well, certainly –

MARTHA LOCK. Until I get this letter. And I do learn that she's not safe and sound at all.

She hands a letter to MOULE.

I cass'n read it all meself like, but I had it read out, and I get the gist.

MOULE. Uh, Mrs Lock –

MARTHA LOCK. Which be, and not to beat around it, as she's been a-seeing this young gentleman. And in the way of such things, as there'll be another joining 'em. In a few months' time.

Slight pause.

A young gentleman, to whom you be related, Mr Moule.

MOULE. Uh – I –

MARTHA LOCK. And they say that troubles never come, but they do come in regiments.

MOULE. I must –

MARTHA LOCK. And that 'the heathen are sunk down into the cess-pit they have dug'. Or so we do hear it whispered, Mr Moule.

Another figure emerges from the darkness. It's FLORENCE CHAFFLEY, carrying her possessions in a bundle.

FLORENCE. Well, if 'tisn't parson. Where d'you spring from, eh?

A thin, sick laugh.

The Reverend Moule. As the whole world knows. A-telling folks to change their ways. A-telling me. When I lose my third, at not yet seventeen. And change I do, mind. Be no more young soldiers, off behind the waxworks at the races. No. Takes up a decent trade, I do. And takes in washing.

Pause.

Washing.

Pause.

Don't I, eh?

MOULE *looks from* FLORENCE *to* MARTHA LOCK. *He closes his eyes. When he opens them, he sees little* FLORENCE CHAFFLEY, *with her tray.*

FLORENCE. Well, parson. Mushrooms? Firewood? Lemon balm?

MOULE *looks at* FLORENCE, *desperately, and then stumbles away.*

2.4.7. The Streets of Fordington. *Simultaneously,* CHILDREN *sing and four dark figures – who could but do not have to include* MOULE's *sons and* AUGUSTUS HANDLEY – *recite from four corners the most famous verses from the Book of Revelation; and* HENRY MOULE *mumbles words and phrases from the Book, as he stumbles through the darkness, the* CHILDREN *dancing around him and, at the end of each verse, one falling dead.*

CHILDREN. Eeena meena mino mo
　　　　　Kewska leena lina lo
　　　　　Eggs butter cheese and bread
　　　　　Stick stock stone dead
　　　　　And out goes SHE.

FIRST FIGURE. 'And behold when the Lamb opened one of the seals and I heard, as it were the noise of thunder, one of the four beasts saying, Come and see. And I saw, and behold a white horse: and he that sat on him had a bow; and a crown was given unto him: and he went forth conquering, and to conquer.'

MOULE (*after* '. . . *Come and see*'). And the seven angels said come hither . . .

SECOND FIGURE. 'And when he had opened the second seal, I heard the second beast say, Come and see. And there went out another horse that was red; and power was given to him that sat thereon to take peace from the earth, and that they should kill one another; and there was given unto him a great sword.'

MOULE (*after* '. . . *Come and see*'). And I saw the great whore . . . that sitteth upon many, many waters . . .

THIRD FIGURE. 'And when he had opened the third seal, I heard the third beast say, Come and see. And I beheld, and lo a black horse; and he that sat on him had a pair of balances in his hand. And I heard a voice in the midst of the four beasts say, A measure of wheat for a penny, and three measures of barley for a penny, and see thou hurts not the oil and the wine.'

MOULE (*after '. . . Come and see'*). . . . and I saw a dragon with great horns . . .

FOURTH FIGURE. 'And when he had opened the fourth seal, I heard the voice of the fourth beast say, Come and see. And I looked and behold a pale horse; and his name that sat on him was Death.'

THIRD FIGURE. Was Death.

SECOND FIGURE. Was Death.

FIRST FIGURE. Was Death.

MOULE. . . . and the dragon stood before the woman, to devour her child as soon as it was born . . .

And suddenly there is silence everywhere, and all focus shifts to HENRY MOULE, *kneeling over the body of the last, dead* CHILD. *Then he looks up into darkness around him and before him, and sees.*

MOULE. Who are you?

Pause.

Where do you come from? Why are you here?

Pause.

WHO ARE YOU?

Long pause. And we, too, see something like three white ANGELS, *surrounding some kind of huge, smoking vessel, appear and disappear.*

Saw. Three angels. Saw. Three strangers. And I John . . . saw the Holy City. New Jerusalem. And behold I make all things new.

Suddenly, MOULE *is aware of something wet falling on his upturned face.*

It's – *rain* . . .

2.4.8. The Vicarage. *At first, we see just* ALD. ARDEN. *Then gentle lights fade up in the Vicarage where* MRS MOULE *reads*

ARDEN's *letter.* HANDLEY *is there, working with a ledger, and* HORACE *standing to the side.*

ARDEN. So, Mr Moule. On Saturday four died. On Sunday three. Today but two. And I have to tell you, there has not been a single case in Dorchester. And with the change in weather, in my judgement, now, there will not be. Thanks be to God.

MRS MOULE (*folding the letter*). Amen.

HANDLEY. So. Thirty. Inclusive of four infants and six children under ten. Beginning with George Loder, publican. And ending with Elizabeth Sibley, seamstress. Seamstress and prostitute.

MOULE *enters. He still looks dishevelled.*

HORACE. Father –

MOULE. Mary, please find me Hebrews.

MRS MOULE. Henry, you were supposed to rest.

But she goes to find the Bible.

MOULE. For you see, methought I saw . . . the copper, but I did not see my friend Augustus, and the copper was not as mine is small but nigh unto the height of men . . . And there was not one but three . . . Mary, find, Hebrews, thirteen, please . . .

MRS MOULE. Of course.

She finds the chapter and reads.

'Let brotherly love continue. Be not forgetful to entertain strangers; for thereby some have entertained angels unawares. Remember them that are in bonds, as bound with them, and them which suffer – '

MOULE. Yes. Yes. I saw them. Saw the angels. Yes.

He takes the Bible and reads to himself.

HORACE. Father.

MOULE *turns to* HORACE.

Father, we must speak about this child. We must speak about this – Fanny. Because, you see, despite her station –

MRS MOULE. Horace, please. Not now.

Pause.

HANDLEY. 'And the heathen are sunk down into the cess-pit they have dug. And by the work of his own hands the wicked man is snared.'

MOULE. But . . . shall the needy always be forgotten? Must their expectations perish?

Slight pause.

When there is no need?

He looks at HORACE. *Suddenly bitter, throwing* HORACE's *own words back at him:*

But you. What misery? What poverty of circumstance?

He turns quickly and goes.

MRS MOULE. Well, yes. Well, yes, indeed.

She stands and moves a little apart. HANDLEY *turns to* HORACE *and tries to explain:*

HANDLEY. She will – of course they will both be provided for. The father – Lock – he has been spoken to. Arrangements have been made.

MRS MOULE (*from the doorway*). Oh, Horace. Why couldn't she and you have been the phantoms? and his blessed angels real?

Scene Five

2.5.1. **The Dragon Brewery.** *In the yard, and the parlour. In the parlour,* JOHN JAMES BESANT *sits and waits. In the yard,* SARAH, SOPHIE, EMILY *and* ALFRED MASON. *They are in the middle of a considerable argument.*

SARAH. Well, I really can't imagine what I'm supposed to say.

EMILY. Now, mother, surely it's not necessary to say anything at all.

ALFRED. And isn't it in everybody's best interests –

SARAH. Not necessary? What, 'Good morning, gentlemen, I'm so sorry to have troubled you – '

EMILY. And *I* really can't imagine why you had them sent for in the first place.

SARAH. Oh, you can't? Why, with their loved ones off and disappeared, without the slightest hint of where you'd gone or when you'd be returned, with your beds unslept in, little Katherine and Charles abandoned –

SOPHIE. Oh, mama!

EMILY. They are in Weymouth. With their nurse. And Sophie's –

SARAH. And I must say that it ill becomes you, Emily, as the only one I'd ever thought to be approximately sensible, I must say your involvement in this business is the greatest shock to me.

EMILY (*with a look to* SOPHIE). I was talked into it.

SARAH. And you married to a Borough Councillor besides.

SOPHIE. Now, please, mama –

SARAH. And that's not to say Sophia is absolved, for all she made a foolish marriage. Indeed I wonder sometimes if John James might not have been the innocent in all of this, and the bad influence gone quite the other way.

ALFRED. Now, Sarah, surely –

SARAH. And I'll thank you Alfred to refrain from surelying and telling me what's in my interests, because –

Enter CHRISTIAN. *During this,* JOHN TIZARD *joins* JOHN JAMES BESANT *in the parlour.*

CHRISTIAN. Uh – ma'am. It's Miss, Miss Emily's –

SARAH. Now, see. The Councillor's arrived.

CHRISTIAN. And, um, Miss Sophie's – Mr John James, I do put him in the parlour, like as well.

SARAH. Well, then.

She looks fiercely at her daughters. EMILY *makes the first move into the parlour, followed by* SOPHIE. *We see* JOHN TIZARD *and* JOHN JAMES BESANT *hurry to greet their wives and ask after them as, still in the yard,* SARAH *turns on* ALFRED.

SARAH. I mean. To give them free run of the brewery. I mean, to let them take the dray. I can't think what possessed you, Alfred.

Pause.

ALFRED. Sarah. She is your daughter.

SARAH. Well now, Alfred, that's not strictly so, and I must confess there's times, and this be one of them —

ALFRED. And just imagine, Sarah, standing up to you.

Slight pause.

SARAH. Well, I can't think what you mean.

ALFRED. Oh yes, you can.

ALFRED *gestures* SARAH *towards the parlour.* SARAH *allows herself to be gestured in. As she and* ALFRED *enter:*

JOHN TIZARD. Well, she must have summoned us for *something*.

JOHN JAMES. I'd been on the road two hours —

SARAH *and* ALFRED *have arrived.*

SARAH. Ah, John. How goes the partnership?

JOHN TIZARD. Well, excellently, thank you, mother-in-law —

SARAH. And the corporation? Be the streets of Weymouth lit and clean?

JOHN TIZARD. Well, moderately, on last acquaintance, yes, but —

SARAH. And John James? You were found?

JOHN JAMES. Yes. I was on my way to Salisbury.

SARAH. In pursuit of some arcane scholastic interest, no doubt.

JOHN TIZARD. And now perhaps you will explain —

JOHN JAMES. Well, yes, indeed —

SARAH. Oh, it's quite simple, John, John James. Last night, my daughters took it to themselves to borrow — well, one might say to appropriate a dray, a pair of horses and a vital item of equipment from the brewery —

JOHN JAMES. What's that?

ALFRED. Well, hardly vital, Sarah.

EMILY. Only our old copper.

SARAH. *My* old copper, which they then proceeded — with a member of my household staff as their accessory — to take down to Fordington —

JOHN JAMES. To *Fordington?*

SARAH. That's it.

JOHN TIZARD. What, where the cholera —

EMILY. Don't look at me.

SARAH. And all because —

SOPHIE. And all because we did think that they might have need of it. Because we thought that we might help, down there. That's all.

Slight pause.

And because it isn't on the moon, or in India or the Crimèa. It's half a mile away.

Slight pause.

And after all, she lives there.

JOHN TIZARD. Well, Emily, I — don't know what to say.

JOHN JAMES. Well, I suppose, as Virgil has it in the Georgics, 'Semper hoc — '

SARAH *can stay silent no longer.*

SARAH. And there's another point. Where's 'she'?

Pause.

EMILY. Who's she?

SARAH. Fanny. Your accomplice.

CHRISTIAN. I don't, like I don't rightly know, ma'am. I baint seen her since last evening.

SARAH. Well somebody at least – at last – with a proper sense of shame.

SOPHIE (*very angry*). Oh for heaven's sake mama!

SARAH. And so who d'you think you are? St George? Some great saviour of all mankind, a-charging round the countryside, a-rescuing everyone and everything?

SOPHIE. And who are you, mama? Are you the dragon, snapping and a-snarling round your gates, to keep out anything and anybody you don't know?

SARAH. I mean, did you think once, just once, mind, did you remember *for one moment* that you be a mother, with two children, and if you'd not come back –

SOPHIE. Oh, mama, can you think for a moment it might be *because*.

Pause.

SARAH. Well, no. Maybe I can't.

Slight pause.

Maybe because I see it t'other way.

Slight pause.

Like, folks with such ideals, such visions of the world and how it ought to be, with so much love for everyone, and everything and everybody . . . that they've none left over for their own.

Pause.

You know?

She goes out.

Scene Six

2.6.1. Outside the Vicarage, Fordington. MOULE *appears, takes* MRS MOULE's *arm. They leave their house, to walk into*

Dorchester. NATTY SEALE *and the geriatric* CAROLINE *await them.*

NATTY. Well, morning, parson. You and missus off to pick up your testimonial, like?

MOULE. Yes, that's right, Mr Seale.

NATTY. Be enough red faces up at Town Hall, I do venture. Like, to see you honoured and hosanna'd and all that . . .

MRS MOULE. Yes. Yes, Mr Seale. I think there may well be.

2.6.2. The Town Hall, Dorchester. *Most of the leading citizens of the town are assembling, including* HENNING, ANN HENNING, REV HANDLEY, MR PATCH, JOHN GALPIN, ANN BESANT *and* SARAH ELDRIDGE's DAUGHTERS. *In the chair is the mayor* GEORGE ANDREWS; *beside him sit* CAPT HENNING *and* ALDERMAN ARDEN. *It is clear that none of them are completely happy with the proceedings. The* MOULES *enter and join them at the top table.*

ANDREWS. Ladies and gentlemen. It falls to me to open the business of the meeting. Now, we have met here, as we are all aware, to take part in one of the most pleasurable proceedings that, as I think, a number of persons can be mixed up with.

That hasn't come out quite right, but he ploughs on.

We have met to testify your — approbation of the exertions and self-denying conduct of a very excellent and estimable gentleman, and an equally excellent and estimable lady. I feel myself most inadequate to set before you the qualities of this lady and gentleman . . .

Calls of 'shame'.

Indeed, when I read the list of the subscribers, I cannot think but that I am a most unworthy person to be in this place at all!

Another, perhaps more muted, cry of 'shame'.

And so I hand the business over to my friend and colleague Captain Henning with some considerable relief!

Slight pause.

Who will present the testimonial, on behalf of the subscribers.

ANDREWS *sits,* HENNING *stands.*

HENNING. Um – Mr Mayor. Ladies and gentlemen. It is my
pleasant task to acknowledge our – the feelings of deep gratitude
that must be felt by every honest citizen to, as you said, your
Worship, a most estimable gentleman and lady.

Any form of testimonial we can present must fall far short of
what they both deserve. They will assert no doubt they did their
duty. But how many were there to be found who did that?

Or who acknowledged, even, what that duty was. Or to whom it
should be shown.

And I think that I should best discharge *my* duty, now, by
presenting without further observation this testimonial to Mr
and Mrs Moule, in the name of the subscribers.

*He hands over a silver salver, and gestures to a small cabinet and
set of clerical robes. He sits, relieved.* MOULE *stands.*
HENNING *has forgotten the third part of the testimonial, and
has omitted to describe the gifts,* ANDREWS *whispers to him
furiously and he has to leap straight up again.*

MOULE. My dear sir, my kind friends –

HENNING. The testimonial, in fact, consists –

MOULE *sits.*

– of a silver salver, of chaste design, inscribed, a set of clerical
robes, and a Devonport cabinet, most handsomely fitted up, for
Mrs Moule. And, the contribution being more than expected, a
purse of . . .

He doesn't know the amount. ANDREWS *whispers.*

. . . of 170 sovereigns.

He sits. A smattering of slightly embarrassed applause. MOULE
stands again.

MOULE. My dear sir, my kind friends, my fellow townsmen, I
sincerely thank you. Did I stand here merely as a man, I should

regard this as a proud occasion; but I stand here rather as a Christian minister, and feel bound to say that, had I acted under the influence of more natural feelings, I should not have stood here at all. To God be all the glory!

ANDREWS *and* HENNING *nod, and look relieved.*

As to the blame for the awfulness of this visitation, I have as you might surmise applied my mind, and I must tell you it is my belief that Fordington was not to blame – though one might speak of its vice and degradation, nor yet the county – though one should consider the responsibility of landowners who throw their tenants on the mercy of the urban parishes, nor even Dorchester and its borough corporation – though I must own that for the dereliction of its sanitary duties there are those who sit upon that corporation who should feel ashamed.

The odd look, but MOULE *continues:*

But even so, in my opinion, ladies, sirs, the blame lies in substantive part elsewhere: at the door of those who for the last sixty years have managed the estates of His Royal Highness Albert Duke of Cornwall.

Pause. An intake of breath.

For they, when they might have prevented it, allowed such a state of things to grow up, largely it is true on a piece of freehold land, but one surrounded on all sides by His Royal Highness' property, a property which consists moreover of two thousand acres of the finest soil in England, worked by labourers who live crushed into a space which cannot overreach five acres, and which has become a great sink into which the excremental filth of all the neighbouring parishes is poured.

This is getting near the bone.

In circumstances of such misery and squalor that such a visitation was inevitable. But, I have to say, in one respect at least, and by the simplest and the cheapest means of sanitary contrivance, nonetheless *avoidable*.

He looks round at the citizenry.

I have written I must tell you to Prince Albert to acquaint him with my views.

This provokes shock.

And I have been informed, as I well knew, that the Prince himself has no personal authority, and that the Duchy has no formal and thus will accept no moral responsibility for the state of Mill Street, Ansty Street and Cuckold's Row.

Complete silence.

To which, good citizens, I have already made reply. For I will not rest until this wrong is righted. For it is a species of oppression, and it will and should provoke resistance. And I say all this as one to whom, until these dreadful happenings occurred, such views as I now entertain were strangers.

Pause. He looks at the gifts.

So now, in my own name as well as that of my wife, all that remains to say is that we thank you, from the bottom of our hearts, for these kind testimonials.

Which we receive on behalf of all, those known to us and those unknown, who strove to keep this dreadful plague from spreading from my parish into yours.

He sits. ANDREWS stands.

ANDREWS. Well, now, perhaps . . . If any lady or gentleman would care to lead off with God Save the Queen, there could not, I think, be a more appropriate way of ending these proceedings. Mr Patch – ?

SOPHIE *stands.*

SOPHIE. Mr Mayor. You do not think it even more appropriate, to sing a hymn?

ANDREWS (*not sure, looking around*). Well, yes.

HENNING. Yes, certainly . . .

There is a quick debate between the ELDRIDGE sisters, and then EMILY begins to sing. The others join, followed by

PATCH *and the whole* ASSEMBLY. *Then* MOULE *and* MRS
MOULE *emerge into the street, and begin the walk back to
Fordington.*

2.6.3. The High Street, Dorchester. *As the* MOULES *process back
through the streets of Dorchester to their home, the hymn is sung.
But then, to one side, we see* FANNY LOCK, *standing with a
suitcase.*

HYMN. Praise my soul, the King of Heaven;
        To his feet thy tribute bring,
        Ransom'd, heal'd, restor'd, forgiven,
        Who like me his praise should sing?
        Praise him! Praise him!
        Praise him! Praise him!
        Praise the everlasting King.

The hymn fades enough for us to hear FANNY:

FANNY. And so, ma'am, it do be concluded, by my father and the
parson, it be better for all parties if I go off on a boat, and has
my baby in Australia.

Slight pause.

And I'm sorry that I cass'n tell you properly. But it all fall out so
fast.

Slight pause.

And it do seem a long way. I'll be quite honest ma'am. It do
seem far to have a baby.

Meanwhile the hymn has continued:

HYMN. Fatherlike he tends and spares us;
        Well our feeble frame he knows;
        In his hands he gently bears us,
        Rescues us from all our foes.
        Praise him! Praise him!
        Praise him! Praise him!
        Widely as his mercy flows.

> Angels help us to adore him,
> Ye behold him face to face;
> Sun and moon bow down before him,
> Dwellers all in time and space.
> Praise him! Praise him!
> Praise him! Praise him!
> Praise with us the God of Grace.

And the MOULES *are back home together, clasping each other's hands tightly.*

MRS MOULE. And now – and now you'll rest?

MOULE. Today. Tomorrow. And forever. What transpires is in His hands, not ours.

And suddenly we see SARAH, *holding* FANNY's *letter. She cries, as if to Fordington:*

SARAH. So who'd you think you are, St George?

Scene Seven

2.7.1. The Roof of King's College Chapel, Cambridge. *Dawn. Brilliant, low light. It is a few years later.* CHARLES MOULE, *in his academic gown, with* HORACE.

HORACE. The towers of Jerusalem.

CHARLES. I'm sorry?

HORACE. Don't you think? Through the morning mist? The spires of Ely, gleam and glisten, like unto the Towers of Jerusalem?

CHARLES. Yes. Yes, indeed.

HORACE. Now, Charles. This is my privilege. To introduce you to this sight. The vision from the roof of King's, King's College Chapel, at the very break of dawn. You might at least affect to be impressed.

CHARLES. I am impressed.

HORACE. Your right, of course, to witness, as a distinguished fellow of the University. Mine as an undistinguished, undeserved MA.

CHARLES. You are entitled –

HORACE. A mere, honorary honour. Coupled with what I imagine is a more or less unique distinction, to have plucked at *both* our ancient universities.

CHARLES. Look, Horace, are you –

HORACE. Charles. Do you know what I do with my days?

Pause.

CHARLES. You are an Inspector of the Poor Law for the District of East Anglia. You are, if I may say so, Horace, increasingly occasionally an Inspector of the Poor Law for the District of East Anglia.

HORACE. Or, put another way, I visit unions. Workhouses. It is not attractive work, I have to tell you, Charles.

CHARLES. I have no doubt. But nonetheless –

HORACE. Last month. An aborted baby, rammed into a soil-pipe. Another, well, newborn, found strangled on a doorstep. As 'a deadborn baby, sirs, please put it underground'. So is it any wonder that my duties are occasionally – occasional?

CHARLES. It is no wonder. But it is a fault.

HORACE. Aha. A *fault*. Oh, how I hear our father. Ah. A *fault*. The genus Moule. *Flagrante.*

CHARLES *says nothing.*

How is he?

CHARLES. He is well. He has patented a scheme for converting shale to gas, which has engaged his interest.

HORACE. Ah, yes, the schemes. And the contrivances. How go the sales of his earth closet?

CHARLES. Not as well as hoped. But they are used in several prisons. And our cabbages and roses grow in great profusion.

Slight pause. CHARLES *smiles.*

In fact, he preached upon the subject. On the seventh Sunday after Trinity. Drawing his inference from Deuteronomy.

HORACE *smiles.*

HORACE. I see.

Slight pause.

Oh, Charles. Do you know my difficulty? With my father?

CHARLES. No, I do not.

HORACE. It's that I can't believe the truth of everything can be drawn from Deuteronomy. Is actually seared down in that book for ever.

CHARLES. Horace, you know that I believe that what is in that book is for all time.

HORACE. Oh, Charles, I am. So full of fear.

He tries a smile.

Fear and Foreboding.

Pause.

CHARLES. Our brother Handley spoke to me of you.

HORACE. No doubt he too had faults to speak of.

CHARLES. No. He spoke of when he was a child and you and he would walk together through the corn, translating Hesiod. Or you'd draw a plan of ancient Rome with lines of pebbles on the lawn. He said — you were the greatest educator he had ever met.

HORACE (*suddenly angry*). Do not — don't talk to me of waste.

Pause.

My son would be a man. I didn't draw a plan of ancient anything for him.

Pause.

CHARLES. Your son?

HORACE. Or daughter. I don't know.

Slight pause.

Whose mother was my mistress. Who for that 'fault' was packed off half-way round the world.

Pause.

D'you see?

CHARLES. Horace, I'm going down.

HORACE. A moment, and I'll follow you.

CHARLES. I'll wait.

HORACE. A *moment*, Charles.

CHARLES *shrugs and goes.*

From here, you see, in the brilliant light of morning, you can see no workhouses. And yet too bright. Oh, far, oh far too blinding bright to bear.

Lights cut back to MRS MOULE, *standing where we left her, but without her husband.*

MRS MOULE (*surprised*). Oh, Henry. Henry?

She realises.

Oh, Henry, I can't *see* . . .

Lights back to the roof of King's.

HORACE. For George, Prince George, what have you done.
You have slain your own beloved son.
You have cut him down, in the morning sun.

HORACE *throws himself from the roof into the darkness below.*

Scene Eight

2.8.1. Fordington: The Churchyard and Streets. *Where* HORACE's
body would have fallen, a DEAD MUMMER *lies on the ground,
the flag of St George lying by his side. The* PRESENTER *comes to
the* DEAD MUMMER *and we realise we are watching a group of
actual* MUMMERS *performing their play around the houses of
Fordington, within sound of the churchyard.*

As the scene gets under way, lights come up on HENRY
MOULE, *kneeling by the grave of his son* HORACE *in St George's
churchyard, and a* WOMAN *standing behind him. It is Christmas
time.*

PRESENTER. Is there a doctor to be found
           All ready near at hand,
           To cure this dread and deathly wound
           And make the champion stand.

Enter the DOCTOR.

DOCTOR. I am a doctor.

PRESENTER. Doctor?

DOCTOR. Ay.

PRESENTER. From whence and why?

DOCTOR.   From whither of the world around,
           For why to cure him on the ground.
           Of the stich, itch and ague, the blight of the lame
           And for half a pence more, the dead raise up again.

2.8.2. The Churchyard. *The* WOMAN *speaks to* MOULE. *It's*
SARAH.

SARAH. Well, once again. We overhear a pagan ritual.

MOULE. I'm sorry?

SARAH. This is – his grave?

MOULE. It is – a grave. And may I ask – ?

SARAH. Of course. It is quite a time ago. You may not readily remember.

MOULE. Well, you will forgive me –

SARAH. I am Sarah Eldridge. Of the Dragon Brewery.

Slight pause.

MOULE. Oh, yes. And what, may I enquire –

SARAH. Well, let's say, I do feel that in this, season of goodwill, that it do seem appropriate . . .

MOULE. Yes? What?

SARAH. To offer my condolences to you.

Slight pause.

In the tragic loss of your dear son. Whose mortal part – I think – lies there.

Pause.

MOULE (*thickly*). I thank you.

SARAH. A loss that bears comparison, you see, with my loss of my son. But perhaps, as well, with mine of my dear husband.

MOULE. Mrs Eldridge, I'm not sure –

SARAH. Which loss, I think, that you do term a suicide.

Pause.

MOULE. The balance of my son's mind was disturbed.

SARAH. Both your son and my husband had disturbed their own minds over many years.

MOULE. Mrs Eldridge, what is the purpose of this visitation?

SARAH. Oh, Mr Moule, we share so much. Why not a little understanding?

Pause.

MOULE. So, ma'am. What would you have me understand?

SARAH. Well, maybe, how harsh the burning light of virtue feels. To those whose own virtue burns less bright. To those who stand in shadow.

Pause.

And that while it is indeed a fault to think all strangers immanently good, it is perhaps as grave a one, to think that those we know and try to love are, well – 'beyond reprieve'.

Pause. MOULE *stands and looks at* SARAH.

MOULE. And are you still a brewer, Mrs Eldridge?

SARAH. Well, retired.

MOULE. You will not expect me, ma'am, to grieve at that.

SARAH. Well, no. No more do I. But there are always things, that one is sad to lose.

MOULE. I must confess, that in this case, I can't imagine –

SARAH. There is of all things an old and battered copper set, which I used for boiling hops, back in my first days, to which I am peculiarly attached.

MOULE. A what?

SARAH. A copper. You know, like an ordinary, domestic copper boiler. Larger, naturally . . .

MOULE. You mean, within the brewery –

SARAH. That's right. Though, in fact, the one I'm thinking of has not been used for many years. Not indeed, I think, since 1854.

Slight pause.

September 1854.

Slight pause.

The night when my two daughters, without my permission or consent – and aided and abetted by what I had thought to be four loyal stablehands – loaded it up on the back of my biggest dray and rode it down to Fordington, and set it down, and built a fire, to boil and disinfect the clothing of the dying and the dead, to try and help some strange old parson stop the pestilence from spreading into Dorchester.

Pause. MOULE looks wild-eyed.

Uh – Mr Moule?

MOULE. Mrs Eldridge. Did you say – two daughters?

SARAH. That's right. My Sophie and my Emily. Though I have to say in this – adventure, not alone. But assisted by a third.

Slight pause.

MOULE. A third.

SARAH. That's right.

MOULE. So it was three.

SARAH. I'm sorry?

MOULE. I did not understand. I had been entertaining angels unawares.

SARAH. Oh, I assure you, Mr Moule –

She stops herself.

Well, maybe. In a way.

Pause.

And it do take me some time to appreciate. That until we loose the bonds of strangers, then the cup we raise behind our gates is gall.

But also, that the strangers we must entertain include our own. And the bonds we loose are not just theirs, but ours.

A moment. Then HANDLEY JNR appears. He is in clerical clothes.

HANDLEY JNR. Now, father. *Here* you are.

MOULE. Why, Handley. What's the matter?

HANDLEY JNR. Father, it's a young woman, from the back of Ansty. She can't be more than seventeen. And she's come to talk to us of marriage.

MOULE. Then certainly, we have to talk to her.

HANDLEY JNR. And she is obviously –

Conscious of SARAH:

– considerably, far gone.

MOULE. I see. Where is she now?

HANDLEY JNR. She's in the Vicarage. She's reading to mama.

MOULE. Well, that's kind.

HANDLEY JNR. No doubt, in order to ingratiate –

MOULE. No doubt.

Slight pause.

And you're quite right. Her fault is grave. And we must tell her so, in no uncertain terms.

HANDLEY JNR *turns and goes off, back towards church. Perhaps he just hears his father.*

But, maybe. There are even graver.

SARAH. Yes.

Slight pause.

MOULE. Who was the third?

SARAH. You know.

Slight pause.

MOULE. Fanny Lock.

SARAH. Our maid. The mistress of your dear, dead son. The mother of your grandchild.

Pause. MOULE's *voice is thick.*

MOULE. Yes.

SARAH. Oh, Mr Moule. St George.

MOULE. I beg your pardon?

SARAH. Your St George. And his true story. Who of course was
not a dragon-slayer, but a martyr. Who was told by God he
would be killed three times. And after his first martyrdom, his
body was cut up and spread about the land. But St Michael the
great angel gathered up the pieces, like a harvest, and God made
him live again. And sometimes he be called Green George, the
dead king who is burnt, and scattered on the frozen earth, to
bring it back to life.

For we must remember, must we not, that like trees men have
roots and trunks, which thrust up to the sky, but also branches
which stretch out to other men, and touch them.

Pause.

For only thus may we divine — from what, strange soil, may
green things grow.

MOULE *looks at* SARAH. *Then he turns and sees:*

2.8.3. The MUMMERS. *The* DEAD MUMMER — *the Horace
Mummer — stands, picks up his flag and moves towards* SARAH
and MOULE. *Neither is sure if what they see is real.*

RESURRECTED MUMMER.
        Oh George, King George, where have I been,
        What strange and wondrous sights I've seen;
        What places there,
        What scenes appear,
        Since I the harrow entered in.

        A hundred echoes round me cross
        From hill to hill the voices tossed,
        From high to low
        They singing go
        And not a single word is lost.

        Behold on yonder risen ground,
        The Holy City all around,
        Never from wending,
        Never be ending,
        Hark to its eternal sound.

*And at first in the distance, but then drawing closer, we hear an old
wassailing song, which as it grows brings all the* COMPANY *on to
the stage — the survivors and the victims, the living and the dead —
who first surround and then swallow up* HENRY MOULE *and*
SARAH ELDRIDGE, *as, in the end, all voices join together:*

COMPANY. How far have we travelled, how far do we hie
Some good cheer to bring now that Christmas be nigh
And our wassail be made of the good ale and true
'Tis nutmeg and ginger the best we can brew

Our wassail is made of the elderberry bow
And so my good neighbours we drink unto thou
We pray that on earth you'll have plenty in store,
And let us come in for 'tis cold by the door.

Up and down, through all the town
and all around,
so far we been:
Sing wassail sing a-wassail
And call you us in

For we know by the moon that we are not too soon
And we know by the sky that we are not too high
And we know by the stars that we are not too far
And we know by the ground that we are within
    sound

Up and down, through all the town
and all around,
how far we been:
Sing wassail sing a-wassail
And call you us in

There's a master and a missus sat down by the fire
While we poor plough boys stand here in the mire
And you pretty maid with your silver-headed pin
Pray open the door and let us come in

So fair maidy so fair lady
with your silver headed pin —
Won't you come to, to your window
And let us come in

Methuen World Classics *and*
Methuen Contemporary Dramatists

Methuen Modern Plays

include work by

Methuen Student Editions